GERONTOLOGICAL SOCIAL WORK

GERONTOLOGICAL SOCIAL WORK

A TASK-CENTERED APPROACH

Matthias J. Naleppa and William J. Reid

COLUMBIA UNIVERSITY PRESS NEW YORK

COLUMBIA UNIVERSITY PRESS

Publishers Since 1893

New York   Chichester, West Sussex

Copyright © 2003 Columbia University Press

Library of Congress Cataloging-in-Publication Data

Naleppa, Matthias J.

Gerontological social work : a task-centered approach / Matthias J. Naleppa and William J. Reid.

p. cm.

Includes bibliographical references and index.

ISBN 0-231-11586-5 (cloth : alk. paper)

1. Social work with the aged—United States.   2. Task-centered social work—United States.   3. Aged—Functional assessment.   4. Aged—Services for—United States.   5. Aged—Care—United States.   I. Reid, William James, 1928–   II. Title.

HV1461.N313 2003

362.6'0973—dc22

2003055413

Columbia University Press books are printed on permanent and durable acid-free paper.

Printed in the United States of America

c 10 9 8 7 6 5 4 3 2 1

CONTENTS

PART III: TASK PLANNERS 257

PREFACE

THE AGING OF POPULATIONS in the United States and around the world continues to lead to an increased demand for trained human service practitioners to serve elderly and frail elderly individuals. As more social workers, nurses, and other health care and human service practitioners work with elderly clients, the number of gerontological practice courses offered by universities, colleges, and various training institutes will grow apace. This book seeks to address the need for comprehensive gerontological practice textbooks. It integrates the fundamentals of work with the elderly and basic practice skills, an intervention approach—the task-centered model—and its applications across various practice settings and offers in-depth coverage of ways to address specific problems of clients. Throughout the book an effort is made to present skills and the practice model in a clear, straightforward, and structured manner so that they can be adapted to various gerontological and geriatric practice settings (e.g., community-based practice, counseling, case management, hospital-based practice, or home health care). Although the book is intended primarily for social workers, it is directly applicable to the work of others who provide services to the elderly.

The book is subdivided into three parts. Part I (chapters 1 through 4) introduces the reader to gerontological human service practice and details practice skills with elderly clients, couples, and caregivers. The practical knowledge and skills presented can be seen as a foundation for any type of intervention with elderly clients. Chapter 1 introduces demographic background information and common problems and needs of the elderly client population. In chapter 2 we present the aging network, the continuum of care, and the principal providers of services. Chapter 3 focuses on basic competencies for communication in gerontological practice. We also introduce communication skills required for practice with special groups of older adults (e.g., persons with hearing impairments or dementia). Chapter 4 focuses on general principles of geriatric assessment and the use of standardized instruments. The chapter concentrates on both the process of assessment as well as the most important standardized assessment instruments and the way they are used.

Part II (chapters 5 through 10) provides a framework for intervention based on the task-centered model. The usefulness of the task-centered model for working with elderly clients has been confirmed in the literature, and numerous articles have described research and practice experiences in using the model with older adults (e.g., Dierking et al. 1980; Fortune and Rathbone McCuan 1981; Rathbone McCuan 1985; Scharlach 1985; Naleppa and Reid 1998, 2000). The basic steps of the model as they have been adapted for gerontological practice are presented and illustrated in chapters 5 through 7. Here, the practice model is presented with a focus on work with individual clients and their families while group applications are illustrated in chapters 9 and 10. Chapter 5 concentrates on the initial phase of the intervention and covers how to conduct intake and assessment, explore problems, and set treatment goals. Chapter 6 presents the middle phase of treatment and includes subjects such as developing and selecting tasks, implementing task-centered interventions, and evaluating their success. Termination-phase activities are the focus of chapter 7. Throughout these chapters we provide examples of rating scales, schedules, or other forms that can assist practitioners and clients in the intervention process. While a practitioner may not use all of these forms, we emphasize the significance of measuring and tracking intervention outcomes.

Chapters 8, 9, and 10 focus on applications of the model to various forms of gerontological practice. Each chapter provides detailed background information on how to apply the model. The applications are then illustrated through extensive case examples. Chapter 8 features the geriatric task-centered case management model, an adaptation of the model that has been tested in several field trials. While work with caregivers has already been introduced in chapters 5 through 7, chapter 9 focuses specifically on practice with caregivers. Chapter 10 shows how task-centered practice can be applied in long-term care and institutional settings.

Part III provides task planners. A task planner is an intervention module that can be drawn upon in addressing specific client problems or issues. Each task planner consists of a brief description of the problem, references to relevant literature, and a menu of possible actions that can be undertaken to resolve the problem (Reid 2000). Task planners relating to service delivery issues, such as nursing home placement or nutritional needs, also provide an overview of the particular services. The task planners presented in this book focus on a wide range of gerontological topics, including health, mental health, caregiving, home and personal safety, senior living, and long-term care arrangements. Finally, the appendix lists several hundred Web sites, classified by topic, that should prove useful in work with the elderly.

A number of individuals and organizations provided assistance in the preparation of this volume. The book project has been supported through the Hartford Geriatric Social Work Faculty Scholars Program. In this context we would like to thank especially Laura Robbins of the John A. Hartford Foundation, Barbara Berkman, principal investigator of the Hartford Geriatric Social Work Faculty Scholars Program, and Linda Harootyan of the Gerontological Society of America.

We are also indebted to Kristina Hash and Debra Lacey for their chapters (9 and 10 respectively) as well as to Miranda Koss for her help in locating and classifying the Web sites. The assistance of the practitioners, students, and researchers who contributed to the task planners is gratefully acknowledged. Their names follow the task planners they helped create.

We would like to thank Connie Corley for her helpful suggestions and feedback at various stages of writing the book. Finally, we are grateful to the graduate assistants who performed essential research and editorial tasks— Lisa Nolf, Kimberly Karanda, and Bonnie Kenaley.

GERONTOLOGICAL SOCIAL WORK

PART I

A FOUNDATION FOR GERONTOLOGICAL PRACTICE

In part I, we lay a foundation for gerontological practice in social work. We present basic knowledge essential to working with elderly clients and their caregivers, regardless of the intervention model used.

Chapter 1 provides a profile of older adults, examining demographic indicators, and common problems and needs faced by elderly and frail elderly clients. Chapter 2 introduces the aging network and the continuum of care as well as the most important service providers. We provide a brief overview of the human service professionals involved in gerontological practice generally and review the role of the informal support network. Chapter 3 focuses on knowledge and skills for communication in gerontological practice. The basic proficiencies for communicating with older adults are considered, and skills for communicating with special groups of older adults are introduced (e.g., communicating with persons with vision or hearing impairments or persons with dementia). Finally, in chapter 4, we take a look at general principles of assessment and the use of standardized instruments.

CHAPTER 1

A PROFILE OF OLDER ADULTS

W E WOULD LIKE to begin with a profile of the older adult population. First, we will offer a general overview of the composition of the older adult population and provide information on some important demographic indicators. This will be followed by an overview of the more common problem areas and typical needs that a gerontological practitioner should know about. Specifically, we will introduce problems with activities of daily living, health and mental health and discuss the economic situation of the older adult population. In our brief discussion we cannot do justice to the complex and diverse conditions faced by the elderly, but we hope that this introduction will nevertheless provide sufficient background for the gerontological human service practice skills we will describe in the subsequent chapters of this book.

DEMOGRAPHICS OF THE OLDER ADULT POPULATION

Older adults, that is, those over the age of 65, constitute the fastest growing segment of the population, both in number and in percentage. This is the case not only in the United States but also in nations around the world. In fact, many European countries already have a much higher percentage of older adults and are thus sometimes referred to as the "aging countries." The graying of populations is a worldwide phenomenon. Furthermore, not only are societies aging but so are the elderly themselves as more and more older adults reach higher ages.

In demographic terms, "older adult" and "elderly person" typically refer to individuals over the age of 65. This definition currently describes about 13 percent of the US population (U.S. Census Bureau 2000). Within this population group, the elderly are often classified into the young old (age 65–74), the middle-old (age 75 to 84), and the oldest-old (over 85 years). In 2000, this latter group numbered 4.2 million. These age groups represented 6.5 percent for 85–89-year-olds, 4.4 percent for 90–94-year-olds and 1.5 percent for those over 95 years of age. Of these three, the oldest-old are the most rapidly growing group. The number of older Americans has increased more than tenfold since 1900, when there were 3 million people age sixty-five or older (4 percent of the total population; U.S. Census Bureau 2000). During the 1990s the population of those age 85 and over increased by 38 percent, from 3.1 million to 4.2 million. In contrast, the population of those 75 to 84 years old increased by 23 percent, and the population of those between the ages of 65 and 74 increased by less than 2 percent, from 18.1 million to 18.4 million (U.S. Census Bureau 2000). This latter group already constitutes 12 percent of the elderly population and 1.5 percent of the general population (U.S. Census Bureau 2000).

For most of this century, the United States has been on a "demographic roller coaster" (U.S. Census Bureau 1996). A baby bust during the 1930s was followed by the much-discussed baby boom of the 1950s. Overall, the percentage of elderly persons increased from 5 percent of the American population in 1930 to about 13 percent today. This in turn was followed by another baby bust in the 1970s and a "baby boomlet" in the 1980s, caused by children born to baby boomers. In 2011, the baby boom generation will begin to turn 65, and it is projected that by 2030 one in five people will be 65 or older. The population is projected to double over the next thirty years and to reach 70 million by 2030 (Federal Interagency Forum on Aging 2000). There were about 65,000 people at the age of 100 or older in 2000, and the number of centenarians is projected to grow quickly so that there may be as many as 381,000 by 2030 (Federal Interagency Forum on Aging 2000). About one in eight Americans were elderly in 1994, but about one in five would be elderly by the year 2030 (U.S. Census Bureau 2000).

With increasing life expectancy and the baby-boomer cohort entering old age, the U.S. Census Bureau estimates that the elderly population will double to 80 million and will comprise 20 percent of the population within the next fifty years (U.S. Census Bureau 2000). Projections for 2050 predict that 2.5 percent of the total population will be over the age of 90, and .3 percent of this group will be 100 years or over.

These trends are concurrent with a decrease in mortality, primarily as a consequence of a reduction in acute health problems. The two most important contributors to the decline in mortality have been significant decreases of stroke and heart disease as causes of death since the 1970s (Manton and Soldo 1985). At the same time that mortality has decreased, an increase in morbidity has been seen (Wolfe 1993). Since age-dependent chronic conditions, for example, cognitive impairments and limitations in performing activities of daily living, do not follow the same pattern of delay as mortality, the proportion of this population group increases (Brody and Schneider 1986). Thus, the increase in the older population leads to a growth of chronic conditions correlated to old age, such as cognitive impairment and impairments in the performance of activities of daily living (Wolfe 1993).

Presently the life expectancy in the United States is 74.2 years for men and 79.9 years for women, and a person reaching age 65 can expect to live another seventeen years (U.S. Census Bureau 2000). Across all ethnic and racial groups elderly women outnumber elderly men. About 41 percent of the older population is male and 59 percent is female. This gender difference increases even further with age. For the oldest-old, the ratio for women to men is 5 to 2. Older men living in the community are more likely to be married (about 75 percent) than older women (44 percent). Only 14 percent of older men are widowed, compared to almost half of the elderly women (45 percent). Approximately 80 percent of the noninstitutionalized elderly living alone are female (U.S. Census Bureau 2000). Although still lower than in the general population, the divorce rate among older adults is also increasing. Currently about 7 percent of older individuals are divorced, which represents a 200 percent increase since 1980 (U.S. Census Bureau 2000).

When one population segment changes so drastically and fast as is occurring with older adults, this has notable consequences for the population as a whole. To help us better understand the changing conditions, demographers have developed several indicators that describe subgroups of the population in relation to the entire population. One such measure is the dependency ratio, which expresses the degree of demand placed on society by the young and the aged (Ward 1984). Currently, there is a stable dependency ratio because the increase in elderly dependents is offset by a decrease in dependents under 18 years of age (Soldo and Agree 1988). However, a shift toward dependency of the aged has taken place, showing an increased need for elder care. Simultaneously, the financial burden of caring for elderly persons is growing.

It should be noted that this is the first time in history that most middle-aged and young old individuals have parents who are alive. Two family support ratios, similar to the dependency ratio, are used to describe the demands placed on middle-aged family members. The parent support ratio describes the number of adults over 85 years per adult between the ages of 50 and 64 (U.S. Census Bureau 2000). This family support ratio has increased significantly. In 1950, 3 percent of persons between 50 and 64 had a living parent. Today this number stands at 29 percent (U.S. Census Bureau 2000). The sandwich generation ratio describes the ratio of those between the ages of 18 and 22 enrolled in college plus the persons aged between 65 and 79 per individual in the age bracket from 45 to 49. It addresses the fact that middle-aged individuals often bear the financial responsibility for their children's college tuition as well the costs related to the care of their elderly parents. However, this double burden is not as common as many believe. While there has been a small increase in the sandwich generation ratio, only 15 percent of middle-aged persons have children attending college full-time, and the percentage of those having to combine this with taking care of their ailing parents is even smaller (U.S. Census Bureau 2000).

In 1997 only 11 persons per 1,000 between the ages of 65 and 74 resided in nursing homes, compared with 46 per 1,000 persons in the age bracket from 75 to 84 and 192 persons per 1,000 aged 85 or over. About half of the older nursing home residents in 1997 were 85 years old or older (Federal Interagency Forum on Aging-Related Statistics 2000). It has been estimated that the total inflation-adjusted expenditures for long-term care for the elderly will grow annually by 2.6 percent between 2000 and 2040. Long-term care spending is projected to reach $207 billion in 2020 and $346 billion in 2040, in inflation-adjusted year 2000 dollars (U. S. Census Bureau 2000).

For noninstitutionalized elders, the annual out-of-pocket expenditures on health care for 1998—which include expenditures on health insurance, medical services and supplies, and prescription drugs—ranged from 9 percent to 16 percent of total expenditures among households headed by older persons at different levels of income. Average dollar expenditures on health care increase with income. In 1998 households headed by older persons in the bottom fifth of the income distribution spent an average of $1,654 per year on health care, compared with $3,614 among households in the top fifth of the income distribution (Federal Interagency Forum on Aging 2000).

Although dollar expenditures increase with income, the relative burden of health care costs is much higher among low-income households and households in the middle range of the income distribution. In 1998 households in the bottom fifth spent an average of 13 percent of their expenditures on health care. Those in the middle fifth spent an average of 16 percent, and those in the top fifth spent 9 percent (Federal Interagency Forum on Aging 2000).

The racial and ethnic composition of the older adult population is becoming increasingly diverse. Although presently 10 percent of the elderly are nonwhite, projections for the next fifty years indicate that this population group will grow to over 20 percent. The Hispanic elderly population will grow faster than any other group, from currently 6 percent to approximately 16 percent by the year 2050 (U.S. Census Bureau 1997).

The proportion of elderly individuals who live in nursing facilities is smaller than is commonly believed. According to the most recent data available, 4.5 percent of people aged 65 or over live in nursing homes, a decline from 5.1 percent in 1990 (U.S. Census Bureau 2000). The risk of institutionalization increases with age, however. Almost 18 percent of the oldest-old, those over 85 years of age, live in a nursing home (U.S. Census Bureau 2000). Projections suggest that two out of every five persons who turned 65 in 1990 will enter a nursing home at some time before they die. One in four will spend at least a year in a nursing home, and one in 11 will spend five or more years (Mayo Foundation 2002) in such a facility (see box 1.1). Thus, as the population ages, the need for long-term care arrangements will continue to increase.

COMMON PROBLEMS AND NEEDS

FUNCTIONAL LIMITATIONS Many older adult clients have functional limitations that prevent them from completing one or more aspects of personal care and managing their home. The term *activities of daily living* (ADL) refers to the ability to perform these basic personal care tasks (see box 1.2). Typically, ADLs include eating, dressing, toileting, bathing, and transferring (e.g., getting out of bed into a chair and vice versa). While most ADL measurements are based on the Katz Activity of Daily Living Scale (Katz et al. 1963), it should be noted that there are more than forty-three different published ADL indexes assessing from five to nine different ADLs (Feinstein, Josephy, and Wells 1986).

BOX 1.1 DEMOGRAPHIC FACTS

- 13 percent of the population is over 65; this is the fastest growing segment
- 41 percent male and 59 percent female
- Life expectancy is 72 years for men and 79 years for women
- 80 percent of noninstitutionalized elderly living alone are female
- Racial and ethnic composition is becoming more diverse
- Currently 10 percent are nonwhite
- 5 percent of the population will spend some time of life in a long-term care facility
- 1 percent of the young old reside in a nursing home

BOX 1.2 ACTIVITIES OF DAILY LIVING (ADL)

- Eating
- Dressing
- Toileting
- Bathing
- Transferring

The term *instrumental activities of daily living* (IADL) refers to the ability to perform important tasks of home management. It was developed as an additional measure of independent functioning because the ADL measures do not capture the full range of activities necessary to live independently (Lawton and Brody 1969). Typically, the IADLs include activities such as housework, shopping, preparing meals, managing money, using the telephone, and taking medications (see box 1.3).

In 1994 approximately 14 percent of older Americans had difficulties in carrying out one or more ADLs, and 21 percent had problems with IADLs (U.S. Census Bureau 2000). However, these percentages also indicate that the majority of older adults (86 percent) have no significant limitations regarding activities of daily living. The percentage of older adults with ADL limitations increases with age. Of the older adult population residing in the community, approximately every third person over the age of 75 and every second person over the age of 85 needs assistance with everyday activities (U.S. Census Bureau 2000). Over half (57.6 percent) of those aged 80 and over had one or more severe disabilities, and 34.9 percent of that population reported needing assistance as a result of a disability (U.S. Census Bureau 2000). Between 1984 and 1995 older Americans reported improvements in physical

---

BOX 1.3 INSTRUMENTAL ACTIVITIES OF DAILY LIVING (IADL)

- Shopping
- Preparing Meals
- Managing Money
- Using Telephone
- Taking Medications

---

functioning—e.g., in their ability to walk a quarter mile, climb stairs, reach up over their head, and stoop, crouch, or kneel. Both men and women reported improvements in each of these categories. The percentage unable to perform at least one of nine physical activities without assistance or special equipment was higher among women than among men, but on the whole declined for both groups: from 23 percent to 20 percent for men and from 34 percent to 29 percent for women (Federal Interagency Forum on Aging 2000). However, institutionalized elderly have significantly higher percentages of ADL limitations. Major national surveys indicate that over 91 percent of the institutionalized elderly receive assistance with at least one ADL (Wiener et al. 1990). According to these surveys, the most common activity for which institutionalized elderly individuals require help is bathing (90 percent), followed by dressing, transferring, toileting, and eating (about one third).

Another sample of older adults, the participants in the National Channeling Demonstration Project, provides us with an indicator of the functional limitations of older adults encountered by human service professionals in the community. The major areas of functional limitations encountered by program participants were identified as: traveling (87 percent), housework (80 percent), bathing (80 percent), preparing meals (75 percent), managing money (70 percent), shopping (59 percent), and dressing (59 percent) (Manton, Vertrees, and Clark 1993). Although these percentages may be higher than average, they point to the typical responsibilities that are faced by caregivers of the elderly and by human service practitioners.

HEALTH Many of the functional limitations described are direct consequences of health conditions the person suffers from. However, not every health problem will lead to a limitation in daily activities of living. Many older adults enduring an acute or chronic health problem are able to adjust their lifestyles and continue to live independently (see box 1.4). In 1995 about 58 percent of persons aged 70 or older reported having arthritis, 45 percent reported having hypertension, and 21 percent reported having heart disease. Other chronic diseases included cancer (19 percent), diabetes (12 percent), and stroke (9 percent). About 64 percent of older women reported having arthritis, 48 percent reported having hypertension, and 19 percent reported having heart disease. Older men were less likely to report having arthritis (50 percent) and hypertension (41 percent) but were more likely to report having heart disease (25 percent). Men were also more likely to have had cancer (23 percent) than women (17 percent) (Federal Interagency Forum on Aging 2000).

BOX 1.4 FACTS ON ADL AND IADL

- ADL and IADL are typically assessed using standardized instruments
- 14 percent of older adults have difficulties with one or more ADLs
- 21 percent of older adults have problems with one or more IADLs
- Percentages of individuals with ADL limitation increases with age
- Institutionalized persons have more ADL limitations than those not institutionalized

---

Although acute health problems are less prevalent among persons over the age of 65, the consequences of such problems are often more serious for older adults than for younger persons (National Center for Health Statistics 1993). Chronic conditions frequently have no clear onset and often progress slowly. The usual treatment focuses on maximizing the person's ability to function with the chronic condition rather than on attempting a cure. The most prevalent chronic conditions of older adults are arthritis, hypertension, and heart disease (National Center for Health Statistics 1993). Other common chronic conditions include diabetes, hearing impairment, cataracts, orthopedic conditions, chronic sinusitis, tinnitus, and visual impairment. Heart disease, cancer, and stroke combined account for approximately 70 percent of the deaths among the older adult population (U.S. Census Bureau 1996). Before we describe the more prevalent acute and chronic health problems, it should also be noted that the majority of the noninstitutionalized young old rate their health as good, very good, or excellent.

Broken bones and hips are acute health problems that often leave the person with severe long-term consequences beyond the need of addressing the immediate medical condition. Many of these fractures are caused by falls, but osteoporosis, a deterioration of bone tissue that leaves bones more porous and brittle, is often a contributing factor. Due to the reduced bone strength caused by osteoporosis, the bones fracture more easily. Osteoporosis may be caused by calcium deficiency, but a lack of physical activity and family history may also play an important role. The loss of estrogen production during menopause is an established risk factor, which is why more women than men have been affected by osteoporosis. Many placements in supported living facilities and nursing homes immediately follow a hospitalization for a fractured hip.

Another common health problem is pneumonia. Pneumonia characterizes a group of inflammatory diseases of the lungs. Bacterial pneumonia is an acute infection caused by bacterial strains. Symptoms include high fever, chest pain, cough, and coughing blood. Pneumonia can be a very acute health problem for older adults. It frequently leads to hospitalization, and in about 10 percent of cases pneumonia is a fatal disease. Influenza or flu is an infectious and contagious disease of the respiratory tract. It is caused by virus strains that mutate over time. Influenza is an epidemic disease, often affecting a broad spectrum of the population.

The term *cancer* describes a group of diseases caused by malignant growth of tissue or tumors that often metastasize throughout the body. About one half of cancer cases occur in the older adult population. Cancer has been on the rise among older adults since the 1960s and continues to be one of the most prevalent causes of death among older adults (U.S. Census Bureau 1996). The increased risk of cancer among older adults may be due to several factors, including prolonged exposure to contributing genetic, environmental, dietary, or lifestyle factors. Even though early detection can help in the treatment of cancer, many older adults do not regularly seek preventative physical exams.

Acquired immune deficiency syndrome (AIDS) is a destruction of the immune system that results from an infection with the human immunodeficiency virus (HIV). A person does not die from the HIV infection but from opportunistic infections that occur when the immune system can no longer protect the body. While the highest rate of death caused by HIV-AIDS occurs among those aged 25 to 54, about three times as many older adults die from AIDS as persons under the age of 20. In contrast to the death rate among children, which has remained relatively stable, the rate for older adults has almost doubled from 1987 to 1992. Between 1996 and 2000 as many as 8,373 individuals (3.2 percent of the AIDS population) were 60 years of age or older and had AIDS (U.S. Census Bureau 1996).

Arthritis is a chronic inflammation of the joints. The most prevalent chronic condition, it affects every second older adult (Federal Interagency Forum on Aging-Related Statistics 2000). Arthritis is characterized by chronic pain, stiffness of the joints, and may be accompanied by significant swelling. Osteoarthritis, the more common form of arthritis, is caused by degenerative changes and breakdown of cartilage in joints. It is caused by wear and tear, thus becoming more common as we age. Rheumatoid arthritis is a chronic autoimmune disease. It is characterized by inflammation, pain, and deformity of the joints and can afflict individuals in all age groups.

Hypertension, elevated blood pressure, involves an increased pressure on the walls of the arteries. If undiagnosed and untreated, high blood pressure increases the risk of heart attack and heart disease. Similar to osteoporosis, hypertension does not occur suddenly. Rather, it is a slow process that develops over years. Individuals may not feel their blood pressure rising and often only notice the condition when their blood pressure has reached very high levels. High blood pressure is especially prevalent among older women. Of the elderly population, 63 percent of the women have been diagnosed with hypertension (National Academy on an Aging Society 2000). Elevations in blood pressure are more prevalent in African-Americans (54 percent) than in whites (38 percent). Cardiovascular disease or heart disease is caused by a narrowing of the coronary arteries and disruptions of the blood flow to the heart. Over time this insufficient blood supply can cause heart tissue to die and lead to an infarct. Even though heart disease continues to be a major cause of death among the elderly, there have been significant improvements since the 1960s (U.S. Census Bureau 1996).

Cerebrovascular disease or stroke is the consequence of disturbances and interruptions in the blood flow to the brain. It is caused by a blockage or hemorrhage of blood vessels leading to the brain that reduces the blood flow, thus causing an undersupply of oxygen in the brain. Cerebrovascular disease often has very severe long-term effects. Persons who had a stroke may endure reduced movement or completely impaired functioning of parts of their body. Although cardiovascular and cerebrovascular diseases are not the most prevalent chronic condition among the elderly, they may have the most serious consequences and continue to be the leading cause of death among older adults. The leading cause of death in 1998 was heart disease. However, the total has decreased by 31.7 percent since 1980. The second most common cause of death is cancer, followed by stroke, which decreased by 8.1 percent since 1980. Number four is chronic obstructive pulmonary disease, with an increase of 60.9 percent since 1980 (Federal Interagency Forum on Aging 2000). Thus, prevention of heart disease and stroke has received increased attention. Prevention has focused on addressing hypertension, unhealthy lipid levels (cholesterol), sedentary lifestyle, smoking, obesity, and diabetes (Hess 1991). (See box 1.5.)

BOX 1.5 PREVALENT CHRONIC AND ACUTE HEALTH CONDITIONS

- Arthritis
- Hypertension
- Heart Disease
- Hearing Impairment
- Cancer

MENTAL HEALTH Some mental health problems faced by older adults are unique or at least much more prevalent in this age group than in the population as a whole. Senile dementia is an example of a condition that is unique to the older adult population. Other mental health problems manifest themselves in similar ways as in the rest of the population. Depression is an example of such a mental health condition. Consequently, some mental health problems faced by older adults are assessed using the same diagnostic criteria and assessment instruments that are used for the general population while special geriatric assessment instruments have been developed for others. The chapter on assessment (ch. 4) will describe the geriatric assessment process and some of the more commonly used instruments in more detail.

Dementia and delirium are the two most prevalent cognitive disorders among the elderly (Kaplan and Sadock 1998). Dementia describes a category of usually slowly progressing cognitive disorders that involve memory loss and loss in intellectual and mental functioning. It afflicts mostly older adults. Five percent of persons over sixty-five experience severe dementia, and the percentage rises to 20 percent of those over the age of eighty (Kaplan and Sadock 1998). Senile dementia of the Alzheimer's type (SDAT) is the most common type of irreversible dementia among older adults. It accounts for about 50–60 percent of all dementia cases, and 50 percent of all nursing home residents have been diagnosed with it (Kaplan and Sadock 1998). SDAT is characterized by a slowly progressing loss of cognitive functioning and an increasing disorientation regarding time and place. In the early phases of SDAT, many individuals continue to live independently. Even as the disease progresses, many individuals suffering from SDAT remain at home and can be cared for by a spouse or a family member. As the disease progresses, however, caring for the person and management of behavior may become overwhelming for the caregivers. Alzheimer's disease is one of the most trying mental health conditions for family members involved. They see their loved one, who may still be in good health otherwise, slowly lose all memory and increasingly become confused and disoriented.

Delirium is an impairment of consciousness with a sudden onset. It follows a brief, fluctuating course, but when treated, it can potentially improve rapidly. The person experiencing delirium is temporarily disoriented and may have delusions or hallucinations. Causes of delirium include diseases of the central nervous system, systemic diseases such as heart failure, and intoxication or withdrawal from toxic or pharmaceutical agents (Kaplan and Sadock 1998). It has been estimated that between 30–40 percent of all hospitalized patients over the age of 65 experience an episode of delirium (Kaplan and Sadock 1998).

Depression is a mood disorder that lasts for more than two weeks and is not due to a general medical condition or hallucinations (APA 1994; Kaplan and Sadock 1998). Although depression may be underdiagnosed in the elderly population, it is more prevalent among this group than in the general population (Kaplan and Sadock 1998). A relatively small number of elderly have major depression. However, experiencing depressive symptoms and or reactive depression (in response to a significant life event, such as physical illness, loss, and relocation) are more common forms of depression among older adults (Cohen and Weisman 1990). Suicide is a serious problem among older adults. Most suicide attempts are made by individuals with depression or depressive symptoms (Belsky 1990). More suicides are attempted by men than by women. This is especially true for white elderly men, who have a significantly higher suicide rate than any other race or ethnic group. More elderly men die from suicide than from car accidents (U.S. Census Bureau 1996).

Parkinson's disease is a progressive neurological disease that afflicts adults and older adults. It is characterized by tremors in fingers and hands, muscle rigidity, and difficulties with associated movements (Kaplan and Sadock 1998). Parkinson's disease is caused by a deterioration of brain cells that produce dopamine. Although there is currently no cure, the progression of the disease can often be halted for extended periods of time if it is identified and treated with medication. (See box 1.6.)

ECONOMIC CHARACTERISTICS The elderly population is very heterogeneous in regard to economic status (see box 1.7). Overall, the income situation for older adults has significantly improved over the last thirty years. U.S. Census Bureau data indicate a median income in 1996 of $17,768 for elderly men and $10,062 for elderly women (U.S. Census Bureau 1996). However, these improvements have not been shared equally among all subgroups of the older adult population. Married older couples are generally financially better off, as are older men. While the income of elderly married couples has

---

BOX 1.6 PREVALENT MENTAL HEALTH PROBLEMS

- Senile Dementia and Alzheimer's Disease
- Delirium
- Depression
- Suicide
- Parkinson's Disease

risen significantly in the 1980s, there have been only modest gains for older women and no improvements for single older African-American women (U.S. Census Bureau 1996). The introduction of Social Security benefits has contributed to the better income situation of older adults. Social Security and pension benefits combined account for 42 percent of the income of retired persons. Property income and private pensions are other significant sources of income for retirees. As with income distribution, the poverty rate is significantly higher for elderly women (13 percent) than for elderly men (7 percent). African-American elderly continue to have the highest poverty rate (26 percent), followed by 23.8 percent for Hispanics, and 9 percent for whites.

In 1959, 35 percent of those aged 65 or over lived in families with incomes below the poverty line. By 1998 the percentage of the older population living in poverty had declined to 11 percent (Federal Interagency Forum on Aging 2000). Although there is a general trend toward improved economic status for the elderly, many older adults still live in poverty or only slightly above the poverty level. In 1998 poverty rates were 9 percent for persons between the ages of 65 and 74, 12 percent for those between 75 and 84, and 14 percent for those aged 85 or older (Federal Interagency Forum on Aging 2000). The oldest-old are the most likely to be poor of any adults over the age of 25 (U.S. Census Bureau 1996).

Among the older population, poverty rates are higher among women (13 percent) than among men (7 percent), among the nonmarried (17 percent) than the married (5 percent), and among minorities than among non-Hispanic white persons (Federal Interagency Forum on Aging 2000). In 1998

BOX 1.7 ECONOMIC FACTS

- Economic situation has improved for the older adult population
- 42 percent of income is from Social Security and pension benefits
- Improvements not uniform for all older adults
- Poverty rate is higher for elderly women than for elderly men
- Poverty rates among the elderly are 26 percent for African-Americans, 23.8 percent for Hispanics, and 9 percent for whites
- Among older adults the poverty rate increases with age
- Many live only slightly above poverty line
- 78 percent of older adults own their home, and 22 percent rent
- 6 percent of homes owned by the elderly have physical problems

divorced black women between the ages of 65 and 74 had a poverty rate of 47 percent, one of the highest rates for any subgroup of older adults (Social Security Administration 2000).

Some older adults continue to work after reaching retirement age, but older workers constitute a small proportion of the workforce. Those who continue working are for the most part employed in part-time positions. An increasing number of older women in their fifties are part of the workforce. At the same time, fewer older men participate in the workforce than in past generations. More and more older men retire early, even before they become eligible for Social Security retirement benefits at age 62 or for Medicare benefits at age 65. The older elderly individuals are, the less likely they are to work.

According to the American Housing Survey, about 78 percent of the elderly own the home they live in and 22 percent rent (1995). White older adults are more likely to own their home (72 percent) than African-Americans (64 percent) or Hispanics (59 percent) (U.S. Census Bureau 1996). Although the rate of ownership is comparatively high, it should be emphasized that most older adults also live in older homes. Thus, they have to spend more time and financial resources on maintenance and repair of their home. Approximately 6 percent of homes owned by older persons have significant physical problems (U.S. Census Bureau 1996).

SUMMARY

Overall, American society is aging. This trend will continue well into the next century as the baby-boom generation bulge broadens and squares the top of the age pyramid (Soldo and Agree 1988) and as birth and death rates decline (Riley 1987; Wolfe 1993). Our discussion, condensed though it had to be, has revealed that older adults are a very heterogeneous group. Diversity is the term that probably best describes this population group. As we continue, we would like to emphasize that this diversity should be kept in mind when applying the practice concepts we present.

We described several areas of problems and needs older adults are often faced with. Activities of daily living and instrumental activities of daily living were introduced as two concepts describing the functional abilities of a person. Although many older adults suffer limitations in ADLs and IADLs, the majority of older adults continues to live independently and is able to manage daily life well. The health status of older adults has been improving over the course of the twentieth century. Older adults are less likely than in earlier times to encounter acute health problems, but when they do become ill, the consequences are often serious. Chronic illnesses, such as arthritis, hypertension, and heart disease, are common among older adults. About 80 percent of the elderly endure at least one chronic health problem. Dementia, Alzheimer's disease, delirium, and depression are the most prevalent mental health problems among older adults. Finally, the economic situation is becoming increasingly positive for a growing segment of older Americans. However, a lack of financial resources continues to be a problem for many elderly and frail elderly individuals who still live in poverty or uncomfortably close to the poverty line.

CHAPTER 2

THE AGING NETWORK AND SERVICE PROVIDERS

I N THIS CHAPTER we will introduce the aging network, a hierarchical structure of programs and agencies that was developed under the Older Americans Act to coordinate the delivery of services to the older adult population. This will be followed by an overview of the continuum of care and the major providers of formal services for elderly clients. We will then turn to the various human service professionals involved in providing these services. Next, we will provide an overview of the informal support network older adults regularly turn to for assistance. The chapter concludes with a case example that will illustrate some of the concepts presented.

THE AGING NETWORK

The term *aging network* describes a system of formal services for older adults. At the heart of this aging network are the provisions of the Older Americans Act (OAA), enacted in 1965 and amended several times since (see box 2.1). The OAA set forth policy objectives and created a structure of services for older adults (Wacker, Roberto, and Piper 1997). The overall goal of the aging network is to establish a coordinated system of services on the local level. This is achieved through coordinated advocacy, planning, and delivery of services.

At the top of the aging network is the Administration on Aging, with the commissioner of the AoA responsible directly to the Department of Health and Human Services. The AoA has ten regional AoA offices that coordinate the fifty-seven State Units on Aging. These State Units on Aging in turn coordinate the efforts of 670 local Area Agencies on Aging (AAAs). The largest program of the OAA is governed by Title III. Resources for programs funded under this title are channeled through the State Units on Aging to the local AAA. The primary role of the local AAA is to assess local needs and ensure that needed services are available. To this end, each AAA is responsible for a local planning and service area (PSA). For its planning area, the AAA develops

---

BOX 2.1 STRUCTURE OF THE AGING NETWORK UNDER THE OAA

DHHS

Administration on Aging (AoA)

10 Regional AoA Offices

57 State Units on Aging

670 Area Agencies on Aging

Local Service Providers

---

a plan for comprehensive coordinated services, funds providers to fill the service gaps it identifies, and advocates for those older adults living within its PSA (Wacker, Roberto, and Piper 1997). Although the AAAs may provide services directly, they usually subcontract with outside providers. There is no means test for those services provided through the OAA. Rather, they are universal age-based programs, available to all older adults. While the AAA is central to planning and coordination, local for-profit and nonprofit providers deliver the majority of services.

Title III of the Older Americans Act is at the core of establishing the aging network. Under Title III, Part A, of the OAA the State Units on Aging and Area Agencies on Aging are required to devise multiyear plans indicating the coordination and delivery of services. Multipurpose senior centers are an outgrowth of this title. Focus of Title III, Part B, of the OAA is the development of a continuum of care. The goal of the continuum of care is to develop a graded system of services that will help older adults to continue living independently in the community. Part C of Title III regulates the delivery of congregate and home-delivered meals programs. Home care services are funded under Title III, Part D, a 1992 amendment to the OAA. Several of the services we will describe in the following section are funded under this title (e.g., personal and home health care, respite programs, homemaker services, telephone reassurance). Another amendment to the OAA in 1987, Part F of Title III, regulates disease prevention and health promotion services.

THE CONTINUUM OF CARE

Provisions in the Older Americans Act led to the development of a continuum of care. The continuum of care is a graded continuum of service options to

---

BOX 2.2 SELECTED SERVICES IN THE CONTINUUM OF CARE

- Senior Centers
- Telephone Reassurance
- Nonmedical Home Care
- Nutritional Services
- Personal Care
- Skilled Home Health Care
- Hospice
- Respite Care
- Adult Day Care
- Retirement Community
- Assisted Living
- Hospital
- Nursing Home

---

assist a person with social, financial, medical, and personal care services. The goal is to match individual needs with the appropriate level of care, thus enabling the older person to continue living at home and preventing unnecessary hospital or nursing home admissions. On one end of the continuum are community-based in-home services that assist the person with one or more activities of daily living. At the other end of the spectrum are acute care hospitals and institutional long-term care facilities that provide twenty-four-hour care and support with all ADLs and IADLs. In the following sections, we will introduce the major service providers in the continuum of care, starting with the least restrictive service options and ending with the most comprehensive service environments (see box 2.2).

SENIOR CENTERS Senior centers offer older adults an opportunity to come together and fulfill many of their social, physical, and intellectual needs (Lowy and Doolin 1990). They offer a wide range of services and activities for older adults, which is why they are often referred to as multipurpose senior centers. Most services and activities fall into four groupings: social and recreational activities, educational programs, health and nutritional programs, and information and referral. Social and recreational activities include arts and fitness classes and socialization groups. Educational programs offered by senior centers focus on topics such as health, nutrition, and finances. The health and nutritional programs offered by senior centers range from blood pressure checks and hearing and vision screenings to providing congregate meals and nutrition screenings. Many senior centers assist their clients in locating and accessing services and resources.

TELEPHONE REASSURANCE Telephone reassurance is a service typically performed by volunteers and usually includes daily phone calls to make sure that the person is doing well. The callers also offer emotional support. If the telephone call is not answered, a professional is sent to the person's home to check on the status of the individual. Another type of telephone reassurance program is the lifeline service. The older adults participating in this program always wear a small lifeline device with a button they can press in case of an emergency. Pushing the button automatically sends a message to the lifeline agency, which immediately sends out professional help to the client's home.

NONMEDICAL HOME CARE Nonmedical home care includes nonmedical services that ease the daily life of an older person with limitations in activities of daily living. Examples of nonmedical home care services are homemakers and home aides. Respite care and home-delivered meals, which we describe separately, may also be considered nonmedical home care services. Homemaker services are provided in the client's home environment with the primary goal of supporting the independent living capabilities of the older person. Services include light housekeeping, shopping, and other small chores (Wacker, Roberto, and Piper 1997). The service can also be provided to those elderly persons who move in with a relative or a friend. However, usually only services that are specifically customer-related are approved for reimbursement. Homemakers do not provide personal or medical care or any other activities that involve touching the client.

NUTRITIONAL SERVICES Several programs offer nutritional services. The two most common meals programs are congregate meals and home-delivered meals. These services are regulated and financed to a large extent through provisions of the OAA. Congregate meals are often offered in senior centers as well as in some alternative living arrangements, such as retirement communities and congregate housing programs. In addition to offering low-cost meals, these programs also offer nutritional education and an opportunity for socializing. In 1995 about two and a half million elderly people took part in congregate meals programs, and nearly a million participated in programs involving home-delivered meals (Weimer 1997). In most communities home-delivered meals (meals-on-wheels) are provided by private nonprofit agencies that are funded through the OAA. In addition to congregate and home-delivered meals, low-income older adults may qualify for food stamps programs and take advantage of food banks. Finally, more and more communities are offering shopping assistance programs for older adults who have problems with grocery shopping (Wacker, Roberto, and Piper 1997).

PERSONAL CARE Personal care activities are often carried out by nonprofessional trained workers. They perform certain personal care tasks, such as bathing, toileting, and dressing the client. However, these trained workers are usually not allowed to administer medication, and they cannot provide other services related to health care. Trained personal care aides are supervised and are usually part of an interdisciplinary home health care team.

SKILLED HOME HEALTH CARE Skilled home health care describes a range of services intended to promote or restore health after illness or disability. It is the largest public expenditure for home-based services to older adults (Wacker, Roberto, and Piper 1997). Home health care providers offer a diverse range of services. A typical skilled home health care agency will provide health and nutritional assessments, skilled nursing care, rehabilitative therapy, mental health assessment and counseling, educational services, and coordination of services. Consequently, most home health care agencies employ an interdisciplinary staff that includes nurses, nutritionists, medical social workers, case managers, physical and occupational therapists, and home health aides (Martin 2000). Many home health care providers are certified under Medicare, indicating that they have met a minimum federal standard of patient care. A referral by a physician is required if the client is to receive Medicare or Medicaid reimbursement for home health care.

HOSPICE Hospices developed to address the need of terminally ill patients and their families for assistance in dealing with death and dying. Convinced that people do not want to spend their last days in depersonalized institutional settings, hospices attempt to move the dying back to a more personal home and family setting. The focus, then, is on supportive care for the terminally ill through offering comprehensive medical, psychological, and spiritual services. This includes honoring the individual values and wishes of the dying person and his or her family. More than anything else, "hospice is a philosophy about caring for others" (Hayslip and Leon 1992:3). Hospice work usually includes the family members in the dying person's life. It thus tries to address the emotional and spiritual needs of the terminally ill person as well as those of the family. Usually, hospice work occurs in the client's home. Professional hospice workers are available around the clock to assist the family and the patient. Hospice services are provided by professionals, such as physicians, nurses, social workers, home health aides, pastoral counselors and clergy, and by trained volunteers. About 33 percent of the hospice providers are community-based organizations, 29 percent operate out of a hospital, and 22 percent are part of a home health agency (Harper 1995). While most hospice patients are elderly, hospice services are offered to individuals of any age. According to the National Home and Hospice Care Survey, 61 percent of the male and 75 percent of the female hospice patients are over 65 years of age (Haupt 1997). There are more than 3,000 hospice programs in the United States caring for over half a million people (Hospice Foundation of America 2001).

RESPITE AND ADULT DAY CARE Adult day care is designed mostly as a respite service for caregivers. Elderly individuals may have a number of conditions that prevent them from staying at home alone when their caregivers are at work. Other caregivers may simply need a respite form the highly demanding tasks of caring for an elderly person. Three types of adult day care can be distinguished, social adult day care, medical day care, and day care for persons with Alzheimer's disease (Naleppa 2001a). Social adult day care programs offer meals, administration of medication, and socializing, but they typically provide no personal care services. Medical and Alzheimer's day care programs are for elderly individuals in need of medical, nursing, physical, or occupational therapy and requiring more intensive personal care or supervision. Many day care programs offer transportation services for their program participants.

HOUSING AND SENIOR LIVING ARRANGEMENTS Most older adults live in the community, and many of the services described so far are focused on sustaining individuals in their own environment. However, a wide range of alternative senior living arrangements exists, from retirement communities to nursing homes (Mitty 2001a). A living arrangement favored by more and more older adults who are able to live independently is the planned retirement community. These retirement communities usually have minimum age requirements and some do not permit the long-term stay of children. Planned retirement communities often have extensive social and recreational offerings. Continuing retirement communities offer a continuous range of living alternatives, from independent living to residence in a nursing home. Older adults can move from one level of supported living to the next according to their individual needs.

In congregate housing facilities, older adults have individual apartments and use common areas for meals and social activities. Adult foster care provides room and board, supervision, and other specialized services to older adults with physical, mental, and behavioral problems (Sherman and Newman 1988; Fokemer et al. 1996). It differs from other residential care settings in the size of the homes and the familial nature of the care. After being admitted to adult foster care, an annual reassessment of the residents' needs is conducted to determine whether a more advanced level of care is needed. Adult foster care homes are approved by local Departments of Social Services. Adult care residences (ACRs) and assisted living facilities are licensed to provide care and maintenance to four or more adults. This type of arrangement is appropriate when the older adult needs assistance with activities of daily living but does not require the level of care provided by a nursing home. Assessment of the appropriate level of care is performed using a uniform assessment instrument.

HOSPITALS Hospitals are the primary provider of acute care in cases of injury and disease, offering a comprehensive array of health care services under one roof. While some hospitals specialize in certain client populations or specific illnesses, many hospitals offer a wide range of health care services and have specialized departments within their facilities. Most hospitals do not specifically target older adults, but they serve an important role in the continuum of care. Some hospitals have designated geriatric care units, specializing in addressing the medical needs of elderly patients. A recent trend is for hospitals to provide health care services through community-based units. Professionals in hospital settings include physicians, nurses, occupational and physical therapists, and social workers.

NURSING HOMES The nursing home or long-term care facility offers the most comprehensive level of care. In a skilled nursing home, all aspects of life and care are fulfilled by the facility. The target groups of the nursing home are frail elderly persons who need around-the-clock-nursing care and extensive assistance with activities of daily living. Rooms are usually private or semiprivate, but the rest of the living space is shared. Nursing homes provide personal and medical care, medications, meals, social activities, and a comprehensive range of therapeutic services as needed (Mitty 2001b). Many individuals enter the nursing home as private pay residents and then, as they run out of money, apply for Medicaid to cover the expenses. In order to receive Medicaid reimbursement, the elderly person's physician must certify that the person's condition requires skilled nursing home care. Furthermore, the person must pass a stringent financial test to establish eligibility. Nursing homes may be public or private facilities, but more and more of them are private for-profit providers. More than 40 percent of nursing homes in the United States are operated by chains (Phillips and Hawes 1996). Two thirds of investor-owned facilities are chain operated, compared with 40 percent of the nonprofit facilities and 8 percent of the public facilities (Harrington et al. 2001).

Medicare's prospective payments system has led to the creation of subacute care units in long-term care facilities for those patients whose needs fall between nursing home and acute care hospital (Wacker, Roberto, and Piper 1997). Another recent trend is the development of specialized units within a long-term care facility for residents with Alzheimer's disease or other forms of dementia. It should be noted that only about 5 percent of the population will enter a nursing home at some point in their life. Most people choose nursing home placement as a last resort after extended periods of caregiving and after the demands of care can no longer be met by the caregivers (see also chapter 10).

In this section, we gave a brief overview of the service providers in the continuum of care. The task planners presented in part III will further describe many of these services and provide more detailed instructions on how to access them.

HUMAN SERVICE PROFESSIONS IN GERONTOLOGICAL PRACTICE

Several human service professionals offer services in the continuum of care (see box 2.3). Some of the professional roles described here require specialized professional training and a higher education degree. For example, social workers and nurses require extended formal education and training in an accredited institution of higher education. Other human services practitioners are identified by the role they assume in the service delivery system. They may be members of a profession or may have received specialized training without a formal degree. An example are case managers; typically they are social workers, often referred to as social work case managers, or they are nurses, referred to as nurse case managers. However, in some cases they may be trained human service workers without a formal degree.

SOCIAL WORKERS Social workers are professionals with a bachelor of social work (BSW), a master of social work (MSW), or a doctoral degree in social work (DSW or Ph.D.). According to the National Association of Social Workers (NASW), more than half of the mental health services in the United

BOX 2.3 SELECTED HUMAN SERVICE PROFESSIONS IN GERONTOLOGICAL PRACTICE

- Social Worker
- Nurse
- Case Manager
- Discharge Planner
- Therapist
- Home Health Care Worker
- Physical Therapist
- Occupational Therapist

States are provided by professional social workers (National Association of Social Workers 2002). Most states license social workers. To obtain a license, a professional must have completed a social work education from an accredited social work program and fulfill additional postgraduate requirements. Most states require a licensed social worker to complete two years of supervised social work beyond the master's degree and pass an additional clinical licensure examination. A recent development has been the growing emphasis on the inclusion of gerontological content in the training and education of social workers. Most MSW programs now offer gerontological content in their curriculum, and some offer special gerontology certificate programs.

Social workers assume a variety of roles in the aging network. As case managers, professional social workers help clients to access and coordinate needed services. They also monitor the proper implementation of these services. As discharge planners in hospitals, social workers assist the older adult in planning for the return home. Hospital social workers also work with older adults and their families providing crisis intervention in the emergency room and in the hospital units. Social workers are often employed by service providers such as home health care agencies, hospices, and nursing homes to offer counseling and psychosocial education to elderly clients and their families and caregivers. More and more social workers in private practice specialize in working with elderly clients and offer services such as case management and counseling. Social workers often take on administrative functions in agencies of the aging network, for example, as directors of the social service department of a hospital, as nursing home directors, or as the head of a social service agency. Finally, some social workers participate in the policymaking process as advocates or lobbyists, or they hold political offices.

NURSES Nurses are the primary professional group working with older adults in the health care system. Certified nursing assistants (CNAs) or patient care technicians (PCTs) are entry-level providers of direct patient care and work under the direction of registered nurses (RNs) (National Council Licensure Examination for Practical/Vocational Nurses 2001). Licensed practical nurses (LPNs) or licensed vocational nurses (LVNs) provide a significant amount of basic nursing services and also work under the supervision of a RN (National Council of State Boards of Nursing 1998). To acquire the status of RN, a candidate must graduate from an approved nursing education program and pass a state RN licensing exam. Advanced nursing education is offered through master's of nursing programs and is one of the qualifications required for a license as a nurse practitioner. In a growing number of states, nurse practitioners are allowed to provide primary care and have the privilege of writing prescriptions.

According to the American Nurses Credentialing Center (2002), there are three types of specializations for nurses working in the field of gerontology. The certified gerontological nurse has at least a bachelor's degree, is licensed as an RN, and has extended practice experience in gerontological nursing. Registered nurses specializing in gerontology and having passed a modular or specialty exam may be awarded the credential of RN, C (Certified) or RN, BC (Board Certified) in gerontology. A gerontological clinical nurse specialist (CNS) is an advanced practice nurse with a master's degree whose work focuses on the development and implementation of treatment plans for the geriatric population. Finally, a gerontological nurse practitioner has graduated from a gerontological nurse practitioner (GNP) master's degree program or has completed a formal postgraduate GNP program. It should be noted that nurses working with older adults may have a specialization in home or community health. After social workers, nurses are the most likely professionals to provide case management functions. They are often called geriatric care managers.

CASE MANAGERS The most common type of geriatric case manager is a practitioner who works directly with clients, focusing on assessment, helping clients access and link to services, and monitoring service delivery. In addition, case managers may provide counseling to the elderly and their caretakers. In many geriatric care settings case managers will work as part of interdisciplinary teams that include social workers, nurses, other medical staff, and case aides (Austin 2001). Case managers in administrative and supervisory positions attend to such functions as program administration, network development, and training. Recently several case management licenses have been proposed and established. However, there is currently no widely accepted or required case management license.

The educational level of case managers ranges from high school to doctoral degrees. Nonprofessionals might not be suitable to carry out certain case management tasks, and there is some concern whether even a bachelor's degree represents adequate education to handle the range of responsibilities with sufficient expertise (Kantner 1987; Schmid and Hasenfeld 1993). Professional associations, such as the National Association of Social Workers and the American Nurses Association, call for qualified case managers to have at least a baccalaureate or masters degree. Furthermore, case managers should be responsible for tasks appropriate to their level of education, skills, and experience (Brennan and Kaplan 1993; National Association of Social Workers 1992) (see also chapter 8).

DISCHARGE PLANNERS Discharge planning is an activity that is incorporated into the continuum of care of acute care hospitals. It addresses the need to assist clients in making plans for their lives after leaving the hospital. Discharge planners serve as intermediaries in the transition between different levels of care, usually at the interface between the hospital and the community. Discharge planning has been a traditional professional activity at many hospitals but did not receive much attention before the early 1980s when prospective payment systems for Medicare patients compelled hospitals to find ways to discharge patients earlier. This led to an increased focus on planning the transition of patients back into the community as soon as medically possible.

Elderly clients often enter the hospital under unforeseen circumstances. They may need to make adjustments to their environment and lifestyle in order to return home. Since not all patients require extensive preparation for discharge, the discharge process begins with the identification of patients who require comprehensive planning. Next, discharge planners may complete a multidimensional assessment to find out which needs a patient will have to deal with upon returning home. An interdisciplinary team frequently completes this assessment. Based on the information gathered, the team develops a discharge plan that lists the problems and needs of the client and how these will be addressed. During this process, the discharge planner helps the client to identify, access, and coordinate needed services and resources. In most hospitals, discharge planning is completed by professional social workers or nurses.

PSYCHOTHERAPISTS/COUNSELORS The role of a therapist or counselor may be assumed by a psychologist, social worker, or psychiatrist. Therapists working with older adults will provide psychotherapy and counseling for a wide range of psychological and emotional problems. Therapy with older adults can take the form of individual therapy, family counseling, or group therapy. An additional area that therapists working with older adults often emphasize is intergenerational counseling. Therapists integrating an intergenerational perspective pay special attention to the interactions between older adults, their adult children, and any other generations involved in therapy. They usually include family members from different generations in at least some of the therapeutic sessions and tasks. Many geriatric case managers will not only perform the case management functions discussed earlier but will also offer counseling as part of their practice (Austin 2001). In particular, this may be the case for the growing number of private geriatric case managers. "Clinical" case management, which addresses the entire range of problems and needs, from personal care needs to psychological problems, has been described as the hallmark of gerontological practice (Morrow-Howell 1992).

HOME HEALTH CARE WORKERS As described earlier in this chapter, home health care agencies often work with interdisciplinary teams that include nurses, social workers, and physicians. In addition, home health care agencies also employ trained nonprofessional workers, such as home health aides and homemakers. Home health aides customarily receive some special training qualifying them to provide personal care services under the supervision of a nursing professional. They assist clients with the performance of activities of daily living, for example, bathing, toileting, and dressing them (Martin 2000). Homemakers and chore workers assist their clients with light housekeeping tasks such as preparing meals, going shopping, and doing the laundry. However, homemakers are usually not qualified to perform any personal care activities.

PHYSICAL AND OCCUPATIONAL THERAPISTS Physical and occupational therapists assist in the process of rehabilitation and in restoring mobility and managing pain after illness, injuries, or surgery. Physical therapists attend to the rehabilitation and improvement of gross motor skills. For example, a physical therapist might use an exercise regimen combined with massage and special equipment to improve the strength and agility of a person's arms and legs after surgery.

Occupational therapists focus on improving the fine motor skills of an individual. For example, they assist the injured or ill individual to become as independent as possible by using directed activities and exercises. Such exercises could focus on the improvement of a person's eye-hand coordination, self-feeding abilities, writing skills, and ability to dress. Occupational therapists also train patients in the use of adaptive equipment, such as walkers. Typically, physical and occupational therapists will provide information and patient education on lifestyle changes that will improve physical mobility and the rehabilitation process.

INFORMAL SUPPORT SYSTEMS

Now that we have covered the continuum of care and the human service professionals, we will focus on the informal systems that provide care to older adults (see box 2.4). Included here are spouses, sons, and daughters as well as friends, neighbors, and various religious and community groups. Informal support systems and formal service delivery systems supplement each other, each fulfilling important functions in the provision of support and resources. Family members may take on most of the personal care tasks, such as bathing and toileting, with the daily assistance of a personal care aide. And while a family member can administer the medications, a home health nurse might provide a daily checkup on the health and the vital signs of the person. A case manager from a home health care agency might coordinate personal care and the delivery of other formal services, while an adult day care center may offer respite for the caregiver.

Before going into detail about informal supports, we should emphasize again that by and large the majority of older adults are able to live independently with little or no support and caregiving. Furthermore, giving and receiving care and assistance is not unidirectional. In fact, many older adults provide significant amounts of assistance and resources to their adult children and their grandchildren. This said, informal systems nevertheless play a very important part in the life of any individual. Elderly clients often come

---

BOX 2.4 INFORMAL SUPPORT SYSTEMS

- Spouses
- Daughters and Sons
- Friends
- Neighbors
- Religious Groups
- Community Groups
- Informal Support Groups

in contact with formal services only after their families and caregivers have exhausted their capacities and resources. According to Rothman (1994), the most important functions informal supports fulfill include: friendship, emotional sustenance, guidance and advice, social integration, and the provision of a buffer against stressors. The contributions of informal supports often remain unmatched by anything the formal service delivery system can offer. Social interaction provided by family members and friends not only gives the individual meaning and prevents isolation, but it is something a formal service cannot provide in the same way or quality. Furthermore, older adults, like members from any other age group, prefer to receive help through informal supports. Research suggests the existence of a clear hierarchical preference structure, sometimes termed as the principle of substitution. According to this preference structure, older adults turn to their spouses and children for assistance first and then to their close friends and neighbors before turning to the formal service delivery system if none of the others can help (Cantor 1991; Litwak 1985). Cultural norms of independence and self-reliance as well as embarrassment about the fact that they need help prevent many older adults from seeking help. Family members and friends are often the first to identify the need for assistance. Many older adults manage to live independently for extended periods of time despite difficulties in performing one or several tasks of daily living. It is often at the time of discharge planning from a hospital that a thorough assessment identifies the person's need for assistance and leads to contact with formal service providers.

FAMILIES AND CAREGIVING Within the informal support network, family members are the primary source of help to older adults. They contribute by far the majority of resources, assistance, and caregiving supports. Gatz, Bengtson, and Blum (1990:410) categorize the assistance given by family caregivers as follows "(1) emotional support, advice; (2) direct instrumental assistance (meal preparation, housecleaning, laundry, shopping, transportation); (3) personal care (bathing, dressing, feeding, etc.); (4) managing money; (5) making decisions about care and providing linkage to formal services . . . ; and (6) providing direct financial assistance." The makeup of this typology can be seen and understood as yet another indicator of the overlapping and supplementary nature of the formal and informal support networks.

A growing body of research has focused on various aspects of family caregiving. This research supports the common belief that spouses are most likely to be the primary caregivers of elderly persons living in the community (Zarit, Birkel, and MaloneBeach 1989). Having the closest ties to the care recipient, they are usually able to offer the strongest social and emotional support. They also provide the majority of instrumental support. Many formal services, especially those offering financial resources, will take the presence of a spouse into account when deciding about the eligibility for services. Spouses are often seen as the first line of defense. Only when they are no longer able to help will certain services and resources become available. As we discussed in the first chapter, the number of divorced older adults has been increasing. A related fact that may come as a surprise is that it is not unusual for caregivers to provide assistance to a divorced spouse (Gatz, Bengtson, and Blum 1990). Among adult children, daughters have traditionally been more involved in caregiving than sons. This trend continues even as more and more women are entering the workforce (Scharlach, Lowe, and Schneider 1991). However, adult sons, as the third primary group of caregivers, contribute more to caregiving than is often thought. Estimates indicate that over one third of caregiving adult children are sons (National Alliance for Caregiving 1997). Thus, adult sons should be considered an important source of caregiving assistance. When sons become involved, they are as committed and motivated as daughters in their assistance to the elderly parent (Harris 1998).

Relationships with siblings hold different meanings for different individuals. Those that had close ties throughout their life usually also stay close in old age. For many older adults, the sibling relationship becomes even more important in later life. Positive sibling relationships can offer significant support through joint participation in mutually enjoyable activities, reminiscing about family issues, providing emotional support, and providing assistance in resolving the developmental tasks of later life (Scott 1990). Finally, children-in-law are often overlooked as a source of caregiving. Contrary to commonly held beliefs, research indicates that children-in-law offer comparable levels of care and have caregiving experiences that are very similar to those of caregiving adult children (Peters-Davis, Moss, and Pruchno 1999).

There has been an increasing interest in the provision of services by caregivers and also in the ways caregivers can be supported and prevented from suffering burnout. A good deal of research has focused on individual counseling for caregivers (e.g., Schmidt et al. 1988; Smith, Tobin, and Toseland 1992) as well the use of caregiver support groups (e.g., Clark and Rakowski 1983; Gonyea and Silverstein 1991; Bourgeois, Schulz, and Burgio 1996). More specifically, studies have focused on training caregivers in coping skills and stress reduction techniques (e.g., Lazarus et al. 1981) and on the combination of several of these treatment modalities (e.g., Mittelman et al. 1995). A common theme in all these studies is the recognition that psychological, emotional, and social support must be offered to caregivers in an effort to reduce their burden and stress levels and to improve their abilities to provide care. It is important to mention that caregiving is not only seen as a burden and a stressor; rather, it also leads to personal rewards for the caregiver. Caregivers frequently report personal gains that range from reduced levels of guilt and increased feelings of self-worth to closer relationships with the care recipient and an enhanced sense of purpose and meaning (Kramer 1997).

CAREGIVING AND INSTITUTIONALIZATION If caregivers are involved in the life of an elderly client living at home, they are usually also involved in decisions about nursing home placement, if this becomes an issue. Institutionalization is not a decision that is easy to make. Despite the myth of families abandoning their relatives, institutionalization is usually used only as a last resort after caregivers have gone beyond their capacities to provide care (Chenoweth and Spencer 1986; Morycz 1985; Naleppa 1996). While predictors of placement naturally include characteristics and needs of the elderly person, the family's and caregivers' attributes also play an important role. Such family attributes include: being overwhelmed by the demands of providing care, relationship to the person cared for, the caregiver's health and mental status, and the acceptance of the caregiver role by the caring family member (Chenoweth and Spencer 1986; Colerick and George 1986; Pratt, Wright, and Schmall 1987; Montgomery and Kosloski 1994; Pruchno, Michael, and Potshnik 1990). Numerous studies also point to the significance of the caregiver's subjective distress as a deciding factor (Brown, Potter, and Foster 1990; Cohen et al. 1993; Lieberman and Kramer 1991; McFall and Miller 1992).

It is important to note that family ties are maintained and caregiving continues after institutionalization (Zarit and Whitlatch 1992). Family involvement is the norm, and most families visit their relatives frequently (Bitzan and Kruzich 1990). Many family members continue to take over caregiving tasks in the nursing home. For example, on any given day, you can see a daughter or a son helping with feeding at dinnertime or taking their elderly parent for a walk. Family members continue to be a main source of social and emotional support. Due to this ongoing involvement, the caregiver's stress and burden often remain at very high levels even after institutionalization occurs (Brody, Dempsey, and Pruchno 1990; Monahan 1995; Pruchno and Kleban 1993; Riddick et al. 1992; Zarit and Whitlatch 1992).

FRIENDS, NEIGHBORS, AND COMMUNITY GROUPS Friends and neighbors are another important source of support. Friends often have long-standing and strong ties. Next to family members, they may have the best insight into the life and the needs of the individual. For example, in the case of a widowed person with no family members living close by, friends may have the most intimate knowledge about the individual's needs and problems. The familiar face of a friend may also also establish a sense of security and connectedness to the outside world. However, long-term friendships are not the only source of assistance a person may rely upon. Sometimes new friendships develop after clients become involved with the same formal services. Two clients might meet at the dialysis unit were they regularly run into each other. Dealing with similar needs, they may become acquainted and end up not only becoming friends but also providing mutual aid to each other.

Neighbors play an important role in the provision of other assistance, but they usually do not provide the caregiving support and direct instrumental supports a family member could offer. By definition, neighbors live close to the person. This proximity is a considerable advantage for the elderly person, in crisis situations as in day-to-day life. Neighbors can drop in without having to plan their visit ahead of time. Sometimes, neighbors informally develop a support network by sharing tasks and resources. The neighbor with the car might drive the other to appointments and run errands, while the other neighbor in exchange might help with chores around the house that cannot be accomplished by one person alone.

Spirituality and religion play an important part in the life of many older adults, addressing important existential and emotional needs (Tobin 1991). Religious groups should not be underestimated as a source of social support and friendship. Older adults are more likely to be members of churches and other religious groups than of any other type of community group. In addition to receiving support, individuals who actively participate in religious activities were found to be of better health than those only attending church or not involved in religious activities at all (Rowe and Kahn 1998). Prayer, meditation, and other spiritual activities provide a sense of grounding, peace of mind, and connectedness. Finally, it should be mentioned that many religious institutions are also involved in the delivery of formal services. All major religious institutions in this country maintain social programs and agencies that provide services to older adults.

There are numerous community groups that offer a range of social, emotional, and in-kind supports to older adults. These community groups range from local community centers and social clubs to volunteer groups and informal support groups. Although some of these community groups could be described as formal organizations, they can be considered part of the informal support network if their primary purpose and intention is not to offer a service. Other groups, such as AA or Al-Anon, may not have the assistance of older adults as their primary intent, but membership nevertheless can offer considerable support for an elderly person who joins the group. This also holds true for many social clubs, volunteer groups, and political organizations. Their primary goal may not be to provide social support, but they nonetheless offer friendship and companionship, guidance, and advice as well as social and emotional support. Being a volunteer for a community organization can provide a sense of accomplishment and belonging. The older adult may derive a feeling of enrichment and purpose from the volunteering experience. Other community activities may also contribute to the well-being of the person. Going to Wednesday night bingo provides emotional and social support. Moreover, it also offers an opportunity to maintain old friendships and build new social networks that might be utilized for support.

CASE EXAMPLE: GEORGE

We conclude this chapter with a case example. George is 92 years old and a resident of St. Mary's Home for Adults, a skilled nursing facility in the suburbs of a midsized town. His life story may make him a typical example of a male nursing home resident his age. George grew up in a small farming community where he also spent most of his adult life. He married his late wife Martha when he was 28. Together they had two sons. For most of his life George worked as a sales manager for a local grocery store, and Martha raised the children and attended to the housework. They were a fairly typical family for the place and time they lived in. After the children left home to go to college, Martha started working part-time in the town library. In addition to their jobs, Martha and George worked a small field adjacent to their home. George retired at the age of 65 but continued to work occasional part-time jobs. For example, during the busy holiday seasons he regularly helped out in the store he had managed for so many years. George and Martha relied mostly on his pension plan and their Social Security benefits as well as on some small savings they had accumulated over the years. They also had an additional source of income from selling a part of their property to a younger couple and investing the money in a small retirement investment fund.

George and Martha enjoyed their life as retirees. They frequently traveled to visit relatives and spent a lot of time with their sons and their grandchildren. Both George and Martha led most of their adult and older adult life without major health problems. George had slightly elevated blood pressure, and Martha had mild arthritis, but neither condition significantly impacted their lives. Aside from their contacts with members of the medical professions, they had very little interaction with health care providers, social workers, or other human service professionals.

Martha became ill shortly after George's eighty-first birthday. She was hospitalized for testing and diagnosis after a period of dizziness that culminated in an incident of fainting. When she was diagnosed with cancer in the advanced stages, they decided that she should return home to die in her own home environment. The discharge planner at the hospital had made arrangements for Martha and George to be visited by a social work case manager who would assist them in accessing and coordinating the services they needed. With assistance from a health care worker, who helped with some of the personal care needs, George took care of Martha until her death. The social worker also introduced them to the concept of hospice and assisted them in accessing the meals-on-wheels program. Although George had always enjoyed cooking, at times he felt too overwhelmed by the caregiving demands placed on him to prepare meals. A long-time neighbor and friend supported him and Martha by occasionally preparing some of the meals. Other meals were delivered once a week by the local meals-on-wheels program. The friend and her husband ran errands for George and Martha and provided emotional support by frequently coming over for afternoon visits.

After Martha died, George became depressed, but he did not want the case manager to continue her visits. George's disposition eventually improved, and although he missed his wife, he slowly started adapting to his new life as a widower. George continued tending his garden, spent time with his sons, and started traveling again. Sometimes he went on these trips on his own, and at other times he was joined by a friend from high school who had also lost his spouse. George also became involved as a volunteer in the local senior center. One day, returning home from a visit to the senior center, he fell on an icy sidewalk and broke his leg. While he was hospitalized, the hospital's interdisciplinary assessment team conducted an extensive multidimensional assessment. George was diagnosed with senile dementia of the Alzheimer's type (SDAT). George had recently felt disoriented at times and had stopped driving his car as a consequence, but he managed to hide his condition from his friends and his sons. As he was slowly recovering from his surgery, a discharge worker started to assist George in making plans for his time after the hospitalization. Although he was at times a little disoriented in regard to time and place, George was able to participate in the discussion of where to live after being discharged from the hospital. Since George would have difficulties living on his own and neither of his sons was able to take care of him, a decision was made that George would enter the nursing home directly from the hospital. Fortunately, a nursing home placement for George was secured within a very short period of time.

George has been residing at St. Mary's Home for Adults for the last two years. Initially he had a very difficult time adjusting to his life in the nursing home. He was very withdrawn and felt left alone even though one of his sons came to visit almost daily. Over time, George became more involved and friendly with some of the more alert residents, and although his disease has slowly progressed since he entered the nursing home, most days he continues to participate in the social activities offered. His sons continue to visit frequently. Occasionally they take him to their homes for the weekend or on short weekend trips to visit some of his old friends.

CHAPTER 3

COMMUNICATION FOR GERONTOLOGICAL PRACTICE

AS WE INDICATED in the first two chapters, older adults are a heterogeneous group. Practice activities for the gerontological practitioner range from counseling the well elderly living in the community to intervening with frail elderly nursing home residents. The way we build relationships and communicate will differ depending on our target audience as well as on the function of our agency. In this chapter, we will look at some of the basic proficiencies for communicating with older adults. We will start with information on various aspects of verbal and nonverbal communication. This will be followed by a review of skills for communicating with special groups of older adults, such as persons with vision or hearing impairments and persons with Alzheimer's disease or other types of dementia.

COMMUNICATING WITH ELDERLY CLIENTS

Communication is the mechanism by which we connect to the world. Much of a person's self-image develops through his or her communication with others. The ability to connect and communicate with a person is the primary foundation of interacting with any client. Therefore, communication skills play a fundamental role in interpersonal practice with elderly and frail elderly clients. Communication researchers studying how communication changes across the life span maintain that older adults are a very heterogeneous group in terms of their communication styles and abilities (Hummert, Wiemann, and Nussbaum 1994; Kemper 1992; Ryan et al. 1994). Contrary to common belief, they assert that no general pattern of severely declining communication abilities for older adults exists. They point to some age-related differences in communication but suggest that the majority of older adults communicate in ways that are similar to those of people in other age groups.

If older adults experience communication difficulties, they are often associated with age-related cognitive and sensory changes. Cognitive changes

associated with normal aging include some slowing of a person's information processing, selective attention, and problem-solving ability (Siegler et al.
1996). However, individuals vary significantly in regard to cognitive changes,
and not all older adults experience them in the same way. These individual
differences can be attributed to personal lifestyle, psychosocial factors, and
genetic risks (Finch and Tanzi 1997; Gottlieb 1995). The memory problems
often associated with becoming older may also be a sign of late-life depression rather than of aging per se. Sensory changes that occur as the body ages
include changes in vision, hearing, taste, smell, and sense of touch. Since they
are the means through which we receive verbal and nonverbal messages, certain changes in vision and hearing can effect communication (Rau 1993). We
will discuss them in more detail in the respective sections on communicating with people having hearing and vision problems. Some changes in communication that a gerontological practitioner encounters are actually caused
by illness or chronic health conditions rather than by being elderly. For
example, suffering a stroke often leads to short- and long-term communication problems. We will talk about some of these medical conditions in the
second part of this chapter.

Despite the changes we just outlined, communication researchers claim
that older adults are not necessarily viewed as poor communicators. In some
areas, in fact, they are seen as considerably better communicators than other
population groups. A study by Kemper and associates (1989) found that older
adults tend to use more straightforward and less complex narratives. Consequently, their listeners perceived them as more precise and easier to understand than their younger counterparts. Ryan and associates (1994) summarize
research that also substantiates the notion of older adults being better communicators. Some studies show that the elderly exceed younger adults in the
ability to express sociability traits such as friendliness, warmth, and sincerity.
Older adults are experienced as considerably better in telling a story. Research
also indicates that older adults are identified as using a more extensive vocabulary. This is supported by the fact that the vocabulary of a person continues
to increase until the person reaches the midseventies (Carman 1997).

As communication involves two or more participants, it is important to
recognize that the perceptions and stereotypes a younger person may hold
about the older adult have an impact on the communication process. Thus,
it may not be the older adult but the partner in conversation who is changing the style of communication. For example, when talking to an elderly person, a younger adult may use patronizing speech or so-called elder talk.
Patronizing speech is characterized by simplification strategies (simple
grammar and slow speech), clarification strategies (simple sentences and
overly careful articulation), and a demeaning tone (overbearing and direc-

tive) (Ryan et al. 1986). Elder talk may include inappropriate expressions of familiarity, such as addressing someone as "hon" or "sweetie."

Research suggests that when older adults are negatively stereotyped, they are more likely to become targets of this patronizing speech (Hummert 1990, 1993, 1994). It is important for a practitioner to avoid patronizing speech when talking with elderly or frail elderly clients. There may be no faster exit from a successful practitioner-client relationship than treating the older adult client like an "elderly child." Hence, we would like to emphasize again that the majority of older adults continue to communicate well and in ways similar to those of other groups in the adult population. For that reason, we will first turn to more generic information on the two primary ways of communicating, i.e., verbal and nonverbal communication.

VERBAL COMMUNICATION

Human beings communicate verbally through the use of language. Language plays a critical role in interpersonal communication. We will look at verbal communication from two angles, i.e., from the perspective of listening and the perspective of responding to a client's message.

LISTENING As important as sending a message through verbal communication is receiving it through listening (see box 3.1). Verderber and Verderber (2001) identify four skills they consider to be essential elements of effective listening: attending, understanding, evaluating, and remembering. Attending is defined as the perceptual process of selecting specific stimuli we have heard. If you close your eyes and listen to the sounds around you, you will hear tones that your ear received but you did not attend to while you were reading this text. Effective listening includes attending to the words and the meaning of the words of your communication partner. It is helpful to prepare yourself physically and mentally for listening. Sit up and take a deep breath, look directly at your client, and establish eye contact. Research has shown that reduced eye contact leads to a loss of some information that is verbally communicated (Verderber and Verderber 2001). Think about the goals of your listening. For example, are you listening for general assessment purposes or are you trying to establish whether there is tension between a client and a caregiver? Focus entirely on listening and try to completely shift your role from speaker to listener. Shifting to "listening mode" is less difficult when you are listening to a longer presentation. In a dialogue with a client, however, you are constantly moving back and forth between listening and speaking. Try to avoid formulating your answer while the other person is still talking and has

---

BOX 3.1 ATTENDING

- Prepare yourself physically and mentally for listening
- Establish eye contact
- Focus entirely on listening
- Completely shift from speaker to listener role
- Listen to person until he/she is completely finished

---

not finished the sentence. This is particularly important with communication-impaired older people who may have difficulty finding the right words. Also, avoid prematurely ceasing to listen because you "already know the rest of the story," for example, with a client who is apparently reminiscing.

The second step in listening is understanding (see box 3.2). It is defined as the ability to decode a message by assigning a meaning to it (Verderber and Verderber 2001). If a person talks to you in a foreign language, you may be able to attend to what the person is saying. You may be able to hear the sounds and may even recognize some words, but you still may not understand the meaning of the words. As a rule, practitioners should avoid using unnecessary professional terminology that may be unclear to the client. If professional terms need to be used, for example, in discussing a client's medical diagnosis, the practitioner should always include an explanation of the vocabulary in plain language. Since clients with memory problems may not recall a term you explain, an explanation may need to be repeated several times.

A second element of understanding is active listening. Active listening goes beyond hearing the words to consciously thinking and trying to understand what the message may mean. Simultaneously attending to nonverbal cues of a person, such as facial expressions, will offer additional information on how to understand the meaning of the words. If you are at all unclear about what the client is saying, paraphrase what you understood and request feedback from the client. At times it may even be useful to isolate the key points in a complex message and write them down. Sharing this list with the client can be a useful instrument for paraphrasing the information.

Critical listening is the third element of effective listening (see box 3.3). It is defined as the process of critically analyzing what has been understood and interpreted in order to determine how truthful, authentic, or believable we judge the meaning of a message to be (Verderber and Verderber 2001). One important aspect of critical listening is the ability to separate fact from inference. Facts are assertions that can be confirmed. An inference is a conclusion

---

BOX 3.2 UNDERSTANDING

- Avoid overuse of professional terminology
- Explain terminology that may be unclear to client
- Concentrate on the verbally conveyed words *and* additional nonverbal cues.
- Paraphrase to ensure you understand the meaning of a message
- Isolate the key points to better understand complex messages
- Write down key points and share list with client

---

we draw based on our own observation and interpretation. This inference may be true or false. One way to prevent erroneous inferences is to paraphrase in your own words and ask the client about the correctness of your interpretation. Another approach is to compare it to other sources of information. Does what the client says concur with the information you have from the referral source? Is the information congruent with what the client said at the beginning of the session? You may also examine the congruence with the client's nonverbal cues. For example, are the facial expression and gestures supporting the inferences you make?

The fourth element of listening is remembering, i.e., retaining what we have heard in our memory (Verderber and Verderber 2001) and being able to recall it (see box 3.4). Among other information, practitioners need to remember details directly related to the intervention process. For example, the practitioner needs to recall assessment facts and information on the client's problems. We will describe this process of systematically recording information in the next chapter. Several techniques can assist a practitioner in remembering information in the short term. One approach is repeating information several times, which improves our ability to remember. For

---

BOX 3.3 CRITICAL LISTENING

- Paraphrase information
- Ask for feedback about your interpretations
- Compare different sources of information
- Examine congruence with nonverbal cues

BOX 3.4 REMEMBERING

- Repeat and paraphrase information
- Use mnemonic techniques
- Take short notes
- Regroup notes

---

example, you can repeat and then paraphrase the information a client offers. Another approach is the use of mnemonic devices, i.e., techniques that aid our memory. For example, as a mnemonic for remembering the clients' names you may use "MARCH" for Mary and Archie. Taking notes is the most common activity practitioners use to remember and recall the content and facts of their communication with clients. Except for the purpose of assessment, extensive recording may hinder the communication process since your focus on documenting may distract you from listening with full attention. However, it may help to take brief notes. After discussing a topic, you may regroup your notes, i.e., sort them under a few separate headings. Involving the client in the activity of regrouping your notes may be a practical approach to eliciting active participation and to receive feedback on the accuracy of your information.

Finally, a listening skill that may occasionally be useful in practice with older adults is reading lips. For instance, you may begin working on the care plan of a hospitalized elderly patient shortly after a trachea tube has been removed. Such patients will take several days or even weeks to regain the vocal strength to speak with enough loudness and an understandable voice. While the person may be able to make some sounds or whisper words, your understanding will be greatly enhanced if you can follow the person's lips while he or she is speaking. See table 3.1 for basic cues for reading lips.

RESPONDING

Responding is the activity that directly flows from listening. When you respond, you shift your role from being the receiver to being the sender of a message. In social work, as well as in counseling and psychotherapy, responding to clients has been the subject of considerable study and classification effort over the past half-century (Fortune 1981; Greenberg and Pinsof 1986;

TABLE 3.1 CUES FOR READING LIPS

LIP MOVEMENT:	LETTERS PRODUCED:
Lips come together	p, b, m
Lips are or become rounded, one syllable	u, o, y, q
Lips are or become rounded, three syllables	w
Upper and lower teeth come together	c, z
Upper and lower teeth come together, tongue tip raised behind teeth	t, d
Upper and lower teeth come together, lips are protected	g, j
Upper teeth on or close to lower lip	f, v
Mouth open, teeth apart	a, e, I, r, k
Mouth open, teeth come together, hissing sounds	x, s
Mouth starts open, teeth come together, lips protected, hissing sound	h
Mouth open, tongue tip raised behind upper teeth	n, l

Based on Cohen 1977; Greenwald 1984

Reid 1990; Fortune and Reid 1999b). A method of classifying the practitioner's responses compatible with most forms of social work practice (Reid 1978; Fortune and Reid 1999b) is summarized in table 3.2 with examples illustrating applications in work with the elderly.

Next, we will elaborate on the categories of the system and comment on their use in work with the elderly.

EXPLORATION Exploration will be given particular emphasis since it is doubtlessly the most common mode of response in work with clients. Asking questions is the most frequent activity used in exploration (see box 3.5). Some techniques can aid in sensitive questioning. Before formulating a question, first think about what additional information you may need. Have you

TABLE 3.2 TYPOLOGY OF PRACTITIONER RESPONSES

TYPE OF TECHNIQUE	DESCRIPTION	EXAMPLES
Exploration	Communication intended to elicit information, including questions and restatements or "echoes" of client's communications.	"What medications are you taking?" "You said your daughter seldom visits."
Structuring	Communication intended to enhance client's functioning in role of client within the interview, including (1) focusing client's communications and (2) structuring the intervention relationship.	(1) "Let's stick to what happened with the doctor for the moment." (2) "This is an area both you and your daughter can work with me on."
Direction	Communication intended to guide client's behavior outside the interview, including direct statements, leading questions, and professional opinions.	"Don't you think you it might be wise to take your medication as prescribed?" "I think the first step would be to talk this over with your daughter."
Encouragement	Communication supporting client's behavior, attitude, or feelings.	"Hey, that's a good idea." "You're able to do that. Look how well you did last time."
Overt understanding	Communication expressing recognition and approval of client's capacities, needs, and feelings, such as expressions of understanding, sympathy, and concern.	"Your getting angry at that is quite understandable." (Paraphrasing what the client has said) "It is hard to go for a long time without seeing any of your family."
Explanation	Communication intended to enhance client's awareness of (1) his or her social and physical environment, (2) significant others, and (3) the client's own behavior.	(1) "The application procedures at both clinics are very much alike." (2) "It seems as if your roommate is taking out her anger on you." (3) "Perhaps you are a little reluctant to go to the clinic because you think you may get bad news about your condition."
Modeling or role-playing	Communication while demonstrating appropriate behavior or actually engaged in modeling or role-playing with the client.	Mrs. G and practitioner role-play client asking doctor to change her medication.

Adapted from Fortune and Reid 1999b.

BOX 3.5 QUESTIONING

- Ask yourself what information you need
- Ask question in a way that clarifies what information you need
- Use open, closed, swing, indirect, and projective questions, based on the information needed
- Use positive nonverbal cues

---

missed only parts of the message or are you completely unclear about the client's comments? Then phrase your question in a way that is not too abrupt. Instead of using short questions like "What date?" or "Who?" include information that clarifies what additional facts you are requesting. "What was the date of your initial visit to the physician?" and "When you visited the senior center, do you recall who talked with you?" would be smoother and less abrupt questions. Another approach is the use of positive nonverbal cues. Use a sincere tone of voice and avoid facial expressions that may be interpreted as evaluative. Finally, it may sometimes be beneficial to "own" the need for clarification. For example, you could say: "I always have difficulty distinguishing between those two words. Can you clarify what they mean for you?" By doing so, you avoid making the client feel inept or put down.

One can distinguish between five basic types of questions: open questions, closed questions, swing questions, indirect questions, and projective questions (Sommers-Flanagan and Sommers-Flanagan 1999). Open questions cannot be answered by yes or no. Rather, they are aimed at advancing the flow of information. Typical open questions begin with words like "what" and "how." For example, the practitioner might ask: "What did they say when they told you that Medicare would not cover this procedure?" Closed questions, on the other hand, can usually be answered by a simple yes or no. An example of a closed question would be: "Did Medicare already approve the procedure?" Swing questions are often used to engage clients in discussing their problems or needs. They usually begin with words like "could" or "would." Although these questions are aimed at a more elaborate response, they leave clients the option to answer with yes or no, if they do not want to engage in a more detailed discussion of the topic (Sommers-Flanagan and Sommers-Flanagan 1999). An example of a swing question would be: "Could you explain a little more what they told you when you called them?" Indirect questions use words like "You must" or "I wonder." They can be very useful to find out what clients

BOX 3.6 CLASSIFICATION OF QUESTIONS*

WORD	TYPE OF QUESTION	TYPICAL CLIENT RESPONSE
What?	Open question	Actual information
How?	Open question	Process information
Why?	Somewhat open question	Explanations
Where?	Less open question	Information on location
When?	Less open question	Information on time
Who?	Less open question	Information on a person
Do/Did?	Closed question	Specific information
Could/Would?	Swing question	Diverse information/sometimes rejected
I wonder/ You must?	Indirect question	Exploration of feelings and thoughts
What if?	Projective question	Information on values and judgment

*Based on Sommers-Flanagan and Sommers-Flanagan 1999

are thinking or feeling without pressuring them to respond (Sommers-Flanagan and Sommers-Flanagan 1999). A typical example would be: "I wonder what you thought when they told you that you would not be eligible?" Finally, projective questions are used to explore the client's values, judgments, or thoughts, or to speculate about certain issues. A typical projective question would be: "What if they decide not to approve the benefits you are seeking?" (See box 3.6.)

Another mode of exploration is the use of comments to clarify what the client has said or to encourage further revelations (see box 3.7). Paraphrasing is a useful exploratory technique when you receive information and want to make sure you properly understand the meaning (Hepworth, Rooney, and Larsen 2001). Rather than simply repeating the information in the same words, paraphrasing involves saying what you understood in your own words. One can distinguish between two types of paraphrasing, the content paraphrase and the feelings paraphrase (Verderber and Verderber 2001). When we use a content paraphrase, we verify the facts of a message. For instance, you might summarize the facts in your own words: "I understand the situation to be as follows. . . ." When we paraphrase feelings, it is our intention to clarify the emotions we think our client is experiencing. For

---

BOX 3.7 PARAPHRASING

- Use content paraphrasing to ensure the proper understanding of facts
- Use feeling paraphrasing to clarify the emotions a client may have
- Both are achieved by summarizing facts or feelings in your own words
- Ask client for feedback on your paraphrase

---

example, you might say: "It sounds like you are unhappy that you have not yet heard back from the health insurance." To avoid misinterpretation, it is important to elicit feedback on the accuracy your paraphrase. A paraphrase of feelings may also be used to express "overt understanding." Its use in that context will be taken up subsequently.

STRUCTURING Structuring consists of the practitioner's efforts to organize (1) communication within the interview or (2) his or her relationship as a whole. In some approaches, such as the task-centered model, the practitioner might impose a considerable degree of structure on the communication process in the session—for example, following a sequence of procedures in helping clients develop and plan tasks. In other approaches, for example, in some forms of psychodynamic psychotherapy, there may be a minimal degree of structure: clients more or less say what is on their minds, and practitioners respond to what the clients say. However, even in such unstructured forms, practitioners impose structure when they focus on certain topics and ignore others. Although practitioners may structure communication in an authoritative way—e.g., "I think we need to talk some more about your feelings"—this kind of control of the communication process should not be confused with *direction*, in which the social worker gives advice concerning clients' actions in their life situations.

Structuring the relationship as a whole provides the framework in which practitioner-client communication occurs. Such structuring involves decisions as who is to be seen, the length of the sessions, and the timing of termination. Again the degree of structure may vary. For example, in some approaches there may be a preplanned number of sessions; in others clients may continue for as long as they please. However, practitioners usually impose some degree of structure, e.g., in limiting sessions to a certain length of time. As far as possible, decisions about structure should be made collaboratively with the client.

In work with cognitively impaired elderly clients the practitioner may need to do a considerable amount of structuring of the interview process; this might include maintaining a focus on clearly defined issues the client can grasp. The same principle would apply to structuring the relationship. Still, cognitively impaired clients should be given as much choice as possible. In some cases the choices may be limited to a narrow range, such as the time of day or day of the week for an appointment, but even such limited choice may be important for the client and supports whatever autonomy he or she may still have (Abramson 1988). When adult children are in the picture, the wishes of cognitively impaired elderly clients are sometimes neglected. Thus, in decisions about which family members to work with, the practitioner should make every effort to include any elder who can participate. Similarly, when the cognitively impaired elder is the first client seen, he or she should be involved collaboratively, if it is all possible to do so, in decisions about which other family members or caregivers should be involved.

A particular challenge in structuring communication in work with the elderly is handling reminiscence. "Reminiscence occurs when a person recalls long-forgotten incidents, dwells on them, and recaptures the emotions that originally accompanied them, often while trying to convey these felt experiences to a listener" (Magee 1988:1). Its primary functions can be described as "self and mood enhancement, coping and adaptation, reparation, retention of the past, self-narrative, and life review with its relationship to ego integrity status in old age" (Sherman 1991:25). The therapeutic value of reminiscing and life review has been described by numerous authors (e.g., Bender, Bauckham, and Norris 1999; Hendricks 1995; Sherman 1991). While it is a common activity for elderly persons, a therapeutic use of reminiscing is not part of the practice model we are presenting. Furthermore, continued reminiscing can hinder constructive problem-solving work and may require the use of refocusing skills by the practitioner.

Nevertheless, reminiscence can be integrated into problem-solving practice in a helpful way. Talking about past events and their meaning for the client can aid in establishing rapport. It can also assist in assessing previous problem-solving attempts. Letting clients reminisce can provide them with a respite during the session and a possibility to retreat to "safer ground." Brief episodes of reminiscence should be anticipated as part of the normal course of working with some elderly and frail elderly clients, but the general focus should be on the "here and now." This focus on the present can be derailed by excessive reminiscence, which can interrupt the problem-solving work and may require constant refocusing by the practitioner. If a client starts to reminisce, it may be helpful to let the client reminisce for a short period of time. However, at some point the practitioner should gently redirect the conversation to the here and now. When a client starts repetitious or excessive reminiscing in a way that hinders work, it may be helpful for the practitioner to immediately attempt refocusing the communication. Examples include sentences that lead back to the topic, such as "Let me get back to. . ." "Before we started talking about your family . . ." "May I ask you a couple more questions . . ." or a direct refocusing on the topic, such as "How are you planning to get things done around the house?" In a study of the geriatric task-centered model, a review of the session audio recordings indicated that brief (one or two sentence) communications by the practitioner were usually followed by continued reminiscence, while longer communication sequences by the practitioner seemed helpful in refocusing and staying in the present (Naleppa 1996). Thus, it may be advantageous for the practitioner to talk for a short while to ensure the client has the time to leave the past and reenter the present.

Box 3.8 presents an example of reminiscing and refocusing. Sequences of repetitious reminiscing frequently occurred throughout the practitioner's work with this client.

This client repeatedly started reminiscing throughout the session. While there were parts of the sessions in which constructive problem-solving took place, many times unsuccessful refocusing prevented any meaningful problem-solving work. These questions used by the practitioner in refocusing typically did not relate to past events but to the here and now. The pattern of repetitious reminiscence seems to be related to the personality of the client. In the sequence, the client starts talking about the past, which was helpful in assessing the history of the problem, possible causes, and previous attempts to solve it. However, the client goes on to talk about her mother and reminisces about issues not directly related to the problem at hand. The practitioner tries to refocus, but the client immediately starts reminiscing again. Finally the practitioner is successful in refocusing the interview.

DIRECTION Direction, or giving advice, is used conservatively in social work because practitioners, with good reason, prefer to help clients develop their own solutions. However, it has been found that many clients want more advice than practitioners usually provide (Davis 1975). Some clients may want advice (even though they may not agree with it or may not use it) because it may stimulate their own thinking about alternative actions they might take to lessen their difficulties. They simply want to know what the "expert" has to recommend.

BOX 3.8 COMMUNICATION EXAMPLE—REMINISCING

Practitioner: There are a couple of things you just made me think of. First, you and I could work on reducing your anxiety. Maybe we can do some relaxation techniques.

Client: I have been that way all my life. I have always been very nervous. As a young person, I had a lot on my mind. My mother had a stroke when she was a young woman. She was about fifty years old. That was young for strokes. It may run in our family, my mother's sister had a stroke too and died from it.

Practitioner: It sounds like you are concerned you might end up having a stroke.

Client: No, I am not, because I went too long. My mother had high blood pressure, and they did not know what to do in the early days, and she worked very hard, you know. She worked for the mill, and when they closed the mill, she started working for her uncle's grocery store. My mother always worked very hard. She used to always get up early . . . and then she had the stroke. Well, my mother was always . . . [*Client starts reminiscing about her mother.*]

Practitioner: I would like to go back to our previous question. Would you be interested in working together on trying to reduce your anxiety?

Client: With you, sure. It is part of my nature. I am a worry lord, because I told you my mother had a stroke when we were young, and that left us with a lot of responsibility. She couldn't leave the bed, so I used the bedpan. It's hard on kids when your mother is sick and you are young. My mother . . . [*Client continues to reminisce.*]

Practitioner: I would like to get back to your anxiety. You mentioned that you are a very anxious person, and that this sometimes worries you. You said that you sometimes don't do certain things that you would like to do, because of your anxiety. There are some methods that can help someone better deal with their anxiety. Would you be interested in looking into some of these techniques?

Client: Yes.

[*They focus on assessing the client's anxiety—client discontinues reminiscing.*]

In working with older people, direction may be needed with cognitively impaired clients around such practical but important issues as taking medication. One should be careful, however, about using cognitive impairment as a rationale for the unnecessary use of direction. To the extent possible, cognitively impaired clients should be helped to explore alternatives and reach their own solutions, especially in regard to placement decisions.

ENCOURAGEMENT When providing encouragement, the practitioner expresses praise or approval of thoughts, feelings, or behavior the client has already expressed. The message, however expressed, is "Good, keep it up!" In work with the frail elderly encouragement is often used to reinforce evidence of progress clients have made in coping with illness or disability, to support constructive adaptations to relocations, and to maintain efforts to promote health and quality of life. Encouragement should not be used to push clients in particular directions when they have not made up their minds. For example, Mrs. Ross may be considering whether or not she should give up her house and move into an assisted living complex, but she is still quite ambivalent. In mulling over her decision she may say some positive things about the assisted living facility she is thinking of moving to. Although the practitioner may think her moving is a good idea, it would be an error to express encouragement whenever Mrs. Ross says something in favor of moving. To do so would be manipulative and might well be resented by the client. In such circumstances it is better to use appropriate forms of explanation to help clients achieve a clearer understanding of the advantages and disadvantages of the alternatives. In that way they can be helped to make up their own minds.

OVERT UNDERSTANDING A main means of expressing understanding is the use of paraphrases supporting feelings. We do not make a statement about whether we think the client should have a particular feeling. Rather, we acknowledge that the client has the feeling. Responding to positive feelings is usually easier than responding to negative feelings. When we support positive feelings, we use can use such approving statements like "that must feel wonderful." Responding to negative feelings is more complex. The practitioner's goal is usually to help the client work through the negative feeling. A first step is to use a response that is in agreement with the feelings the client is expressing. When a person has very strong negative feelings, it may take him or her time to calm down enough to gain a more rational perspective. Rather than immediately confronting the problem, which may intensify the client's feelings, it may at times be better to acknowledge the feelings and wait to address the issue at a later time. By offering understanding and support, we are letting the client know that we can see how troublesome or painful the feeling must be. Again, we are not making a statement about the appropriateness of the feeling. Once you consider the timing and the client's state of mind appropriate, let him or her know that you are willing to assist in the process of working through the negative feelings.

Supporting responses express a certain level of empathy, which can be defined as the understanding of a client based on the client's frame of reference and perspective rather than on your own. We often talk about "starting where the client is," and this implies that we are trying to understand where the client actually "is" and what he or she may think and feel. On a general level, it requires that we are able to understand and identify with the client. An empathic response is one in which the practitioner attempts to "think with, rather than for or about a client" (Brammer, Shostrom, and Abrego 1989:92). Communicating with empathy serves several purposes in the intervention process. It helps to reduce the client's anxiety, assists in building a positive relationship and rapport, and promotes a positive tone. Being able to convey empathy makes the client feel that the practitioner is interested and attentive and facilitates the process of client self-exploration (Cormier and Cormier 1998).

As a gerontological practitioner, you may be younger, have less life experience, and may find it difficult to connect with an elderly client's feelings. You have never been in the client's situation and do not know what it feels like for an older adult. Empathy is a skill that requires you to take on the client's frame of reference. However, in order to be empathic, you need not have experienced the same feelings. If that were the case, only a recovering alcoholic could be empathic with a substance-abusing client. In fact, when we share similar negative or stressful experiences with a client, our own preoccupation may impact on our ability to respond with empathy. Moreover, loneliness, sadness, fear, and anxiety are feelings we all share, regardless of age.

Being empathic also includes responding in an empathic way (see box 3.9). Hepworth, Rooney, and Larson (2001) distinguish between sympathetic responding and empathic responding. They define sympathetic responding as supporting or condoning the other person's feelings. Empathic responding, on the other hand, entails "understanding the other person's feelings and circumstances without taking that person's position" (Hepworth, Rooney and Larson 2001:100). As Nathanson and Tirrito (1998) suggest, empathic communication includes keeping the focus on the client and not prematurely changing topics. Since some elderly clients may require more time to talk through an issue, you should be aware of the potential need for an altered tempo. Nonverbal behavior, such as facial expression, eye contact, and body posture also convey empathy. Research by Maurer and Tindall (1983) supports the importance of nonverbal behavior, suggesting that clients perceive their counselors as more empathic when their body postures are similar.

EXPLANATION The primary purpose of explanation is to point out different views and meanings (see box 3.10). Persons requesting assistance may have limited views of their problems, needs, or circumstances. As a practitioner,

---

BOX 3.9 COMMUNICATING WITH EMPATHY

· Think with the client, not for the client
· Keep focus on the client
· Avoid prematurely changing the topic
· Adjust tempo of communication to the client's needs

---

your role is to help the person analyze his or her perceptions from various angles. The first step in explanation is to listen carefully to what the client is saying or describing. Point out that the client's interpretation is one way of portraying a situation or behavior, and that there may be other ways to look at it. Formulate alternative interpretations. Present your explanation to the client and request feedback. It sometimes helps the client to hear your interpretations, if you preface your message with a supportive statement. For example, a practitioner might say "You sound very upset about the way you were treated, and that is understandable. I am not sure whether I understood it correctly, but it sounds like they first gave you information that contradicts what they are saying now. You are feeling that they are trying to deny your claim. Could there be some other way to look at it? Could it be that they made a mistake, and the person you are talking to now does not know about the misinformation you were given?"

As illustrated above, the first two types of explanation aim to help clients understand their situations or the actions of others. The third type is directed at helping clients enhance their understanding of their own behavior. Most such explanations should help the client clarify what he or she is trying to grasp, for example, helping an elderly woman verbalize her half-recognized fears of going to a clinic, as in the illustration presented earlier. Occasionally, however, the explanations may be more confrontational, for example, in helping an elderly person realize that interfering in the affairs of his adult children may be counterproductive. Verderber and Verderber (2001) have developed some guidelines for this kind of explanation, which they refer to as constructive criticism. First, such explanations are most effective when they are received with open ears. Thus, the first step is to ensure that the other person is responsive to hearing what he or she may view as criticism. Before offering the explanation, it is important to describe the subject matter as accurately as possible and ensure that you have the right facts and information. It is usually

---

BOX 3.10 EXPLANATIONS

- Ensure that the explanation relates to something over which the client has control
- Describe the subject of the explanation as exactly as possible
- Preface negative assertions with positive statements
- Keep the goal of the explanation in mind, e.g., improvement in the client's situation or behavior
- Be as specific as possible

---

helpful to preface a negative assertion with a positive statement. For example, a practitioner may offer some praise to the client beforehand. When providing explanations that may be taken as criticism, be as specific as possible. If your explanation is unclear or held to be too general, it is more likely that you will elicit a negative response from the client. Moreover, use such an explanation only for matters over which a client has control, i.e., behaviors the client can change. Explanation is enhanced if it leads to suggestions about how to improve the behavior at issue. The client should play a leading role in coming up with suggestions for improved behavior.

MODELING OR ROLE PLAY Modeling and role play are usually used together in work with clients. If the goal is to help the client learn a particular behavior, the practitioner, in a role play, may take the role of the client and model the behavior. In a subsequent role play the client, playing himself or herself, may be asked to rehearse the behavior the practitioner has modeled. In work with the elderly modeling and role play is frequently used to help elders learn certain skills or behaviors that would enhance their coping. For example, elders often feel quite dependent on caregivers and service providers and are reluctant to make requests that might alienate them. They may benefit from help in being effectively assertive in such situations. Mrs. Ivanoff is reluctant to request an earlier appointment with her eye doctor although she would like to have one since her vision problems have recently gotten worse. She doesn't want to be seen as a "nuisance," and besides with her poor English she has a hard time putting her problem into "the right words." Role plays in which the practitioner models and the client rehearses how she might make the request may help her take this action.

NONVERBAL COMMUNICATION

We would now like to turn to the nonverbal aspects of communication. As communication theorists explain, "you cannot not communicate" (Watzlawick, Beavin, and Jackson 1967). Even when you are not engaging in verbal communication, you still offer nonverbal communication cues through facial expressions, eye contact (or lack of eye contact), gestures, and so on. While much, but by no means all, content of communication is expressed verbally, nonverbal behavior contributes cues for the communicators on how to understand a message. Nonverbal and verbal communication are interrelated. As Cormier and Cormier (1998) point out, nonverbal behavior supports verbal messages by regulating its flow, repeating, substituting, accenting, or contradicting it. One function of nonverbal behavior is to regulate the flow of communication. For instance, an approving nod of the head is often followed by continued talking of the other person, while a disapproving shake of the head tends to elicit feedback. A message can be repeated through nonverbal behavior. For example, if you invite someone into your office and move your arms in a welcoming gesture as the person enters the room, you are repeating the message "come in." Nonverbal messages can also substitute for verbal information. For example, instead of answering to a question, a person may smile approvingly. Another function of nonverbal communication is to accent a message. For instance, a sad message can be intensified by the presence of tears, and an angry facial expression can emphasize a verbal message of aggravation. Finally, verbal and nonverbal messages may contradict each other. There is some indication that when a lack of congruence exists, we gravitate toward believing the nonverbal cues (Cormier and Cormier 1998). In our discussion, we will focus on the more common dimensions of nonverbal behavior, i.e., kinesics, paralinguistics, proxemics, environment, and culture (see box 3.11).

BOX 3.11 DIMENSIONS OF NONVERBAL BEHAVIOR THAT AFFECT COMMUNICATION

- Kinesics (Body Motion)
- Paralinguistics ("How" of a Message)
- Proxemics (Use of Informal Space)
- Environmental Factors
- Cultural Factors

KINESICS One way we communicate nonverbally is through our body motions or kinesics (see box 3.12). This includes eye contact, facial expressions, gestures, and posture. Eye contact, and lack thereof, plays a fundamental part in our nonverbal communication. In Western cultures, direct eye contact indicates a willingness to communicate, while lack of eye contact may suggest avoidance, withdrawal, or deference (Cormier and Cormier 1998). Being at eye-level with the partner of interaction facilitates communication. While many interactions will occur with practitioner and client both sitting or standing, special considerations should be given to individuals who are wheelchair-bound or bedridden. In both cases, if the practitioner sits in a chair with the head at the same level as the client's, it enables the client to better communicate than if he or she needs to look up. Usually, the practitioners should sit opposite the person in a wheelchair much the way one would face a person sitting in a regular chair. Depending on the preferences of a bedridden client, the practitioner should sit opposite or at an angle to the person's face. If you can sit on either side of the bed, ask the client on which side he or she prefers you to sit.

A second set of body motions through which we communicate nonverbally are our facial expressions. Facial expressions encompass the ways we use our eyes, eyebrows, nose, cheeks, mouth, and chin. Through facial expressions we communicate feelings such as happiness, sadness, fear, or anger. For example, we purse our lips together to express anger or stress, bite our lips in sadness or anxiety, and open our mouth without speaking to show surprise or fatigue. Movements of our head often reinforce facial expressions. We nod our head in agreement, shake it in disagreement, and we lower it to express sadness or concern. Other parts of our body also convey nonverbal messages. By

---

BOX 3.12 ELEMENTS OF KINESICS

- Eyes
- Mouth
- Facial Expressions
- Head
- Shoulders
- Arms and Hands
- Legs and Feet
- Overall Body Posture

tapping our feet, for instance, we can express impatience or anxiety, while continually crossing and uncrossing them may indicate an increased level of anxiety. Gesture refers to how we move our hands, arms, and fingers. We use gestures to supplement information or emphasize what we are saying. Posture, on the other hand, refers to the overall position our body takes. For example, keeping one's arms folded indicates an avoidance of interpersonal exchange, while arms in an open position reveal a willingness to engage. We shrug our shoulders to express ambivalence or uncertainty, and we lean forward to show our openness to communicate.

PARALANGUAGE Paralanguage refers to the "nonverbal sound of what we hear—how something is said" (Verderber and Verderber 2001:145). The vocal characteristics assist the listener in interpreting what is being said. Three prominent vocal characteristics are pitch, volume, and rate (see box 3.13). Pitch refers to how high or low a voice sounds. Volume is how loud or soft a person's voice is. Rate refers to the speed of the speech. They all provide additional information that qualifies the message sent. With the volume and tone of our voice, for instance, we emphasize certain aspects of our message. A simple example is the way you say a person's name. How the name is said already gives you an indicator of what is being expressed. If a person says your name softly, a friendly message would be anticipated. If someone shouts your name, anger may be expressed. Another example is the use of a rising voice, which will often lead directly to a question.

In gerontological practice, you may encounter older adult clients who have difficulty hearing. Thus, you may at times decide to increase the volume of your voice. However, raising your voice increases the high-pitched sounds you make, which are the most difficult to hear for many hearing-impaired persons. A more useful approach may be to talk slower, look directly at clients so they can follow your lips, and use clear pronunciation. Rather than repeating the same words several times with an increasing volume, rewording or rephrasing your message may be a more useful approach. In general, slowing

---

BOX 3.13 ELEMENTS OF PARALANGUAGE

Pitch
Volume
Rate

the speed of speech a little may greatly improve how well the client will understand you as long as it does not convey a sense of patronizing. As a general suggestion, when you first meet an elderly client, begin speaking with a normal volume, pitch, and rate. Adjust the voice accordingly once you get to know the client as a listener.

PROXEMICS Proxemics are concerned with the management of personal or informal space (Cormier and Cormier 1998; Hall 1966). Personal space is the amount of physical space we need to feel comfortable. This space moves with us as we move around. One can distinguish between four zones of personal space: intimate (up to 18 inches), personal (1.5 to 4 feet), social (4 to 12 feet), and public space (more than 12 feet) (Hall 1966). These distances vary based on cultural norms. Practice typically occurs in the far personal and close social space, with the practitioner sitting approximately 3 to 5 feet from the client.

It is very common in gerontological practice to work with clients in their own home environment. Entering an elderly client's home brings specific challenges that require the practitioner's attention (Naleppa and Hash 2002). First and foremost, the practitioner has to adapt to the client's environment, rather than being in control of the environment. Since you are on the client's turf, most decisions regarding the use of the environment have already been made. For example, the client usually decides where to sit, what lights are on, how warm or cold the room is, how clean it is, and so on. Moreover, the practitioner may encounter distractions that do not exist in the agency environment, such as phone calls or unplanned visitors. Until you have built a relationship with the client, it may be difficult to actively change environmental factors without running the risk of hurting the client's feelings. Nevertheless, the practitioner should take an active but respectful role. For instance, instead of asking the client to sit somewhere else, you might explain that you think it would be helpful to sit at the table because you can see the client better and have some paperwork to fill out. Box 3.14 provides an overview of some considerations for working in a client's home.

Finally, cultural factors play an important role since the use of verbal and nonverbal communication varies in different cultures. A lack of verbal mastery of a language is easily detected and the communication can be adjusted accordingly. Differences in the use of nonverbal behaviors, however, are more covert and harder to notice. Some clients may speak English well and be in strong command of verbal language skills but may continue to use and understand nonverbal communication cues differently. For example, the use of personal space can vary significantly in different cultures. In some cultures, being

---

BOX 3.14 WORKING IN THE CLIENT'S ENVIRONMENT

- Respect the client's decisions regarding environmental factors
- If changes are needed, take an active and respectful role in requesting them
- Sit close enough to the client and make sure light is not coming from behind you
- Make sure the client can hear you and that you can hear the client
- Try to reduce distractions, such as street noise, radio, and television
- Ensure privacy, especially if noninvolved other persons are in the client's home.
- Make use of environmental cues, such as family pictures
- Observe the client's level of comfort with you in his or her environment
- Avoid being perceived as an intruder by letting the client make decisions about his or her personal space
- Always keep in mind that you are in the client's personal environment

---

close and holding someone's hand while talking to the person may be an important part of communication. In other cultures, again, this would make a person feel uncomfortable. Verderber and Verderber (2001) use the example of white American and Arab men. For the Arab man, it is common to be very close to the other man when talking, but the white American man is accustomed to having more distance and personal space. Consequently, one of the two men will feel uncomfortable in the use of space. Either the American will feel that his space is being "invaded," or the Arab man will experience the distance too great to hold a serious conversation. Since so many differences exist in the use of nonverbal communication, it is always important to clarify your perceptions by asking the client for feedback on your interpretations.

COMMUNICATION WITH SPECIAL GROUPS OF OLDER ADULTS

In the previous section of this chapter, we described a variety of skills for communication with older adult clients. We also indicated that most elderly clients communicate much like other individuals do. Nevertheless, conditions may exist that impact on the person's abilities to communicate. We will now turn to some of these special situations and conditions. For each, we will provide an overview of the problem and describe ways to adjust communication when working with clients affected by these conditions.

COMMUNICATION AND HEARING PROBLEMS

The occurrence of hearing impairment is significantly higher for older adults than in the general population (see box 3.15). It is the most common sensory impairment older adults encounter (Williams 1995). The prevalence of hearing impairment increases from 4.9 percent for persons between the ages of 18 and 44, to 27.4 percent for persons between 65 and 74, to over 38 percent for those over the age of 75 (Shewan 1990). The prevalence of hearing loss has been increasing over the last thirty years and is expected to continue rising in the future (Wallhagen et al. 1997). Hearing impairments can range from slight trouble with hearing or difficulty distinguishing certain sounds or consonants to complete deafness. As hearing loss increases, communication becomes more difficult and frustrating for the person experiencing the deficit. It can also pose a significant burden on the caregiver. Hearing loss can lead to withdrawal from social interactions and feelings of loneliness and isolation, which in turn can increase the susceptibility to depression. However, as Aldwin (1991) asserts, rather than withdrawing from communication, many older adults use proactive strategies to adapt and cope with their hearing loss. Some will use inferencing strategies to fill in words they do not understand. Others may try to lip-read. It is important to note that persons of all ages may be embarrassed by their hearing loss, and as a consequence they may not let you know about their difficulties. Thus, it may be wise to ask new clients about possible hearing impairments if they seem to have problems comprehending what you are saying.

Proper hearing requires three parts of the ear to work concurrently. The outer ear and the ear canal are responsible for picking up the sounds. Tiny bones in the middle ear then transfer the sounds to the auditory nerve. In the inner ear, the sounds are converted and transmitted to the brain (Williams 1995). Two common types of hearing loss in the elderly are conductive hear-

---

BOX 3.15 AGE-RELATED CHANGES IN HEARING

- Loss in ability to hear high-frequency sounds
- Decreased ability to discriminate consonants such as s, z, th, f, and g
- Increased sensitivity to loud noises
- Decreased ability to hear background noises
- Potential for the condition of "recruitment"
- Decreased hearing due wax or fluid buildup in ear

ing loss and sensorineural hearing loss. Conductive hearing loss is a problem of the outer or middle ear. Common causes include wax or fluid buildup in the ear canal or behind the eardrum, inflammation of the ear canal, and otosclerosis, the buildup of bony material in the ear (Santo Pietro and Ostuni 1997). Typical consequences of conductive hearing loss are increased pressure and pain in the ear and fuzzy hearing. Conductive hearing loss can be improved to some extent through medical treatment, cleaning out the earwax, or removing the fluid buildup in the ear. Sensorineural hearing loss, sometimes also termed nerve deafness, is caused by a malfunction in the inner ear or the auditory nerve. Common causes include prolonged exposure to high noise levels, high fever, and presbycusis. Whereas medical treatment usually does not heal the condition, hearing aids can significantly increase a person's hearing. Older adults with sensorineural hearing problems have more difficulty hearing high frequency tones than low frequency ones. Consequently, they have trouble distinguishing between different consonants. They may not hear whether the consonant was "f," "s," or "th" (Villaume, Brown, and Darling 1994). Thus the client may not understand whether you are saying "sick" or "thick." Background noise or simultaneous side-conversations may further intensify a person's trouble distinguishing higher pitched sounds. Older adults may have more trouble understanding female voices because of this difficulty in hearing sounds at higher pitches. For many older adults with sensorineural hearing problems, the ability to hear is also impacted by a condition called "recruitment" (Santo Pietro and Ostuni 1997). While someone with recruitment may not hear soft-spoken sounds at all, loud sounds or shouting abruptly activates the auditory system, and the person hears the sound at its true level of loudness. Another common consequence of sensorineural hearing loss is tinnitus, a continual ringing in the ears. Tinnitus is makes it difficult to hear what someone is saying, especially in noisy environments.

Several skills can improve a practitioner's communication with hearing-impaired clients (see box 3.16). Schneider, Kropf, and Kisor (2000) suggest that the practitioner should face the person directly, as hearing-impaired individuals often compensate by reading lips. Sitting close to the client and not talking from a different room addresses this problem. The practitioner should catch the client's attention before starting to speak. If possible, the eyes should be on the same level as the client's head. The hands should be kept away from the face, as they can impede the client's ability to follow the practitioner's lips and read the nonverbal aspects of communication. At the same time, practitioners should use facial expressions and gestures to convey the meaning of their message (Voeks et al. 1990). The practitioner should speak in a

---

BOX 3.16 SUMMARY: COMMUNICATION WITH HEARING-IMPAIRED CLIENTS

- Sit at 3–6 feet distance
- Make sure there is enough light
- Face the person and sit at the visual level of the other person
- Give listener a clear view of your face
- Let client read your facial expressions and follow your lips
- Use natural speech, not too fast and not much slower than usual
- Speak clearly and, if needed, a little louder, but do not shout
- Find out whether client uses or needs hearing aid
- Use shorter sentences and avoid lengthy monologues
- Do not repeat sentences, but rephrase them
- Get the client's attention before starting to speak
- Introduce topic in summary fashion before going into detail
- Reduce background noise
- Avoid simultaneous side-conversations by other persons

---

normal manner and voice, i.e., not too fast or too loud. When sitting down, make sure that the light or sun is not shining directly into the client's face, since this makes it more difficult to read your lips and follow your facial expressions. If a client did not understand something, you may try rephrasing what you said, rather than using the same words again. Obviously, it is always advantageous to reduce interfering background noise. For example, if you are working in the client's home, the TV or radio may be running or street noise may be entering through open windows. Finally, as Williams (1995) points out, more than two-thirds of people over the age of 70 who have a hearing aid wear it for less than eight hours a day. Thus, if a client with a hearing aid has difficulty hearing you, it may be useful to check whether it has been turned on.

COMMUNICATION AND VISION PROBLEMS

Approximately 15 percent of persons aged 65 and almost 30 percent of persons at the age of 85 and older experience vision impairments (Williams 1995). More than 90 percent of older adults require eyeglasses to see properly. However, while the occurrence of vision impairments increases with age, there is no significantly higher prevalence of blindness in the older adult

---

BOX 3.17 AGE-RELATED CHANGES IN VISION

- Adjustment for near and far vision becomes more difficult
- Adaptation from light to dark becomes slower
- Color discrimination decreases
- Eyes require more light to see
- Eyes become more sensitivity to glare
- Range of vision decreases

---

population (Hooyman and Kiyak 1999). Several changes in vision occur as part of the body's aging process (see box 3.17). The eye lens of an older person becomes more rigid, and the muscles controlling the shape of the lens atrophy. Therefore, focusing on nearby objects becomes more difficult. The eye has a harder time to quickly adjust for near and far vision, and the ability to adapt from light to darkness slows down. An older person's eyes are more sensitive to glare. As a consequence, the eyes requires up to 70 percent more light to identify an object close to a source of glare (Williams 1995). Throughout a person's life, a yellow-brown pigmentation builds up on the eye's lens. This buildup leads to a reduction in the amount of light entering the eye and a need for more light to see accurately. The buildup on the lens also leads to a decrease in color discrimination. Thus, to the older person's eyes blue tones may appear greenish blue (Williams 1995).

Three common diseases that affect the vision of older adults are cataracts, macular degeneration, and glaucoma. Cataracts are a clouding of the eye that impairs the range of vision. This condition can usually be corrected through surgery. Macular degeneration is a vision disability that is characterized by a progressive loss of central vision. It leads to difficulty in clearly distinguishing colors and objects. Laser treatment can postpone but not prevent the continued loss of vision caused by macular degeneration. Finally, glaucoma is marked by high fluid pressure within the eyeball that causes damage to the optic nerve. Glaucoma can be treated through medical therapy, but in some cases surgery may be required (Williams 1995).

A first step in communicating with persons suffering from vision impairments should be to directly ask them about ways to best assist them. For example, some visually impaired persons may see general outlines well but not every detail. Thus, you need not describe what item the person is looking at, but only point out the details. A useful approach for clients with serious vision problems is to announce when you are entering the room and indicate who is present. However, rather than stating, "Mrs. Smith, Mr. Smith, and I are in the room," this information can be integrated into normal conversation. For example, when entering the room, you might address each person with a word of welcome. When you speak to a visually impaired person, include information on who you are addressing. For example, you may start your sentences with the addressee: "Mrs. Smith, you just suggested that we should look at finding an apartment in one of the assisted living facilities. Mr. Smith, what is your thought on this?" Although this may feel repetitious, it helps the visually impaired person follow a conversation with several participants. Especially the nonverbal aspects of communication are reduced or lost by a visually impaired person. If content and tone of voice leave the interpretation of a message ambiguous, the listener will look for facial expressions or other nonverbal clues to interpret the meaning. This becomes difficult or impossible for a visually impaired person.

If a visually impaired person is moved to a new environment, share information on the environment in which the person typically moves around. Include information on smell, sound, temperature, and so on. Take the person on a walk through the entire place and indicate where you are, what sounds you hear, what smells are present, and where they come from. When walking around, offer your arm to the person for guidance. To better manage the environment, the visually impaired will use routines and memorize locations. Thus, you should avoid moving things around, except if the visually impaired person asks you to do so. At the end of a client visit, announce when you are leaving. If several persons are present, let the visually impaired person know if anyone remains in the room.

Lights that are too dim or too bright, produce a glare, or reflect from shiny surfaces can further reduce a person's already poor vision. This negative effect can be intensified by overstimulation of the eyes. For example, the combination of various sources of light, a flickering computer monitor, standby lights from electronic fixtures, and clutter may provide too much visual stimulation for a person who already has trouble seeing and identifying the basic outlines of things. Thus, it is essential to keep the amount of visual stimuli low and the environment clear of clutter. Along the same lines, printed materials should use large enough font sizes for visually impaired clients to read. When designing forms for use with older adult clients, a font size of at least 14 points should be used. A summary of this section is provided in box 3.18.

BOX 3.18 SUMMARY: COMMUNICATION WITH VISUALLY IMPAIRED CLIENTS

- Ask person about ways to assist him or her
- Announce yourself when you are entering the room
- Share layout of room and information about who is present
- Always include who you are addressing in your communication
- Take client on a tour of new environment
- Let client know if you move any objects
- Announce when you are leaving the room
- Let person know if someone remains in the room
- Make sure there is enough light
- Reduce glare and shiny or reflecting surfaces
- Avoid visual overstimulation

COMMUNICATION AND SPEECH AND LANGUAGE DISABILITIES

Several speech and language disabilities may directly impact on the communication capabilities of older adults. Some of the more prevalent conditions include aphasia, agnosia, and apraxia. Aphasia is caused by damage to the left brain hemisphere and is often a direct consequence of a stroke, brain tumor, brain trauma, or dementia (Williams 1995). One can distinguish between fluent and nonfluent aphasia. Fluent aphasia is characterized by speech that sounds normal in terms of inflection, speech melody, and length of sentences. However, the sentences produced contain very little information or content. Individuals with fluent aphasia may also exhibit difficulties with calculations, telling left from right, and ordering a series of tasks (Dreher 2001; Williams 1995). Nonfluent aphasia, on the other hand, is characterized by problems with pronunciation, effortful speech, and reduced length of sentences, or even relative lack of speech. The speech of an aphasic person often is in telegram style, sounding almost automatic. A person suffering from aphasia may have problems comprehending spoken or written language and may not understand what is being said. Patients with aphasia may also have problems with memory retention and recall. This is why patients in the early period after a stroke often have difficulties remembering simple words, such as the hospital's name. While aphasia significantly impacts a person's ability to communicate, it is usually possible to achieve at least partial recovery through speech and language therapy (Williams 1995). One should keep in mind that aphasia manifests itself in many ways. A person's aphasia may be mild, i.e., he or she may hardly notice the difficulties in finding the proper words or symbols. On the other end of the spectrum, a person with severe aphasia may not be able to connect a meaning with any words or symbols.

Articulatory apraxia is a disorder of the speech movement. Individuals suffering from articulatory apraxia have difficulties positioning their lips and tongue properly to make a desired sound. The rhythm and flow of speech becomes broken up. This difficulty with speech movement also causes words to be mispronounced. For example, a person intending to say "platform" might say "flatporm" instead (Dreher 2001). Agnosia is another condition that may be the consequence of a stroke or brain tumor. The brain of a person with agnosia does not receive and process sounds properly. Thus, the person is often able to hear the words but unable to understand their meaning. Individuals with agnosia at times may be able to draw an object even though they are not able to name it (Dreher 2001).

Patience is the key to communication with persons who suffer from aphasia, apraxia, and agnosia. As practitioner, allow sufficient time for work with individuals with one of these conditions. It is important to let the person complete his or her thoughts before jumping in and finishing sentences. Ask the client directly how to best communicate with him or her. If family members or friends are involved, you may ask them for feedback as well. However, make your request in a manner that does not make the client feel left out. Sometimes it may be helpful to ask the person to write down his or her thoughts. If this approach is taken, the practitioner should read the words or sentences aloud and look for verbal or nonverbal feedback. Pictograms can be used for communication. Using this approach, the person can point to the drawing or the word to indicate what he or she wants or needs. Writing aids may be used if a person cannot speak, especially with persons who have mild forms of nonfluent aphasia. While the person may have to use the nondominant hand for writing, this is usually not a big hurdle. A bigger problem is typically that the person with aphasia has lost some vocabulary and may not have the words available. Consequently, without being able to first formulate a word in the mind, the person will not be able to write it down. Useful communication tools are alphabet charts, pictograms, and charts with printed words. The patient communicates by pointing to the appropriate letters, pictures, or words. Finally, many of the communication techniques described for persons with early stage dementia may also prove practical for individuals suffering from the speech and language problems described (see box 3.19).

BOX 3.19 SUMMARY: COMMUNICATION WITH CLIENTS SUFFERING FROM
SPEECH AND LANGUAGE DISABILITIES

- Be patient
- Allow additional time for communication
- Ask elderly person and caregiver about best ways to communicate
- Avoid completing words or sentences prematurely
- Encourage written communication if appropriate
- Use pictograms, alphabet charts, or word charts if appropriate

---

COMMUNICATION WITH PEOPLE AFFECTED BY ALZHEIMER'S DISEASE AND DEMENTIA

Although dementia is not a normative part of the brain's aging process, its prevalence increases with age. Approximately 5 percent of individuals over the age of 65 and 20 percent of those over the age of 80 display signs of dementia (Kaplan and Sadock 1998). Dementia usually starts slowly and is characterized by an increasing impairment of the person's cognitive functioning. It is caused by damage in the brain tissue. One can distinguish between reversible and irreversible dementia. Causes of reversible dementia include drug and alcohol use, nutritional deficits, brain tumor, or severe depression. If treated early, the cognitive decline can be reversible (Kaplan and Sadock 1998). Irreversible dementia, however, cannot be cured. The two most common types of irreversible dementia are senile dementia of the Alzheimer type and vascular dementia, also called multi-infarct dementia. Together, they account for 75 percent of all dementia cases (Moody 1994). Parkinson's disease, Huntington's disease, Pick's disease, Creutzfeldt-Jakob disease, and HIV are other causes of dementia. Since dementia is a slowly progressing disease with significant changes over time, one distinguishes between early, moderate, and late stage dementia. We will use these categories to discuss communication strategies for dealing with persons suffering from dementia.

EARLY STAGE DEMENTIA A person's memory, understanding, and speech and language skills change as the dementia progresses. During early stage dementia, memory problems include beginning problems with orientation to time and some loss of short-term and long-term memory (Kaplan and Sadock

1998). However, these difficulties may not be very apparent in a regular conversation. Impairments of language and communication are often the earliest symptoms of dementia (Kemper and Lyons 1994). Spouses and family members describe difficulties with finding words or naming objects and understanding aspects of a conversation as the first signs that their relative may have dementia (Bayles and Tomoeda 1991). The person may lose some ability to understand faster paced speech and may find it difficult to understand complex and abstract conversations. The ability to rapidly name things may begin to decrease, and the person may occasionally switch related words. For example, the person may switch the words "sugar" and "salt" but still have the ability to self-correct these mistakes (Santo Pietro and Ostuni 1997).

Communication with persons in early stage dementia requires comparatively few and easy adjustments. First, it becomes even more important to use simple and direct language. A message stated in active voice (e.g., "The doctor will complete the form") is easier to understand than the same statement made in passive voice (e.g., "The form will be filled out by the doctor") (Rau 1993). Utilize several shorter sentences instead of longer and more complex ones. A client with early stage dementia will occasionally have difficulties finding or remembering a word. Circumlocution, the use of alternative words, is a technique that can be used if a person cannot remember a word (Rau 1993). For example, you can ask the client to describe the item or ask whether he or she can say it in a different way. At the same time, avoid prematurely filling in words or talking for the person. Rather, provide the elderly client with additional time to process and think about what he or she wants to say. Clearly structuring your communication will enhance the client's ability to follow and understand what you are saying. Begin with an introduction to the topic, provide some general information, and then move to the more specific issues. Summarizing, rephrasing, and repeating important messages will also foster the client's comprehension of the information. Focusing and paying attention may already become more difficult for persons in early stage dementia. Thus the practitioner should watch the elderly client's attention span. Nonverbal cues, such as wandering eyes, provide useful information about whether a client is still able to concentrate. If needed, provide time for the client to rest and talk about less demanding topics. If a client likes to reminisce, you may include time for this communication activity. However, as we described earlier, extended periods of reminiscing may hinder the problem-solving work you can still accomplish with clients in the early stages of dementia. Finally, the use of written materials enhances the client's understanding of what is being discussed. It offers an additional advantage of serv-

---

BOX 3.20 SUMMARY: COMMUNICATION WITH CLIENTS SUFFERING FROM EARLY STAGE DEMENTIA

- Use simple and direct language
- Carefully watch client's attention span
- Encourage the use of alternative words if a client cannot remember a word
- Avoid filling in words or talking for the client
- Provide client with additional time to process what you say
- Begin with general topics and then move to more specific issues
- Use techniques of summarizing, rephrasing, and repeating important messages
- Provide space and time for reminiscing
- Use written materials and memory aids

Based on Toseland and McCallion 1998:35

---

ing as a memory aid. As we will describe in more detail later, assessment and practice forms can be shared with the client. Furnishing written copies of these forms can have a positive impact on the outcome of client activities (Fortune and Rathbone-McCuan 1981; Naleppa 1996). A summary of this section is provided in box 3.20.

MODERATE STAGE DEMENTIA As in early stage dementia, characteristic changes in memory, understanding, and speech and language skills can be identified for individuals with moderate stage dementia (Kaplan and Sadock 1998; Santo Pietro and Ostuni 1997). Memory changes associated with the middle stages of dementia are a slowly increasing loss of orientation to time and place. However, the individual is still able to identify family members and other familiar persons. Losses in short-term and long-term memory begin to become more apparent in regular conversation. The ability to process abstract concepts or vocabulary decreases, and the person begins to exhibit difficulties in retaining new information (Kemper and Lyons 1994). Prolonged conversations, especially in distracting and noisy environments, become more difficult. While the person can still read, the ability to understand what he or she reads is slowly being lost. The person's language becomes less fluent, includes more pauses and revisions, and sentences become more fragmented (Kemper and Lyons 1994). The ability to self-correct also begins to decrease, and the person uses language in a less creative manner. Moreover, the person will often leave sentences unfinished (see box 3.21 for an overview).

Begin any visit to a client suffering from moderate stage dementia by addressing him or her by name. Introduce yourself, if there is any possibility that the client may not remember you. Rather than using "he," "she" and so on, use persons' names, and if appropriate, indicate their roles. For example, you might say, "Mrs. Smith, your daughter Jean told me that you saw the physician, Dr. Morris." Always face clients directly and speak only when they can see you. This helps the client to pay attention. It also makes it easier to follow your nonverbal clues, such as gestures and facial expressions. The use of visual cues, such as pictures and familiar objects, can help you lead the client to a new topic. For example, a practitioner interested in finding out what informal supports the elderly client relies upon, may ask: "This is a nice picture of your family. Who is everyone in the picture?" The practitioner may then continue and ask what they are doing today, where they live, and how often the client sees them. This would be followed by questions on who helps with tasks and chores.

A client with moderate stage dementia may have difficulties expressing what he or she wants to say. Thus, it is often helpful for the practitioner to concentrate on nonverbal cues. Likewise, slightly overemphasizing facial expressions and gestures can enhance the client's ability to understand the meaning of your message. Individuals with moderate stage dementia need additional time to process communication. Thus, it is important to provide enough time for the client to listen, think, and respond to any questions. If a client does not respond after one or two minutes, you may need to repeat the question. If you believe that the client may have difficulty understanding, try rephrasing the message rather than repeating words. Keep your statements short and straightforward. Avoid lengthy, complex sentences, as well as any professional jargon. Moreover, avoid sudden topic changes. At times, you may not be certain whether the client understood what you said. Thus, if you are offering specific information, ask the client to repeat it. Finally, routine activities and tasks are easier to follow for clients with moderate levels of dementia. Hence, it is beneficial to develop a predictable routine for your client visits. For example, it may be advantageous to keep the visits to a similar length of time, in the same setting, and with the same persons present.

LATE STAGE DEMENTIA Characteristic for late stage dementia is a person's lack of orientation to person, time, and place (Santo Pietro and Ostuni 1997). Difficulties in recognizing family members arise and the ability to create new

---

BOX 3.21 SUMMARY: COMMUNICATION WITH CLIENTS SUFFERING FROM MODERATE STAGE DEMENTIA

- Speak only when the client can see you
- Begin communication by addressing the client by name and introducing yourself
- Use people's names and avoid using "he," she," "we," and so on
- Face the client when speaking
- Use visual cues, such as pictures and familiar objects
- Focus on verbal and nonverbal cues to understand what a client is saying
- Provide enough time for the client to listen, think, and respond
- Repeat the question if the client does not respond after one or two minutes
- Rephrase rather than repeat words if a client has difficulty understanding you
- Avoid sudden changes of topic
- Avoid lengthy and complex sentences
- If you are providing specific information, ask the client to repeat it
- Develop a predictable routine for client visits

Based on Toseland and McCallion 1998:36–37

---

memories is being lost. The person has problems understanding the meaning of most words and often is not aware that someone is speaking with him or her (Santo Pietro and Ostuni 1997). In the final stages of dementia or Alzheimer's disease the person may completely loose the capacity to speak and become mute.

Communication with individuals in late stage dementia becomes increasingly challenging. Nevertheless, some communication guidelines can be presented (see box 3.22). Again, it is important to speak only when the client can see you and your face. Begin your communication by addressing the client by name. Introduce yourself and explain who you are. Talk with a low and restrained voice. Whenever possible, use pictures, familiar objects, and other visual cues. Adjust the rate of your speech and talk slower. Pronounce and shape your words very clearly. Although the client may show little reaction, always presume that he or she is hearing you. Moreover, continue talking despite the fact that the client may not respond. At times, you may gently touch the client while talking to increase the feeling of "connectedness." For example, you may reassuringly pat the client on the arm (Rau 1993). Since the

---

BOX 3.22 SUMMARY: COMMUNICATION WITH CLIENTS SUFFERING
FROM LATE STAGE DEMENTIA

- Speak only when the client can see you
- Begin communication by addressing the client by name and introducing yourself
- Use a low, affectionate, and restrained voice
- Face the client when speaking
- Use visual cues, such as pictures and familiar objects
- Speak very slowly and shape every word clearly
- Assume that the client is hearing you
- Continue talking, even if the client does not respond
- Touch the client gently and reassuringly while talking
- Look for nonverbal clues

Based on Toseland and McCallion 1998:38

---

person may not be very verbal, it becomes especially important to look for nonverbal clues (Toseland and McCallion 1998). Can you see signs of discomfort or pain? Is the client calm and relaxed or agitated? Do nonverbal behaviors indicate that the client may approve or disapprove of what you are saying?

SUMMARY

This chapter has described the many ways in which communication occurs. In general, communicating with elderly clients is very similar to communicating with other adult clients. Most basic skills of verbal and nonverbal communication apply to practice with all adult and older adult client populations. At the same time, some age-related differences in communication exist. We discussed those we consider most important for practice with elderly clients. In concluding this chapter, we would like to point out that we should not expect any client to communicate with us in a certain way. Rather, communication is always a two-way process in which we need to balance our own professional skills with the abilities and communication habits of our elderly and frail elderly clients.

CHAPTER 4

ASSESSMENT IN GERONTOLOGICAL PRACTICE

I N THIS CHAPTER we present some general principles of assessment in work with elderly clients. We then concentrate on one major form of assessment—the use of standardized instruments. A second major form of assessment—obtaining data about the client's problems and needs through conversational interviewing—is taken up in the following chapter in the context of the task-centered practice model.

In many ways assessment in gerontological practice is similar to assessment with other client populations. The purpose of assessment is the same, namely, to gain an understanding of the client's problems, needs, and strengths and to have information on which to base a decision on what intervention to use. Hence, the assessment is the starting point of a process that should lead to an intervention plan addressing the problems and needs of the client. Despite these similarities, however, assessment with older adult clients differs in several ways. The practitioner conducting a geriatric assessment needs to pay attention to specific issues that are inherent in the nature of the elderly client population. Lichtenberg (2000) identifies four assessment principles that should guide a geriatric assessment (see box 4.1).

BOX 4.1 BASIC PRINCIPLES FOR ASSESSMENT

- Age and functioning are not linearly related in clinical settings
- Clinical gerontologists should emphasize brief assessments
- Assessment results must emphasize clients' strengths and weaknesses and treatment recommendations
- Multiple methods of assessment are optimal

Source: Lichtenberg 2000:2–9

The first principle Lichtenberg (2000) identifies is that age and functioning are not linearly related in clinical settings. Age alone is not a reliable predictor of a person's functioning or susceptibility to disease. Rather than relying on the chronological age of a person, i.e., the age of a person measured in years, it is more useful to think in terms of functional age. Functional age describes the abilities of an older adult to complete functional tasks, such as activities of daily living. While age and the prevalence of certain diseases and chronic conditions show a linear relationship in population-based research, this is no longer the case in health care and other clinical settings (Lichtenberg 2000). In these settings, a person's comorbidity, that is, the coexistence of chronic diseases is a more useful indicator than his or her chronological age. Therefore, instruments that assess comorbidity and functional abilities are widely used in gerontological practice settings. We will describe some of the more common functional assessment instruments, such as the Katz ADL and the IADL instruments, later in this chapter.

A second principle is that clinical gerontologists should emphasize brief assessments. A growing body of research indicates that brief geriatric assessment instruments can be as reliable and valid as longer ones (Lichtenberg 2000). Another consideration is the characteristics of the elderly client population. Some elderly and frail elderly clients no longer have the attention span to sit through lengthy assessments. Fatigue and lack of concentration can lead to inaccurate responses. Furthermore, resource and time constraints on the person conducting the assessment also indicate the use of rapid assessment instruments. To meet the need for brief assessments, a two-tiered, staged approach may be useful. Using this approach, a practitioner starts with a more general, multidimensional assessment instrument to screen for the client's problems and needs. This is then followed by a more in-depth assessment of those areas previously identified as potentially problematic using one or more specialized assessment instruments.

A third principle in Lichtenberg's assessment guidelines is that assessment results should include the client's strengths and weaknesses. The purpose of an assessment is not only to diagnose. Rather, it should also include information on the person's unique characteristics and abilities and should focus on the strengths and weaknesses. Furthermore, it should be kept in mind that the assessment is only the first step in a series of intervention activities. Thus, it is useful to gather additional client information that can aid in the planning of the intervention process. For example, information on a client's cognitive strengths can be incorporated in the planning of the problem-solving strategies that practitioner and client select.

Finally, Lichtenberg proposes the use of multiple methods of assessment as most useful for the geriatric client population (2000). Rather than relying only on self-reports by the client, it may be helpful to include a second source of information, such as a caregiver. Another way to improve the quality of information gathered is to combine self-report and performance-based assessment methods when appropriate. We will take a more in-depth look at some of these assessment approaches later in this chapter.

An assessment can only provide a "snapshot" of a person's situation at a certain point in time. The individual's problems as well as his or her means to deal with them change over time. This may be especially true for elderly clients. The support systems of an elderly client may also change. A caregiving daughter may become unable to provide continued support, the neighbor who helps with shopping may move away, or the spouse who organized the household may become a care recipient as well. Likewise, the needs of the client may change over time. For example, while some of the client's needs for assistance with activities of daily living are attended to, new health-related complications may arise. In view of these potential changes, it is important to regularly reassess an elderly client's problems and available supports.

Another important consideration in the context of geriatric assessment is the setting in which the interview takes place. The two settings in which assessment interviews usually occur are an agency or institutional setting (e.g., hospital or nursing home) or the client's own home. As we discussed in the previous chapter, the practitioner is in control of many environmental factors in an agency setting. He or she can choose the location of the assessment, decide who is present, arrange the seating, and so on. For the client, on the other hand, it may be a very unfamiliar and even anxiety-provoking environment. Thus, the practitioner needs to take additional care and time to comfort the client. The location should be quiet and ensure privacy. If you have difficulty ensuring this, for example, if you have to interview a client in a two-bed hospital room, you should ask the client whether continuing under those circumstances is acceptable. Ordinarily, a small meeting room or the practitioner's office would be preferable locations to meet with the client.

Conducting an assessment in the client's home brings with it a different set of challenges and opportunities. By conducting an assessment in the client's home, you may gather information you could not gain in an agency setting. The home environment offers numerous cues that can aid in the assessment process. Family pictures can lead to a conversation about the client's family and support systems, diplomas on the wall may be used to talk about the client's current or past work experience, and room decorations can lead into a conversation about the client's leisure activities. A second advantage of the home setting is easier access to the client's documents. Records on health care and insurance, financial information, and other documents can be accessed with less effort and delay. Moreover, the home environment offers many visual cues that can aid in the assessment. Home safety, hygiene, or cleanliness of the home can be best assessed in the environment of concern rather than through a discussion in an agency setting. Several questions can easily be answered through direct observation of the client in his or her own environment. Can the client freely move through the house? Which structural changes need to be made to the home environment? Are adaptive devices, such as commodes, walkers, or grab bars needed? All these details can add valuable information to the process of organizing the client's care and service plan.

In either environment, it is important that the client can feel comfortable. One should keep in mind that for many clients and caregivers this could be the first contact with a professional helper. Therefore, it may be especially important to clarify your role and the purpose of your meeting. Explain what type of questions you will be asking and let the client know up front approximately how long the assessment will take. Avoid beginning the assessment interview with intimate or uncomfortable questions (e.g., "have you made burial arrangements?"), but start with general questions that enable the client to relax and get comfortable. Questions about a person's family history, past employment, and so on may be good introductory questions. Use language and terms the client understands and avoid professional jargon. This can at times be intricate when one uses standardized assessment tools. Sometimes the interviewer walks a thin line between asking the questions the way they are asked in the instrument (otherwise you may be changing the measurement's outcome) and making sure the respondent understands the question. To help

---

BOX 4.2 BASIC INTERVIEW GUIDELINES

- Carefully consider the setting for the assessment
- Ensure privacy
- Choose a comfortable environment
- Clarify your role and the purpose of your meeting
- Clarify what will be done with the assessment information
- Avoid beginning the interview with intimate or uncomfortable questions
- Start with questions that enable clients to warm up and build comfort
- Use language and terms that the client can understand
- Do not abruptly end the interview

the interviewer, many standardized assessment instruments provide clear instructions on how to conduct the assessment and how to ask the questions.

Just as at the beginning of the interview, it is beneficial not to abruptly end the assessment interview. Summarizing the major points is often a good way to lead toward the end of the interview. After concluding the interview, clarify again what will be done with the information. Being asked a battery of questions and not knowing what the interviewer thinks or what conclusions can be drawn may feel very uncomfortable. Share your assessment with the client and provide information on how he or she can contact you if there are any further questions. Box 4.2 presents a summary of the basic guidelines discussed here.

CHOOSING ASSESSMENT INSTRUMENTS

We will now turn our attention to assessment instruments often used in gerontological practice. The first step is always the selection of an assessment instrument appropriate for the clients served. Three considerations should be at the forefront of the decision-making process: (1) scientific considerations, (2) practical considerations, and (3) the process used to gather assessment data (self-report versus performance-based assessment).

In general, preference should be given to standardized assessment instruments with sound psychometric qualities. They have undergone extensive research, development, and testing. Furthermore, the developers have established the validity and reliability of their scales, two very important considerations in the selection of an instrument. The validity of an instrument refers to its ability to measure what it is intended to measure. It can be viewed as a gauge of how well the purpose of the measurement is achieved (Fortune and Reid 1999a).

One can distinguish between three basic types of validity: content, criterion, and construct validity. Content validity is concerned with the question of whether the items on a scale tap into the content area one is trying to measure (Fisher and Corcoran 2000). Thus, content validity is a matter of expert judgment. Criterion validity is concerned with whether the variables correlate with other relevant variables, i.e., usually other already established instruments (Fisher and Corcoran 2000). Finally, construct validity deals with whether the instruments accurately measure the constructs of interest. The background information on standardized instruments usually includes a discussion of validity and the procedures the developers used to establish it.

Reliability refers to the consistency of an instrument (Fortune and Reid 1999a). In the case of reliability one is concerned with the question whether the instrument measures consistently—in other words, whether it is stable and dependable. In the process of standardizing the instruments, a researcher establishes a reliability coefficient. These reliability coefficents can range from 0.00 (no reliability) to 1.00 (perfect reliability). Measures used in clinical assessment should generally have reliability coefficients of .80 or higher (Jordan and Franklin 1995).

In addition to scientific considerations, there are several practical considerations to keep in mind when choosing assessment instruments (see box 4.3). One consideration is the purpose of the assessment. Some questions to reflect on include: What is the intent of the assessment? Are you trying to establish eligibility for a service? What will the information be used for? Are you collecting data for clinical assessment, for agency reporting of outcomes, or for research purposes? Another important question to address is the feasibility of administering the assessment instrument. The best scales are of little use if practitioners do not have the resources to complete them or if they are too difficult for the client to respond to. For example, an instrument may be so lengthy that a client may loose the ability to concentrate and give misleading answers. Likewise, an instrument may be too complex for a client with a cognitive impairment. Moreover, the practitioner may not have the resources (e.g., time) to use an instrument. The determination whether to use certain instruments should always include a pilot test of the instrument with clients. Several areas should be the focus of such a pilot test. Does the client understand the questions? Is the client able to recall important information? How long is the instrument? How much time does it take to complete it? Some clients may not be able to participate in lengthy assessment interviews. Balancing the length of the assessment interview and the quality of the data gathered can be a difficult task. One positive development is that many developers of geriatric assessment instruments are making use of advanced statistical procedures to shorten the number of items on their measurements, thus reducing the time it takes to administer them. You should consider the clarity of the instrument and whether clients are able to understand its terminology. While instruments are developed with the respondent in mind, a client with dementia, for example, may not be able to understand complex questions. The time required for completion of the assessment is also an important consideration. While some clients may not mind a long assessment instrument, others may not feel comfortable answering a lot of questions. Furthermore, some older adult clients may no longer

---

BOX 4.3 CONSIDERATIONS FOR SELECTING ASSESSMENT INSTRUMENTS

- Validity of instrument
- Reliability of instrument
- Purpose of assessment
- Clarity of instrument
- Feasibility and pilot test results
- Length and time required for completion
- Mode of assessment

---

have the ability to concentrate for longer periods of time. Thus, whenever possible, practitioners should use short assessment instruments. Finally, the mode of collecting the assessment information is important. As we will describe below, instruments can follow various formats, including self-reports, observations, or a performance-based format.

Two primary approaches to gather information in gerontological practice are self-reports and performance-based assessments. A self-report assessment can use a self-rating approach or be administered by an interviewer. In either case, the client is asked a series of questions by an interviewer or through a self-administered instrument, thus offering a self-report based on his or her own judgment and memory. Proxy reports by caregivers or other respondents who know the client well can be used for clients with cognitive impairments. Proxy reports otherwise follow the same format as a self-report assessment. Self-reports and proxy reports have several advantages. Clients may fluctuate in their functional or cognitive abilities. Self-reporters or proxy reporters are able to include their knowledge and experience regarding these fluctuations in the assessment. They can base their account on observation over a longer period of time in the client's own environment. Thus, they can report how problems in the area being assessed manifest themselves on "average." The outside interviewer, on the other hand, can only make a judgment based on the client's functioning at the time of the assessment. Another advantage is that self-reports are usually quick and easy to administer. Answering eight or ten questions usually takes much less time than performing the respective eight or ten activities. Some areas also do not lend themselves to direct observation and performance-based assessment. For example, while a nursing assistant may be able to assess a client's incontinence based on her daily care of the patient, most practitioners have to rely on self-reports based on the person's self-care experience.

In a performance-based assessment, the client is asked to perform certain activities. The interviewer then rates the client's abilities to perform the tasks. The actual performance of a task, especially when conducted in the client's own environment, can provide a very accurate picture of the problems or needs of a client. Performance-based assessments can reduce cultural, educational, and linguistic biases (Loewenstein and Mogosky 2000). Some self-report instruments, for example, do not perform well with less educated respondents. Likewise, the respondent may not speak English well enough to correctly understand all the questions asked.

Research does not endorse one or the other method of assessment as a better approach. Some studies indicate that self-reports can be very reliable (Loewenstein and Mogosky 2000). A study of elderly persons living in the community found that clients' self-reports of how well they performed in their home environment correlated highly with the performance-based assessment of their abilities (Myers et al. 1993). Other studies, however, paint a more mixed picture. Sinoff and Ore (1997), for example, found that among the old-old, the quality of self-reports on functional abilities could be problematic. Their findings indicate that self-reports may be less reliable for cognitively impaired clients. Another study by Weinberger and associates discovered that clients usually overestimated their functional abilities. At the same time, they found that caregivers do not always assess the clients' abilities well, often underestimating or overestimating their capabilities (Weinberger et al. 1992). Thus, self-reports may be more useful with elderly clients whose cognitive functions are intact while the use of proxy reports and performance-based assessment instruments should be emphasized for clients with increased cognitive impairments. In some cases it is possible to embrace the advantages of both approaches by conducting self-report and performance-based assessments in sequence. A practitioner may conduct an initial multidimensional assessment to identify potential problem areas. Next, she may select a more refined assessment instrument that taps into the potentially problematic areas. This may then be followed by a performance-based assessment. An example might be the assessment of a client's sleep disturbance. The practitioner may identify potential sleeping problems as a result of the assessment battery she conducts. A more in-depth assessment of insomnia may follow, using a sleep assessment interview. The client may also be asked to keep a sleep diary. Finally, if indicated, the client may undergo a polysomnography, a recording of brain activity, eye-movement, and muscle tension while he or she is sleeping. In this example, the first three assessment methods used client self-reports, which were then followed by an observational method.

ASSESSMENT INSTRUMENTS

The remainder of this chapter will focus on standardized gerontological assessment instruments. It will include a description of the more common standardized geriatric assessment instruments. However, since there are many more instruments than we can include in this overview, we would like to refer the reader to the growing literature of assessment resources. Comprehensive reviews can be found in *Assessment in Clinical Gerontology* (Lichtenberg 2000), the *Handbook of Geriatric Assessment* (Gallo et al. 2000), and *Assessing Older Persons* (Kane and Kane 2000). Other useful assessment resource books can be found in the social work literature (e.g., Fisher and Corcoran 2000; Jordan and Franklin 1995), the nursing literature (e.g., Beaton and Voge 1998; Frank-Stromberg 1992), and the literature on long-term care (e.g., Beaton and Voge 1998; Teresi et al. 1997). A comprehensive review of instruments to assess the health status of older adults can be found in Andresen, Rothenberg, and Zimmer (1997).

MULTIDIMENSIONAL ASSESSMENT

First, we will consider multidimensional assessment instruments. Many agencies use multidimensional assessment instruments as part of their regular agency practice, often combining standardized and nonstandardized measurements. The ways in which agencies combine different instruments and construct their own instruments vary greatly. In addition to the many measurement tools developed at the agency level, several standardized multidimensional assessment instruments have been developed. We will present three, the Uniform Assessment Instrument (UAI), the Older Americans Resources and Services Questionnaire (OARS), and the Minimum Data Set (MDS). With exception of the UAI, these multidimensional assessment instruments have undergone extensive development and validation research.

Uniform Assessment Instruments (UAIs) are measurements that many states mandate. They vary from state to state. UAIs are used to measure general characteristics of clients and outcomes across populations served. While they may include parts of standardized assessment measurements, they are not necessarily standardized instruments per se. An example of a UAI is the Virginia Uniform Assessment Instrument. The Virginia-UAI comes in two basic versions, a two-page short form and an extended version. Areas the UAI covers include: identifying information (e.g., name, address, birth date, gender, marital status), functional status in the areas of activities of daily living (e.g., bathing, dressing, toileting), ambulating (e.g., walking, climbing stairs, mobility), instrumental activities of daily living (e.g., preparing meals, housecleaning), and medication management (independently or with assistance), psychosocial status in the areas of behavior (e.g., wandering, abusive behavior), and orientation (e.g., oriented, disoriented, comatose) as well as a summary that includes prohibitive conditions, levels of care needed and approved, and information on the person conducting the assessment.

The Older Americans Resources and Services Questionnaire (OARS) is a multidimensional assessment instrument that focuses on social and economic resources, physical and mental health, activities of daily living, and instrumental activities of daily living (Fillenbaum 1988). Rankings from 1 (excellent ability) to 6 (total incapacity) are assigned to all eleven areas the OARS appraises. For example, a person may have a mental health score of 3, indicating mild mental impairment, a social resources score of 1, indicating excellent social relationships and adequate social resources, and so on. The OARS can be utilized in community and institutional settings and is applicable for clinical practice as well as research. It follows a structured format and requires a trained interviewer to conduct the assessment. A major drawback of the OARS is that it is a rather lengthy instrument, requiring about one and a half hours to complete. However, it is possible to use only some sections of the instrument for specific assessment purposes.

The Minimum Data Set (MDS) is another widely used multidimensional assessment instrument (Hawes et al. 1995; Morris et al. 1990). It has undergone several revisions in a rather short time (i.e., MDS, MDS+, and MDS-V2) (Salamon 2000). The MDS was designed for the Health Care Financing Administration to become the universal assessment instrument that the Omnibus Reconciliation Act of 1987 mandated for Medicare and Medicaid reimbursement, home care, and nursing home placement (Salamon 2000). It is also utilized in some community-based settings. The seventeen sections of the MDS include assessment of cognitive functioning, mood and behavior, ADLs, physical functioning, health and mental health, activity patterns, and the individual's discharge potential. Although the MDS is a very comprehensive instrument, it takes less than one hour to complete the assessment. The MDS has to be readministered on a regular basis. Box 4.4 provides an overview of the assessment instruments discussed here.

FUNCTIONAL ASSESSMENT

Medical disease by itself is a poor predictor of a person's ability to function independently (Gallo et al. 2000). For example, while one person with rheumatoid arthritis may be able to perform most activities of daily living

---

BOX 4.4 MULTIDIMENSIONAL ASSESSMENT INSTRUMENTS

INSTRUMENT	AUTHORS (YEAR)	AREAS ASSESSED
Uniform Assessment Instrument (UAI)	N/A	Varies, typically identifying information, functional status, medical information, psychosocial status
Older Americans Resources and Services Questionnaire (OARS)	Fillenbaum and Smyer (1981)	Social and economic resources, physical and mental health, ADL, IADL
Minimum Data Set (MDS, MDS+, MDS-V2)	Morris et al. (1990); Hawes et al. (1995)	Cognitive, mood, behavior, ADLs, physical functioning, health, mental health, activity patterns, discharge potential

---

independently, albeit with a lot of pain, another person with the same diagnosis may need considerable assistance. Thus, measures of functional abilities were developed to better assess and describe a person's need for assistance. These measures provide valuable information for developing a person's care and service plan. Furthermore, measures of functional ability have been established as good predictors of mortality (Gallo et al. 2000).

The Katz Index of Independence in Activities of Daily Living (Katz-ADL) is probably the best known measure of functional activities of daily living. It was developed to measure treatment results and provide a prognosis for elderly and chronically ill clients (Katz et al. 1963). Many of the newer measurements of functional autonomy are based on the framework provided by Katz and his associates. The activities of daily living measured by the Katz-ADL schedule include bathing, dressing, toileting, transfer, continence, and feeding (see box 4.5). For each of these items, the rater assesses whether the patient can complete the activity independently, requires some assistance, or is completely dependent. The index provides a hierarchical grading of independence levels.

The Barthel Index (BI) is another widely used functional assessment instrument. It was initially developed to measure the functional independence of patients with neuromuscular and musculoskeletal disorders, but it

---

BOX 4.5 GRADES OF INDEPENDENCE/DEPENDENCE IN THE KATZ ADL*

A = independent in all six functions

B = independent in all but one of these functions

C = independent in all but bathing and one additional function

D = independent in all but bathing, dressing and one additional function

E = independent in all but bathing, dressing, going to the toilet, and one additional function

F = independent in all but bathing, dressing, going to the toilet, transfer, and one additional function

G = dependent in all six functions

Other = dependent in at least two functions, but not classifiable as C, D, E, F

*Based on Katz et al. 1963:915

---

has since been applied in a wide range of hospital and institutional settings (Mahoney and Barthel 1965). The items of the index refer to eleven different functional activities. Each individual item is weighted (scores = 0, 5, 10, 15), based on the time it takes a person to complete the activity and the amount of physical assistance that is required. Repeated applications of the Barthel Index enable the assessment of general improvements or declines in the physical functioning of a patient. As a straightforward and easy-to-use instrument, the Barthel Index is still widely used in long-term care and rehabilitation settings.

An Instrumental Activity of Daily Living (IADL) measurement is part of the OARS assessment battery and should be combined with an ADL assessment (Duke University 1978). It measures the performance in seven activities of daily living, including the abilities to use the telephone, travel, shop, prepare meals, complete housework, take medication, and manage money (Fillenbaum 1988). On each of these items the IADL instrument measures whether a person is independent, needs some assistance, or is completely dependent. Although the OARS-IADL is part of the multidimensional OARS assessment battery, it has been used independently for the measurement of IADLs.

The Determination of Needs Assessment (DONA) is one of the combined ADL and IADL assessment instruments. It was originally developed by

Paveza and associates for assessment in community-based practice settings (Paveza et al. 1989). These instruments differ from other functional assessment tools by separating the measurement of an individual's impairment from the measurement of his or her needs. For each of the fifteen ADLs and IADLs of the DONA, the interviewer separately rates the client's level of impairment and the level of unmet needs, using a four-point rating scale. Based on the overall scores, respondents can be grouped into different levels of impairment and levels of need.

The Physical Performance Test (PPT), developed by Reuben and Sui (1990), is one of the newer functional assessment tools. It is a performance-based measure that asks the client to complete the following activities: walk, climb stairs, write a sentence, simulate eating, lift a book to place it on a shelf, put on and take off a jacket, pick up a coin from the floor, and turn by 360 degrees. The PPT has been developed for outpatient use, but it can be adapted to hospital and inpatient settings. Observation of clients' actual performance makes the PPT suitable for use with individuals suffering from dementia and cognitive impairments where a self-report instrument may not yield reliable results.

Similar to the PPT, the Direct Assessment of Functional Status (DAFS) uses performance-based indicators for the assessment of a person's functional abilities. It was developed out of a concern that most functional assessment instruments rely on self-reports, thus making them difficult to use with demented or cognitively impaired clients (Loewenstein et al. 1989). The DAFS assesses an individual's skills in the areas of time orientation, communication skills, transportation, finances, shopping, grooming, and eating. Items are weighted differently, based on their importance for predicting whether a person can live independently in the community.

The MDS, described as one of the multidimensional assessment instruments, includes a battery of measurements of activities of daily living (MDS-ADL). Since a person's ADL performance may vary from day to day, the MDS requires the assessment of the individual's performance over the last seven days. The scoring of the MDS-ADL is based on sequential levels of performance. For each of the ADLs, the rater scores whether the person can complete the task independently; requires supervision, limited assistance, or extensive assistance; or is totally dependent. Multiple sources of information are used for assessment. For example, the rater may question direct care staff from different shifts, ask the patient for information, and review nurses' reports and other forms of documentation. (See box 4.6 for a summary of functional assessment instruments.)

BOX 4.6 INSTRUMENTS FOR FUNCTIONAL ASSESSMENT

INSTRUMENT	AUTHORS (YEAR)	AREAS ASSESSED
Katz Index of Independence in Activities of Daily Living (ADL)	Katz et al. (1963)	ADLs, different levels of dependence/independence
Barthel Index	Mahoney and Barthel (1965)	Levels of self-care and mobility in physically impaired persons
Instrumental Activities of Daily Living (IADL)	Duke (1978)	Range of IADL abilities, e.g., shopping, using telephone, preparing meals, taking medication
Determination of Need Assessment (DONA)	Paveza et al. (1989)	Combined assessment of common ADL and IADL measures
Physical Performance Test (PPT)	Reuben and Sui (1990)	Performance-based measure of ADLs
Direct Assessment of Functioning Scale (DAFS)	Loewenstein et al. (1989)	Performance-based measure of ADLs for persons with dementia or cognitive impairments
Minimum Data Set ADL Battery (MDS-ADL)		Basic ADL functioning over the last seven days

SOCIAL ASSESSMENT

Practitioners assessing a person's social network rely to a large extent on tools such as eco-maps, genograms, and open-ended questions about family members, friends, and other support systems. Several standardized instruments have been developed to assist in the collection of such information (see box 4.7). Two of the instruments we present assess a person's network and support. The third instrument, the Burden Interview, assesses caregivers' perceived feelings of burden. Other social support and caregiver burden scales exist. However, many of them are designed as data collection instruments for research purposes.

BOX 4.7 INSTRUMENTS FOR SOCIAL ASSESSMENT

INSTRUMENT	AUTHORS (YEAR)	AREAS ASSESSED
Lubben Social Network Scale	Lubben (1988)	Nature of support system
Norbeck Social Support Question- naire (NSSQ)	Norbeck, Lindsi, and Carrieri (1981)	Functioning (affect, aid, affirmation) and network (size, duration, frequency)
Burden Interview	Zarit and Zarit (1990)	Effect of caregiver burden on health, personal and social life, emotional well-being, finances

---

The Lubben Social Network Scale is an instrument that can be utilized to assess a person's social network (Lubben 1988). It is appropriate for the assessment of the social networks of older adults as well as those of their caregivers. The brief nine-question instrument provides a general description of the size and nature of the respondent's social network. It also includes information on the accessibility of the network to assist the individual with making decisions and providing care.

The Norbeck Social Support Questionnaire (NSSQ) is a self-administered nine-question instrument that can be used to assess the social supports of clients and/or their caregivers (Norbeck, Lindsi, and Carrieri 1981). Respondents are first asked to make a list of their informal and semiformal supports, and based on these they then answer the questions of the instrument. Since the NSSQ distinguishes between different areas of social support, it allows the assessment of those areas in which a client has good supports and those in which adequate social supports are lacking.

The Burden Interview is a twenty-two-item scale to measure the perceived burden of caregivers (Zarit and Zarit 1990). It assesses the perceived adverse effects that caregiving has on the caregivers' health, emotional well-being, social and personal life, and finances (Whitlatch, Zarit, and von Eye 1991). The Burden Interview includes two subscales that assess the caregiver's personal strain and role strain. The authors of the instrument suggest that the Burden Interview should be supplemented with clinical observations (Zarit and Zarit 1990).

MENTAL STATUS ASSESSMENT

Illness and disease may bring about changes in a person's mental status. Since these changes can significantly alter a person's behavior, patterns of communication and interaction, and capacity to perform activities of daily living, the assessment of a person's mental state is a very common screening activity. The common assessment instruments are very similar in content and design. They typically focus on the person's orientation, feeling states, cognitive skills, and thought patterns (Fraser 1992). Most instruments are rather short, often comprising fewer than ten or twelve questions. We will briefly describe four widely used mental status assessment instruments that are quick and easy to administer.

The Mini Mental Status Examination (MMSE), developed by Folstein and associates, is one of the most frequently applied tests of cognitive functioning (Folstein, Folstein, and McHugh 1975). It has strong psychometric properties and offers population-based normative data according to educational level and age (Crum et al. 1993). The eleven-item instrument has two parts. Part one assesses memory, orientation, and attention using verbal responses. Part two of the MMSE evaluates the respondent's writing and naming abilities and success in following verbal and written commands. The responses are weighted differently (individual scores ranging from 1–5), with a total possible score of 30 points. The instrument's authors indicate that respondents scoring 24 points and below should be considered cognitively impaired (Folstein, Folstein, and McHugh 1975).

The Short Portable Mental Status Questionnaire (SPMSQ) is part of the OARS assessment battery. Developed by Pfeiffer (1975), the ten-item instrument is based completely on verbal responses, requires no additional prompts, and is easy for the clinician to memorize. The unobtrusiveness of the SPMSQ makes it one of the more widely used tests of mental status. Although the SPMSQ has shown to correctly identify over 90 percent of older adults without cognitive impairments, the test may not differentiate well enough between respondents with mild cognitive impairment and those with normal cognitive functioning (Smyer, Hofland, and Jonas 1979).

The Mental Status Questionnaire (MSQ) is a screening instrument developed for use with institutionalized elderly clients (Kahn et al. 1960). It consists of ten questions that cover the areas of orientation to current location, time, person, and current events. Based on the number of erroneous responses, a respondent is classified into one of the following categories: intact, nonsignificant impairment, mild to moderate impairment, and severe impairment.

BOX 4.8 INSTRUMENTS FOR ASSESSMENT OF COGNITIVE AND MENTAL STATUS

INSTRUMENT	AUTHORS (YEAR)	AREAS ASSESSED
Mini Mental Status Examination (MMSE)	Folstein, Folstein and McHugh (1975)	Cognitive impairment in orientation, attention, registration, recall, and language
Short Portable Mental Status Questionnaire (SPMSQ)	Pfeiffer (1975)	Orientation to person, time, and place
Mental Status Questionnaire (MSQ)	Kahn et al. (1960)	Orientation to current location, time, person, and current events
MDS-Cognitive Performance Scale (MDS-CPS)	Morris et al. (1994)	Comatose state, decision making, short-term memory, dependence in eating

---

Finally, the MDS-Cognitive Performance Scale (MDS-CPS), developed by Morris and associates, is a mandated component of the Resident Assessment Instrument that all nursing homes participating in Medicaid or Medicare programs have to complete (Morris et al. 1990). The instrument is used to classify residents into one of seven cognitive performance categories, ranging from cognitively intact to severe cognitive impairment. (See box 4.8 for an overview.)

GENERAL HEALTH STATUS

The instruments measuring general health status are sometimes referred to as measures of health status or of health-related quality of life. As this terminology indicates, they do not measure narrowly defined concepts, such as functional abilities or certain types of health problems, but are broader multidimensional measurements of a person's general health status (see box 4.9). The four instruments we will describe are the Sickness Impact profile, the Short Form 36, the General Health Questionnaire, and the Duke Health Profile.

BOX 4.9 INSTRUMENTS FOR GENERAL HEALTH ASSESSMENT

INSTRUMENT	AUTHORS (YEAR)	AREAS ASSESSED
Sickness Impact Profile (SIP)	Bergner et al. (1981)	Physical, psychosocial and other areas of health
Short-Form 36 (SF-36)	Ware and Sherbourne (1992)	Physical functioning, bodily pain, health perceptions, social functioning, vitality, role disability, mental health
General Health Questionnaire (GHQ)	Goldberg (1972)	Somatic symptoms, anxiety, insomnia, social dysfunction, and depression
Duke Health Profile (DUKE)	Parkerson, Broadhead, and Tse (1991)	Physical, mental, social, general, and perceived health

---

The Sickness Impact Profile (SIP) is a comprehensive measure of health status (Bergner et al. 1981). It provides a physical, a psychosocial, and a general health score. The SIP is widely used and has undergone extensive validation. It can be used in an observation, interview, or self-administered format. Since the instrument contains 136 questions and takes about forty-five minutes to complete, shorter versions of the SIP have been developed. For example, a shorter sixty-six-item version was developed for respondents in nursing home settings (Gerety et al. 1994).

The Short Form 36 (SF-36) is a health-related quality of life questionnaire that is used as an assessment and screening tool in primary care (Ware and Sherbourne 1992). Eight different functional health concepts are assessed by the SF-36, namely, physical functioning, bodily pain, general health perceptions, social functioning, vitality, role disability due to physical health problems, role disability due to emotional problems, and general mental health. The SF-36 can be a useful screening instrument for identifying the need for a social work assessment of elderly primary care clients (Berkman et al. 1999).

The General Health Questionnaire (GHQ) screens for the presence of psychiatric disorders (Goldberg 1972). It was developed specifically for primary practice settings and is established as screening instrument around the world (Gallo et al. 2000). The self-administered instrument contains sixty items; however, a shorter twenty-eight-item version is often used. This scaled version of the GHQ assesses somatic symptoms, anxiety, insomnia, social dysfunction, and depression (Goldberg and Hiller 1979). For each question the respondent is asked to indicate whether during the last four weeks the symptoms described were experienced "not at all," "no more than usual," "more than usual," or "much more than usual."

The Duke Health Profile (DUKE) is a seventeen-item questionnaire that assesses respondents' health outcomes in the areas of physical, mental, and social health as well as general and perceived health status (Parkerson, Broad, and Tse 1991). The instrument also provides scores for disability, self-esteem, anxiety, depression, and pain. The DUKE is easy to use and is administered using a self-report format.

ASSESSMENT OF DEPRESSION

Many of the scales used for screening depression have been adapted for use with elderly clients. Among the most widely used depression screening instruments for older adults are the Beck Depression Inventory (BDI) and two scales specifically developed for the older adult population, the Geriatric Depression Scale (GDS) and the Zung Self-Rating Depression Scale (see box 4.10).

The best-known screening instrument for depression, the Beck Depression Inventory (BDI), is also widely used with the older adult population.

BOX 4.10 INSTRUMENTS FOR MENTAL HEALTH ASSESSMENT		
INSTRUMENT	**AUTHORS (YEAR)**	**AREAS ASSESSED**
Beck Depression Inventory (BDI)	Beck et al. (1961), Beck and Beck (1972)	Depression, with cutoffs for mild, moderate, and severe depression
Geriatric Depression Scale (GDS)	Yesavage et al. (1983), Sheikh and Yesavage (1986)	Depression, with cutoffs for normal, mild, and moderate severe depression

The BDI comes as a twenty-one-item inventory (Beck et al. 1961) and a shorter thirteen-item version (Beck and Beck 1972). Some examples of BDI items are mood, pessimism, feeling guilty, self-accusation, lack of satisfaction, and sense of failure. Since the shorter version drops the somatic items, it may be more accurate for screening older adults (Ossip-Klein, Rothenberg, and Andresen 1997). The BDI yields a single composite score and provides standard cutoff points for mild, moderate, and severe depression. It takes about five to ten minutes to complete.

The Geriatric Depression Scale (GDS) is another common tool for the screening of depression. It was developed by Yesavage and his associates specifically for the use with the older adult population. (Yesavage et al. 1983). The GDS uses a straightforward "yes/no" response format, which makes it easy to use. It can be administered as an interview or in a self-report format. Like the BDI, the GDS is also available as a longer form with thirty items (Yesavage et al. 1983) and as a shorter version with fifteen items (Sheikh and Yesavage 1986). It provides standard cutoff points for normal and mild depression and moderate to severe depression.

GOAL ATTAINMENT SCALING

Although it is not an assessment instrument to establish the manifestation of a problem, goal attainment scaling should be mentioned in the context of assessment. Goal attainment scaling is concerned with measuring practice outcomes. It takes into consideration the problem status at the beginning of treatment, anchoring changes in the information gathered during assessment. A first step in rating goal attainment is to prepare a goal attainment follow-up guide when planning the intervention. In such an approach, client and practitioner develop specific indicators for each of the levels of goal attainment. The indicators that are developed are later used for the evaluation of goal attainment. Although this approach is more time consuming, developing the indicators is helpful when discussing possible treatment outcomes and their consequences. It can add additional structure to the process of exploring target problems and setting treatment goals. Furthermore, this format of goal attainment scaling leads to a more accurate measurement of treatment outcomes. Figure 4.1 is an example of a goal attainment guide. Practitioner and client develop a description of indicators that would be evidence for the level of goal attainment and mark them in the right-hand column of the form.

Figure 4.2 is a follow-up guide developed for measuring goal attainment with an eighty-seven-year-old client one week after hip fracture surgery. It was completed while the client was still in the geriatric rehabilitation unit of the hospital. The various levels of goal attainment were developed together with the client.

FIGURE 4.1 GOAL ATTAINMENT GUIDE

Date: _____ Client: _____ Practitioner:_____

Treatment Goal: _____

GOAL ATTAINMENT LEVEL: DESCRIPTION OF GOAL STATUS:

(-2): Most unfavorable treatment outcome

(-1): Less than expected success

(0): Expected level of treatment success

(+1): More than expected treatment success

(+2): Best possible treatment outcome

KEY:

X = Level at beginning of treatment
* = Level at first follow-up
** = Level at second follow-up

GOAL AREAS

	Personal Care	Mobility	Future Care Situation
Much less than expected (-2)	Feeds self and washes upper body with set up. (X)	Chairfast; two- person assist for transfer; decreased dynamic sitting balance . (X)	Stays on the geri-atric rehabilitation unit (X)
Somewhat less than expected (1)	Dependent in lower limb care and in bathing ; achieves goals in more than six weeks.	One-person hands-on transfer, walks 15 feet with walker, meets goal in four weeks.	Is discharged to a nursing home.
Program goal (0)	Independent in personal care; wife is able to supervise bathing; goal is achieved within 5–6 weeks.	Independent transfer, walks 75 feet with assistance of a walker; reaches goal at three weeks. (*)	Home with eight hours of outside supports per day. (*)
Somewhat better than expected (+1)	Same as in program goal (level 0), but achieved in four weeks; able to do modest household chores.	Meets the goal in two weeks or is fully mobile within the house and able to walk to the car.	Home with four hours of outside support per day.
Much better than expected (+2)	Same as in level +1 achieved in less than four weeks or return to premorbid condition. (*)	Fully mobile within the house, able to walk 100–200 feet outside with assistance of a walker.	Home with no additional sup-ports required.
Comments	Premorbid ADL independence, did some household chores and banking.	+2 describes the pre-morbid level of functioning. Goal is needed for further outpatient rehabilitation	Caregiver indicates that she would be able to take the client home if he can become inde pendent in pesonal care

SUMMARY

In this chapter, we provided an overview of basic principles for geriatric assessment. We examined guidelines for choosing measurements and introduced the reader to some of the more common standardized assessment instruments used in gerontological practice. The following chapters will focus on the application of the task-centered model to practice with older adults. As an integral part of this discussion we will provide additional information on the clinical assessment of clients' problems and needs.

PART II

TASK-CENTERED PRACTICE
WITH THE ELDERLY

In part II we describe the gerontological task-centered model. Chapters 5, 6, and 7 will introduce this model of practice. We will focus on individual and family adaptations of the model with a brief overview of its use with groups. Chapters 8, 9, and 10 will focus on special applications of the model (case management, caregivers, institutional settings). Group applications will be dealt with more extensively in chapters 9 and 10. Although we may use shorthand expressions, such as "work with the elderly," to describe the model, we have in mind work not only with elderly persons but also with others that matter in their lives, such as caregivers, partners, and family members.

Throughout these chapters we will provide examples of rating scales, schedules, or other forms that can assist practitioners and clients in the intervention process. While a practitioner may not use all of these forms, we would like to emphasize the significance of measuring and tracking intervention outcomes. Moreover, instruments such as the task-planning form provide the client with additional support in accomplishing tasks. For example, the form can serve as a reminder to carry out specified actions and increase the likelihood that they will be done.

CHAPTER 5

INITIAL PHASE OF INTERVENTION

THE TASK-CENTERED model consists of clearly defined and sequenced activities that are collaboratively carried out by the practitioner and the client to solve problems. It has been adapted to practice in a wide range of settings, problems, and client populations (Reid 1992, 1997; Tolson, Reid, and Garvin 2002), including geriatric social work (Cormican 1977; Dierking, Brown, and Fortune 1980; Fortune and Rathbone-McCuan 1981; Rathbone-McCuan 1985).

The task-centered model for practice with the elderly consists of three phases (see box 5.1). In the initial phase, the stage for the intervention is set. This includes conducting intake and assessment, selecting the problems to work on, and setting intervention goals for each of these problems. The middle phase focuses on the process of developing tasks to address the client's problems. It includes developing and selecting intervention tasks, anticipating potential obstacles to the intervention, carrying out the tasks, and reviewing how well they were accomplished. The final phase addresses the ending of the intervention process and includes termination, reinforcing of accomplishments, and making plans for the future.

BASIC CHARACTERISTICS OF TASK-CENTERED PRACTICE

Before proceeding with an elaboration of the steps of the initial phase, it may be useful to discuss the basic characteristics of the task-centered approach. What is distinctive about the model is found not in any one characteristic but in the combination of all of them. (For an overview see box 5.3.)

EMPIRICAL EMPHASIS The model has evolved through a program of research and development begun in the 1970s. Numerous studies, including eight controlled experiments, have been used to test and improve the model (Reid

---

BOX 5.1 PHASES OF THE INTERVENTION MODEL

INITIAL PHASE: SETTING THE STAGE

Intake

Explaining Role, Purpose, and Intervention Procedures

Assessment and Problem Identification

Selecting and Prioritizing Problems

Exploring and Specifying Problem

Setting Goals

Completing an Intervention Plan and Contracting

MIDDLE PHASE: ADDRESSING THE PROBLEMS

Developing Task Alternatives

Selecting Tasks

Agreeing on Tasks

Establishing Incentives and Rationale

Planning Details of Implementation

Anticipating Obstacles

Rehearsal, Guided Practice, and In-vivo Implementation

Summarizing Tasks

Implementing Tasks Between Sessions

Monitoring Through Task and Problem Review

FINAL PHASE: ENDING INTERVENTION

Recontracting, if necessary

Final Problem and Task Review

Reinforcing Accomplishments

Reviewing Problem-Solving Skills

Future Plans

1997). In case applications, preference is given to methods and theories tested and supported by empirical research. Hypotheses and concepts about the client system are grounded in case data. Speculative theorizing about the client's problems and behavior is avoided. Assessment, process, and outcome data are systematically collected in each case.

INTEGRATION The model draws selectively on theories and methods from compatible approaches—e.g., problem-solving, cognitive-behavioral, cognitive, and family structural ones. Essentially the model provides a structure for incorporating concepts and techniques from any source that can contribute to helping social workers and clients understand the latter's problems and to developing actions to alleviate them. Given the empirical orientation of the model, preference is given to importing those components that are based on research.

PROBLEM FOCUS Like other problem-solving models, the task-centered model focuses on alleviating clients' problems. Emphasis is on problems and goals defined by the client, thus fostering clients' decision-making and increasing clients' autonomy. Problems arise in the context of the systems in which the client is embedded. To resolve a problem and prevent it from recurring, the context in which it occurs may need to be changed. Likewise, successfully solving a problem may bring about planned as well as unanticipated changes in the context in which it occurs. Consequently, the systems surrounding a client as well as the context in which the problem arises should be carefully appraised and taken into consideration when planning interventions. While the terminology of problems is used in writing about the model, practitioners may wish to substitute "need" for "problem" in their communication with clients. Although conceptually the notions of problem and need can be regarded as equivalent, some elderly persons may prefer seeing themselves as having "needs" rather than "problems." Another option is to refer to goals once they have been established.

Given the recent emphasis on client strengths in social work practice, it should be noted that the task-centered model has always attached considerable importance to such strengths (Reid and Epstein 1972). From a task-centered perspective, having strengths and problems is not incompatible. Most people, old and young, have their share of both. A "target problem" in the task-centered model is simply a condition the client wants to improve or rectify. This may be as simple as the erratic delivery of Meals on Wheels or as complex as an unsatisfactory relationship with a caregiver. In this view problems are a normal part of existence; they are not to be equated with personal failure or pathology.

TASKS AS THE MEANS OF CHANGE Tasks are seen as the primary vehicle for change. Changes are brought about through these tasks, i.e., through specific problem-solving actions. Tasks can be implemented by elderly persons, their caregivers, practitioners, or others involved in the intervention process. Yet, whenever possible, preference should be given to tasks that elderly persons implement on their own. Undertaking and successfully completing tasks is an empowering experience that can heighten self-esteem and self-efficacy and can lead to further problem-solving activity (Bandura 1982). This kind of experience is particularly important for older people because their confidence in their own actions has been often undermined by stereotypes equating age with dysfunction.

While tasks may be worked on during the session, the critical actions are carried out between client contacts. Work during the session lays the foundation for implementation following the session. For example, in hospital discharge planning, a great deal of effort in the session may be devoted to developing the plan, but it is the carrying out of the plan that matters. The nature of tasks and ways to develop them will be discussed in more detail in the next chapter.

CLIENT PARTICIPATION AND DECISION MAKING The task-centered model follows a clearly structured step-by-step approach. It spells out a sequence of intervention activities that the practitioner and client collaboratively undertake. By following such a clear structure, clients are enabled to take on a more active role in efforts to help them. The practitioner-client relationship is seen as a collaborative partnership. Since we ask our clients to participate in planning and implementing care-related decisions, they should have at least a basic understanding of how we will proceed. Therefore, a practitioner using this model should explain to the client how it works. This can be accomplished in a number of ways. It is helpful to provide a general outline of the service activities at the beginning, usually during the first or second client contact. This explanation should include an overview of the basic practice approach and also a review of the client's and the practitioner's roles. It should emphasize the importance of active participation by the client in planning and carrying out tasks. A more detailed description of specific intervention activities may best be introduced when they first take place during the intervention process.

Gerontological practitioners will encounter situations that may require a departure from this collaborative client-directed approach. For example, a crisis situation may occur in which a client with cognitive impairments requires immediate attention but is not able to actively engage in problem-solving at that point in time. Likewise, situations can occur where it would constitute neglect or imminent risk to self or others not to intervene. There may also be legal requirements to intervene, regardless of a client's agreement to do so. A possible case scenario, for instance, is the Adult Protective Service worker who initiates certain legal actions on the client's behalf without his or her explicit cooperation. Using this model, the practitioner would still try to actively engage the client in other service decisions and actions.

Our guidelines for decision making and autonomy with elderly clients are based on a framework developed by Collopy (1988). Among the autonomy issues categorized by Collopy, the distinctions between decisional and executional autonomy may be the most relevant. Decisional autonomy refers to the ability to make self-determined decisions, and executional autonomy refers to the ability to carry out these decisions. A client may no longer be able to implement a decision but may still have all the capacities to make decisions. Likewise, a client may no longer be able to make completely autonomous decisions but may still be able to carry out all or a significant amount of the problem-solving activities. The decision-making guidelines summarized in box 5.2 offer specific instructions on how to address varying levels of capabilities in clients.

PLANNED BREVITY Task-centered practice is a brief intervention modality that uses time limits. Typically, practitioners using this approach in geriatric settings will plan for four to twelve sessions during a period lasting up to four months. Time limits are usually introduced at the onset of the intervention process, when practitioner and client develop a time frame for the length of service. Several decades of research have indicated that outcomes are generally as good for short-term time-limited as for long-term service (Bloom 2000; Koss and Shiang 1994; Reid and Shyne 1969), but it needs to be noted that this research relates primarily to psychotherapy and counseling models. Caution is needed in extrapolating results to other forms of work with the elderly.

Some of the principles of brief service definitely apply to geriatric practice. Time limits can mobilize clients and practitioners to become more effective. Working on solving a problem with a set time goal in mind may help the client to "see the light at the end of the tunnel" and thus provide additional motivation to work toward achieving it. Client motivation, in turn, has a positive impact on successful completion of service activities and the attainment of goals.

However, as some of our case illustrations will show, service limits often do not become an issue in work with the elderly because service by nature is often for a short term only. Problems may be specific and the course of their resolution delimited, as in discharge planning. Historically, time limits have been used in psychotherapy and clinical social work to control the length of service in work with problems that may be more or less interminable, such as many psychological and interpersonal problems. For such problems intervention may accomplish only so much, and the point of diminishing returns soon arrives. Time limits may capture the period when most change is likely

---

BOX 5.2 AUTONOMY GUIDELINES

- Clients should be enabled to make decisions when they need assistance in executing a choice. Inability *to execute* decisions should not affect the right to *make decisions.*
- Clients should be enabled to execute decisions when they need assistance to make a decision. Inability to *make decisions* should not affect the right to *implement decisions.*
- When clients delegate autonomy, practitioners must make sure that all parties understand and agree on the contents, extent, and consequences of this delegation.
- A client's level of competence has to be assessed in context and should not be generalized beyond the context. All information needed to make a rational, informed decision should be available to the client. A competent choice that is coherent with an elderly person's values should be respected, regardless of differing professional or agency norms.
- The values, morals, and life history of a client should be taken into account.
- Decisions should not be based solely on rationality or the caregivers' expectations.
- Immediate and long-range considerations should be carefully weighed. For elderly clients the autonomy in the immediate situation is often more significant.
- A client's desire for noninterference should have precedence, except when this would constitute neglect. Positive entitlements, e.g., having the right to be cared for in a veterans' facility, should not be used as an excuse to intervene against the client's preference for noninterference.
- Whatever the specific autonomy issue under consideration may be, the client should be involved in making and carrying out decisions to the greatest extent possible. Clients' "doing for themselves" takes precedence over "doing with the client," which in turn has priority over "doing for the client."

Based on: Collopy 1988; Naleppa 1999.

---

to occur, and their mobilizing effects may enhance the amount of change attained (Reid 1992). When problems are delimited, there may not be any need for durational limits to control the length of service. What is often more important is the orientation that the service will be directed as expeditiously as possible at helping clients with problems of concern to them with the

---

BOX 5.3 BASIC CHARACTERISTICS OF TASK-CENTERED PRACTICE

- Developed and tested through empirical research
- Preference for empirically supported methods and theories
- Integration of methods from compatible approaches (e.g., problem-solving, behavioral, cognitive, and structural family therapy)
- Theories about client problems grounded in case data
- Emphasis on client-defined problems
- Tasks are the primary vehicle for change
- Tasks carried out by the client are preferred over tasks implemented by others
- Collaborative practitioner-client relationship
- Use of time limits, typically 4–12 sessions during a period of four months, with the recognition that such limits are frequently unnecessary since service will be brief in its nature
- Primary focus on the present (here and now)

---

option of providing additional services in the future in case those problems recur or new ones emerge. Even so, it is often helpful to provide the client with an estimate about the likely duration of service.

In the context of gerontological practice, pace and brevity of intervention merit specific mention. It is a commonly held misperception among those not working with the elderly that practice with these clients moves slowly. In fact, gerontological social work is often a particularly fast-paced form of intervening. Hospital workers see their elderly clients at a time of health crisis, discharge planners see them when they are getting ready to leave the hospital, home health care and case management service providers are contacted at times of immediate crisis. All of these situations are characterized by a limited time to intervene and a need for quick action. In discharge planning particularly, a practitioner will have a few client contacts over very short time periods, often only a few days. For example, think about the problems of an elderly hip replacement patient at the time of hospital discharge. This client may need home health services, home-delivered meals, coordination of medical treatment and physical therapy, transportation, and so on. Not only can the number of problems be quite extensive, but the services also have to be in place before the client can move back home.

By and large, our experience with time limits in gerontological practice has been very positive. At times, a practitioner using the task-centered approach with frail elderly clients may need to be more flexible in the application of time limits. Time limits also require special consideration in geriatric case management. At first glance, short-term intervention and long-term case management seem at opposite ends of the spectrum. However, time-limited task-centered strategies can be successfully integrated with a long-term case management approach (see chapter 8; Naleppa and Reid 1998, 2000). While case management is usually characterized by ongoing, long-term efforts of practitioner and client, new problems can be viewed as recurring service episodes, most of which can and should be addressed within a short and limited time period. For example, a client may receive assistance with accessing services upon discharge from a hospital. All related activities are completed within a few days, and the required services should be in place by the time the client leaves the hospital. Several months later the client voices concern over not having enough money to pay for medication. Again a few weeks later the client indicates that she may have problems with insomnia. Each of these problems can be seen as an "episode" that can be addressed using brief intervention strategies. An intervention time frame is set for each new problem as it arises. If problems are likely to recur or are "on the horizon," a case may be kept open but remain dormant. Such cases may be monitored through periodic reassessments (see chapter 8).

EMPHASIS ON THE PRESENT The primary focus of task-centered practice is on the present (here and now) and the future rather than on the past. Looking at the past may play an important role at various points in the intervention process, for instance, when collecting assessment information. Yet, many problems can be resolved without extensive knowledge about the past. Moreover, many problems of elderly clients have a present and future orientation by their very nature. Think again about the example of the client at the time of hospital discharge following hip replacement surgery. The role of the discharge planner is to ensure that the client can return home or to another environment in which the services and supports are in place to ensure safe living conditions. In this case, the client's past successful and unsuccessful approaches to dealing with such difficult situations may provide some useful information. Some questions that would be addressed include: How has the client dealt with similar situations? What help can be mustered from the client's informal support system? Are any modifications to the home environment needed? However, an intensive analysis of the client's psychological or emotional past may not add much information to assist in addressing the immediate need.

INTAKE

Intake is the first actual contact with a potential client. In many agencies support staff rather than the practitioner who will later work with the client conduct the intake interview. Parts of the initial intake interview are frequently completed by phone at the time a client or a referring person contacts the agency for information. The purpose of the intake interview is to assess the appropriateness of the client for agency programs or services and to obtain a first indication of the client's problems. This may also include an assessment of whether there is a crisis situation that requires immediate attention.

During intake the client or referring person is asked to describe the presenting problems in general terms. This assists in prescreening potential clients' eligibility for the services provided by the agency. It also furthers an assessment of the urgency of intervention. Sometimes it is necessary to provide crisis intervention quickly. If the intake worker does not have the training and qualifications to provide crisis intervention, a procedure for immediate referral to a trained worker should be in place. The services provided by the agency should be explained to the potential client. If a person agrees to "become" a client, the case can be activated. Engaging the elderly client early on is an important part of building a trusting helping relationship (Vourlekis and Greene 1992). For many elderly clients it is important to arrange a rapid follow-up meeting. If you are conducting a home visit, it is beneficial to contact the client by phone shortly before the planned visit. This may prevent an unsuccessful trip to the client's home. Clients may forget about the home visit; they may have had a medical emergency, or they may be afraid to open the door to someone they do not yet know (Naleppa and Hash 2001). The dialogue in box 5.4 serves as an example of how to start a telephone intake interview.

EXPLANATION OF ROLE, PURPOSE, AND INTERVENTION PROCEDURES

When clients first come into contact with a practitioner or an agency, they may know very little about what they can expect. Explaining the roles, purpose, and intervention procedures serves an important function in the context of a client's role induction. In order to actively participate in planning and implementing service-related decisions, a client needs to know what can be done, by whom, what the expectations of the client are, and so on. One important question in that context is what the client knows about the role of the practitioner. The practitioner may come into contact with the client just after discharge from a hospital, a place where doctors, nurses, physical ther-

---

BOX 5.4 TELEPHONE INTAKE INTERVIEW

Practitioner: Hello, I am trying to reach Mrs. Warner.

Client: That is me.

Practitioner: This is Karen White. I am with Community Care.

Client: You are with whom?

Practitioner: I am with Community Care. We are part of St. Mary's Hospital. Dr. John, your physician, may have mentioned that someone will call you.

Client: Oh yes, I remember. He said that someone would call me with more information, like on the meals program.

Practitioner: That's right. Do you have a few minutes?

Client: Yes.

Practitioner: What we do is we assist with finding out what needs someone has and then try to help them find ways to make their life easier—like the meals programs you mentioned. What I would like to do, if it is OK with you, is to get some information from you about the areas that you could need help with, and then I would like to set up a time when I could come and meet with you.

Client: I don't have a car.

Practitioner: I could come to your home, if it is all right with you.

Client: That would be good.

Practitioner: So, the doctor said that he talked with you about . . .

---

apists, and a range of other professionals may have been involved in providing care. Now, back in the client's own home environment another set of professionals is engaged in assisting him or her. Under such circumstances it can become difficult for anyone to keep track of each professional's role. Some simple steps can help prevent ambiguity and role confusion. Provide the client with your name and information on ways to reach you. Clarify why you are working with the client and what the goals of your efforts will be. It is important to ensure that the client has a clear understanding of why you are assisting him or her. This can prevent boundary problems that may arise in the course of service. For example, a client may become unclear about your role and the purpose of your work and begin to see you as "part of the family" or as a friend. Provide a clear explanation of what you can and cannot do. You may need to restate your role and the purpose of your visits more than once over the course of working with a frail elderly client. An elderly client with moderate stage dementia may be oriented to time and place most

---

BOX 5.5 CHART OF SERVICE PROVIDERS

NAME OF WORKER	AGENCY	SERVICE PROVIDED	FREQUENCY	PHONE
Mrs. White	VNA	Personal care nurse	1 x day	713–3232
Dr. James	Physician	Family physician	as needed	717–2967
Mr. Rich	A&M Clean Home	Light housecleaning	1 x week	713–9562
Sally, Rick	Meals-on-Wheels	Meals	1 x day	715–6666
Mrs. Jones	Case Management services	Coordinates	2 x month	713–7536

---

of the time but not always. By the time of the next visit, he or she may have forgotten some of the information you had previously provided.

In addition to explaining the practitioner's role, you should also inform clients about the function of your agency and what it has to offer them. The practitioner may ask clients what they know about the agency and add to that information. This may include an explanation of the services the agency can and cannot provide. In many cases, as noted, a number of service providers will be involved in the older person's life and care. This is especially true for clients in case management, home health care, and other community-based programs. Clarifying the roles of those other service providers helps reduce role confusions. Charts of the service providers involved in the client's life and care serve as a useful and clarifying tool. To be helpful to the client, a service provider chart should include the name of the contact person, the name of the agency, the services provided, and a phone number. Since it is a very straightforward activity, the development of a chart of service providers is a good "warming up" device (see box 5.5 for an example).

Next, we should clarify the client's roles and expectations. Our practice model invites active participation by clients in making and implementing decisions. In order to become an active participant in the intervention process, or in any other activity for that matter, it is imperative that the person has enough information about his or her roles, the expectations, and the process that will be followed. Thus, summarizing the intervention procedures is an important step in preparing the client for active participation. Box 5.6 can be used to explain these to the client.

Some elderly clients have conditions that limit their autonomy in making or implementing decisions. However, that does not mean that the client can-

---

BOX 5.6 EXPLANATION OF INTERVENTION PROCEDURES

1. Clarify roles (practitioner, agency, client, others)
2. Clarify active participation of client and others involved
3. Clarify that focus is on areas that client wants help with
4. Explain the use of time limits if they are used
5. Explain confidentiality and any limits to it
6. Explain the basic steps of approach:
   Conduct an assessment
   Identify problems
   Select the problems to work on
   Set priorities
   Set goals
   Develop tasks to achieve goals
   Carry out the tasks
   Review success of tasks
   Review whether problems have changed

Based on Tolson, Reid, and Garvin 2002

---

not participate in the intervention process. In such situations it is the practitioner's responsibility to make every effort to include the client to the greatest extent possible. The intervention procedures should therefore still be explained to the less "active" client.

Finally, if caregivers, spouses, or family members are involved in the initial sessions, the extent and nature of their involvement also needs to be clarified. One important question is whether the client wants the active involvement of family members and to what extent. This brings us back to the unfortunate reality that elderly clients' own care-related decisions are too often and too easily overlooked by family members and practitioners. Clarifying the roles of caregivers and family members also helps to keep service boundaries clearer.

ASSESSMENT AND PROBLEM IDENTIFICATION

In part I we presented an overview of assessment in geriatric social work practice (chapter 4), with special attention to standardized assessment instruments. The principles and methods in that chapter are applicable to assessment within the context of the task-centered model. The model itself presents a problem-focused approach to assessment, which in turn can be applied to other forms of practice.

A key process in planning an intervention is identifying the client's problems. While the term "problem" is used in reference to any potential object of an intervention, the term "*target* problem" is defined as the problem a client explicitly agrees to as the focus of service. This is not to say that a client initially has to agree that these problems exist. Rather, the client has to agree on the importance of addressing them after a process of deliberation and exploration—the focus of collaborative client and practitioner efforts during the first one or two sessions. As observed earlier, terms such as "need" or "goal" may be used instead of "problem" in discussions with elderly persons or their caregivers.

Most information for assessment and problem exploration is obtained by interviewing the elderly individual or his or her caregiver. In the chapter on assessment, we discussed the importance of making a decision whether to obtain information directly from the client or to apply other procedures such as using a proxy respondent. Another basic decision that has to be made is where to conduct the assessment interview and the following client contacts. When working with clients in a hospital or nursing home, the setting is usually predetermined. In community-based practice, however, there may be a choice between the client's home and an agency location. In general, working in the client's home is preferable. Being in one's own home environment will make the process easier for the client. It also reduces anxiety and increases his or her comfort level. Moreover, as discussed in chapters 3 and 4, the client's home environment provides useful information for assessment and for communicating with the client.

Assessment is the first step toward achieving the goals of an intervention. A thorough geriatric assessment should be comprehensive and multidimensional and should include information on the presenting problem, personal background, bio-psycho-social, medical, and economic factors, mental and functional status, physical environment, and the client's social network (Kane and Kane 2000; Lichtenberg 2000). An assessment should also appraise the extent to which a client already uses services. The assessment can be augmented with standardized instruments, such as the ones we presented in chapter 4. In conducting the assessment, attention must be paid to special characteristics of the frail elderly client population, such as possible difficulties in remembering the chronology of events, the desire to reminisce, fatigue, and fear (Gwyther 1988).

A thorough assessment is usually completed during first home visit or client contact. The assessment guides specification of the problems for initial task planning. Using the task-centered approach, case planning directly flows from the initial problem assessment. As already indicated, the task-centered model focuses on working with problems acknowledged by the client. It should be emphasized that standardized multidimensional assessment instruments (chapter 4) should not be seen as an alternative for exploring the issues the clients want help with. Rather, they serve as a tool to guide the process into fruitful directions. Multidimensional assessments may be augmented by the use of rapid assessment instruments (RAIs). These are brief standardized assessment instruments that tap into specific problem areas such as anxiety, depression, or cognitive abilities. They can assist in fine-tuning the assessment. If they are administered on repeated occasions, they provide useful information on the client's changes in the problem areas the RAI assesses. Finally, evaluating the scores together with the client provides helpful prompts for the assessment interview.

A study on social, environmental, and economic variables for outpatient geriatric assessment identified the following elements as the most essential: identifying data, financial information, type of living arrangement, primary caregivers, insurances, estate planning, beneficiary designation, and psychosocial assessment (Saltz, Schaefer, and Weinreich 1998). Box 5.7 provides a more comprehensive list of areas for multidimensional assessment.

Problems may be introduced in a number of ways. A client may begin the process by expressing his or her concerns. Likewise, the practitioner may introduce potential problems, for example, based on information gathered through a multidimensional assessment or based on his or her observations. Another approach is the identification of problems by the client and practitioner through an interactive process. Finally, a third party, such as a referring agency, may refer the client with an identified problem. A hospital discharge planner might refer an elderly client to a case management program for assistance with accessing and coordinating certain home-based services. It should be noted, however, that these "referrer-identified" problems do not become part of the intervention process until the client or the practitioner introduces them as potential targets. In order to assess the client's acceptance of problems indicated by the referring party, it is usually best to give clients themselves the opportunity to introduce the problems (see box 5.8). If they do not, the practitioner can bring them up.

It is advantageous to request the client's input on problems the client sees as important before conducting a standardized assessment. While the assessment ensures that a comprehensive range of typical problem areas is exam-

---

BOX 5.7 COMMON AREAS OF A MULTIDIMENSIONAL ASSESSMENT

AREA	EXAMPLES
Identifying Information	Address, phone, SS#, insurance, physician, primary caregiver
Financial	Assets, social security, pension, public assistance, veteran benefits
Legal	Power of attorney, advance directives, attorney
Health and Medical	Assessment of health conditions, hospitalizations, medications
Nutritional Status	Diets, allergies, consistent food intake
Physical Functioning	Activities of daily living, use of adaptive equipment
Housing Conditions	Access, home safety, structural issues, cleanliness
Mental Assessment	Mental status, cognitive functioning, memory
Psychological Status	Depression, anxiety, coping, family conflicts
Current Services	Any services the client already receives

---

ined, it may push to the background other issues the client sees as most important. Moreover, if a client introduces a problem as a target of intervention, he or she will have a stronger sense of "ownership" and may be more motivated to address it. In a field test of task-centered practice with elderly clients, problems that were initially identified by clients led to better service outcomes (Naleppa 1995).

To become a target problem, i.e., the target of intervention, the problem's existence must be explicitly acknowledged by the client, and the latter must agree that he or she wants to address it. Therefore, the practitioner should establish early on how motivated a client is and whether the client even acknowledges a need for intervening. Many elderly individuals become clients involuntarily; thus, not all clients will acknowledge the existence of problems or a need for intervention.

Like any other social worker, therapist, counselor, or case manager, a gerontological practitioner is likely to encounter involuntary clients. Rooney (1992) makes a useful distinction between voluntary, involuntary, and legally mandated clients. Voluntary clients want assistance. Frequently, they are the ones initiating service by actively seeking support from a practitioner or an agency. These clients are usually able to describe their problems in much detail. An example of a voluntary elderly client is the patient at the time of

BOX 5.8 EXAMPLE: INTRODUCING A PROBLEM IDENTIFIED BY THE REFERRER

Practitioner: You were referred to our program by the hospital discharge planner. What is your understanding of the reasons for which they sent you to us?

Client: I am not really sure.

Practitioner: They indicate in the referral here that you might benefit from assistance with various tasks around your home. Are there some things that you see as possibly problematic when you return home?

Client: Well, I think I will be all right. I haven't been home for a while now, and I hope everything is OK. I have really nice neighbors. They watered my plants and took care of my mail.

Practitioner: They sound like wonderful neighbors. Getting back to the referral, one of the things Mrs. Greg, the hospital social worker, wrote down is that you might benefit from some assistance with preparing meals. Is that something you would like to look into a little more?

Client: Oh, I always liked to cook, but in the last few years that has changed. A lot of times, I just do something small. I don't know how it will be now. I do still have a lot of difficulties with walking and standing for a long time.

Practitioner: So, would some help with preparing your meals be something that we could look into a little more?

Client: Yes, I suppose, well, it may make it easier to have some help when I get home.

hospital discharge who wants to return home. This client is interested in "making it happen" and is likely to pursue all options that allow him or her to move back home. Involuntary clients, on the other hand, may become involved with an agency because of social pressures from family members, friends, physicians, or others. While the client's problems may seem obvious, the practitioner first has to address the client's motivation for help before attending to them. For example, Mr. Johnson, an 86-year-old widower, was referred by his daughter who is concerned that her father, who lives alone, is "forgetting" to take medication for his heart condition. When contacted, Mr. Johnson informed the social worker that he didn't want any outside assistance and was able to manage quite well on his own. The social worker mentioned the reason for the daughter's worry and asked if Mr. Johnson had any concerns about his health. In the ensuing discussion, in which Mr. Johnson did acknowledge some health worries, the social worker was able to describe some of the services that might be of use to him, such as helping him develop ways of managing his medication or having regular visits from a nurse. As the example illustrates, practitioners should focus on eliciting from the client what problems he or she acknowledges and what might be done to resolve them.

Legally mandated involuntary clients are "more involuntary" but not necessarily less open to active participation in intervention activities. An example of a legally mandated involuntary client would be an abusive "caregiver" who comes to the attention of an Adult Protective Services worker. Such an investigation may lead to specific court-ordered actions required of the client. However, even legally mandated clients have choices. For example, they have the option of not complying with the required actions and instead shouldering the negative consequences. Since intense pressures may exist, many legally mandated clients are open to taking action. For instance, the abusive caretaker might agree to a service package that would include anger management training as preferable to facing charges.

The process of identifying problems leads to an agreement by client and practitioner on which ones will become the target of the intervention. These target problems are specified as clearly as possible, stated in terms of conditions to be changed, and summarized in a problem statement. We will now turn to the procedures for prioritizing target problems.

SELECTING AND PRIORITIZING PROBLEMS

After problems are identified and agreed upon, they are prioritized, i.e., a decision is made about their relative importance and the sequence in which they will be tackled. The setting of service priorities should be explained to the clients, and the rationale for undertaking this step should be provided. Whenever possible, the client's priorities should be respected. However, the practitioner may express concerns about the way a client ranks target problems. For example, based on the practitioner's professional knowledge and experience, she may know about obstacles the client could encounter if certain problems do not get addressed expeditiously. Prioritizing problems is especially important when more than two or three problems have to be addressed. Any step that provides additional structure to the elderly client is helpful and usually welcome.

The Problems and Goals Statement (see fig. 5.1) is used to record the results of the initial problem exploration and serves as a preliminary care plan. It also includes space for information on the goals and progress of the intervention, two areas we will discuss later. The form serves as the basis for selecting the target problem and is the first monitoring tool in the sequence

FIGURE 5.1 PROBLEMS AND GOALS STATEMENT

Client: _____ Case Manager: _____ Date: _____

PROBLEM: GOAL: PROGRESS:

#1: _____ _____ _____
_____
_____

#2: _____ _____ _____
_____
_____

#3: _____ _____ _____
_____
_____

#4: _____ _____ _____

of problem exploration, problem formulation, task development, and task review. Problems are entered in the order of their priority.

Whenever caregivers are involved, the practitioner needs to ensure that the client has the opportunity to participate adequately in prioritizing problems. If caregivers are asked to carry out the step of prioritizing problems, for example, because the client may not have the cognitive abilities to do so, the client should at a minimum be asked for agreement after the list has been established. Practitioners often need to be more directive with clients suffering from cognitive impairments. Again, however, an effort should be made to involve the clients by having them agree to the list. The dialogue sequence in box 5.9 provides an example of a practitioner prioritizing problems with her client.

The communication sequence in box 5.9 represents a fairly typical process in setting service priorities. At the beginning, the practitioner recaps the different problems that have been identified as target problems. She then asks the client about the order in which the problems should be addressed. During the process of prioritizing, the practitioner recounts the areas that are still left. At the end, she repeats the listing and asks for the client's agreement. The process of prioritizing problems may look different in cases where caregivers participate, as the two examples in box 5.10 show. In both cases, a client and a daughter are present at the session.

The two examples in box 5.10 illustrate some varieties of caregivers' involvement. The caregiver in the first vignette was somewhat controlling

---

BOX 5.9 PRIORITIZING PROBLEMS

Practitioner: There are a couple of things we have identified today: the senior housing, the senior transportation van, the health care proxy, and the EPIC program. How do you want to prioritize these? With that I mean which ones do you want to start working on first?

Client (*without hesitation*): The housing. That's really the most important for me.

Practitioner: OK, and what do you think is next after that? Transportation, health care proxy, or the EPIC program?

Client: Transportation.

Practitioner: And then, what would you put next?

Client: Whatever is best . . . [*Laughs*] I don't know . . .

Practitioner: Assistance with medication, which is the EPIC program, or health care proxy.

Client: The medication program, I think.

Practitioner: [*Shows client the following list*]

[*The practitioner completes the form, recording information about the problems and goals previously obtained*]

Problem Area	Problem Statement	Goal
#1: Housing	Unable to negotiate stairs	Move to senior housing
#2: Transportation	Surrendered driver's license	Obtain senior bus pass
#3: Prescription coverage	Not taking medication due to cost	Pursue EPIC or AARP
#4: Advance directives	Lacks advance directives	Health care proxy

Practitioner: I wrote them all down in the sequence that we could work on them. Does this look like the order in which we should address them?

Client (*looks at list*): Yes, this looks good to me.

Practitioner: Great. So why don't we start looking at the housing situation a little more, and see how far we get today. And then we can look at transportation and the other areas next week.

Client: That sounds good.

---

and directive throughout the entire session. Being alert to this, the practitioner tried to ensure that the elderly person was adequately involved in the process. However, when the client was not clear about the task at hand, the caregiver took over again. In the second example, the client also seemed unable to prioritize her problems. She may have been overwhelmed or not

BOX 5.10 SAMPLE COMMUNICATION SEQUENCES

EXAMPLE 1

Practitioner: What I would like to do next is write down what we will be working on together. I think we have identified two primary areas. One is the admission into the adult home; the other one is determining eligibility and applying for the heating assistance program. Which one should we address first? Which one do you think is most important?

Daughter: St. Mary's home first.

Practitioner (*to client*): Do you agree? Do you think working on admission is the first priority?

Client: I don't know what you mean.

Practitioner: If you were to order the two things we are going to work on, getting admission into St. Mary's and applying for the heating benefit, which one would you put first?

Daughter: Which one is the most important for you?

Client: Most important for what?

Daughter: For you. Is it to get into this short-term home?

Client: Yes.

EXAMPLE 2

Practitioner: So, let me go over the things you think we should work on. Getting the medical equipment . . .

Client: Right . . .

Practitioner: . . . follow up with a neurologist, you will appoint a power of attorney and a health care proxy . . .

Client: Right . . .

Practitioner: . . . and you want a companion to do some light housekeeping and errands . . .

Client: That's right.

Practitioner: In which order would you tackle them? What do you think is most important?

Client: They are all important.

Practitioner: What order would you put them in?

Client: Just the safety first.

Practitioner: So you want to prioritize the things that make you feel safer first.

Client: Yes, is that OK? [*Does not stay on task, talks about her phone, seems overwhelmed or not sure what to do. After several attempts, the practitioner turns to the daughter.*]

Practitioner (*to daughter*): How would you prioritize these?

Daughter: I would like to get the tub bench and grab bar first and then set up the appointment with the neurologist and check on the power of attorney . . .

Practitioner (to client): How do you feel about this? These are the things we will do. Let's go through this. [*Practitioner goes through the list of problems in the order prioritized by daughter.*]
Practitioner: Do you agree with how we prioritized them?
Client: Yes, yes I do.

---

clear about what to do. After unsuccessfully trying to involve the client, the practitioner directly asked the caregiver to prioritize the problems and then elicited feedback from the client. These two incidents point to the importance of trying to include the client. Even if the caregiver needs to do the prioritizing, the practitioner should always ensure that the client agrees to whatever list is developed. Even if a client's cognitive abilities seem to prevent a meaningful participation in the process, the practitioner should at least share the information with the client, as the interaction in box 5.11 illustrates.

Throughout the intervention process this client with a cognitive impairment required more directive interventions by the practitioner. In the example several attempts by the practitioner to include him in the decision-making process were unsuccessful. After identifying his first priority, the client forgot again what he had selected by the time he had to choose the second most important problem. The practitioner finally asked the client whether she should rank the problems for him. In this case it was helpful that the practitioner was more directive and finally prioritized for the client. It was also valuable that she explained to the client why she prioritized a certain way.

EXPLORING AND SPECIFYING TARGET PROBLEMS

Some information on the target problems has already been gathered during the process of identifying and prioritizing the client's problems. This information should provide an initial glimpse of the nature and scope of the client's problems. However, more detailed and in-depth knowledge about the target problems is usually required for planning an intervention. Problem exploration is a process with shared activities by practitioner and client. While the practitioner initially leads the interaction by the questions she asks, the client has the personal "expertise" regarding the problem. He or she has the knowledge of the unique way the problem manifests itself, what contextual factors have an impact, and what has been done to solve the problem.

BOX 5.11 SAMPLE INTERACTION

Practitioner: So, I will summarize what areas we will work on together. I want you to think about them and how you would prioritize them. The first one was the medical follow up with your doctor . . .

Client: We have to find a doctor now, right?

Practitioner: No, you already have a doctor. The second concerned the medications . . .

Client: What is the situation with the medications? I don't know about that.

Practitioner: To help you access your refills. Then there was learning about the interaction about alcohol and your medications. I was going to get you some written information.

Client: Yes.

Practitioner: And there was the legal and financial end of things, housekeeping, pocket notebook calendar . . . and then you were going to think about working on improving your hygiene, but you are not sure what you want to do . . . and increasing your opportunities for socializing.

Client: I got kicked out of the Lion's Club. That was a social thing.

Practitioner: So how would you order them? Out of all of those things, what is the most important?

Client: List them again and I will tell you. [*Practitioner goes down the list, client forgot items but identifies medical follow-up as most important.*]

Practitioner: So what do you think would be the number two priority?

Client: What did we make number one?

Practitioner: Physician follow-up. I could try and rank them, but it is more important that you do that.

Client: Go ahead, you do it, and I will tell you if it's OK. [*Pause*]

Practitioner: OK, here is how I would rank them, and you tell me if you agree with this. I would keep physician follow-up as number one and medications as number two, because those are very important for you day-to-day. And I think I would bring financial and legal matters as number three. . . . What do you think? [*Client agrees but is confused again about some of the problems.*]

The guidelines in box 5.12 can be used for exploring problems in task-centered practice.

Problems manifest themselves differently for each client. A first step is to develop a factual understanding of the typical occurrences. The practitioner may ask clients to describe in their own words a recent occurrence of the problem. Questions that can guide this process include: What does the prob-

---

BOX 5.12 BASIC CONSIDERATIONS FOR PROBLEM EXPLORATION

- Factual description of typical occurrences
- Frequency of occurrence
- Duration of problem
- Seriousness or severity of problem
- Previous problem-solving attempts by client
- Success of previous problem-solving efforts
- Context of problem

---

lem look like for the client? Where does the problem occur? When does it typically occur? A second consideration is the frequency with which the problem occurs. In most cases, retroactive baseline information is used. The client is asked to describe the frequency with which the problem occurred during the past days, weeks, or months. The time frame chosen for a retroactive baseline will depend on the type of problem.

Many problems faced by frail elderly clients are not behavioral or psychological. For example, problems may relate to a lack of resources or to chronic health conditions. Therefore, the question regarding the duration of that problem, i.e., how long it has existed, may be more meaningful. Typical questions include: When did the problem first occur? What happened that brought it on? This may also be a suitable time to assess previous efforts by the client to solve the problem and the success of such attempts. The client may have had difficulties for long periods of time and may have been very adept in dealing with the problem. Practitioners might ask questions such as: What worked for the client? Why did it work? Which attempts failed? Why did they fail? An elderly client who has been coping with mobility problems over several years will have important information on what problem-solving strategies have or have not worked in the past. What assistive devices have helped her? What resources have or have not made a difference? When did it become so problematic that the client needed outside help?

Next, practitioners should assess the seriousness of the problem from the client's perspective. This should be done even when using standardized assessment instruments that provide an indicator of the problem's severity. For example, pain, stress, or being overwhelmed are to some extent subjective and will feel very different for each client. Assessing the client's perspective may be especially important when working with caregivers and family

---

BOX 5.13 COMMON QUESTIONS FOR PROBLEM EXPLORATION

- What occurs that is troubling?
- Where does it occur?
- When does it occur?
- Who else is present when it occurs?
- How often does it occur?
- What is the duration or length of the phenomena?
- How severe is the problem?
- What has been done by the client or others to try to solve the problem?
- What has been the result of previous problem-solving efforts?
- What are the client's expectations about what will solve the problem?
- What is the meaning of the problem to the client?
- What is the client's affective reaction to the problem?
- What are the antecedents or stimuli to the occurrence?
- What are the consequences or responses to the occurrence?
- What other contextual factors bear on the problem?

---

members, since they may have opinions on the severity of problems that differ from the client's viewpoint.

Finally, the context in which the problem manifests itself is explored. Can specific external causes be identified? Do certain situations exist in which the problem typically occurs? Who is present when it occurs? During the entire process of problem exploration, the practitioner makes available any professional knowledge and information that can assist in specifying the problem. These and other aspects of problem exploration can be covered through a series of questions developed by Tolson, Reid, and Garvin (2002, see box 5.14).

The process of specifying target problems leads to the completion of a Target Problem Form (see fig. 5.2). The purpose of this form is to guide clients and practitioners in their efforts to establish target problems. The form also documents the baseline of a problem and previous attempts by the client to solve the problem. It is the second tool for monitoring changes. As such, it provides information on the process and structure of implementing the model. Moreover, using the forms helps to establish client agreement on the target problems.

The following example illustrates the application of these problem exploration questions. It is a sequence of questions that the practitioner asked an elderly client who indicated that she had difficulties falling asleep. The client

---

BOX 5.14 EXAMPLE: QUESTIONS IN PROBLEM EXPLORATION FOR INSOMNIA

- So, you say that you have problems with falling asleep. Can you tell me a little more about that?
- How often do you have trouble falling asleep?
- When the problem occurs, how long does it usually take until you actually go to sleep?
- How does lack of sleep affect you the next day?
- I assume you have tried different approaches to deal with your sleeplessness. What are some of the things you have tried?
- Did that provide any help?
- Have you tried anything else?
- What about alcohol?
- Do you take any medications at night that might wake you up?
- You say that you tried over-the-counter sleeping aids. How well do they work for you?
- Do you have any thoughts about anything you haven't tried that might help your sleeping problem?
- Can you tell me a little about what you do in the evening before you go to bed?
- When you cannot fall asleep, is there anything you usually think about?
- Are there any special things that happen when you cannot fall asleep?
- Do worries keep you awake?
- Do you eat or drink certain things at night that might wake you up, like coffee or certain teas?
- Are there any other things that you think might be related to your sleeping problem?

---

stated in her own words that she has "insomnia." Note that the question list has been somewhat modified to make it more appropriate for this particular problem and some illustrative probes have been added. Also in an actual interview not all questions would be asked since some answers would have been obtained in responses to previous questions.

SETTING GOALS

Next, practitioner and client develop and operationalize short-term and long-term service goals. Goals are the end point of an intervention. They are

FIGURE 5.2 TARGET PROBLEM FORM

Date: _____ Client, including caregiver _____ Practitioner: _____

Who initially formulated the problem?

Client(s) Name(s) _____ Practitioner _____

Describe the problem as it was first formulated with client(s):

Preintervention baseline (frequency, duration, severity):

How long has problem existed?

What have clients done to address the problem?

---

the condition or status the client wants to reach. Goals should be problem-related, specific, measurable, and stated as achievable objectives. If possible, they should also include a time frame for achieving them. Goals should be specified as a condition to be reached, not as the activity to be undertaken. Like a beacon at night, goals can serve as valuable motivators and provide guidance. At times, however, a goal may seem too big or too far away. It may become difficult to muster the energy to work toward it. Consequently, goals that take substantial time and effort to attain should be broken down into shorter term subgoals. Thus the goal of setting up home in an assisted living facility can include a series of subgoals that relate to selecting the facility, visiting it, successfully completing an application, selling the house, and moving.

The steps undertaken on the way to developing a goal contribute to how well a goal can be defined. Clearly specifying a problem facilitates the formulation of the related goals. Accountability and measuring service outcomes continue to become more important practice considerations. Goals that are stated in specific terms enable practitioners and clients to establish whether the goals have been achieved.

COMPLETING AN INTERVENTION PLAN AND CONTRACTING

This phase of the intervention, i.e., identifying, selecting, prioritizing, and exploring problems as well as setting goals, culminates in the completion of

BOX 5.15 SUMMARY: PRACTICE GUIDELINES FOR INITIAL PHASE

Intake
- Assess whether a crisis situation exists
- Ask client to describe the presenting problems in general terms
- Explain agency and services
- Arrange assessment meeting and location

Explaining Role, Purpose, and Service Procedures
- Explain roles of client, practitioner, and agency
- Explain purpose of intervention
- Provide overview of intervention procedures
- Clarify client's role and expectations

Assessment and Problem Identification
- Obtain assessment information from clients
- Conduct a comprehensive and multidimensional assessment
- Focus on problems acknowledged by the client
- Request client's input on the problems
- Ask client for explicit acknowledgement of the problem
- Ask client for agreement that problem becomes a target of intervention
- Specify target problems as clearly as possible
- If possible, state problem as condition to be changed

Selecting and Prioritizing Problems
- Prioritize problems
- List order and sequence in which problems will be addressed
- Respect client's choice of prioritizing problems
- If necessary, express concerns about priorities

Exploring and Specifying Problem
- Gather detailed information on frequency of occurrence, seriousness of problem, previous problem-solving attempts, the context in which problem occurs
- Assess the seriousness of the problem from the client's perspective

Setting Goals
- Develop short-term and long-term goals
- Operationalize goals (problem-related, specific, measurable, and stated in achievable objectives)
- Include time frame for achieving goals
- If necessary, break down goals into subgoals

Completing an Intervention Plan and Contracting
- Complete an initial case plan
- List all problems, priorities, and goals
- Contract on case plan

the initial intervention or care plan. An intervention plan should include a list of all problems, prioritized in the order in which they will be addressed as well as the related goals. During the course of intervention the steps that will be taken to achieve these goals can be added to the case plan. If linkages to formal services are involved, the potential providers should be listed together with an indication of the type and amount of service the client will receive and a time frame for service provision. Furthermore, the intervention plan should clarify responsibilities for carrying out tasks, identify potential obstacles to receiving services, and state alternatives. The Problems and Goals Statement, presented earlier in this chapter, is an example of the outline of such an intervention plan. It is beneficial to use the completion of the intervention plan as another option to elicit the client's agreement on the selected target problems and the goals of the intervention.

SUMMARY OF INITIAL INTERVENTION PHASE

We conclude this chapter with a summary of the practice steps that are completed during the initial phase of service (see box 5.15). In the next two chapters, we will focus on the middle and termination phases of the practice model.

CHAPTER 6

THE MIDDLE PHASE

I N THE MIDDLE phase of the intervention, client and practitioner take direct action to resolve target problems. How much actual time is spent in the middle phase depends mostly on the practice setting and the types of problems the client faces. A hospital discharge planner may spend a few sessions over a short period of time in this phase. A practitioner in a long-term care setting may have a little more time at hand. In both examples, however, the practitioner would put into practice the sequence of activities subsumed under the middle phase. Moreover, in both cases the practitioner would adhere to the same basic principle of task-centered practice, e.g., work within a limited number of sessions over a brief time period.

Before explicating the practice activities carried out in the middle phase of the task-centered model, we would like to familiarize the reader with the nature and function of tasks. Tasks are planned problem-solving actions. They are the primary medium for change in task-centered practice. The goal of intervention is to solve clients' problems. These problem changes are primarily effected through the elderly person's actions, or, in the case of the more frail elderly, through actions caregivers or practitioners carry out on their behalf. An overview of the basic change functions of tasks is provided in table 6.1.

TASK PARTICIPANTS

One way of categorizing tasks is by who carries them out (see box 6.1 for an overview). A single person, i.e., the client, the practitioner, a caregiver, or others involved in the intervention process, can implement an individual task. Two or more participants can also carry out a collaborative activity, i.e., a shared task. The nature of the problem and actions needed to alleviate it will require a decision on whether an individual task is the best route or whether

TABLE 6.1 CHANGE FUNCTIONS OF TASKS (BASED ON REID 1992)

FUNCTION:	EXAMPLE:
1. To take direct action to affect a problem, need, or the context in which it occurs	Mrs. B. applies for and obtains home heating benefits.
2. To test one's ability	Mr. Y.'s failure to limit his alcohol intake to five drinks a day convinces him that he needs help with his drinking problem.
3. To heighten one's sense of self-efficacy and mastery.	By successfully making adjustments to her diet, Mrs. K. feels more confident.
4. To learn through doing.	Mrs. D.'s efforts to obtain home health care services help her learn how to deal with community agencies.
5. To try out understanding gained in session.	Having achieved awareness about his tendency to monopolize discussion in a residents' group, Mr. S. tries to invite the opinions of others rather than to give his own.
6. To acquire information	Mrs. G. visits an assisted living residence to gain different views about the possibility of living in such an environment.
7. To challenge or test beliefs	Mr. C. develops a list of constructive things he is able to do to challenge his belief that he is "totally useless"; Ms. Y. tests her belief that other residents don't like her by asking one to have lunch with her.

a shared task should be implemented. In working with frail elderly clients, the practitioner may at times share tasks that better functioning clients regularly carry out as individual tasks. For example, a practitioner in a geriatric case management program may make phone calls for an elderly client with hearing difficulties or fill out a form for a visually impaired client. At the same time, while most clients would be able to make a phone call to a

---

BOX 6.1 POSSIBLE TASK PARTICIPANTS BY TASK PARTICIPANTS

INDIVIDUAL TASKS:

Elderly client
Caregiver client
Practitioner

SHARED TASKS:

Elderly client and caregiver
Elderly client and practitioner
Caregiver and practitioner

---

provider or fill out an application, practitioners all too readily fulfill these actions for clients despite the latter's ability to do so themselves.

If a practitioner assumes responsibility for a task, the same process for developing, agreeing on, and implementing tasks would be used as for clients. The practitioner's tasks should also be reviewed and rated at the beginning of each subsequent session, much in the same way clients' tasks are reviewed.

The practitioner can assume different roles, depending on the actions the tasks require. As a broker, the practitioner may carry out service linkage actions. By resolving a dispute with a health insurance company that refuses to cover service costs, she can take on the role of mediator. As an advocate, she may carry out tasks to assist a client in gaining access to a scarce resource. All of these tasks can be carried out in a way that facilitates clients' tasks or as an independent practitioner action. Facilitating practitioners' tasks are used when a practitioner carries out actions that make it easier for the client to implement a task. For example, the practitioner may find out about eligibility and application procedures for medical adult day care in preparation for a client's tasks of applying to and visiting such a program. An independent practitioner task consists of a separate individual task aimed at achieving a particular goal. In such a case, the practitioner's actions do not directly assist the client in the performance of his or her task. Rather, she acts as the client's "agent." Whether to use facilitating or independent practitioner tasks depends on the specific situation. Yet, facilitating tasks have the advantage of fostering the notion that clients should be assisted in doing for themselves rather having things doing for them.

Our experience with using the model with the frail elderly supports the importance of active client involvement. In a field test of geriatric task-centered case management, the highest task completion ratings were achieved for practitioner tasks; however, they were closely followed by shared tasks and tasks completed by the frail elderly. Caregiver tasks had the lowest levels of completion (Naleppa 1995). That almost all practitioner tasks were successfully completed should not come as a surprise. As professionals, practitioners have an obligation to follow through with their tasks. They also have the knowledge and experience to complete the tasks. Furthermore, practitioner tasks typically include fairly straightforward actions, such as making a call to another service provider or finding out additional information on a problem or need. The positive finding was that the frail elderly clients carried out approximately two thirds of their tasks with complete success.

It is important to make a planned decision about who should implement a task. We would like to emphasize again that preference should be given to individual client tasks. If this is not feasible, shared tasks that include the client as participant should be preferred over tasks carried out by the practitioner or a caregiver on behalf of the client.

TYPES OF TASKS

Tasks can be categorized as cognitive, behavioral, or situational (see box 6.2). *Cognitive tasks* are directed at increasing understanding, thinking through a problem, or examining beliefs. As in the following example, they can be the first step in a sequence of tasks. The practitioner had worked with an elderly couple after the wife had articulated a need for help. She expressed feeling overwhelmed and physically and emotionally exhausted. Several target problems were developed and addressed in a collaborative effort by husband, wife, and practitioner. One problem related to the husband's reluctance to use his wheelchair. He stated that he did not want to advertise his physical limitations and dependence on others. A task was developed that took advantage of his

---

BOX 6.2 TYPES OF TASKS

- Cognitive Tasks
- Behavioral Tasks
- Situational Tasks

former career as a newspaper journalist. It was to write a short story about a fictitious friend, discussing the advantages and disadvantages of using a wheelchair to get around in public. After he successfully completed this largely cognitive task, a behavioral task was developed, i.e., that he would utilize the wheelchair at least once outside the house by the following week.

Behavioral tasks are aimed directly at changing clients' behaviors or at changing interactions between clients. The ultimate goal of a behavioral task is the alteration of enduring behavioral or interactive patterns. An example of a behavioral task can be found in the intervention with an isolated and lonely elderly client. Although the client had led an active social life, he stopped his social activities during the two previous years when he provided intensive caregiving to his frail wife, who had recently died. The client came to the attention of the social worker at the time of his discharge from the hospital for minor surgery. He did not need any supports to return home but complained about his lack of outside contacts. An assessment by the social worker did not indicate the presence of major depression; however, it was very clear that the client felt lonely and socially isolated. At first a task was developed to make one new contact before the next home visit. After reviewing ways to achieve this, the task was stated as follows: Mr. B. will visit the social gathering at the local Elks Club at least once to try connecting with former acquaintances before the next home visit on May 22.

Situational tasks involve efforts to change or alter a client's situation. Many of the tasks in practice with older adults fall into this category. This is especially true for elderly clients seen in home health care, geriatric case management, and hospital discharge programs. Situational tasks can relate to seeking information, obtaining resources, changing living arrangements, or altering the environment. Examples of situational tasks include seeking information about a client's social security benefits, applying for a heating program, or moving into an assisted living facility. Unlike behavioral tasks, situational tasks often consist of one single action or a series of one-time activities. An example of such a sequence of situational tasks is an elderly couple's move to an assisted living facility. A succession of one-time tasks was developed and carried out over a period of six months. It included individual as well as shared tasks for each of the spouses. It also included several practitioner tasks. The tasks that were implemented related to reviewing potential assisted living facilities, making visits to the two most promising ones, selecting a facility, completing the required application procedures, putting the house up for sale, downsizing the amount of personal belongings and furniture, planning the move, moving to the new home environment, and making a conscious effort to establish a new social network.

THE TASK PLANNING AND IMPLEMENTATION SEQUENCE

The task planning and implementation sequence (TPIS) describes the succession of activities undertaken by the practitioner and client when they develop tasks and carry them out. It includes the steps of generating, selecting, and agreeing on tasks, planning how tasks are to be done, reviewing potential obstacles, implementing and reviewing tasks, analyzing actual obstacles, and revising unsuccessful tasks. When there is more than one client participating in a session, the practitioner can make use of *structured client interaction* to complete steps of the TPIS. The practitioner suggests that the participants try to work out a particular step together—e.g., coming up with different task possibilities or developing a plan for carrying out a task— and takes the role of facilitator. In that role, the practitioner keeps the participants focused, attempts to draw out anyone remaining silent, and offers suggestions as needed. Structured interactions provide an excellent means of empowering clients to solve their problems in their own way—a way that is often far superior to what might result from the practitioner-client dialogues. Moreover, the interactions can help the participants develop more effective ways of relating to one another and of problem-solving together.

The TPIS is the result of systematic research and development. Studies have shown that clients who engage in TPIS activities are more likely to complete tasks following the session than those who do not (Reid 1975, 1994). In one of these studies (Reid 1975) clients were randomly assigned to two conditions. In one condition a task was simply assigned to the client in a given session, in the other condition the steps of the TPIS were used. Clients using the TPIS were significantly more likely to complete their tasks than those in the "assigned only condition."

A fundamental objective of the TPIS is to empower the client. As discussed in the previous chapter, empowerment of clients enables them to make full use of their abilities in making and implementing decisions. Thus, it is important to address a frail elderly client's decisional and executional autonomy throughout all steps of the TPIS.

DEVELOPING TASK ALTERNATIVES

Developing task alternatives is a brainstorming activity carried out by client and practitioner. Together they try to establish different actions that might improve the problem or address the need. The practitioner should start this process with a brief explanation of the practice step at hand. Since the model emphasizes the active engagement of the client, mentioning the client's role in developing task alternatives is beneficial. Asking clients for their input can be accomplished with questions such as: What do you think could be done to solve this problem (or address this need)? Both the client and the practitioner should suggest task alternatives. If caregivers or others participate in a session, they should also generate task alternatives, if possible by using methods of structured interaction as described above. In one case, for example, a father and his two daughters developed a postdischarge plan for the father that involved decisions about selling his house and where he would live. The plan led to a variety of tasks. Although the practitioner is the professional, tasks suggested by the practitioner are not necessarily completed more successfully. In a field test of task-centered case management with elderly clients tasks that were initially suggested by elderly clients, practitioners, or caregiver clients led to similar levels of task completion (Naleppa 1995).

At this point in the process, the focus should be on generating alternatives. A more in-depth evaluation of the alternatives should be delayed until a comprehensive list of options is developed. An evaluation that is carried out too early can sidetrack the process of task generation. It can also narrow the focus prematurely and possibly prevent the development of better task alternatives. In some situations, of course, the preferred task may be an obvious choice, and generating or evaluating alternatives may not be necessary.

The first task a client is asked to implement should have a strong likelihood of success. A successful experience will further motivate the client and increase his or her sense of self-efficacy. A failure, on the other hand, may be demoralizing and reduce the client's enthusiasm to continue with the intervention. At the same time, the initial task should be significant enough to make a difference in the problem or need. If a client begins to carry out tasks that can be easily achieved but that do not seem to make any real difference, the result may be a sense of frustration and a lack of confidence in the intervention process.

In order to increase the chances of success, it is sometimes useful to split a task into several subtasks or introduce it with a low frequency. For example, Ginnie, age 76, was not able to get over the loss of her husband who had died over a year ago. She seemed to deny his death at an emotional level. Thus, she had put away all remembrances of him because it was "too painful" to have reminders around. The social worker had suggested she try to create a photo album of the many pictures she had of him and of the two of them together. In this way she might be able to experience, and ultimately resolve, her feelings of loss. Ginnie agreed to the task but found it to be "too over-whelming" to attempt. She was asked to think of some small way of beginning the task. She thought for a moment and said with a smile, "Well, I could actually buy a photo album, since I don't have one."

Task planners (see part III) can be utilized to identify task options and develop task alternatives. A task planner provides essentially a menu of task possibilities for a specific client situation, problem, or need. It also contains information about the problem and references to current literature or Web-based resources. Task planners will be described in more detail at the beginning of part III of this book.

ESTABLISHING MOTIVATION

Client motivation is a fundamental element of successful task work. The task-centered model views a client's task behavior as occurring in response to an unsatisfied want (Reid 1992). This unsatisfied want gives rise to the problem. This way of viewing the problem reinforces the critical idea that problems in the model represent the *client*'s concerns and not difficulties defined by others.

A person has an incentive to carry out a task because of the potential benefit of completing it, i.e., satisfying the want/solving the problem. A task may not completely solve a problem, but it may be a step in that direction. Or it may achieve a partial solution, which the client may be satisfied with. Attaining goals and successfully completing tasks provide additional motivation to the client. Consequently, goals as well as the task to achieve them should be set in a way that makes them attainable.

Tasks should enable clients to achieve what they want. Thus, practitioners have to be careful not to impose their own goals onto their clients. If the practitioner thinks that a goal the client has not considered is important, he or she is free to point this out to the client. Sensitivity to the client's motivation for undertaking tasks is essential. Clients may agree to tasks because they feel pressured to consent, but when it comes to actually implementing such tasks, they will often not follow through.

The reason for completing a task, i.e., the rationale, provides the client with an understanding of why completing the task will be of benefit. The rationale makes the incentives clear. Thus clients may come to realize the incentives for adhering to a medical regimen (and be more inclined to undertake the appropriate tasks), if they understand how taking a particular medication as prescribed will help them with their health problems.

SELECTING TASKS

When more than one possible task has been developed, practitioner and client proceed to select one for the client to try. Again, the client's active involvement is imperative. Before asking the client to select from the task alternatives, the practitioner should review the different options. This is especially important for clients with memory problems and for those having trouble staying focused. The practitioner could introduce task selection with questions, like: "We just developed three approaches as to how we could address your financial problems. (The practitioner reviews the alternatives.) Of these three possibilities, which one should we try?"

Often it will be very clear which task seems most appropriate. At other times, however, this may not be so obvious, and two or more alternatives may have to be evaluated in more detail. In such cases, benefits and disadvantages of each option have to be appraised (see box 6.3). Several questions can guide the selection process. A first set of questions relates to the likelihood of success. Are all task alternatives achievable? Are any tasks easier to undertake than others? Can the client implement the task or is it too difficult to complete? A second question relates to the connection between the task and the problem. Is one task alternative better than others in addressing the problem? Another question addresses the clarity of the task. Are the task alternatives stated clearly enough? Does the client understand them? As has been noted, the client's motivation is an essential factor in successful task completion. Thus, questions about motivation can help in selecting from several task alternatives. Is the client more motivated to undertake one of the task alternatives? Finally, who will undertake the task? If there is a choice between a task to be done by a practitioner, caregiver, elderly person, or a shared task, preference should be given to the option that includes the elderly person as much as possible.

BOX 6.3 CHOOSING FROM MULTIPLE TASK ALTERNATIVES

- Is the task achievable?
- Is the task manageable?
- Does it address the problem?
- Has it been specified clearly?
- Is the client motivated to undertake the task?
- Is the client given as much responsibility for the task as is feasible?

AGREEING ON TASKS

The elderly client must be willing and able to carry out tasks or agree that the practitioner or a caregiver will implement them on his or her behalf. The level of the client's commitment has an impact on the achievement of the task. Reid (1978) found that when the client's commitment was rated low or neutral, 30 percent of the clients successfully completed their tasks; however, when the client's commitment was rated high, task completion increased to 63 percent. Moreover, the client's expressed commitment to implement a task was found to be a better predictor for completion than whether the task had initially been suggested by the client or by the practitioner (Reid 1978). While generating and selecting alternatives may often imply implicit approval of the tasks by the client, the practitioner should always ask for an explicit agreement on the selected task.

Some frail elderly clients may have difficulty actively agreeing to tasks, especially if they suffer cognitive impairments or if they foresee difficulty in implementation because of their frailty. In such cases, the client's decisional and executional autonomy (chapter 4) should be kept in mind. Even if a client is no longer able to implement a decision, his or her autonomy to make such a decision, i.e., in this case agree to the task, needs to be respected. If the client's abilities to cognitively process this activity are limited, the practitioner should at least inform the client about any tasks others have decided upon. In most such cases, a caregiver will be the primary partner of the practitioner in the TPIS. When a caregiver takes on this active role, he or she would be planning and selecting tasks on behalf of the care recipient. Consequently, he or she would also provide agreement to the task. But even clients with severely limited cognitive capabilities can still be provided with the basic information—e.g., this is the problem we are addressing, this is the task we are carrying out.

PLANNING DETAILS OF IMPLEMENTATION

In this step, client and practitioner develop a plan for carrying out the task. The amount of detail and structure to be included in the plan will depend on the nature of the task and the capacities of the client. In most cases including certain "ingredients" in a task plan helps to clarify the actual process of implementation. Box 6.4 provides an overview of key questions that should be considered in developing a task plan.

BOX 6.4 QUESTIONS TO BE CONSIDERED IN DEVELOPING A TASK PLAN

- Who is to do what?
- When?
- How often?
- How long?
- Where?
- With whom?

In this context, "who" refers to the individual(s) responsible for carrying out the tasks. As stated, tasks can be carried out by individuals or combinations of two or more participants. "What" refers to the action that will be taken. The clearer and more precise this description, the easier it will be to implement the task. Ambiguous descriptions make it more difficult to follow through with a plan of action. "When," "how often," and "how long" a task should be carried out depends on the problem being addressed. Many situational tasks related to resource linkage will be one-time actions. Behavioral tasks, on the other hand, often include repeated activities over longer periods of time. In planning one-time actions, it is useful to work out an agreement with the client as to when the task will be done, as a means of avoiding procrastination. In most cases this should be a time between the development of the task and the next meeting, as in Mr. Childs will make an appointment with his eye doctor before next Tuesday (the next scheduled session).

"Where" refers to the location in which the task will be implemented. While the location is obvious in many instances, there are situations in which the setting for task performance is critical. "With whom" may be an indicator of the target of a task, as in "Mrs. Jones will ask her husband to attend the next counseling session," or it may suggest a shared task, as in "Mrs. Smith and her daughter will visit Sunnydale Home on Saturday."

As should be obvious from this discussion, not all questions presented will apply to all tasks. When generating task alternatives, it is helpful to keep these key questions in mind. At the very least, the first two questions (who is to do what and when) should be included in all complete task plans.

In sessions with several participants, structured interactions among participants provide useful vehicles for task planning. Participants can stimulate one another to think of things that otherwise might not surface and that the practitioner, unfamiliar with the details of their lives together, would never have thought of. For example, Mr. and Mrs. S. may plan an activity outside of their home that is mutually enjoyable and can be done while Mr. S. is still wheelchair bound. The kinds of mutually enjoyable activities they might engage in are likely to emerge more readily in face-to-face dialogue between the couple than through the practitioner's questioning. Task planning can also occur in connection with longer range strategies to address a problem. Mr. and Mrs. S. may discuss their long-term options regarding living environments and consider the alternatives should one of them become too frail to be cared for by the other.

MODELING, REHEARSAL, AND IN-VIVO IMPLEMENTATION

After the task is planned, modeling, rehearsal, or guided practice may be used as part of the preparation process. Role plays are often used. For example, Mrs. Gartner becomes upset when her daughter-in-law (her caregiver) is late taking her to the clinic, but she has been reluctant to voice her dissatisfaction. After planning a task for Mrs. Gartner to speak to her daughter-in-law about her concern, the practitioner in a role play might model how Mrs. Gartner could address her caregiver. Mrs. Gartner might then rehearse what she will say to her daughter-in-law, now played by the practitioner.

In in-vivo implementation clients actually carry out a task with the assistance of the practitioner. A client with a memory problem may practice an exercise designed to improve memory, or under the practitioner's guidance, a client may practice methods of progressive relaxation. In a structured interaction a father and his caregiving son might practice communication skills as a way of improving their relationship.

As the foregoing suggests, modeling, rehearsal, and in-vivo implementation can be used in social skills training. Such skills can be situation specific, such as learning how to be assertive (as in the case of Mrs. Gartner above). Or skills may be cross-situational, that is, applicable to a wide range of situations. An isolated resident in an enriched living facility may be helped to develop skills in making friends. The practitioner might facilitate skill development by accompanying the client on a "friends-making" venture at meal time.

Although in-vivo implementation may take place during the session, it may also occur in the client's "real-life" environment, as in the friends-making example above. Task work of this kind may consist of a variety of activities: for example, joining clients in meetings with health care personnel to make sure their wishes are heard, accompanying anxious or intimidated clients in visits to social and health agencies, helping recently disabled clients learn to cope with their home environments, or using exposure methods to enable phobic clients to overcome fears.

One of Mr. Allen's problems was his reluctance to use the microwave oven in his enriched living apartment to which he had recently moved. He had heard that microwave ovens could blow up if they were not used properly. His fears about the microwave oven appeared to be part of a generalized anxiety disorder with many worries about health, finances, etc. Since the microwave oven was his only means of cooking, and he did not like the food in the common dining facility, the problem was not a minor one. After Mr. Allen failed to attempt a task to use the microwave, the practitioner proposed a more direct intervention. They agreed she would visit his apartment expressly for the purpose of helping him overcome his fears of the microwave oven. During her visit, she tried out the microwave oven while Mr. Allen stayed in his bedroom. After determining that the appliance was in working order, she invited Mr. Allen in and gave him a demonstration of how to use it. An anxious Mr. Allen gave it a try, without the catastrophic consequences he feared. Subsequently he was able to use the microwave oven without difficulty.

Such in-vivo task work takes intervention beyond the largely verbal "sessions" that customarily define task-centered and other forms of clinical practice. Through in-vivo tasks practitioners can help clients develop skills, as with Mrs. Gartner, or solve a particular problem, as with Mr. Allen.

In-vivo implementation may be begun during a session with the client finishing the task later. For example, a lengthy application may include medical and psychological information that practitioner and client jointly fill in, and the remainder of the form is completed by the client between sessions. A client may be asked to begin a cognitive task in the session, such as identifying advantages and disadvantages of remaining in his or her home, and continue it on his or her own afterward.

The dialogue box 6.5 illustrates use of rehearsal as well as elements of in-vivo implementation in helping a client access the senior transportation system. The client had suggested this task.

When two or more clients are involved in the session, structured client interactions can be used as a basis for in-vivo implementation of tasks. For example, having a mother and her caregiving daughter discuss residential care options in the session enables them to engage in an actual dialogue leading to real decisions—a task in every sense. However, since the task is carried out in the session, the practitioner can facilitate the process in the ways described earlier.

BOX 6.5 EXAMPLE 1

Practitioner: OK. Let's go over how to use the senior transportation van.

Client: Yes.

Practitioner: So this is what you do: You call them . . .

Client: I called them and they said any time between 9:00 and 3:30.

Practitioner: See, the van comes and picks you up.

Client: No, they didn't say they would.

Practitioner: They didn't say they would? Let me call them, because that's the way it always used to work. They would come and pick you up, they would take you down to the County Office for the Aging, you would have your picture taken. and you pay them the two dollars and then they bring you back home. . . . Let me go and call. [*Practitioner calls for information.*]

Practitioner: I called STAR van directly, and this is what you have to do: You call STAR van, and then you tell them that you just got your certification letter and that you need to go to the County Office for the Aging. Here is the address [*provides the address*]. What you need to do is make a reservation to go. Let's say you want to go next week on a Wednesday. So, you call STAR van at that number and you say: I would like to go the Office for the Aging next Wednesday morning at ten o'clock . . .

Client: How far ahead do you have to call?

Practitioner: As soon as you know that you have an appointment, call them. A week in advance is great. There is some flexibility. You call the STAR van and tell them where you want to go and at what time. And then, the day before the appointment, you call them again and they give you the time that they will come and pick you up. Now, the obstacle sometimes to using STAR van is that if you have an appointment at 10:30 and you call and say I want you to come and pick me up at 10:00 and they have other people scheduled, they might say we will pick you up at 10:15. When you make the appointment you should leave enough time for that sort of thing. It's good to use when you go to the supermarket, because if you arrive 15 minutes later it does not matter.

Client: Right.

Practitioner: This is a good test run for you to call STAR van, decide what day you want to go to the Office for the Aging and say I would like to be picked up at 10:00. The day before you call them back and see what time they will pick you up and bring you. It might be good to get that experience now so that you know how it works.

Client: [*Rehearses what needs to be done and asks the practitioner to write procedures down.*]

Tasks using structured interactions can take a variety of forms. They can make use of established couple or family problem-solving methods (Reid 2000). The sequence of steps may include defining the problem, clarifying each person's position, developing alternative solutions, making concessions, and selecting a solution. Obstacles blocking progress on tasks and problems often consist of clients' lack of understanding of one another's behaviors, feelings, or beliefs. Tasks can be designed to help clients gain such awareness. Through informative discussions, clients can tell one another "where they are coming from." For example, clients can share their thoughts and feelings about emotional issues such as having life-threatening surgery, entering a nursing home, or dying. Or a once independent woman can share with her caregiving partner how it feels to be in the role of receiver of help. Family members or partners in conflicted relationships often fail to see anything positive in each other. A corrective task is to ask clients to disclose what they like about one another or the way the other does certain things. A care recipient may be asked to express to her daughter what she likes about the way she assists her. The caregiving daughter would share what she likes about the way her mother responds to her caregiving.

Tasks involving several participants do not necessarily need to take place in a conventional session. For example, in order to gain insight into what her care recipient might be experiencing, a caregiver might maneuver a wheelchair through the house or a public space and then share her reactions with the care recipient.

ANTICIPATING OBSTACLES

Before concluding the planning process, practitioner and client review potential obstacles that could impede the successful implementation of the task (see box 6.6). This process of identifying and resolving obstacles is a key element in the practice model. In the context of task-centered practice, obstacles can be defined as what prevents clients from solving their problems (Reid 1992). One can distinguish between potential obstacles, those that might come up, and actual obstacles, those that have already occurred. Potential obstacles are dealt with during the planning phase. They are the obstacles that could impede successful completion of the task. Thus, potential obstacles are elicited through "what if" questions. Potential obstacles can be identified through a process of thinking through the contingencies that might obstruct the implementation of a task. One approach is to ask the

---

BOX 6.6 COMMON OBSTACLES

- Client Motivation
- Cognitive-Emotional Problems
- Client Skills
- Physical Functioning
- External Systems

---

client what could go wrong. The client's intimate knowledge of previous attempts—both effective and ineffective—to solve the problem provides useful insight into potential obstacles.

Actual obstacles are those that have already occurred in the process of undertaking a task, i.e., a client has tried to perform a task but without success. In such circumstances, the practitioner will discuss with the client what hindered completion of the task. Common questions include: Did the client lack the abilities, skills, or physical capabilities to undertake the task? Was the client not motivated enough? Did others, or an external system, prevent completion of the task?

Several options for dealing with actual obstacles can be distinguished. A first approach is to resolve the obstacle itself. A second option is to modify the task in a way that avoids the obstacle. A third possibility is to develop a new task that avoids the obstacle but still addresses the problem. Finally, if these three options fail, practitioner and client should evaluate whether the problem can be resolved. In light of the new information, is it still feasible to work on the problem or need? If not, it may be necessary to defer work on the problem, if that is possible, and revisit it later.

We would now like to turn to types of obstacles that might be encountered and discuss some strategies to address them. Common obstacles relate to motivation, cognitive-emotional problems, clients' skills, physical functioning, and issues with external systems (Reid 1992). Obstacles that relate to *motivation* may surface during task planning or after unsuccessful attempts to complete a task. They are often caused by conflicted motives or low motivation. Conflicted motives stem from incompatible wants. The client is ambivalent about which of these wants should be satisfied. The basic strategy is to clarify the ambivalence and generate a strategy that helps select one option or find a compromise. A caregiving wife who wants to initiate a move of her husband into a skilled nursing facility can be taken as example. On the one hand, she may be thoroughly overwhelmed by the demands of caregiving and may think that her husband would receive more appropriate levels of care in the nursing home. On the other hand, she has strong feelings of guilt and failure as a caregiver for even considering this option. One strategy is to find a compromise and develop a task that is sensitive to this ambivalence. For example, the client might consider temporary respite placement, or she could consider moving into a continuum of care facility that offers skilled care for her husband and a regular assisted living apartment for herself. Another strategy is to ask the client to visualize what the future would look like for each of the choices and then select the more agreeable choice.

Low motivation is another common obstacle to task completion. For example, a client who is not suffering from memory problems forgets to carry out a task, makes only half-hearted attempts, or keeps postponing efforts to undertake it. If low motivation stems from previous unsuccessful tasks or low self-efficacy, using smaller subtasks is a useful strategy. While clients' involvement in developing, selecting, and agreeing on tasks should reduce such incidents, clients may consent to tasks because they feel coerced. They may feel that they have to satisfy the practitioner, a family member, or the referring agency. In such cases, reexploring and reevaluating the problem could be a useful approach. If the client comes to a different understanding and "ownership" of the problem, additional efforts to solve the problem may be undertaken with more success. At times, however, a client will not have the same opinion about the existence of a problem. If the client does not see a problem and does not want to address it, possible consequences of not carrying out the task should be pointed out. With the exception of those situations where not addressing the problem would constitute neglect, pose imminent harm, or in situations where clients lack the cognitive abilities to make decisions, clients have the option of not addressing a problem and taking the consequences.

Clients need to possess sufficient cognitive abilities to actively participate in planning and implementing tasks. As we have argued, clients with limited cognitive capacity can participate in task work in a meaningful way. However, the practitioner needs to adapt the intervention process to pay special attention to the client's abilities and autonomy.

Obstacles to task performance can occur in the client's emotions and beliefs. For example, a client's anxiety or feelings of inadequacy may hinder efforts to undertake the task. In the task-centered model, it is "assumed that feelings can be most effectively changed by identifying and modifying controlling beliefs" (Reid 1992:76). Common steps in this process include identifying beliefs and involving the client in cognitive restructuring. The practitioner's role is to assist clients in identifying the distorted belief in a way they can understand and accept. A client's self-reflection on the belief is often the first step in changing it. The practitioner guides this process through questions and comments that promote reflection. She may also present facts that challenge the client's beliefs. While it is desired that clients make their own corrections, the practitioner may directly suggest modifications of beliefs. Since the focus at this time is on obstacles to carrying out tasks, these modifications need to be substantial enough to enable the client to perform the task successfully even if they do not result in fundamental or even enduring change. In the present model, change is effected largely through tasks. Cognitive change is not the primary goal, but it is used for purposes of task completion.

A client may *lack appropriate skills* to undertake a task. If so, skills training following the procedures suggested earlier in the chapter may be used (see "Modeling, Rehearsal, and In-Vivo Implementation"). For example, a client may need to learn assertiveness skills before he or she is able to complete a task that involves expressing concerns about medication to a physician.

Tasks may focus on addressing a *limitation in physical function*, such as problems with mobility, physical safety, and activities of daily living. At the same time, physical limitations can pose an obstacle to a client's efforts at implementing a task. Usually, a thorough assessment will make the practitioner aware of any major limitations to physical functioning. Based on this knowledge, she will help devise strategies that take this physical limitation into account. One option is to revise or adjust the task in a way that minimizes or circumvents the impact of the physical limitation. Another option is to develop a shared task in which the practitioner or a caregiver takes on a supportive function. The task can be devised in such a way that the client implements as much as he or she can, and then the task partner takes supportive action. Finally, tasks addressing the client's physical limitation can be implemented as an antecedent. An example is the client with hearing difficulty who has difficulty making phone calls to a service provider. Before addressing the client's other problems, the hearing could be chosen as target problem. Tasks could focus on acquiring a hearing aid and phone equipment with assistive technology. Once these tasks are completed, client and practitioner can continue work on the other problem areas.

Obstacles to the client's completion of tasks frequently arise in external systems. Different types of such obstacles can be identified. External obstacles can be caused by beliefs and behaviors of significant others. Mrs. H., for example, may feel provoked by the frequent antagonistic evening phone calls from her sister, making it difficult for her to complete her task of trying to go to bed at a prescribed time. The obstacle may be located in one or more organizations. Staff may label the client as manipulative and not answer her requests in a timely manner. The service delivery may be problematic, for instance, if a service is denied despite a client's eligibility. Multiple service providers may be involved, making it challenging for the client to comply with conflicting demands. The neighborhood or surrounding community can cause an obstacle to task implementation. An example is the elderly client who is too fearful to leave the house because of recent crime in the neighborhood, which in turn prevents her from making a required visit to a service provider. Finally, the source can reside in the physical environment. For example, since her fall two months ago, Mrs. K. has difficulty taking a shower, since it is located on the second floor of her home. This hinders her from undertaking tasks related to improving her personal hygiene.

When the strategy is aimed at *expanding the intervention system*, the effort focuses on including the external obstacle in the intervention process. For example, multiple service providers can be asked to attend a case conference that includes the client. The difficult sister could be asked to attend a joint session. However, consideration has to be given to the possibility that a joint session with the "antagonist" might make matters worse. If outside persons are asked to participate, it is important to clarify the purpose of the session ahead of time.

When empowerment of clients is used as a strategy, clients confront the obstacles themselves. The practitioner may support the client in this effort, for example, by providing in-session skills training on how to face the external obstacle. As with other practice activities, direct client actions may be the most effective means of removing the obstacle. Finally, successful confrontation of external obstacles provides additional motivation for the client to undertake other tasks. However, if the external obstacle is too complex and difficult to resolve, practitioner tasks may be more appropriate. Practitioners can facilitate the client's action or undertake tasks themselves. A facilitating task can foster the empowerment of clients, for example, if the practitioner action helps a client to successfully perform a task. Alternatively, through an independent task, the practitioner can try to alter the obstacle without direct action by the client. Frequently, such tasks will involve organizations that are unresponsive to the client's needs. Such actions by the practitioner may more often be necessary in geriatric case management, which we will discuss in a later chapter.

SUMMARIZING TASKS

The last step in planning the implementation of tasks is to summarize and restate them. Usually, the practitioner will ask the client to state the task in

FIGURE 6.1 PRACTICE FORM 1:

TASK PLANNING FORM

Date: _____ Client _____ Practitioner: _____

Target Need: _____ Goal: _____

Describe Task:

Who will carry out task?

When will task be completed?

What are possible obstacles? How will they be approached?

his or her own words. This ensures that the client understands the task. It also conveys the expectation and importance of completing the task. Attending to the way the task is presented offers the practitioner another opportunity to assess the client's motivation to carry it out.

The Task Planning Form is used to record the tasks client and practitioner agree to implement. This sample form is more comprehensive than a simple statement of the task, because experience has shown that the repetition and the additional information are helpful to many frail elderly clients (see fig. 6.1). Since this form is routinely shared with the client, duplicate write-through copies are practical. Displaying the form at a prominent place in the client's environment serves as a useful memory aid and may increase the likelihood that the task will be completed. For example, a practitioner might provide the client with a magnet carrying the agency's phone number and use it to attach the task planning form to the client's refrigerator.

IMPLEMENTING TASKS

Most tasks developed during the session are undertaken between sessions, typically before the next session. However, between-session contacts can be included as part of the task. A client's task may include a phone call to the practitioner between sessions. For example, he or she may update the practitioner on the progress made. The client may share information gained from a service provider. A phone call to the practitioner may also be used as a way to raise the expectation of performing the task. Some clients may be forgetful and benefit from telephone reminders by the practitioner. This can increase the likelihood that the task will be carried out. Since a phone call could be considered rather intrusive, it should be done only if the client has agreed to it beforehand.

REVIEW OF TASK PROGRESS

At the beginning of each subsequent session, the practitioner initiates a review of the tasks that had been planned in the previous session. Like most steps in the task-centered model, the task review is a collaborative activity in which the practitioner leads the process, but the client also contributes actively. Reviewing task performance is a significant activity that should be systematically incorporated into the beginning of each session. The systematic use of tasks as the key means of change includes not only the structured process of developing and implementing them, but also a methodical evaluation of their success. As Tolson, Reid, and Garvin point out, employing tasks but not reviewing their completion would be like a teacher assigning homework but never checking whether it was completed (2002).

The task review focuses on the extent to which each task has been implemented. Was it performed as planned? How did it work? If the task is an ongoing one, how many times did the client carry it out? Which results were achieved? It is also advantageous to ask the client whether any other actions were undertaken to address the problem. A client may have carried out other problem-solving actions than the tasks that had been planned. All these questions assist in the decision how to proceed, i.e., whether to continue, modify, or discontinue the task. If one-time tasks have been completed and the problem is alleviated, usually no more task work is required for that target problem. If ongoing tasks have been completed and have led to a change in the problem; however, they often require continued performance. The importance of continued task performance should be emphasized. Every so often, problems resurface after some time. If this can be anticipated, strategies for addressing the recurrence should be planned ahead of time. Generally, those tasks that were successful in the past would be applied again.

As part of the task review, clients are asked to rate the success of task performance using a scale with points like minimally completed, partially com-

FIGURE 6.2 PRACTICE FORM 2:

TASK REVIEW FORM

Date: _____ Client _____ Practitioner: _____

Target Need: _____ Goal: _____

Instructions: Rate task completion together with client using the following scale

Task completion ratings:
4 = completely achieved, 3 = substantially achieved, 2 = partially achieved,
1= minimally achieved, N = not able to carry out task

Task Completion Rating: _____

Is problem/need still present?

Were obstacles encountered in carrying out the task?

How were they dealt with?

Indicate on new task plan if the task is a revision of a previous task.

---

pleted, substantially completed, fully completed, or not able to carry out the task. Practice form 2 (see fig. 6.2) provides an example of how to track task review information. The Task Review Form is used to record the task completion ratings that are part of the process of reviewing how well a task was achieved.

Not all external tasks will be successfully completed. Tasks that are not performed fall into two general categories: (1) attempted but unsuccessful tasks, and (2) tasks not performed. We will first review unsuccessful tasks (see box 6.7).

Tasks may not have been successfully completed because they were not performed or because they did not achieve the planned effect of changing the problem. If a task was not performed, the first question is whether the expectations were perhaps unclear. In such cases, the task does not have to be revised. Rather, the practitioner would clarify the task and provide additional information on the details of performing it. Role-playing the task may also

---

BOX 6.7 COMMON REASONS FOR UNSUCCESSFUL TASKS

- Unclear expectations
- No opportunity to implement task
- Emergence of an unanticipated obstacle
- Lack of appropriate skills on the part of the client
- Lack of motivation on the part of the client

---

be helpful. It enables the practitioner to observe what may have caused the lack of success.

Another possibility is that the client had no opportunity to implement the task. Circumstances beyond the client's control may prevent the completion of a task. The review of potential obstacles minimizes this occurrence but cannot completely prevent it. For example, a client may have tasks related to her depression but falls and is hospitalized. During this time, it would be difficult for her to implement her cognitive tasks, especially since she is receiving strong pain medication. Another example is that a client's appointment with a service provider may be canceled by the agency due to a family emergency of the social worker. This situation was not foreseeable and could not have been anticipated when practitioner and client discussed potential obstacles. In most cases, these types of unsuccessful tasks can be attempted again with no or only few changes.

At times, unanticipated obstacles emerge during the implementation of tasks. One type of such an unanticipated obstacle can be a lack of skills on the part of the client. This can occur despite diligent task planning and anticipation of obstacles. Practitioner and client should assess the obstacle and its impact on the task. The development of a new task may be required, taking the obstacle into consideration. Such tasks are generated the same way as any other task during the middle phase of service.

Finally, a client may have lacked sufficient motivation. Again, even a thorough assessment of the client's motivation will not always prevent this obstacle to task performance from surfacing. This type of obstacle would usually lead to a discussion of the rationale and incentives for the task. If problems are not critical to the client's day-to-day life, the client may have forgotten about the problem and viewed the task as not that important.

Sometimes tasks are fully completed, but the desired effect on the target problem does not occur. Many problems faced by elderly clients are multifac-

---

BOX 6.8 COMMON REASONS FOR NOT PERFORMING TASKS

- Lack of interest in changing the specific target problem
- Lack of interest in working with practitioner
- Lack of interest in changing anything

---

eted and complex. A task may have successfully dealt with one part of the problem, but left other, more significant components unchanged. In such cases, the typical strategy is to separate the problem into its various parts and examine which of them would lead to a change if successfully dealt with. Next, new tasks would be generated that focus on these aspects of the problem.

Occasionally, a client consistently does not perform his or her tasks (see box 6.8). Three common reasons for nonperformance of tasks are that a client has no interest in changing the specific target problem, has no interest in working with the practitioner, or has no interest in changing anything (Tolson, Reid, and Garvin 2002).

If a client lacks the interest in changing a specific target problem, the strategy is to identify problems the client wants to resolve. Before doing so, practitioner and client should evaluate the consequences of not addressing the target problem. If changing the target problem entails a significant shift in focus, a partial or complete reassessment may be indicated. In cases in which a client does not want to work with the practitioner, the approach is to find out whether a different practitioner is available to work with the client. However, most clients are reluctant to share this kind of information with a practitioner. They may also not be aware of their reservations. If a client is not interested in changing anything, termination of service should be considered. In cases where this is not possible due to ethical or legal reasons, the practitioner may employ strategies for work with involuntary clients (see Rooney 1992 for a detailed account of strategies for involuntary clients).

Our experience in using the task-centered model with elderly clients suggests that it may be beneficial to have a phone contact to follow up on task completion if meetings with a client are more than two weeks apart. Anecdotal evidence indicates that this phone contact fosters successful task performance on the part of the client. During this phone contact, the progress made on the tasks as well as problem changes are reviewed. If the task has not yet been completed, a review of the above-described aspects can be completed by phone. Even if task accomplishments and problem changes are evaluated by phone, the more formal review and rating of the task accomplishments is still carried out at the beginning of the next in-person contact.

REVIEW OF TARGET PROBLEMS

The review of target problems is integrated into the task review. As in the task review, the focus is on the specific target problems that were addressed. Taking into consideration the starting point, i.e., the detailed information gathered during problem exploration, a determination is made whether any changes occurred. Based on this comparison and an appraisal of the current problem status, practitioner and client decide what further actions to take. If the problem has been completely alleviated, no further action may be needed. If only partial changes occurred, the review should focus on which parts were left unchanged and how these specific aspects of the problem can be addressed.

Practitioners working with the task-centered model often ask clients to rate the changes in their problems using a simple scale like the following: problem is unchanged, minimally changed, substantially changed, or completely alleviated. The Problem Change Form in figure 6.3 serves as an example of how problem changes can be assessed and tracked. Clients and practitioners complete the form at the time the target problems are reviewed. At times it may be a useful tactic to have client and practitioner first rate the changes in the problem separately. They then compare and discuss their ratings. If ratings are not in agreement, the difference is a good starting point for a discussion of the client's and the practitioner's perceptions of the changes in the problem.

ASSESSING NEW PROBLEMS

A thorough assessment and problem exploration notwithstanding, new problems will often arise throughout the intervention process. Clients may present one problem but have others on their mind. They may be too anxious or insecure to share their more significant problems during the first sessions, or they may be unsure whether it is an appropriate focus for the practice setting. Clients may have been genuinely unaware of an underlying problem. Or they may test the practitioner to see whether he or she can establish trust before sharing their more important issues. A referral may have highlighted a specific problem, and the client is not sure whether other

FIGURE 6.3 PRACTICE FORM 3:

PROBLEM CHANGES RATINGS

	Session								
	1	2	3	4	5	6	7	8	9
Target Problem:									
#1: _____	—	—	—	—	—	—	—	—	—
#2: _____	—	—	—	—	—	—	—	—	—
#3: _____	—	—	—	—	—	—	—	—	—
#4: _____	—	—	—	—	—	—	—	—	—

Note:

Rate problem changes by comparing the current status to the status at the beginning of service. Use the following scale:

3 = Problem completely alleviated

2 = Problem substantially changed

1 = Problem minimally changed

0 = Problem unchanged

concerns can be included. In many cases, the new problem may not have existed when the initial assessment was conducted. Solving one problem may have uncovered a related problem. Finally, the collaborative work during the middle phase of service produces additional information on areas such as the client's personal situation, environment, social networks, and the manner in which they problem solve.

In all of these cases, the fact that new information has become available does not by itself cause a problem to become the target of intervention until a client agrees to this. If a new problem is chosen as a target for intervention, practitioner and client examine the current problems and how they were prioritized. The client is asked to reprioritize the problems, i.e., rank the new problem in relation to the ones already identified and prioritized. Once a new problem becomes the focus of intervention, which may be immediately, it is explored and tasks are developed in the same way as for problems that were identified during the initial assessment.

RECONTRACTING

If the situation requires it, client and practitioner may recontract for an additional period of time. The practitioner may communicate to the client: "We have two more sessions to go. Some of the goals that we planned to reach have been achieved. However, there still are two areas that we have not worked on. As we are coming toward the end of the sessions that we contracted on, we might need to reconsider contracting for a few more sessions." Like the initial contract, recontracting includes a fixed number of sessions and a timeline to be followed.

While an extension of the time limits is always an option, routine postponement of termination should be avoided. Client and practitioner alike should accept that some uncertainties always remain. If the previously determined time limits are extended too easily, practitioners and clients begin to take them less seriously, and they lose their capacity to mobilize and concentrate their effort. Moreover, service may be extended unproductively without agreeing on a clear focus and new time limits. Nevertheless, the practitioner needs to be flexible. Some problems may need more work than the original contract allowed for, or new problems may arise during the course of service. Thus, while the durational limits of the model can be reasonably adhered to in most cases, there are inevitable exceptions.

In deciding about recontracting, client and practitioner need to consider whether additional time and effort would be likely to result in appreciable gain. In making a collaborative decision, client and practitioner should take into account the amount of progress that has been made and the likelihood that their continued task work can lead to additional progress. A summary of the middle phase is provided in box 6.9.

WORK WITH GROUPS

A considerable amount of gerontological social work takes the form of work with groups. Work with groups of caregivers and residents and with support groups in relation to different illnesses are common examples of such work. Since its development by Garvin (1974), the task-centered group model has been used with a range of problems and populations (Tolson, Reid, and Garvin 2002), including the elderly (Toseland and Coppola 1985). Combined psycho-educational and task-centered work with groups of younger adults around health issues can be readily adapted to work with older people

---

BOX 6.9 SUMMARY OF MIDDLE PHASE OF SERVICE

- Possible tasks are formulated together with the client
- The client should actively engage in generating possible tasks
- Practitioner can suggest tasks
- All task alternatives are evaluated and one task is selected
- The client must be willing to participate in carrying out the selected task or agree to have the practitioner carry out the task
- An agreement is made on the task
- A plan to execute the task is developed
- If it is not already clear, practitioner and client develop a rationale for the tasks in the session, e.g., they consider the potential benefit of carrying out the task
- Another in session activity is the clarification of potential obstacles
- Through analyzing the context, the practitioner can assist the client in identifying and resolving potential obstacles
- Tasks are selected that avoid the obstacles or plans are made to deal with them
- Finally, the task is operationalized in concrete terms, stating what the task is, how it should be carried out, by whom, and by when (*Task Plan Form*)
- If needed, the task can be broken down into subtasks
- The task should be of such a nature that the client can work on it prior to the next meeting
- A task plan should always include at least one, but no more than three client tasks (if the client has appropriate levels of functioning to carry out tasks)
- Practitioner and client review how the task will be carried out
- The client is asked to present the task plan from his or her view

---

(Pomeroy, Rubin, and Walker 1995). The most recent presentation of task-centered group methods can be found in Tolson, Reid, and Garvin (2002).

The task-centered model for working with groups in the context of geriatric social work is presented in more detail in chapter 9, where working with caregivers is discussed. Methods outlined there can be applied to other groups relating to work with the elderly. Here we present only a brief overview of the approach.

While procedures for forming and conducting task-centered groups vary, the following format is typical. Preliminary individual interviews are held with prospective group members to determine primarily if the applicant has at least one problem that would fall within the prospective focus of the group and to orient him or her to the general structure and purpose of the group intervention model. In the initial group meeting, clients are asked to state the problems they wish to work on and to assist one another in exploring and specifying problems. A contractual agreement is reached on the purpose of the group and its duration (which is planned for the short term, just as in individual work). In subsequent sessions, each member in turn formulates, plans, practices, and reviews tasks with the help of the practitioner and other group members. As in individual and family approaches, the TPIS serves as a procedural outline. In addition, the practitioner may undertake tasks outside the session on behalf of an individual client or the group as a whole, or group members may perform tasks outside the sessions to help one another with their problems.

CHAPTER 7

FINAL PHASE: ENDING SERVICE

THE FINAL PHASE of the task-centered model focuses on the ending of service. The purpose of termination goes beyond simply providing closure for the intervention process. It should also help clients generalize their problem-solving skills and maintain the goals that were achieved. The final phase of the model includes the steps of evaluating tasks and problem status, reinforcing accomplishments, reviewing problem-solving skills, and discussing the client's future plans. In addition, this is a time for clients to discuss their feelings about termination.

THE TERMINATION PROCESS

When time limits are used, the termination process begins when the number of sessions is planned in the beginning phase (Reid and Epstein 1972). During the middle phase, the practitioner periodically reminds the client about the time limits contracted for as well as how much time and how many session are left. This reminder should include an indication of the progress that has been made up to that point and further goals that still need to be achieved. When time limits are not used, revisable estimates of service duration keep the client informed about when termination is likely to occur.

Termination is the focal point of the last one to three sessions. The time frame for the termination phase depends on the type of interventions and settings. Discharge planning, for instance, is characterized by a rather short time period. Rarely will termination in discharge planning take more than two sessions or client contacts. A gerontological practitioner working in a setting that focuses on counseling and therapy would typically follow the one to three session format. A case manager may also adhere to this plan. However, as we will describe in the next chapter, the nature and purpose of case management make termination less final. In this approach it is more common to temporarily discontinue or reduce the active phase of intervention until new problems arise. However, when new problems appear, the practitioner-client relationship is revived.

In most cases the durational limits of the model produce a positive, uneventful termination. As noted earlier, stipulating an end point at the beginning energizes both client and practitioner to attain agreed upon goals within the predetermined time frame. Usually, these goals are achieved to the extent it is possible to achieve them, or it becomes apparent that they cannot be achieved.

As useful as they may be, durational limits should not be used to deny clients needed services. Fundamentally, a case is terminated if a client no longer needs the services provided by the practitioner or her agency. The main determining factor is a client's wish to terminate. In some cases, all problems will have been solved with success. In other cases, some of the target problems may still be unresolved, but the client decides that the most important issues have been settled, and the remaining problems are not that important at this point in time. In still other cases, however, problems may remain that the client wishes to work on. In these situations the client and social worker may recontract for a predetermined number of additional sessions devoted to working on the remaining problems, as discussed in chapter 6. Recontracting, even if it is repeated, is preferable to offering service for an indefinite period of time. Like the original durational limits, recontracting helps all participants to focus energies on accomplishing specific goals in the most efficient manner possible.

Other factors may affect termination. Service goals may be achieved before the projected end point. In such cases the practitioner may suggest termination. A determination by the funding source to reimburse only a certain number of sessions may affect decisions about the length of service. Some clients may choose to pay for additional services out-of-pocket. In other cases the agency may waive the fee if additional service is required.

While it is preferable that the original practitioner completes the case from beginning to end, this is not always possible, even when using short-term interventions. Termination may include a transition of the client to a different practitioner in the same setting. For example, the original practitioner may be a student whose field placement is ending. If a practitioner needs to end the relationship prematurely, he or she should anticipate the possibility that the client may become upset and address such feelings as they arise. Another type of transition is transferring a client to a different service provider. For example, Mrs. Rollins had been seeing a social worker for help with her grief after the recent death of her husband. Before completing the planned interventions, she decided to move closer to her adult daughter. Unable to provide service herself, the social worker helped Mrs. Rollins find a practitioner at the new location and facilitated her first contact with this new social worker.

REACTIONS TO TERMINATION

From the client's perspective, termination usually involves a separation from a caring and helpful person. This separation often entails mixed feelings for the client as well as for the practitioner. If the practitioner thinks the client may have such feelings, he or she should ask about them.

Research has suggested that clients' reaction to termination is usually positive and characterized by a sense of accomplishment (Fortune, Pearlingi, and Rochelle 1992). The emphasis on using time limits and reminders throughout the intervention process help reduce negative reactions to termination. Some clients, however, have very strong reactions to termination (Strom-Gottfried 2001). Six common reactions of clients to termination are presented in box 7.1.

Termination may cause a client to feel anger at the practitioner. This may be especially strong in situations where a practitioner leaves the agency, as in the example cited above. Client reactions to such unforeseen termination can cause feelings similar to a crisis situation. In such circumstances, practitioners should encourage clients to express themselves. Practitioners should respond in an empathic yet constructive manner (Strom-Gottfried 2001).

Denial or avoidance of termination is another common reaction of clients. It can take various forms. If sessions take place in an agency setting, clients

---

BOX 7.1 COMMON REACTIONS TO TERMINATION

- Anger
- Denial
- Avoidance
- Complaints about the recurrence of problems
- Trying to prolong service
- Finding substitutes for the practitioner

Based on Strom-Gottfried 2001

may not show up for their final session. In home-based practice, the client may not open the door or may not be home at the time of the practitioner's visit. Clients may try to evade any dialogue that focuses on termination by switching topics or getting sidetracked on insignificant details. In such cases, it may be useful to refocus on termination and remind the client of the process and the time limits that were determined at the beginning of the service.

Some clients report the recurrence of old problems or introduce new ones at the time of termination. The former may be based on anxieties created by the upcoming termination. The latter may be an attempt to extend service. Although these new problems may often be insignificant, clients may bring up information they previously withheld. If the new or recurring problems require more attention than can be provided in a final termination session, client and practitioner may decide to recontract for a limited number of sessions to work on these problems.

At times clients may try to prolong contact with the practitioner. For example, they may suggest social or business contacts after termination. The more careful the practitioner was to keep the boundaries clear during the service process, the less likely and problematic these actions by clients become at the time of termination.

Finally, clients may try to find a substitute for the practitioner, for example, another person who can help them address their needs. In general, this can be seen as a constructive undertaking as long as it does not lead to an overdependence of the client on others (Strom-Gottfried 2001).

FINAL PROBLEM REVIEW

Reviewing target problems and task achievements is an ongoing activity in the middle phase of the model. The final problem review is conducted much in the same way. However, the final review is more comprehensive because all problems will be considered at the same time (see box 7.2). Moreover, the review covers the entire service period.

One objective of the final problem review is to appraise the changes that have occurred. Jointly, practitioner and client compare the problems at the beginning of service with their respective current status. All problems, including those that may not have been addressed, should be included in this evaluation. The practitioner should ask the client to express his or her perceptions regarding the status of current problems. What does it mean for the client to have alleviated the problem and achieved the service goal? If problems were not completely solved, how do clients perceive their current situation?

BOX 7.2 FINAL PROBLEM REVIEW

- Review target problems
- Describe current problem status
- Identify the client's current perceptions regarding the problem
- Review problem changes during service
- Establish a final rating of problem changes
- If appropriate, collect posttest data
- Review problems that were not the focus of intervention
- Evaluate the client's general situation in regard to the problem
- Establish how gains can be maintained

Next, intervention outcomes should be evaluated. If problem change scores were systematically collected as part of the intervention process, they can provide the basis for reviewing the progress made. The visual graphing approaches used in single-subject designs offer a simple way of charting improvements. They have the additional advantage that clients easily understand them. If problem change scores were not collected on an ongoing basis, client and practitioner can still rate outcomes at the end of the service using the problem change ratings presented in figure 7.1 or adopting a similar approach. The client is asked to rate the current problem status as it compares to that at the beginning of service. Such rating scales serve two purposes. For the client, the rating may lead to a better appreciation of the changes that occurred during service. For the practitioner, it provides another means of demonstrating service outcomes.

If practitioner and client used a target problem scale as described in chapter 6, they can utilize these ratings for the final problem review. Scores can be charted as in figure 7.2.

If standardized measurements have been used for assessment or monitoring purposes, they can be repeated at this time for the evaluation of outcomes. Many standardized clinical measurements and RAIs used for diagnosis or for establishing a preservice baseline of the problem lend themselves to postservice data collection. Such pre- and postintervention data are useful in assessing the impact of the intervention. Goal attainment scales also provide an indicator of the level of success. As discussed in chapter 4, goal attainment scaling is a process of specifying potential intervention outcomes at the beginning of an intervention and evaluating them after service is completed (Fortune and Reid 1999a; Kiresuk and Sherman 1968; Rockwood 1994). Using

FIGURE 7.1 PRACTICE FORM 1: PROBLEM CHANGE RATINGS

Date: _____ Case #: _____ Case Manager: _____

Please rate the problem changes as compared to the first session.

Problem # 1: _____

| 1 | 2 | 3 | 4 | 5 | 6 | 7 | 8 | 9 | 10 |

| Much
Worse | | Somewhat
Worse | | No
Change | | | Much
Improved | | No Longer
a Problem |

Problem # 2: _____

| 1 | 2 | 3 | 4 | 5 | 6 | 7 | 8 | 9 | 10 |

| Much
Worse | | Somewhat
Worse | | No
Change | | | Much
Improved | | No Longer
a Problem |

Problem # 3: _____

| 1 | 2 | 3 | 4 | 5 | 6 | 7 | 8 | 9 | 10 |

| Much
Worse | | Somewhat
Worse | | No
Change | | | Much
Improved | | No Longer
a Problem |

Problem # 4: _____

| 1 | 2 | 3 | 4 | 5 | 6 | 7 | 8 | 9 | 10 |

| Much
Worse | | Somewhat
Worse | | No
Change | | | Much
Improved | | No Longer
a Problem |

this procedure, practitioner and client discuss possible outcomes at the time that the service goals are developed and agreed upon. After the intervention is completed, they review and rate the progress that has been made toward alleviating a problem and reaching the related goal. A form for goal attainment scaling was presented in chapter 4. A simpler form as shown in figure 7.3 can also be used to track goal attainment. A separate rating scale is used for each goal. When working with subgoals, practitioners should indicate to which overall goal each one relates. Client and practitioner collaboratively complete the form, but the client should be asked to do the ratings. If the client's ratings diverge significantly from the scores the practitioner would have given, client and practitioner can discuss the differences.

FIGURE 7.2 PROBLEM CHANGES RATING IN FINAL PROBLEM REVIEW

	Session:					
	1	2	3	4	5	6
Problem 1:	3	4	4	4	4	4
Problem 2:	n	1	1	2	4	4
Problem 3:	n	n	n	4	4	4
Problem 4:	n	n	n	n	n	n

Note:
4 = Problem completely alleviated
3 = Problem substantially improved
2 = Problem minimally improved
1 = Problem unchanged
n = no work on problem

If problems were substantially improved or completely alleviated, practitioner and client should consider how these gains can be maintained. Since maintaining gains often involves continued task work, this deliberation can be integrated into the final task review.

FINAL TASK REVIEW

If tasks were performed since the previous session, they are reviewed like any other tasks carried out during the intervention process. In addition, a final task review can be conducted as part of termination. The final task review follows a similar format as the task reviews conducted during the middle phase. Box 7.3 provides an overview of the most important steps of the final task review.

The primary purpose of reviewing tasks one more time at the end of service is to reinforce the client's accomplishments and provide the client with an additional opportunity for learning. How much emphasis is given to the final task review depends on the types of tasks that were implemented. Some one-time tasks, for example, those related to accessing resources, may not benefit much from an additional review. On the other hand, many ongoing tasks would profit from an additional review at the end of service. This helps to reinforce the continued performance of such ongoing tasks. In cases with many subtasks, practitioners may decide to stay with reviewing the overall process and emphasize the most significant tasks that were implemented. If

FIGURE 7.3 PRACTICE FORM 2: GOAL ATTAINMENT FORM

Date: _____ Client: _____ Practitioner: _____

Please rate degree of attainment for each of the goals you worked on.

Goal # 1: _____

−2	−1	0	1	2
Much less than expected	Less than expected	Expected level of goal attainment	Better than expected	Much better than expected

Goal # 2: _____

−2	−1	0	1	2
Much less than expected	Less than expected	Expected level of goal attainment	Better than expected	Much better than expected

Goal # 3: _____

−2	−1	0	1	2
Much less than expected	Less than expected	Expected level of goal attainment	Better than expected	Much better than expected

Goal # 4: _____

−2	−1	0	1	2
Much less than expected	Less than expected	Expected level of goal attainment	Better than expected	Much better than expected

the tasks were carried out as part of an incremental task strategy, the process as well as the final tasks should be highlighted.

Task achievements (see fig. 7.4) were rated throughout the intervention process. These task completion ratings can be charted as graphs. For some clients, such a presentation format helps them visualize the progress made.

REINFORCING ACCOMPLISHMENTS AND PROBLEM-SOLVING SKILLS

The reinforcement of accomplishment is integrated into the final problem and task reviews. Practitioners should highlight the client's accomplishments, commending him or her for successful efforts to achieve the goals. In

---

BOX 7.3 FINAL TASK REVIEW

- Review and reinforce task accomplishments
- If there were many subtasks, review the overall task achievements
- Review task completion ratings
- Graph task achievements (optional)
- Reinforce the client's accomplishment of tasks

---

the task-centered model, clients are active participants in the change process. Yet, when assessing the achievements, clients often attribute these changes more to the practitioner's actions than to their own efforts. Thus, it is important to emphasize the positive changes the elderly person's activities brought about. Focusing attention on the clients' contributions increases their sense of mastery. It strengthens their awareness that they are able to take action on their own behalf. If caregivers or spouses are involved, practitioners should make sure that their accomplishments are reinforced as well.

FIGURE 7.4 FINAL TASK RATINGS

	Session:					
	1	2	3	4	5	6
Task Rating:						
(4)			a/b	a	a	a
(3)		a				
(2)						
(1)			c	c	c	
(n)	a					

Note:

a, b, c = tasks

4 = Problem completely alleviated

3 = Problem substantially improved

2 = Problem minimally improved

1 = Problem unchanged

n = no work on problem

This is also a good time to appraise the client's problem-solving skills. One rationale for direct client actions to change the client's problems is that learning occurs. Through their active task work, clients learn new skills in solving problems. The practitioner can reinforce this learning by highlighting the problem-solving skills that have been used during the course of the intervention. The goal is to help clients generalize the skills learned by demonstrating how they can be transferred to other current problems or situations or to those that might arise in the future. For example, the social worker asked Mrs. Burns to recall one of her successes during the intervention process. She remembered telling her doctor about the unpleasant side effects of her medication, and as a result her prescription was changed. She saw that the skill involved was "speaking her mind when she had a right to do so." The social worker then asked her to think about other problem situations in her life where she might apply that skill. She quickly thought of one. She had just bought a refrigerator, but the store did not deliver the one she had ordered. She had thought that perhaps she should just keep it even though it wasn't quite what she wanted. She could see how "speaking her mind" might be used here.

BOX 7.4 SUMMARY OF FINAL INTERVENTION PHASE

- Termination covers the last 1–3 sessions, depending on the type of interventions and settings
- Termination is introduced when time limits are set at onset of service
- Client is reminded throughout service about number of sessions left
- Need for additional service is met through time-limited extensions
- Termination entails mixed feelings, which are explored
- Reaction to termination is usually positive
- Some clients have strong reactions, manifested in anger, denial, and avoidance
- Final reviews of problems are conducted and ratings of problem changes are made
- A final task review is focused on task accomplishments
- The client's problem-solving skills used in the tasks are identified and reinforced
- How skills can be applied to other problems is considered
- Plans for dealing with remaining problems are discussed in a positive and affirmative tone

FUTURE PLANS

Finally, the clients' future plans regarding their problems and needs are discussed. This discussion should be in a positive, optimistic, and affirmative tone (Tolson, Reid, and Garvin 2002). Several questions should be addressed. How does the client plan to maintain changes in each of the areas addressed? How will he or she approach obstacles that may arise in continued performance of the tasks? Are caregivers or the service providers involved aware of the elderly person's future plans? In discussing these questions, the practitioner's overall demeanor should be supportive and positive.

CHAPTER 8

CASE MANAGEMENT

THE CURRENT INCREASE in the older adult population continuing to live in the community is leading to an increased demand for community- and home-based services. Case management has been developed as an approach to assist clients in accessing and coordinating services. This chapter will provide an overview of case management and show how it can be implemented using a task-centered approach. First, an initial definition of case management will be given, followed by a brief summary of its history. The remainder of the chapter will focus on the task-centered case management model and case examples that illustrate how the model is implemented.

DEFINING CASE MANAGEMENT

"Would-be customers must have precisely the right things wrong with them and the right things right, as well as the correct personal characteristics, in order to receive a given service. Further, this consumer must be well-informed, persistent, and lucky to thread the maze many times to find the different agencies that deliver all of the services being sought" (Dinerman 1992:2). This quote describes well how a potential client might see a service system in which delivery, access, and availability vary greatly in type of client, type of need, type of service, and geographic location. Case management is often seen as a response to this somewhat disordered service delivery system. Yet, defining case management is an intricate venture. An initial definition can be given as follows: Case management is a mechanism of linking and coordinating services for clients with multiple needs. It consists of a "set of logical steps and a process of interaction within a service network which assure that a client receives needed services in a supportive, effective, efficient, and cost-effective manner" (Weil and Karls 1985:2). It can be called a boundary-spanning activity to guarantee the "continuity of care across services . . . over time" (Rubin 1987:212). Beyond these basic definitions there are many ways to define case management, as further discussion will show.

HISTORY OF CASE MANAGEMENT

The term case management is presently enjoying great popularity. In its current form, the terminology stems from the early 1970s. However, one of the concept's main components, case coordination, has had a long tradition in social work. Weil and Karls trace the roots of case coordination back to 1883, when Massachusetts established America's first board of charities to "coordinate public human services and to conserve public funds used in the care of the poor and the sick" (1985:4). The settlement houses as well as the Charity Organization Societies included case coordination, and Mary Richmond (1917) already pointed to the importance of a more client-oriented form of interagency coordination. In the 1920s, child guidance clinics explored team approaches to deliver and coordinate services. "One-stop multiservice centers" were established in Los Angeles following World War II (Weil and Karls 1985). The emergence of the various current forms of case management was a response to the rapid growth of human service programs in the 1960s and 1970s. While the availability of services expanded considerably, their funding primarily through categorical channels resulted in a fragmented, uncoordinated, and complex service system (Intagliata 1982). Professionals began to recognize the barriers this posed for clients facing complex problems requiring them to negotiate with multiple different programs. Since the early 1970s, federal, state, and local governments have initiated several demonstration projects to improve service coordination (Rubin 1987). The demonstration projects differed in various ways, such as funding, services delivered or coordinated, and the level and locus of organization. Most projects included case management and expanded community-based services (Austin 1988). Models of case management have since spread to a wide array of services and to diverse client populations.

According to Moxley, the emergence of case management in its current form has been advanced by six distinct factors, namely: "(1) the impact of deinstitutionalization on human service delivery, (2) decentralization of community services, (3) the presence . . . of client populations with significant problems of social functioning, (4) the recognition of the crucial role social support and social networks play . . . (5) fragmentation of human services, and (6) the growing concern with cost effectiveness" (1989:12). The group of vulnerable clients in need of long-term support is growing, and the fragmented service system is becoming increasingly more complex and difficult for clients to negotiate. This is reflected in the ongoing interest in case management as a boundary-spanning approach to ensure that clients with multiple and complex problems will receive appropriate and timely services (Rubin 1987).

CORE FUNCTIONS OF CASE MANAGEMENT

Several ways of structuring case management have been presented in the literature. There seems to be a general agreement among all models on the core functions of case management. Some overt differences between the models are more reflections of individual ways of compartmentalizing the functions than distinctly dissimilar models. All models presented in the literature are flexible and adaptable to the various external and internal factors that guide the practice of case management in different settings. Included in the most basic models are screening, assessment, planning, linking, monitoring, and evaluation (Austin 1983; Moxley 1989; Rubin 1987). A more extensive model encompasses client identification and outreach, assessment, service planning and resource identification, linking, service implementation and coordination, monitoring, advocacy, and evaluation (Weil 1985). A more complex and inclusive model of case management core functions was presented by Rothman (1992, 1994). It is based on a survey of case managers and the synthesis of more than one hundred studies on case management. This empirically based model includes intake, assessment, setting goals, intervention planning and resource identification, linking to formal and informal systems, monitoring, reassessment and evaluation, and the intermittent functions of counseling and therapy, advocacy, and interagency coordination.

The comprehensiveness of a case management program can be evaluated by its intensity, breadth, and duration (Applebaum and Austin 1990). The larger the caseload of a case manager, the lower the intensity of the practitioner-client relationship. Models emphasizing only assessment, brokerage, or gatekeeper functions usually have considerably higher case loads and less intensive practitioner-client contacts. Programs that utilize clinical or therapist case managers generally are characterized by smaller caseloads and a more intensive practitioner-client relationship. The component of breadth refers to the range of services a case manager can coordinate and provide. Some programs are limited to the services the agency has to offer while others permit case managers to coordinate or provide a comprehensive range of services. Finally, one can distinguish between short-term and long-term programs. Some short-term programs include only assessment and linkage, and cases are terminated immediately after successful linking to relevant services. Long-term models, on the other hand, include an ongoing monitoring, coordination of services, and linkage to new services as new needs arise.

CONCEPTUALIZATION OF CASE MANAGEMENT

Several requirements impose restraints on the structure and function of case management. Case management must be flexible to react to the uniqueness of clients and to the timing and variance of their problems. Clients' independence should be a prime consideration. Clients should be encouraged to actively participate in the case management process. Rothman (1994) further delineates components an intervention for highly vulnerable clients must address. He suggests that the main goals are community living and psychosocial enhancement since the focus of case management is on caring rather than on curing. The service structure of the case management intervention should be longitudinal, community-based, and extend across a wide range of resources. Therefore, practice should emphasize support and skill development as well as environmental interventions that are concurrently based on micro and macro practice perspectives.

A distinction can be made between case management as a service and case management as a system. The service component refers to the practice tasks involved in the implementation of a case plan and comprises the tasks and skills a case manager has to use to move a client from intake through implementation and coordination of services. In its totality it includes all activities of case manager, client, service providers, and others involved. The case management system embodies a practice component as well as the resources, arrangements, and administrative systems required to implement a case plan. O'Connor (1988) applies Bronfenbrenner's scheme of environmental levels to the case management system, distinguishing between the micro, meso, exo, and macro levels. Case managers have to attend simultaneously to these different levels. Directly working with a client (micro level), a case manager might have to connect to community resources (meso level) in a way that is governed by structures set forth by the agency (exo level) and consider a client's social and economic environment (macro level).

In addition, case management can be viewed as part of the service delivery system. It is shaped by this system, but the activities of a case manager also serve as a "systems intervention tool" (Austin 1990:399). Through this function the delivery system is influenced by referrals, allocation of resources, and case and systems advocacy.

Goals of case management can be both client oriented and system oriented (Applebaum and Austin 1990). Client-oriented goals include ensuring that services are meeting the elderly person's needs, improving access to services, supporting caregivers, and bridging care systems. System-oriented goals affect the care delivery system and are concerned with the development of services, quality and efficiency of services, effective coordination, adequate targeting, and controlling costs. Client- and system-oriented goals can be contradictory, and the client's best interest may not coincide with the service delivery system's interests. As a gatekeeper to resources, the case manager's responsibility is the well-being of the client and also controlling costs for the system. These competing demands have led to criticism as to whether case managers can balance client- and system-oriented goals.

Case management programs differ in their location within the service delivery system. Programs can be found in agencies on the state, area, or local level. Another factor in the conceptualization of case management is the organizational setting in which a program operates. The freestanding agency is relatively autonomous. Having case management as its main function, it can concentrate on this purpose and give less attention to other interorganizational struggles. But the advantage of autonomy has its limitations, e.g., establishing credibility and maintaining funding can be challenging. A second organizational setting is the special unit in a planning agency, as in many Area Agencies on Aging that provide case management programs. The advantage of this arrangement is the visibility of the agency, easy access for clients, and the agency's influence on other providers. Interorganizational and political requirements and conflicts with service providers stemming from other agency activities might be a disadvantage. Another variation in the organizational setting is the information and referral agency. The benefit of this arrangement is that the agency is not seen as a threatening competitor. Workers in these agencies have extensive knowledge of the services available and are known for documenting and participating in filling service gaps. A frequent approach is the special unit in an institution or multifunction agency. For example, hospitals, multipurpose senior centers, and assisted living and nursing home facilities may coordinate services through case management. Advantages of this arrangement include the established reputation of the larger organization and conceivably better access to services. Some demonstration projects have established consortiums of provider agencies to coordinate services. Such projects have facilitated access to the resources of the respective agencies and built supportive bases. Problems have included a limited period of funding, ambiguity about program responsibility, and conflicting expectations.

ROLES OF CASE MANAGERS

Moxley (1989) identifies several direct service roles case managers commonly assume. As implementor, a case manager completes tasks on the client's behalf. While this is a very directive function, it can be helpful to clients in crisis situations. In the role of teacher, the case manager helps clients to develop skills. The process typically includes modeling, role-playing, and performance feedback followed by transfer to real-life situations. A common example for the case manager as guide is the process of advising and linkage to a service. Making the knowledge of the service system available to a client is the function of the information specialist. Finally, as supporter, the case manager enables the client to engage in self-advocacy through supportive activities. In her discussion of service provision, Weil (1985) further breaks down these roles based on a case manager's responsibility to the client, the service network, and the case management program. She identifies the roles of case managers to be broker, diagnostician, planner, community organizer, system boundary spanner, service monitor, system modifier, record keeper, evaluator, consultant, colleague and collaborator, service coordinator, counselor/therapist, expediter, problem-solver, and advocate.

THE CASE MANAGEMENT TEAM

In many instances an individual case manager is interacting with the client(s) on an ongoing basis. He or she carries out most, if not all, tasks relating to intake, assessment, case planning and implementation, and monitoring. Often, however, this individual case manager has the backing of a case management team. Such a team can include professionals from the professions of social work, nursing, home health care, and others. The case management team may deliberate on each case, may have regular case conferences, or may convene to discuss selected cases. Different team members may assume distinct roles in the case management process. For instance, an intake specialist may collect initial client information, another professional may conduct the multidimensional assessment, and a third case manager may follow up with accessing, coordinating, and monitoring service delivery.

Several studies evaluated the integration of case managers into hospitals and physician practices. Netting and Williams (1999) present a model in which geriatric case managers are integrated into physician practices. These nurse/social work case management teams conducted in-home assessments and brokered and coordinated client services. Anker-Unnever (1999) describes a similar project in which case managers worked in close partnership with primary care physicians. She points to "physician ownership" as one of the primary factors of successful collaboration. The physicians participating in this collaborative model were involved in determining the patient selection criteria, designing the screening instruments, developing a protocol for monitoring, and selecting care pathways.

Families play an important role in caregiving for elderly persons. Partaking in case management can be a part of typical family caregiving activities. As a part of the client's system of support, families can also be included as members of the case management team or even as case managers themselves. Projects in which family members were trained as case managers have led to successful outcomes. A study by Seltzer and her colleagues, for example, found that family members trained as case managers performed significantly more case management tasks than caregiving family members who received only the regular caregiving supports (Seltzer et al.1992).

TASK-CENTERED CASE MANAGEMENT MODEL

We provided an overview of the way case management has been conceptualized. The remainder of the chapter will focus on a task-centered approach to case management with elderly clients. The task-centered case management model adapts the basic methods set forth to case management with elderly clients in need of multiple services. As task-centered case management evolved, features were added, such as modular interventions and parallel functions that could also enhance the basic model.

DEVELOPMENT OF THE MODEL

The model was developed to meet the needs of the frail elderly in the community, a group in need of a variety of services. The clear structure of the model and its emphasis on client participation in making and implementing decisions was considered beneficial for such clients. Although case management is of long-term nature and task-centered practice is a brief service approach, they supplement each other well. The short-term nature of the task-centered approach is useful to case management since planning and making decisions needs to be accomplished within a brief, clearly defined time frame. At the same time, case managers continue to work with clients over extended periods of time, monitoring their continued needs and the implementation and delivery of services. As new needs arise, they can be addressed using time-limited strategies.

The model was developed and first implemented in a midsized urban hospital (Naleppa and Reid 1998, 2000). (The case examples presented at the end of the chapter were drawn from this program.) Three social work case managers served a caseload of approximately eighty primarily frail elderly clients who were living in the community. All three case managers in the team were social workers with graduate degrees. While clients usually were assigned to only one of the case managers, the team met for case consultations and supervision on a weekly basis. In this activity, the team was assisted by nurses, discharge planners, home health care workers, and physicians as needed. An ethics committee consisting of physicians, nurses, directors of the social work and nursing departments, and the three case managers met on an ad hoc basis to consult on cases that posed ethical dilemmas. The case management team had a set of guidelines to decide when to refer to this ethics committee.

The average age of clients was 83, and the average length of stay in the case management program was approximately eight months. Referrals to the program came from the hospital provider system (24 percent), community agencies (38 percent), physicians in the community (29 percent), and previous clients (9 percent). About half of the cases referred to the program were accepted, the other cases were referred to more appropriate service providers or programs. To be eligible for services from this case management program, clients had to be at least 65 years of age and live in the catchment area of the hospital. They had to be at risk of hospital or institutional care, which was very broadly defined and included clients who were referred from other hospital units (e.g., discharge planning), referrals from primary care physicians, or a collaborative decision by the team of case managers.

The model was created through a series of development activities. After conducting a thorough review of the existing program, other similar programs, and the requirements of the local service delivery system, the team synthesized components of three different practice concepts into one case management intervention model (see table 8.1): (1) the empirically based case management core functions (Rothman 1991, 1994), (2) the task-centered model (Reid 1992, 1978; Reid and Epstein 1977), and (3) the notion of modular treatment (Dupree 1994; Liberman, Mueser, and Glynn 1988).

TABLE 8.1 FOUNDATIONS OF THE MODEL

	CASE MANAGEMENT MODEL	TASK-CENTERED MODEL	MODULAR TREATMENT
Authors	Rothman 1991, 1994	Reid 1978, 1992, 1997	Dupree 1994, Reid 1998; Liberman, Mueser, and Glynn 1988
Brief Description	Long-term approach of assisting clients to access, coordinate, and monitor services. Consists of empirically derived core functions.	Brief-treatment model based on clearly defined and structured steps collaboratively undertaken by practitioner and client.	Use of treatment modules describing ways to intervene in specific, clearly defined problems or situations.
Functions of Model (abbreviated)	Intake and assessment Care planning Implementation Monitoring Reassessing Terminating Several additional functions	Identify and select target problems Set goals Develop task alternatives Evaluate potential obstacles Select and contract on tasks Implement tasks Evaluate task accomplishments	Description of specific problem Literature and research on problem Description of intervention strategy
What it Contributed to New Model	Structure of case management; core functions for the initial model	Clearly described and structured intervention strategies that aided case manager and client	Task planners (modules) for typical problems encountered by elderly clients in case management

The model of case management core functions presented by Rothman (1991, 1994) guided the structure of this practice approach. It was chosen as the most complex and encompassing model presented, empirically based on the analysis of over one hundred case management programs. All core functions described are included in our current model and adjusted to fit our design requirements.

Another component of the model is based on the notion of modular treatment, which means that specific intervention modules are devised for particular problem situations (Dupree 1994; Liberman, Mueser, and Glynn 1988; Reid 1999). In the present approach, modular treatment incorporates both task-centered and non-task-centered methods, as will be made clear below.

One additional aspect that had to be addressed was the inclusion of the elderly person in making and implementing decisions related to his or her needs. As recipients of care, elderly clients should play an active role in directing efforts that have an impact on their life. The task-centered case management model sees the client-worker relationship as one of collaborative problem solving. Whenever possible, clients are included as active participants in the process of making and implementing decisions. The framework of maintaining autonomy in decision making, presented in chapter 6, may be especially important when working with frail elderly clients in case management.

THE INTERVENTION MODEL

The task-centered case management practice model consists of parallel practice functions, a core intervention model, and alternative intervention modules (see fig. 8.1).

At the core of the task-centered case management model are those practice activities that are carried out for all individual cases, including: access, intake, and assessment, case planning and implementation, monitoring, reassessment, and termination. The central parts of these core functions are implemented using task-centered strategies that have been adapted to the practice with at-risk frail elderly clients and to the structural requirements of case management.

ACCESS, INTAKE, AND ASSESSMENT Case managers actively reach out to clients in the community in several ways, including networking with local providers, distribution of program brochures, and collaboration with primary care physicians. Potential clients can be located through public outreach, relying on other agencies, formalizing the process of referral, specifying eligibility, or relying on word-of-mouth information by former clients. Intake is the step in which the first actual contact with a potential client occurs. The case manager activities of this phase can be summarized as prescreening potential clients for eligibility, clarifying the presenting problems and expectations of the client, specifying the services of the agency, and performing crisis intervention if necessary. If a person agrees to become a client,

FIGURE 8.1 THE TASK-CENTERED CASE MANAGEMENT MODEL

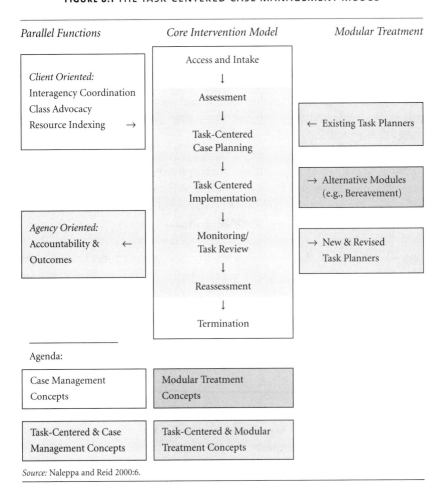

Source: Naleppa and Reid 2000:6.

the case can be activated. Engaging the client early on is an especially important part of building a trusting helping relationship in practice with elderly clients (Vourlekis and Greene 1992). For many clients it is important to arrange a rapid follow-up meeting and contact the client by phone beforehand (Rothman 1994).

During the initial contact, the clients' appropriateness for the program is determined through a brief assessment of their problems and their current involvement with other service providers. The program is explained, including the case manager's role and the importance of the client's choices. A home visit is set up if the client is considered appropriate for the program. During the first home visit a comprehensive multidimensional assessment is administered. This assessment guides the problem identification for the initial task planning. During this assessment session, task-centered case planning begins with collaboration on the initial problem assessment and problem exploration.

TASK-CENTERED CASE PLANNING The emphasis in case planning is on working with the client on defined problems and goals. The case management process is conducted in a way that maximizes the client's autonomy and favors decision making by the client. Only in extreme situations (e.g., where there may be an imminent risk to the elderly person or others or where required by law) is the principle of client centeredness modified. Essentially, case planning follows the basic procedures of the middle phase of the geriatric task-centered model (chapter 6). What follows is a summary of those procedures as they occur in a case management context.

In the first step, client and case manager collaboratively identify the client's problems. The identified problems are then summarized in an initial care plan. Making use of these initial problem definitions, client and case manager work toward defining the target goals. During this process, the case manager makes available all additional information that can aid in the decision-making process, for example, professional knowledge about the client's conditions and the availability of resources. Since problems in case management applications are frequently health related and usually require special services, the case manager needs to be well versed in both geriatric health issues and health and community services.

The client system may include caregivers, other family members, and different service providers may also be involved. Thus, the identification of problems may involve communication with a number of actors over a period of time; it is not always accomplished in a single session with the client. This may be particularly true if the cognitive functioning of the elderly person is impaired or is believed to be impaired.

For example, Mr. Ross, 83, who lived alone in a two-story house, was severely arthritic and suffered from a heart condition; he was referred by his daughter who lives in another state. On a recent visit she was "appalled" at the "deplorable condition" of the house. Her father's difficulty in negotiating stairs made it difficult for him to care for the house. As she described it, it was filthy and so badly in need of repair that it was in danger of being condemned. He was also becoming increasingly confused and forgetful, with the result that he was forgetting to take the medication for his heart condition. Someone, she said, needed to convince him to go to "some kind of home." She tried to talk him into this herself on her last visit, but without success. In her initial visit, the case manager found the house pretty much as the daughter had described it, but was informed by Mr. Ross that his only problem was lack of someone to help him with the cleaning. However, he was agreeable to have the case manager discuss his situation with the local clinic that was treating him for his health problems. Ultimately, in this case identifying and formulating the problem involved contacts with Mr. Ross, the daughter, a nurse from the clinic, a neighbor who drove him to the clinic, and the local housing authority. Finally, Mr. Ross and the case manager agreed to work on getting help with house cleaning, house repair, and medical attention (through a visiting nurse.)

After selecting the target problems, they are prioritized, i.e., a determination is made about the order in which they will be addressed. Again, the client's involvement is a prime consideration, but the case manager may express concerns about the way a client ranks target problems. This a frequent issue in case management practice, since clients may be cognitively impaired, and because of this or other reasons they may not give, in the practitioner's judgment, sufficient attention to issues critical to their well-being. But as with Mr. Ross, it is important to take the client's priorities seriously and to try to negotiate differences. Cognitive and other impairments notwithstanding, older people are usually responsive to rethinking priorities if the reasons requiring it are explained. Thus, Mr. Ross was able to see that something needed to be done about the condition of the house when he learned that it might be condemned.

After agreement on the target problems has been reached, the problems should be specified as clearly as possible, stated in terms of conditions to be changed, and summarized into a "problem statement," which may consist of a listing of needs, as in the Ross case.

Next, the client's short-term and long-term goals in relation to the target problem are established. Goals should be problem-directed, specific, measurable, stated in achievable objectives, and include a time frame. These goals should be specified as a condition to be reached, not as the activity to be undertaken. Rather than stating a goal in terms of services delivered, a specific client status should be determined as goal. If possible, the goals should be broken down into subgoals. In setting the goals, a client's needs, right to self-determination, and the fiscal constraints of the service system have to be carefully evaluated and balanced. The complete problem and goal statement includes at least one target problem, an estimation of the time needed to solve the problem, and the final goal.

Subsequently, possible tasks are formulated together with the client. All task alternatives are evaluated and at least one task is selected. The client must be willing to participate in carrying out the selected task or agree to have the case manager or others carry it out. Task implementors may also be other service providers who may be organized into a case management team. Thus, in the case of Mr. Ross, the visiting nurse agreed to the task of giving Mr. Ross his medication on her weekly visits and checking on how much he had used during the week. The neighbor (and friend) who drove Mr. Ross to the clinic volunteered to help with the house repairs.

Another activity during sessions is the clarification of potential obstacles. Through analyzing the context, the case manager can assist the client in identifying and resolving potential obstacles. Tasks are selected that avoid the obstacles or plans are made to deal with them.

In case management, obstacles often involve difficulty in negotiating the service system. Thus, Mrs. Green's hearing may not be acute enough to make a phone call to a service provider, or mobility problems may prevent her from attending a support group.

TASK IMPLEMENTATION The tasks established in the session are carried out between sessions. Tasks in case management often include formal or informal linkages, but they can also be of a behavioral or psychosocial nature. Formal linking is the process of connecting clients with resources available in the formal service delivery system. Beyond matching client and service, professional linking includes doing whatever is needed to guarantee that a client obtains the needed resources. This can include sharing information about the service, providing encouragement for using it, preparing the client through role play and modeling, putting together a checklist of needed items, completing all necessary paperwork, arranging for transportation, and accompanying clients on visits to health and other facilities. Acting as liaison between client and agency, the case manager often gets in touch with a provider and initiates the service contact. Another possible task for case managers is to mediate any conflicts between clients and service providers. By providing emotional and material support, informal networks supplement formal services. When case managers mobilize support networks, they should focus on enhancing the clients' existing strengths and capacities. Activities of informal linking include sharing the elderly person's case plan with the caregivers, educating the family about services, and assessing its capability and willingness to assist in care and support. Other interventions include the clarification of the supportive functions the family is expected to take over and reaching an agreement between the elderly person and network members about their commitments. The case manager should be available to mediate possible conflicts.

MONITORING THROUGH TASK REVIEW Monitoring is conducted through the ongoing review of task accomplishments. The case manager initiates a review of the target problems and tasks at the beginning of each successive contact with the client. Together client and case manager examine whether any changes in the problem occurred and rate the progress made. The completion of the task is collaboratively reviewed and is rated using the task rating scales. Those tasks that were achieved are emphasized, especially if they were carried out by the elderly client. If a task requires any further work, obstacles and their contexts are reexamined, and the plan for carrying out the task is changed if necessary. Target problems as well as tasks agreed to by caregivers, service providers, and others are also reviewed, sometimes in brief contacts or over the phone.

In addition to monitoring through problem and task reviews, practitioner and client may utilize other approaches to measure progress. In doing so, priority should be given to formal ways of monitoring that emphasize the adequacy, quality, and outcome of the services provided. The participants, times, tools, and format for monitoring should be determined beforehand and can be included in the case plan. On the client level, monitoring should focus on the client's condition, in order to make decisions about maintaining, increasing, decreasing, or terminating services. Regular client feedback should be elicited on the satisfaction with outside services he or she receives. Monitoring should evaluate whether services are delivered and implemented by the formal and informal systems according to the case plan.

REASSESSMENT The case management function of reassessment overlaps to some extent with monitoring—in some case management models, it is considered part of that practice function. Similar to monitoring, a formal reassessment should consider the implementation of the case plan, progress in the client's condition, advancement toward the goals set at the beginning, and the validity of plan and services; reassessments should be conducted on a regular basis. Parts of the assessment instrument can be readministered to evaluate changes. In extended forms of task-centered case management, a formal reassessment is completed every three months. The current care plan is discussed with the client and is updated. This includes a review of the current problem status and the progress made through task work and an assessment of the continued need for case management. All task plans of the period covered are reviewed. The reassessment should culminate in a revision of the case plan.

TERMINATION If case management is no longer needed, the case is terminated. The collaborative decision by the client and case manager to terminate service is based on a reassessment of the client's needs. It includes an evaluation of whether all the client's problems that had been identified have been sufficiently addressed and whether any problems have developed that require further attention. The client's reactions to termination are explored, and he or she is assured that the service of case management can be restarted at any time. If appropriate, the case manager maintains periodic contact with the client.

PARALLEL INTERVENTION FUNCTIONS

The practitioner attends to a second set of functions parallel to the core intervention model. These activities are carried out on behalf of the clients, but contrary to the core intervention model, no explicit client agreement is required. The purpose of such parallel activities can be either client-oriented or agency-oriented. Any activities directly aimed at solving the client's problems are implemented following the practice strategies of the core intervention model.

RESOURCE INDEXING One of the most important skills of a case manager is to match the client with available, appropriate, acceptable, and accessible resources. A client-oriented parallel function of the task-centered case management model is resource indexing. In addition to utilizing the available case management resource guides, case managers track available resources, eligibility criteria, and procedures to access them. A personal resource index typically includes address and phone number, names of contact persons, office hours, services and fees, and quality and reliability of services. Newly identified resources are added to the resource index on an ongoing basis. One section of the index tracks unavailable but needed resources and is used for class advocacy purposes. Information from the index is made available to the client during the task planning process to assist in locating resources and developing tasks. Ongoing development of treatment modules is another way in which case managers can develop systematic data on available resources (see part III). Finally, the Internet and Web-based search engines have developed into very useful resource tools for gerontological practitioners (see appendix).

INTERAGENCY COORDINATION A second parallel function that indirectly benefits the client is interagency coordination. Credibility and positive public relations with service providers have to be maintained deliberately and consistently. Case managers attend to this function through activities that build public relations with the professional community, e.g., through engagements and professional outreach activities. This also includes regularly communicating with other providers about client services and providing information to outside agencies about the case management program. Case management programs enhance coordination between agencies by sharing client information, setting up interagency task forces and teams, establishing joint funding, making mutual referrals, coordinating case conferences, and working out interagency service agreements.

CASE AND CLASS ADVOCACY In case advocacy, a practitioner takes on tasks to influence a system on behalf of a particular client. For example, a case manager may attempt to get a meals-on-wheels program to extend its geographical range to serve a particular client.

Class advocacy goes beyond the direct need of one client to efforts at inducing changes at the systems level that benefit the whole target population. No explicit client agreement is requested since class advocacy is not directly connected to an individual case. An example of class advocacy would be the active involvement in the local Alzheimer's association. Such involvement is important since the case manager, through his or her extensive experience with the service delivery system, has a unique knowledge of inadequate services or injustices experienced by the client population served.

The goal of both advocacy approaches is to secure adequate and accessible resources. As advocate, a case manager uses skills of discussion, persuasion, negotiation, confrontation, and conflict resolution. Skills should be applied judiciously and careful consideration should be given to consequences for the clients and the agency.

ACCOUNTABILITY AND OUTCOMES An important agency-oriented function of case managers is to measure their performance and the outcomes of their interventions. The task-centered approach fosters easy access to such information. As an integral part of the intervention model, task completion and problem changes are routinely evaluated and rated by case manager and client. Collaboratively they establish achievements made and rate task completion for each task on a four-point scale. Changes in the problem status are measured using problem change ratings. Together, case manager and client evaluate the current status of the problem and compare it to the condition before the intervention. Using a ten-point scale they rate the changes in the problem. This dual focus on measuring the process (progress in task work) and the outcome (measuring change in problem status) is especially useful for work with elderly case management clients since changes often do not occur simultaneously with the implementation of the tasks. For example, while all tasks relevant to a nursing home placement may have been success-fully implemented, it may take several months until the actual move occurs. Measures of task progress will indicate that advances were made, while the measures of problem status may not yet indicate a change.

INTERVENTION MODULES

An intervention module is a set of practice methods addressed to a particular problem. In task-centered case management modules augment the core methods of the approach. As noted, two types of treatment modules are used.

TASK PLANNERS The most frequently used type of treatment module is the task planner. A task planner describes a particular problem and presents a menu of possible tasks (including tasks with research support) that could be used to address the problem. Part III of this book provides an extensive array of such task planners. Task planners are descriptive rather than prescriptive, i.e., they serve as a guiding tool for developing tasks, but need to be adapted carefully to the individual client and the unique problem situation.

In task-centered case management task planners are developed on an ongoing basis using a stepwise procedure. As a regular part of their record keeping, case managers keep track of all problems that have been addressed. They also document all related tasks that have been implemented. Periodi-cally, case managers use this documentation to develop new task planners. The first step is an examination of already existing practice modules. If a task planner already exists, it is updated with any new information. If a task plan-ner is lacking, a new one is developed from the case material. Next, a litera-ture search is conducted to determine empirical support for tasks used in other cases as well to identify other tasks (and related research) used for the problem. Literature concerning the problem itself may also be examined. Information from both sources, the case manager's own documentation and the literature, is then integrated into a new task planner.

With this procedure, a set of task planners is developed that is reflective of the agency setting and the local practice environment. This process enables the practitioners to systematically share their experience with all members of the case management team. The task planners also facilitate the training of new case managers. Among the task planners that were developed in the hos-pital-based case management program discussed earlier were those concern-ing resource and linkage tasks, nursing home placement procedures, initiat-ing a social support network, establishing protective services, and care coordination initiated by family members.

OTHER MODULES There may be practice situations in which case managers will decide to depart from the task-centered model. For example, they may decide that clients wish help for issues of loss and bereavement, to work through their feelings in the session with more intensity than is provided by task planners concerning such issues (Reid 2000). For such cases, they may develop an alternative module that can be used for this purpose while returning to the task-centered model for other problems.

CASE EXAMPLE 1: MRS. WALKER

Mrs. Walker is an 82-year old widowed woman who contacted the case management program at the recommendation of a friend. The client's fear of "being stuck" in her upstairs apartment and indications by the landlord that he would like to sell the house prompted her to call the case manager for advice. During this phone call the case manager explained the program and determined the client's appropriateness for case management. At this time the case manager also established that the client was not eligible for or served by other case management programs. They set up a first home visit for the following week.

After introducing herself and providing the client with additional information about the case management program, the practitioner gave an overview of the practice approach she would like to take. She discussed the roles that she and the client would assume in planning and implementing care-related decisions and emphasized the importance of the client's active involvement. During this home visit, the intervention planning process began with the administration of a multidimensional assessment instrument. The client lived alone in a rented apartment. She had no direct family or caregiver involvement, but her landlord, who is a close friend, helped her with many chores. Mrs. Walker perceived her health to be in good condition although she had problems with arthritis, hypertension, and the effects of a recent total hip replacement. She had some mobility problems, especially with walking stairs. A walker and a cane assisted her in moving around. During the assessment, the client identified three areas of need that she would like to address: (1) the need for a housing alternative, (2) lack of adequate transportation, and (3) inadequate prescription coverage. In addition, the case manager identified the client's lack of advanced directives as an area of concern. After exploring these problems and selecting the target problems, the case manager asked the client to prioritize the needs, and they collaboratively developed the initial problem statement (see boxes 8.1 and 8.2 for itemized summaries). No tasks were developed during the first home visit.

BOX 8.1 DEVELOPMENT OF PROBLEM STATEMENT

PROBLEM STATEMENT	GOAL	PID*
1: Unable to get up stairs, house sale	Find senior housing	Mrs. W
2: Lack of transportation	Obtain senior bus pass	Mrs. W
3: Not always taking meds. due to cost	Pursue prescription coverage	Mrs. W
4: Lack of advanced directives	Establish health care proxy	CM

*PID: "Problem Identified" indicates who initially identified the problem

---

At the next home visit, case manager and client began to work on the first problem related to the client's access to the second-floor apartment. Increasing difficulties with walking up and down the stairs led the client to express interest in senior housing alternatives. At the client's suggestion, the case manager provided information on the different alternatives for senior housing. After reviewing her options, the client decided that a senior apartment complex would be the most appropriate living arrangement.

The next set of tasks related to determining the availability of apartments, a subtask that was assumed by the case manager, and applying for the apartment, a task that was completed collaboratively. Client and case manager also visited the senior apartment complex. All tasks related to the need of a housing alternative were successfully carried out, with the exception of a moving-related task. Although the client had been accepted into an apartment, she was put on a waiting list. Thus, she was not yet able to implement this task.

A second problem area related to transportation. The client had purposely let her driver's license lapse and relied on her friends for transportation. Dissatisfaction with depending on other people prompted her to inquire about transportation options. The first task was to call and request an application for using the senior transportation system. After the client received the application package, case manager and client collaboratively completed and submitted it. In reviewing potential obstacles to using the senior transportation system, Mrs. Walker said she felt insecure about how to use it. The case manager and Mrs. Walker rehearsed how to use the senior bus system, and she successfully started using it.

BOX 8.2 SUMMARY OF TASKS - MRS. WALKER

PROBLEM # AND TASK	SUGGESTED	CARRIED OUT	TCR*
1.1: Review alternative living options and select one	CM	Mrs. W and CM	4
1.2: Complete and submit application for senior apartmt.	Mrs. W	Mrs. W and CM	4
1.3: Tour the building and look at an apartment	CM	Mrs. W and CM	4
1.4: Move into senior apartment	Mrs. W	-	n
2.1: Call to request application for senior transportation	CM	Mrs. W	4
2.2: Complete and submit application	CM	Mrs. W and CM	4
3.1: Complete application for prescription plan	CM	Mrs. W and CM	4
3.2: Mail in application	CM	Mrs. W	4
4.1: No task was developed	-	-	-

*TCR "Task Completion Ratings": 4 = task completely achieved, 3 = substantially achieved, 2 = partially achieved, 1 = not achieved, n = unable to implement task.

The third goal was to establish a prescription coverage plan. Due to the costs of the drugs, the client was not taking her medications as prescribed. The case manager provided information on several options to reduce her costs. Tasks of completing and submitting an application for a prescription coverage program were successfully completed. During this home visit, the three-month reassessment was conducted. The case manager and Mrs. Walker reviewed the progress that had been made in the four areas identified in the initial assessment and then rated the changes in the status of each problem (see box 8.3).

In this case, the problem change scores were relatively low for all target problems, despite the high ratings on task completion. All major tasks for the first problem were carried out, but the new apartment was not yet available. Thus, no significant change in the problem status was reported. All tasks relating to the transportation problem were accomplished, but although the transportation pass was approved, the client had not yet received it at the time the problem changes were rated. Also, all tasks relating to prescription

---

BOX 8.3 PROBLEM CHANGE SCORES - MRS. WALKER

TARGET PROBLEM	PROBLEM CHANGE RATINGS *
1: Housing	6
2: Transportation	6
3: Prescription coverage	8
4: Advance directive	5

Notes: *Problem Change Scores at first reassessment: 1–2 = much worse, 3–4 = a little worse, 5 = no change, 6–7 = a little better, 8–9 = much better, 10 = not present or no longer a problem

---

coverage were completed, and the plan was approved. No change had occurred relating to the advance directives, since the client and case manager had not yet started working on this area. Three months later, at the next reassessment, problems related to transportation, prescription coverage, and advance directives were rated with a score of ten. Mrs. Walker was still waiting for an apartment. No change in the status of this problem had occurred. After rating Mrs. Walker's problems, the case manager compared the information to the existing relevant practice modules and updated them.

CASE EXAMPLE 2: THE MURPHY'S

Mr. Murphy is an 85-year-old white man who lives with his wife in the home they own. His physician referred him to the program. Medical conditions that limit Mr. Murphy's activities include the effects of a stroke he had the previous year (which resulted in paralysis on the right side of his body), arthritis, hypertension, and partial vision loss. He perceives his health to be in fair condition. Mr. Murphy is totally dependent on assistance with using a toilet, getting up from a chair, getting out of bed, moving around, housecleaning, preparing meals, and personal care. His adaptive equipment includes a wheelchair and a commode. The client shows no signs of significant cognitive decline. During the initial assessment, two areas of need were identified. The client required assistance in the areas of personal care and physical mobility in order to maintain his independence and his current level of mobility. Related to these needs was an indication by the caregiver that she needed some respite. While this need was not directly stated as a focus of

---

BOX 8.4 PROBLEM STATEMENT—MR. MURPHY

PROBLEM STATEMENT	GOAL	PID*
1. Needs personal care assistance	Maintain independence	Mrs. M
2. Decreasing mobility	Maintain present mobility	Mrs. M, CM
3. Insurance coverage unclear	Ensure reimbursement	Mrs. M
4. Reluctance to use wheel chair	Use adaptive equipment	Mr. and Mrs. M, CM

---

*PID: "Problem identified" indicates who initially identified the existence of the problem, CM = case manager

---

service, it was indirectly addressed through working on Mr. Murphy's problems. Two more target problems were identified during the course of service—questions about finances and insurance and Mr. Murphy's reluctance to use his wheelchair(see box 8.4).

The first set of tasks related to Mr. Murphy's need for help with personal care. Since his stroke and the following right-sided paralysis, he had not been able to walk independently. After further exploration and education about available services, a task to arrange for a meeting with a home health aide was collaboratively developed by the case manager and Mrs. Murphy. The task was agreed to by Mr. Murphy and was successfully completed by the case manager. A second task was for Mr. Murphy and his wife to discuss with a home health aide the nature, times, frequency, and costs of the service and to arrange for service delivery. Mr. Murphy and his wife completed this task during the visit of the home health aide (see box 8.5 for an overview).

A second target problem related to the client's physical mobility. His ability to walk and manage personal care needs without assistance had significantly decreased. It was established that he would benefit from medical adult day care, since the program's physical therapist would offer the needed assistance to maintain and possibly increase his physical mobility. It would also provide him with an opportunity to socialize and would offer some respite to his overburdened wife. Several tasks were implemented to address this target need. The first task, arranging the visit of a representative of the local medical adult day care service (including subtasks of calling the client to coordinate a time for the home visit and contacting the physician to ensure com-

BOX 8.5 SUMMARY OF TASKS—MURPHY CASE

TASK	SUGGESTED	CARRIED OUT	TCR*
1.1: Arrange for home health aide	CM, Mrs. M	CM	4
#1.2: Discuss with aide: times, frequency	CM, Mrs. M	Mr. & Mrs. M	4
#2.1: Arrange visit by adult day care services	C	CM	4
#2.3: Contact MD, ensure medical forms are completed	CM	CM	4
#2.4: Coordinate application, date, transportation	CM	CM, Mr. M	4
#2.5: Write list of questions for day care orientation	CM	Mrs. M	1*
#2.6: Attend medical adult day care for orientation	CM	Mr. and Mrs. M	4
#3.1: Obtain copy of health insurance policies	Mr. M	Mrs. M	1*/4
#3.2: Explore coverage and possible reimbursement	Mr. M	Mr. and Mrs. M, CM	4
#4.1: Try using adaptive equipment	CM	Mr. M	2/3/4*

*TCR "Task Completion Ratings": 4 = task completely achieved, 3 = substantially achieved, 2 = partially achieved, 1 = not achieved, n = unable to implement task,

*Obstacles encountered and comments:

#2.5 and #3.1: Mrs. M. initially forgot to carry out tasks.

#4.1: Some initial resistance to use adaptive equipment.

pletion of the required medical paperwork), was suggested and carried out by the case manager. As a next step, case manager and client coordinated the application process, set a starting date, and arranged for transportation. A final task was for Mr. Murphy to attend an orientation at the medical adult day care program and for the caregiver to write a list of questions to be addressed. They attended the meeting, but Mrs. Murphy had not written a list of questions. Nevertheless, the meeting went well, and Mr. Murphy enrolled in the program.

While working on the linkage with a home health aide, the wife was unclear about their insurance coverage. Mr. Murphy suggested two related tasks. His wife was to obtain a copy of the insurance policies before the next session. Since she forgot to do it, the task was initially not carried out. The second task, to review the policies and establish reimbursement for the service, was carried out after the wife obtained copies of the policies at the second attempt.

The last target problem related to the client's reluctance to utilize his wheelchair. He stated that he did not want to advertise his physical limitations and his dependence on others. The client's self-esteem seemed to be hindering an increase in his mobility. Using persuasion techniques, the case manager convinced the client to begin using the equipment at home, where only his wife could see him. The client started doing so after some further resistance. However, after a period of getting used to the wheelchair, Mr. Murphy began using it to move from his house door to the senior van that picks him up for adult day care.

Overall, eleven tasks were developed to address the four identified problems and most were successfully implemented. As box 8.6 indicates, the status of all target problems improved significantly over the course of service. The status of all four problems was rated as much better, or the problem areas were completely resolved.

In the context of this case, the particular role of the caregiver as a focus of the intervention should be mentioned. The primary focus of the interventions during the period covered was on problems relating to the personal and medical care of Mr. Murphy. The respite for the overburdened caregiver was only dealt with indirectly although it might have been beneficial to address it as a separate area of need. When working with elderly couples, it is often the case that one partner is referred to a service provider as the primary client. While many caregivers are involved in the sessions, attention is directed

---

BOX 8.6 PROBLEM CHANGE SCORES - MR. AND MRS. M.

TARGET PROBLEM	PROBLEM CHANGE SCORE*
1: Personal care	8
2: Physical mobility	8
3: Financial	10
4: Self-esteem/mobility	9

Notes: *Problem Change Scores at first reassessment: 1–2 = much worse, 3–4 = little worse, 5 = no change, 6–7 = little better, 8–9 = much better, 10 = not present

toward problems of the partner with the more obvious and urgent problems. As in this case, the focus of work may change after the most significant problems are addressed, and potential problems of the caregiver may need to receive more attention. If this occurs, practitioner, elderly person, and caregiver should recontract with the caregiver as focus of attention. The case manager should clearly express the reasons for recontracting and what the new contract entails. Explicit agreement of the client to the new contract should be elicited.

DEVELOPMENT THROUGH RESEARCH

Following principles of the design and development paradigm (D&D) (Rothman and Thomas 1994), the model was tested in a small-scale study. The purpose of the study was twofold: (1) to ascertain the promise of the model as a means of delivering services to the frail elderly in the community, and (2) to collect data that would inform the development of the model. As suggested by the D&D paradigm, a more definitive test of the model was planned and is currently in progress.

The summary below suggests some specific revisions that can be incorporated into the model. Other revisions suggested by the study have already been presented and will be noted briefly. The summary also completes our illustration, begun earlier in this chapter, of how systematic methods of designing and testing intervention models can be used to develop services for the elderly.

STUDY SAMPLE AND METHODS

The setting, a midsize urban hospital, and processes of model design were discussed earlier in the chapter. The field test was conducted with ten participants.

SAMPLE CHARACTERISTICS The median age of the participants was 84. This age is typical for a case management program with frail elderly clients and is consistent with the age of clients (noted earlier) served by the program at the field site. Of the frail elderly clients participating in the field test, seven were female and three were male. Nine of these clients were white, and one was African-American. Seven lived independently, one lived with her daughter, and two others lived with their wives. Caregivers participated in three cases.

In three other cases a family member or a close friend were involved in some of the sessions.

The cognitive level of functioning of the frail elderly clients was measured with the Global Deterioration Scale (Reisberg, Ferris, and De Leon 1982). On this seven-point scale, the average 2.0 GDS score of the participants indicates forgetfulness and very mild cognitive decline.

Overall, 55 target problems, an average of 5.5 per case, were addressed in the field trial. The target problems covered a wide range, including access and coordination of services, financial management, assistance with ADLs, medication management, addressing problematic family interactions, lack of socialization, behavioral problems, skills training, and establishing informal support systems.

PROCESS AND OUTCOME MEASURES Two methods of process analysis guided the evaluation of the field trial, informative event analysis and interpersonal process recall. All sessions were audiotaped. These recordings were listened to and reviewed for informative events and segments for the interpersonal process recall. The process analysis used an event-based format of content analysis (Reid and Bailey-Dempsey 1994). This type of content analysis focuses on "informative events"—incidents that are selected because they provide useful factual information about the model, raise questions, or provide new insights into the intervention process. The researcher selects informative events through an inductive process of reviewing the data (Reid 1985). The informative event analysis was structured by describing the antecedent of the event, the event itself, and the implications for the development of the model.

In addition, one event per case was further analyzed using Interpersonal Process Recall (IPR), a special technique of interviewing. The method was originally developed for the study of thought processes and later adapted to the study of interpersonal processes in training and psychotherapy (Elliott 1984, 1986; Kagan and Kagan 1990). Using the basic IPR method, a session is videotaped or recorded on audiotape. The recording is then reviewed independently by all participants, and a facilitator elicits comments on the process that are measured using structured or unstructured response categories. Significant events are then further analyzed. The IPRs in this study were based on tape recordings of sessions and were conducted by the researcher or a second facilitator familiar with the IPR method. Considering the strain placed on the elderly respondents and the fact that playing back the recording and asking questions is time consuming, brief session segments were selected, varying in length from seven to ten minutes. For each IPR, one

segment of a session recording was selected following a multistage procedure. The client IPRs were conducted in the clients' homes and included the
client and in some cases a caregiver.

First, the facilitator explained the procedures and played a section of the
tape to ensure the participants were able to hear it and to familiarize them
with the sound of their recorded voices. Clients were instructed to stop the
tape any time they wanted to comment. In addition, the facilitator stopped
the tape at predetermined points to ask prompting questions, such as: Do you
have suggestions how to do this better? The case manager IPRs followed the
same procedures. For the analysis the recording segments used and the
responses given during the IPR sessions were transcribed. The IPR events
were structured using the same outline as for the informative events described
above.

Data on task completion and problem changes were routinely collected as
part of the implementation of the model (see the Walker and Murphy cases).
Task completion was measured on a four-point scale on which the client and
the case manager collaboratively rated how well a particular task was accomplished. Problem change was measured on a ten-point scale on which client
and practitioner rated the actual change in the status of a client's particular
target problem.

PROCESS FINDINGS

After reviewing all session recordings, four problem areas were inductively
identified as important for improving the model, namely, clients with cognitive impairments, reminiscing clients, caregivers' participation, and practitioner-related issues.

CLIENTS WITH COGNITIVE IMPAIRMENT Based on Collopy's conceptual system of autonomy (1988, see ch. 5), a distinction can be made between decisional and executional autonomy, i.e., between making self-determined decisions and an autonomous execution of these decisions. Some elderly lose the
ability to execute certain tasks, but they are capable of autonomous decision
making. A problematic consequence is that they are often treated as having
lost the decisional capacities. On the other hand, a certain level of cognitive
functioning is needed to make decisions, limiting some clients in their decisional autonomy. As part of the model, the practitioners were asked to consider these two aspects of autonomy in the process of working with a client.
Several informative events and IPRs looked at how the implementation of

the model differed for clients with cognitive impairment. One client had a moderately severe cognitive decline, as measured by the GDS (Reisberg, Ferris, and De Leon 1982). Suffering from frontal lobe syndrome, he had sufficient long-term memory but little short-term memory. In one informative event, the client and the case manager were planning an extensive cleaning to prevent the house from being condemned. While the client had previously acknowledged the problem, he had forgotten what had been discussed. The case manager was leading the session, but always asked for the client's feedback. During the IPR, the case manager expressed that she was more directive than with other clients. This points to a limitation of a task-centered approach with clients whose cognitive impairment prevents them from adequately participating in the decision-making process. When clients' levels of functioning limit their participation in the process of decision making or executing activities, an effort should be made to elicit their feedback and agreement on the decisions made and the tasks to be implemented. The format of such an agreement will depend on the individual limitations. In two other events, clients identified and explored a problem but had forgotten it when the problem was brought up in a later session. When a client's cognitive condition varies, the practitioner has to consider whether to work on problems the client acknowledged when he or she was cognitively aware or only on those the client acknowledges at the present time. In either case, the practitioner should stay within the client-centered framework of the model. As a first step, the problem should be reintroduced, further explored, and the client's agreement obtained. If this is not possible, the case manager may need to use a more directive approach. Another option is to reintroduce the topic in a later session if a delay would not increase the severity of the problem unnecessarily or cause an ethical conflict. Providing the client with a written list of the target problems (needs) and the tasks seemed to be especially helpful for clients with varying cognitive conditions.

REMINISCING AND REFOCUSING While reminiscing is a common activity, its therapeutic use is not part of the model tested. Reminiscence can assist in establishing rapport and assessing previous attempts to address a problem, and it can provide the client with "respite" during the session. Brief episodes of reminiscence should be accepted, but the primary focus of work should be on the here and now. A review of the audio recordings revealed no pattern of antecedents for reminiscing, except that case managers asked questions or opened the communication to input from the client. The informative event analysis and IPR yielded useful information on dealing with reminiscing clients. It may be helpful to attempt immediately to redirect clients who reminisce repetitiously and are not receptive to refocusing to the here and now. Examples of successful refocusing include sentences that lead back to the topic, such as "Before we started talking about this," or a direct refocusing on the topic, such as "How are you planning to get things done around the house?" The practitioner should clearly lead back to the topic and ensure that the client has time to leave the past and reenter the present. A pattern could be identified that one- or two-sentence communication sequences by the practitioner were followed by continued reminiscing, but the clients stayed in the present after longer sequences. Reminiscing may pose a limitation for utilizing a task-centered case management model. Clients who repetitiously reminisce require the case manager to be more leading and directive. The case manager has to make a determination on an individual basis whether such clients are able to participate in the process of deciding on and carrying out activities related to their needs and may need to involve a caregiver or legal guardian in the decision-making process. If such a person is missing in the client's life, the case manager should initiate the process of establishing such a linkage.

CAREGIVERS' PARTICIPATION All cases involving caregivers were reviewed for information on using the approach with caregivers. In addition, a number of IPR sessions covered sessions with the caregivers' participation. Several events revealed a pattern of neglecting the elderly person in favor of a faster process. In one case including a caregiver, an elderly woman, Mrs. R., slowed down the process because she needed time to understand what was talked about. After she started to reminisce, the case manager shifted her focus to the caregiver, neglecting Mrs. R. The case manager and caregiver collaboratively developed a task and presented it to Mrs. R. who was hesitant to accept it. Generally, practitioners should not emphasize work with the caregiver over working with the care recipient simply because progress may be faster when doing so. This would be contrary to the model's emphasis on maximizing the elderly person's inclusion in the process of making and executing decisions. Clients capable of participating in the decision-making process and of executing tasks should be included in all phases of the work. The event points to the need to strongly emphasize the elderly person's involvement when caregivers participate in the session.

A second issue relating to caregivers' participation was the question of how to approach separate sessions with one member of the client system. Sometimes a separate session may be carried out with one partner of a client system. One IPR was based on a session with Mrs. S., a caregiving wife. Her task was to talk with her husband about the possibility of nursing home placement. The task was rehearsed in the session, but Mrs. S. did not implement the task between sessions. This put the case manager in an awkward position at the beginning of next session, since she had not made provisions for noncompletion of the task, and the husband was not aware that this sensitive topic was discussed. The case manager could either not carry out a task review or ask the wife for consent to introduce the issue at that time. Rules for separate sessions should be determined up front and address the following questions: What are the rules for reviewing between-session tasks? Should a follow-up phone call be made preceding the joint session? How will confidential information from the separate session be handled? How can triangulation be avoided? How can the practitioner avoid keeping secrets from the client not participating in the separate session?

PRACTITIONER EVENTS A third element the analysis focused on was events helping to clarify practitioner-related issues. In this context, two areas were reviewed: the use of terminology and practitioners' directiveness.

The need to change the problem-oriented terminology when working with elderly clients was addressed in the initial practice guidelines. Most clients did not have difficulties with the terminology if the process of work was clarified in advance. However, two events indicated that some terms may be hard to understand for clients. The client and case manager IPRs indicate that a better explanation of the terminology or the use of language understandable to the client would have been helpful. Terminology that was identified as problematic included terms such as "prioritizing," "tasks," and "obstacles." Misunderstanding can be avoided by introducing the terminology to the client during the process of presenting the approach.

A consequential question when using a client-centered approach is how leading and directive the practitioner should be. One client indicated during the IPR: "When the case manager asked me what steps do you think need to be taken together? I would have preferred the case manager to tell me what to do." The case manager responded in the IPR that she tried to involve the client in decisions, but the client often wanted her to be more directive than she wanted to be. While practitioners' directiveness varies according to client and situation, many clients prefer practitioners to be directive and tell them what to do. Yet, this is often not beneficial for the client since it may create undue dependency on the practitioner. If a client is cognitively aware and able to execute tasks but resistant to implement tasks, the practitioner should address the issue of independence with the client. The task-centered model suggests starting with small client tasks, which may be especially useful for such clients.

OUTCOME AND RESULTS The model includes a dual focus on evaluating outcomes through task completion ratings and through problem change scores. This has several benefits. Many problems can be addressed by tasks that lead to an immediate change in the problem status. Other problems may not immediately change although practitioner and client are successfully working to resolve them. For example, after acceptance to a waiting list for senior housing, it may take considerable time until the actual move occurs, as was noted in the Walker case presented earlier. In that case, successful task work did not lead to a problem change until later.

Beyond the mere completion of tasks, it was of special interest to see if there were relationships between who identified a problem, who initially suggested a task, who implemented a task, and the successful completion of that task (see box 8.7).

The first column in box 8.7 shows the relationship between who initially identified a target problem and the task completion rating. Those problems identified collaboratively showed the highest task completion ratings. Problems identified by clients or caregivers had a similar success rate, but problems identified by case managers led to the lowest task completion ratings. This last finding may have several reasons, including that clients are more motivated to work on problems *they* identify. The problems for which clients seek help

---

BOX 8.7 TASK COMPLETION RATINGS

MEAN TASK COMPLETION RATINGS BY SELECTED VARIABLES

	Need Identified by	Task Suggested by	Task Implemented by
Case Manager	2.94 (17)	3.57 (55)	3.92 (27)
Collateral/Shared	3.73 (16)	3.55 (13)	3.64 (31)
Care recipient	3.50 (47)	3.31 (19)	3.17 (28)
Caregiver	3.58 (13)	3.60 (6)	2.71 (7)
Grand Means	3.51	3.51	3.51
Total Tasks	(93)	(93)	(93)

Note: Values are based on mean ratings of tasks implemented in relation to a need. Clients and case manager collaboratively rated task completion. Tasks with a rating of n were not included in the calculation. Number of tasks are in ( ). If more than one task was carried out in relation to a target need, the mean completion rating for all tasks was calculated.

Task completion ratings: 4 = task completely achieved, 3 = substantially achieved, 2 = partially achieved, 1 = not achieved, n = no opportunity to implement task.

may be more urgent, thus provide more motivation, and fall into the category of client-identified problems. Furthermore, problems identified by the case manager in the field trial included personal hygiene, substance abuse, and lack of socialization, all areas a client might be resistant to work on.

Only a tenuous connection was revealed between task completion and who initially suggested the task. Tasks suggested by caregivers were the most likely to be completed, followed by those the case manager suggested, collaboratively developed tasks, and tasks initially suggested by the clients. Motivation may not be as influential as it is in the steps of identifying a problem and implementing a task, since "ownership" of the task alternative may no longer be clear after the process of deliberation. The findings also indicate that only tasks that are likely to be completed are selected, regardless of who initially suggested the task.

In regard to task implementation, almost all tasks of the case manager were completely achieved, leading to a mean completion score of 3.92. This should not be surprising since they "know the system" and are in a professional role. Shared tasks received the second highest scores. Care recipients' scores followed with a score of 3.17, indicating that the average task was at least substantially achieved. Excluding tasks that the care recipients were unable to complete due to circumstances beyond their control, i.e., that received a rating of "n", they successfully completed 70 percent of their tasks. The mean score for caregivers' task completion is the lowest, but the score was influenced in one case by a resisting caregiver.

Overall, these outcome findings can be regarded as positive. A typical task was at least substantially achieved and more than two-thirds of the tasks (72 percent) were completely achieved. While case managers show the highest mean task completion rating, the high mean completion rating of care recipients and shared tasks indicate that elderly clients can be successfully included in this step.

It was of particular interest to see whether the level of task completion had an effect on the problem change scores (see box 8.8). As seen in box 8.8, there is a clear progression of problem change scores with increasing task completion ratings. The higher the task completion rating, the more progress was made in alleviating a target problem. A positive relationship exists between the tasks as means of alleviating the problems and a change in the problem status. We also note that the mean problem change rating (7.7) was close to the "much improved" level of the problems scale. Of the fifty-five target needs, twenty-five were rated no longer a problem or much improved, and none of the cases became worse in their level of need. Moreover, in all cases except one the care recipient was able to remain in his or her residence.

BOX 8.8 PROBLEM CHANGE SCORES BY TASK COMPLETION RATINGS

TASK COMPLETION	MEAN PROBLEM CHANGE*	N (TASKS)
n	6.3	9
1	6.3	2
2	6.5	5
3	8.2	5
4	8.2	34
Total	7.7	55

Notes: *Mean problem change ratings: 1–2 = Much worse, 3–4 = Somewhat worse, 5 = No change, 6–7 = Somewhat improved, 8–9 = Much improved, 10 = No longer a problem. Clients and case managers independently rated the problem change. Presented is the mean of the two ratings.

Task Completion: 4 = task completely achieved, 3 = substantially achieved, 2 = partially achieved, 1 = not achieved, n = no opportunity to implement task or no task work. Clients and case managers collaboratively rated task completion.

STRUCTURAL ANALYSIS

Analysis of the cases from the point of view of the structure of the model yielded important revisions, which have already been presented in our earlier presentation of the model. These included developing parallel functions for the model—include resource indexing, interagency coordination, and class advocacy—and the notion of modular intervention.

The task-centered case management model tested in the field trial led to encouraging results. Task completion and problem change measures emphasized the positive potential of including elderly clients in all steps from identifying problems to suggesting and implementing tasks. It will always be a matter of capabilities, judgment, and preference who will implement which tasks, but practitioners should feel comfortable including elderly and frail elderly clients in these steps. The field trial also suggested that a task-centered approach can be successfully integrated into long-term case management for the frail elderly. Task-centered interventions provided an intensive period of service that helped clients work on immediate problems. Moreover, they helped clients actively participate in decision-making processes and in problem-solving activities. At the same time, the case management component maintained the necessary long-term time dimension required by the typical situations and problems of elderly clients.

Several suggestions can be made for the further development of the model. The process findings should be incorporated into the practice guidelines and addressed in future training. As part of further development, the effectiveness of the revised model should be eventually evaluated through a controlled study. Such a study should examine the effects of the model on frail elderly clients both with and without caregivers as well on clients at different levels of cognitive functioning.

CONCLUSION

Task-centered case management provides a well-defined structure and procedures for preserving and strengthening clients' autonomy. The practice model is sufficiently flexible to adapt to the unique autonomy requirements of each individual elderly client. For example, an elderly person may be limited in her ability to carry out certain decisions, but she still may be able to make those decisions. Another elderly person may be unable to come up with a plan of action, but she may be able to implement collaboratively developed tasks. In the first case, the practitioner using this model would enhance autonomy by eliciting the client's active involvement in identifying problems and developing tasks, but she may take a more leading role in carrying them out. In the second example, the case manager may be more leading in identifying problems and suggesting tasks, but she would still try to include the elderly client in their implementation. However, regardless of the level of the client's involvement, the case manager would elicit explicit agreement from the client before carrying out any steps of the model.

The model presented incorporates a systematic way of identifying and prioritizing clients' problems, and it facilitates the explication of problem-solving actions (tasks). This enables clients to actively participate in the intervention process. The systematic intervention process also assists the case manager who works with a client population that has a wide range of problems and intervenes in a service delivery environment that is highly complex and fragmented.

Task-centered case management fosters the development of specific intervention modules through continuing construction and tryouts of task planners. Practitioners and clients monitor task accomplishments, and successfully completed tasks are added to an index of practice modules. As the model evolves, the process of developing and revising practice modules leads to a database of tasks that work in the local service delivery environment. The practice modules are used as a resource for future task planning and as a tool for training. An additional advantage is that these practice modules are grounded in the reality of the local service environment in which the practitioner intervenes.

The modular structure of task-centered case management enables the integration of a core intervention model with alternative approaches for situations that require a departure from regular practice. This addresses the practice reality of certain situations requiring a different approach than the primary intervention model used. The task-centered case management model presented also provides clear guidelines regarding which activities are collaboratively carried out and which activities a case manager undertakes on behalf of clients. This makes the practice model adaptable to the wide range of situations encountered in case management.

The task-centered case management model is a consumer-directed approach that asks for active participation of clients whenever possible. As our experience with task-centered case management indicates, many frail elderly clients can actively participate in identifying their problems and developing tasks to address them. The model seems well suited to elderly clients who want to participate in the decision-making process and the implementation of activities related to their problems. It has been successfully used with caregivers and frail elderly clients alike. While the model may have limitations with clients who lack the cognitive abilities to participate at least at a minimum level, these clients typically have caregivers or legal guardians making care-related decisions. The case management model presented can be applied in the same format with these caregivers and legal guardians.

At the same time, the dual focus of the model emphasizes accountability through tracking progress and outcomes. This may make the model appealing to accountability-oriented systems of care such as managed health care plans. The collection of data on client progress and outcomes is an integral part of the case management model, and it can easily be adapted to particular documentation needs required by such systems of managed care (Benbenishty and Ben-Zaken 1988). The flexible structure of the model lends itself to the implementation in a wide range of case management practice settings.

CHAPTER 9

PRACTICE WITH CAREGIVERS: INDIVIDUALS AND GROUPS

Kristina Hash

GERONTOLOGICAL PRACTITIONERS encounter caregivers for older adults in a variety of settings, including institutions, such as hospitals and rehabilitation facilities, and home-based services, such as home health, hospice, and case management programs. In addition, they may interact with caregivers in support groups and in counseling sessions. In these settings, social workers and other gerontological practitioners are in a unique position to assist caregivers and their loved ones. This chapter will describe the responsibilities of caregiving and common needs and issues faced by caregivers, discuss the opportunities offered by task-centered practice with this client population, and present the application of the model through three case examples. The second part of the chapter will provide an introduction to task-centered group work with caregivers of frail older adults.

PROVIDING CARE: RESPONSIBILITIES AND NEEDS

THE PRIMARY CAREGIVER

When older adults become seriously ill or disabled, they often need assistance with activities of daily living. While older persons are cared for in the community, a loved one typically provides this assistance and assumes the role of "caregiver." This role may involve a variety of tasks and responsibilities, depending on the severity of the illness and level of impairment of the care recipient. Common caregiving tasks include personal care (such as assistance with bathing and grooming), household tasks (such as cooking and cleaning), grocery shopping and errands, budgeting and bill paying, and providing transportation. More complex tasks may include the administration of medical treatments (such as injections) and toileting. These caregiving responsibilities may be accomplished in an hour each day or they may require twenty-

community, including agencies that provide personal care, meals-on-wheels, and friendly visiting. Caregivers may also need help coordinating the various aspects of care, including medication regimes, insurance policies, and physician appointments. Depending on the role of the practitioner, he or she may be in a position to provide this assistance or may refer the family for case management services. As the caregiving situation can be quite isolating, caregivers are often in need of outside socialization and support. Furthermore, caregivers may be dealing with grief, such as feeling the loss of the person they once knew—as is often the case with caring for a person with dementia—or anticipating the impending death of the care recipient. In such cases, the practitioner can connect caregivers with local support groups or provide individual or family counseling or refer caregivers for such counseling.

Chronic illness and the need for care can also have a detrimental impact on the care recipient. Long-term illness involves numerous losses for the individual. They may include physical losses, such as a decline in physical strength and mobility. To accommodate these physical losses, home modifications may be necessary, including outdoor wheelchair ramps and handrails in the bathtub. A care recipient may also experience social losses, especially if the individual must move out of his or her own home and into the home of an adult child. Adding to the physical and social losses, many care recipients are also uncomfortable with being dependent on others. These multiple losses often require great adaptation on the part of the care recipient. Through providing help with the adaptation process, the practitioner can provide a vital service to a client. A practitioner may also refer the individual to a support group whose members share a similar experience of loss.

Strains in the relationship between the caregiver and recipient can compound the difficulties experienced by each individually. At times, tension can extend to other caregivers or relatives who are not seen as full contributors to caregiving or who feel neglected by the primary caregiver. Helping caregivers and recipient work through these interpersonal difficulties is an essential component of geriatric social work practice.

Financial assistance can also be critical in sustaining caregiving. Providing care can become quite costly, and income may be lost when caregivers or care recipients terminate employment. Gerontological practitioners can aid caregiving families by providing information on medical assistance and other programs that reduce the financial burden.

Even when caregivers are adequately supported, the progression of a loved one's condition may require increasingly advanced care. For this reason, long-term planning is beneficial. In many cases, advance directives are needed to ensure that the care recipient's wishes are respected and legitimized. Social workers, case managers, and other gerontological practitioners are usually in a position to assist families in preparing such documents. At times, this progression can necessitate a higher level of care than can be provided in the person's home. Because many caregivers provide care to avoid institutionalization, the issue of nursing home placement can produce a tremendous amount of guilt. This is especially difficult when the care recipient is fearful about institutional care. As a result, planning for institutionalized long-term care is often emotionally distressing and painful for all involved. The practitioner can provide support and education to families during this decision-making process and make referrals to skilled and intermediate care facilities.

SPECIAL NEEDS AND ISSUES OF DIVERSE CAREGIVERS

Most of what is currently known about the caregiving experience has been gathered from studies involving Caucasian wives and daughters as care providers. Only recently have attempts been made to study diverse populations of caregivers. As a result, the experiences and needs of diverse caregivers, including men, persons of color, and gay men and lesbians, have become more visible and better understood.

Several caregiving studies focused on the effects of gender, comparing the caregiving experiences of husbands and wives. Husbands were found to be less depressed, experience lower levels of burden, provide less hands-on care, and have more assistance than their female peers (Horowitz 1985; Miller 1990; Miller and Guo 2000; Prunchno and Resch 1989). However, husbands were less likely to have a confidant while providing care (Prunchno and Resch 1989). Male caregivers, in general, may also seek out formal assistance less often and value the ability to fulfill a commitment over the emotional gratification of caregiving (Kaye and Applegate 1990). Male caregivers, then, may tend to overextend themselves in caregiving and lack the emotional support needed to sustain their caregiving efforts over longer periods of time.

African-Americans may also experience lower levels of burden and depression (Farran et al. 1997; Hinrichsen and Ramirez 1992; Haley et al. 1996; Knight et al. 2000). In addition, some studies have shown African-Americans to have higher levels of mastery and derive more meaning from the caregiving experience than their white counterparts (Farran et al. 1997; Lawton et al. 1992). The support systems of this population are unique, as African-American care recipients are more likely to be cared for by a person other than a spouse and tend to receive more help from extended kin, neighbors, and friends (Cox 1993; Hinrichsen and Ramirez 1992; Lawton et al. 1992;

Wood and Parham 1990). Furthermore, African-American caregivers may rely more heavily on these informal supports than on formal support services (Cox and Monk 1990). In general, these caregivers have been found to have lower incomes and education levels and be in poorer health than their Caucasian peers (Haley et al. 1996; Lawton et al. 1992; Wykle and Segall 1991). With regard to coping, African-American caregivers may employ faith more as a source of support and use prayer more as coping strategy than their counterparts in the white population (Wykle and Segall 1991).

Latinos, Asian-Americans, and Native Americans may rely more heavily on familial rather than formal supports in caregiving (Cox and Monk 1990; John et al. 2001; Lee and Sung 1998). Although great diversity exists within these groups, each culture encourages strong family ties and support systems. Hispanic caregivers have shown high levels of self-reported depression. This has often been tied to a perceived lack of familial support. Serious financial difficulties have also been associated with caregiving in this population (John and McMillian 1998). Many Native Americans experience financial difficulties in providing care. In addition, they frequently lack adequate knowledge about health conditions (John et al. 2001).

Very little is known about caregiving in alternative families, including gay men and lesbians who provide care to partners, family members, and friends. Midlife and older gay men and lesbians who cared for partners were found to experience similar conflicts as those in previous caregiving studies, including physical, financial, and emotional strains (Hash 2001). One unique issue for these caregivers, however, is their interaction with family members, coworkers, and health and human service professionals. These caregivers are often faced with family members who were not accepting of their relationship, which may add additional strain to the caregiving situation. Despite this lack of support, some have the advantage of a strong network of family and friends who are supportive of the partner relationship and provide emotional support and assistance with hands-on care (Hash 2001).

Unfortunately, many gay men and lesbians who provide care to partners may anticipate encountering nonsupportive professionals. Consequently, they may be apprehensive about formal support services in general. As a result, they prefer referrals to "gay-friendly" and other supportive professionals. Other unique issues involve their need to disclose the nature of their relationships to family and to professionals and the need to reengage in the gay community for support. Advance directives may be of particular importance for this population of caregivers, as their partner relationships may not be respected by family or acknowledged by law (Hash 2001).

Practitioners who encounter diverse caregivers, including men, members of ethnic minority groups, and gay men and lesbians, will likely provide many of the same services as they provide to all caregivers, including resource planning, counseling, and education. In their interventions, however, they have to consider the special needs of these populations. For example, when working with African-American and other ethnic minority caregivers, the social worker may find that multiple caregivers are involved and available for emotional support and instrumental assistance. Financial assistance and education related to medical conditions and available resources, however, may be much more important for these caregivers. When working with gay and lesbian caregivers, the gerontological practitioner may need to focus on resources in the gay community or on gay-friendly service providers.

TASK-CENTERED PRACTICE WITH CAREGIVERS

The task-centered model offers great promise for working with caregivers and care recipients. The planned brevity of the approach is in accord with the short-term nature of intervention in most health care settings. Since illness involves a progression, the future-oriented and planning-oriented aspect of the model is beneficial. Its collaborative orientation is empowering for clients who have already suffered great losses in independence and decision making. The model also lends itself well to dealing with crisis situations that may occur in caregiving. General considerations in applying the task-centered model to cases where caregivers are involved have been discussed earlier in this chapter and in part II. These considerations will be further explored and illustrated through three case examples. They will be followed by a detailed description of a task-centered group work model for practice with caregivers.

CAREGIVING CASE EXAMPLES

LETTA AND CATHERINE

Kevin, a home health social worker, had been referred a case by an agency nurse. The case involved Letta, an 80-year-old African-American female, who lived with her 69-year-old sister, Catherine. Letta had a medical diagnosis of congestive heart failure and was not ambulatory. According to the nurse, Catherine served as her caregiver, but she was overwhelmed by her sister's bedridden status. Letta had been non ambulatory for the past two months. She had decubitus ulcers on both heels and had one beginning on her back. The nurse from the home health agency believed that Catherine had not repositioned Letta as often as she should to prevent skin breakdown. Letta's physician insisted that Kevin begin the process of nursing home placement.

During the first home visit, Kevin introduced himself to Catherine and presented his role as part of the plan of care directed by Letta's physician. Letta was asleep during the visit, and her sister claimed that she was often confused. The visit progressed with Kevin conducting an assessment. The sisters had lived together for most of their lives. Neither had married or had children. Other family members lived in other states and were currently not very involved in the lives of the sisters. Kevin presented the concerns of the nurse and physician related to Letta's worsening ulcers and the possible need for nursing home placement. Catherine stated that she was unable to lift her sister and had difficulty repositioning her due to her own lack of physical strength. She was overwhelmed by care but was hesitant to place Letta in a nursing home due to feelings of guilt and hopes of recovery. Because of Catherine's uncertainty about nursing home placement and the fact that persons must wait several months for placement when being placed from home, Kevin and Catherine decided to focus initially on interventions that would meet the immediate care needs. The first problem was identified as the need for in-home assistance. Catherine suggested that looking into respite and similar services could help her better take care of her sister. They agreed on a practitioner task of exploring availability and eligibility requirements for respite services.

At the second home visit, Kevin informed Catherine that her sister was eligible for four hours of sitter services for five days per week, at no cost. This would provide Catherine with much needed respite, so she was eager to begin services. The service was confirmed through a phone call to the provider. Service was to begin in two weeks.

Letta was again asleep during this visit, and her sister reported that she slept most of the day and night. It appeared that the current care situation had caused Letta and Catherine to become very isolated. During both visits the drapes of the house were drawn, and the house was darkened. The isolation, initially identified during the assessment interview, was prioritized by Catherine as the second target problem. Catherine and Kevin spent a significant amount of time during this visit further exploring the problem and generating task alternatives. Catherine indicated that she and Letta had once been active members of a nearby church. They had stopped attending services when Letta became ill. However, she suggested that she might be interested in getting in contact again with the congregation. An individual task for Catherine to contact her pastor was developed. It was broken into several subtasks. First, she would call the pastor, explain her situation, and get his ideas about church activities that she could engage in once her respite service began. Next, she would deliberate on which activities would interest her the most and select at least one of them. Since she was somewhat anxious about reconnecting after such a long period of time, she would focus on her anxieties in a future session if it would become problematic. The forthcoming respite service would enable her to make an appointment with her own physician—another individual task she had developed.

The lowest issue on Catherine's list of problem priorities was Letta's possible need for nursing home care. When Kevin introduced the possibility of looking at this option, Catherine was very reluctant; yet she agreed that she would be open to talking more about it and maybe consider the possibility. Working on the respite tasks and starting to have more time to think about long-term plans, she more and more opened up to this possibility and realized that placement might be inevitable. However, she felt tremendous guilt even thinking about this decision. Two related tasks were agreed on. The first task was for Catherine to write down her feelings about nursing home placement for Letta. She would keep a daily diary of her thoughts and feelings. The second task was to get another opinion by discussing the possibility of nursing home placement with Letta's visiting nurse.

The third and final in-home visit began with a brief contact with Letta, who was awake but appeared somewhat confused. Kevin introduced himself, and she agreed to answer a few questions related to time and her surroundings (Mini Mental Status Exam). She was aware that she was living in her sister's home and that she had been ill for some time. She was unsure of the month or year and who is currently president. Kevin explained the problems and events to date, but Letta was slowly drifting off to sleep. She did not appear to be competent to participate in any care-related decisions.

After a short time, Letta started drifting off again, and Catherine's task accomplishments were reviewed. She had contacted the pastor and planned to attend a meeting of a senior citizens group that the church sponsored. She also shared that her pastor had made a visit to her. Two church members had also dropped by. She remarked that the start of sitter services had made her feel more rested and allowed her to get out of the house. Although she did not write down her feelings about nursing home care for Letta—it was too painful a subject—the task did prompt her to think more about the possibility. She began to realize that Letta's worsening condition might leave her with little choice. She did talk to the visiting nurse, who was supportive of a placement for Letta. Although her social and care supports had increased, Catherine was still physically overwhelmed by the amount of caregiving tasks. She said she was now willing to begin the process of nursing home placement. Catherine was aware of two nursing homes close by. A task for her to visit both in the next few days was agreed upon. The task planner on Relocation (see part III) was used in planning the task. Although she knew that placement was necessary, Catherine talked at some length about placing Letta. She expressed a good deal of guilt, since as the older sister, Letta had always been very protective of her. Kevin reassured her that her feelings were understandable, but he tried to help her see that Letta needed more care than Catherine could provide. He suggested that a placement might be in Letta's as well as her own best interests. Catherine, in tears, nodded her head. Since additional time was needed to work on the nursing home placement, they recontracted on two more home visits. The focus of these visits would be on selecting a nursing home, completing all required paperwork, and submitting it to the facility. Before the next visit, Catherine was to visit two more nursing homes that might have an opening.

The following week, Kevin made a follow-up phone call to Catherine. Catherine had visited two more nursing homes, toured the facilities, and met with staff. She had decided on one of the homes and had collected all paperwork. The focus of the next visit was on completing the application. Letta had to be placed on a waiting list; however, an indication was made that it would probably take less than two months for her to move in. Catherine still felt very guilty about the decision. However, she did not want to focus on this problem during the home visit. She expressed that despite feeling guilty, she also was confident that she had made the best decision for herself and her sister. It was mutually decided that another visit was not necessary at this time. Kevin invited Catherine to call if she needed further assistance with placement or other issues. (See boxes 9.1 and 9.2 for an overview.)

BOX 9.1 PROBLEMS STATEMENT: LETTA AND CATHERINE

TARGET PROBLEM	GOAL	PROBLEM IDENTIFIER
Caregiver overwhelmed by the duties of care	Secure additional in-home care services	Caregiver
Caregiver and care recipient are isolated and lack personal supports	Connect with support persons in the community	SW
Care recipient is possibly in need of a higher level of care	Begin the process of nursing home placement	Physician, SW

BOX 9.2 TASKS: LETTA AND CATHERINE

TASK	SUGGESTED	CARRIED OUT	TCR*
1.1: Explore in-home services	SW	SW	4
1.2: Make referral for in-home service		SW	4
2.2: Make contact with former church	SW, Caregiver	Caregiver	4
3.2: Consult with nurse and physician	SW	Caregiver	4
3.3 Record feelings about placing Letta	SW	Caregiver	1
3.4 Proceed with placement plan for Letta	SW, Caregiver	Caregiver	
3.5: Visit local skilled nursing facilities	SW, Caregiver	Caregiver	4
3.6: Secure placement	SW, Caregiver	Caregiver	2

*Task Completion Ratings 4 = task completely achieved, 3 = substantially achieved, 2 = partially achieved, 1 = not achieved, n = unable to implement task

TIM AND JAMES

Sandy, a hospital social worker, received a referral to assist Tim. He was identified as a 68-year-old Caucasian male who had recently been admitted to the hospital for HIV-related pneumonia. During their first meeting, Sandy also met Tim's partner of thirty years, James, aged 60. Tim's condition had advanced to AIDS, and he currently required assistance with personal care and medication injections. He was alert and oriented and able to make decisions related to his care. During the initial assessment, both Tim and James expressed great fears about the future and the progression of Tim's illness.

Three problem areas were identified as targets for intervention: (1) A general uncertainty about the future financial and care planning, (2) the need for caregiver respite, and (3) dealing with grief and loss issues. The second home visit began with work on the first target problem. The couple was specifically concerned about Tim's family of origin and their involvement with the couple. Tim's family knew about the nature of their relationship and, "on the surface," was accepting. However, although they had offered to relieve James, they were always busy when he called them for respite. Moreover, Tim's family lately seemed primarily interested in what would be left to the family once he died. Because the couple had not drafted advance directives, long-term planning was identified as the first target problem. Sandy suggested that these documents would be important so as to assure that their wishes could be respected in health care and other decisions. She provided very detailed information on the benefits of completing such advance directives. After reflecting on their relationship with Tim's family, the couple decided to complete the advance directive forms. Tim wanted to discuss financial and property issues since he felt the need for some kind of plan. A plan was developed which included Tim's decisions to grant a power of attorney to James and to update his living will. Task planners on advance directives and power of attorney (see part III), which the practitioner shared with the couple, informed the discussion during the session. Since the practitioner had brought the required paperwork for the advance directives, a shared task for Tim and James to complete it was developed. A practitioner task was to bring all required information and paperwork on the power of attorney to the next meeting.

Four days later, Sandy visited Tim again just before his discharge from the hospital. As customary in this particular setting, the work focused on the discharge process and the supports available in the home. James voiced his concern again that since he worked full-time, Tim would be home alone for most of the day. The need for respite or similar assistance had been identified during the assessment as the second target problem. Obtaining in-home services was identified as another related intervention goal. Sandy consulted with Tim's physician, and a referral was made to a home health care agency for physical therapy and assistance with medication injections.

Next, they focused on the additional supports that would be needed once Tim was discharged. James was not "out" to his employer for fear of losing his job and had told his boss that he was taking care of a family member at home. This was seen as a potential obstacle to his continued providing of care. Sandy provided information on meals-on-wheels and a friendly visitor program that was offered by the local HIV health services center. They all agreed that this would be a good idea since it would relieve some of James' fears during the workweek. A referral was made, and an intake worker for the center scheduled a home visit for the initial assessment for services.

The third problem area was the expressed feeling of loss. Sandy asked about their support network, and Tim claimed that in recent years they had not been active in the gay community. They socialized with a group of friends who were "mostly straight." Sandy suggested ways the couple could benefit from other supports in the gay, lesbian, and HIV communities. When Sandy mentioned HIV support groups, Tim and James voiced their opposition to attending these types of groups. They did not feel comfortable sharing their feelings in a group setting. James would be interested, however, in seeing a private counselor for issues related to bereavement. Since this problem was assessed to warrant more time and focus than could be provided in discharge planning, it was decided to pursue the counseling option. Sandy provided a list of clinical social workers in the area that saw members of the gay and lesbian community. James decided to check with his insurance company about mental health benefits and coverage for treatment. The couple was also given information on the HIV health services center and other services in the gay community (see boxes 9.3 and 9.4 for an overview).

BOX 9.3 PROBLEM STATEMENT: TIM AND JAMES

PROBLEM STATEMENT	GOAL	PROBLEM IDENTIFIER
Couple has not developed advance directives or plan for handling finances	Complete advance directive forms and update other legal documents, develop financial plan	SW, Tim
James requires care and other services during the workday	Secure health care and other in-home support services	James
Couple experiencing feelings of loss and fear	Obtain resources to alleviate fear and cope with loss	Tim and James

---

BOX 9.4 SUMMARY OF TASKS: TIM AND JAMES

TASK	SUGGESTED	CARRIED OUT	TCR*
1.1.: Complete durable power of attorney forms and living will	SW	Tim, SW	4
1.2.: Update will and other legal documents	SW	Tim	2
2.1.: Set up in-home medical services	SW/MD	Tim, MD	3
2.2.: Set up meals-on-wheels and friendly visiting	SW	Tim, SW	3
3.1.: Provide information on support groups and counseling services	SW	SW	4
3.2.: Make appointment with counselor	SW	James	2

*Task Completion Ratings 4 = task completely achieved, 3 = substantially achieved, 2 = partially achieved, 1 = not achieved, n = unable to implement task

---

JOHN, LOUISE, AND MARSHA

John, 71, had suffered a stroke and was receiving outpatient therapy at a reha-bilitative center. The social worker, Barbara, was asked to see John by his adult children because they were concerned about their parents' home situation. According to the rehabilitation nurse, John lived with his wife of forty-five years, Louise, age 66, who provided care and supervision but was often over-whelmed. The adult children, Harold and Marsha, were primarily concerned with John's treatment of their mother. Marsha, who lived several miles away, would occasionally come over to help her mother with John's care.

Since the request for intervention had come from the adult children, the social worker first assessed the couple's interest in seeing her. She approached them during one of their visits to the rehabilitation center and introduced herself as one of the social workers and asked whether they would be inter-ested in her assistance. Initially, John and Louise both were unsure what the social worker's role would be and what she could do for them. However, after a brief explanation of the ways a social worker could assist them, John and Louise expressed their openness to receiving some help. They set up a time for a meeting and decided that it should take place in the couple's home.

During Barbara's first visit John was alert and oriented but said he was forgetful and confused at times. He could walk with the assistance of a cane but reported spending most of his day resting on the living room couch. Louise added that John had been depressed and agitated since the onset of his heart disease. His mood had gotten only worse since the stroke. When asked about his mood, John agreed that he felt "worthless" since he cannot even walk to the curb in front of their home. Barbara asked about their relationship. Louise commented that his moods were difficult to handle, but that their relationship was OK.

The assessment process culminated in the determination of two areas that they would like to focus on: John's adaptation to illness and Louise's need for assistance. Somewhat to the surprise of the social worker, they both decided that the need for assistance would have the lower priority and that they would first like to address John's adaptation to illness. An additional six home visits were agreed on with the focus on helping John. The couple also indicated that they would be open to Barbara's following-up with their adult children.

The first target problem was John's adaptation to illness. In the follow-up phone call to their children, Marsha said that her mother was "on the verge of breaking down" due to her father's "demanding, abusive, and hostile" behavior. In addition, she said that a nurse's aide had refused to make subsequent visits to the home because of John's verbal abuse of her when she called to cancel a visit due to personal illness. Neither John nor Louise had mentioned this during the initial assessment visit. According to the daughter, John was a floor supervisor at a furniture factory for many years and was anxious when schedules were not kept. Marsha suggested that she would like to meet with her parents and Barbara together to try to work out a better plan for her father's care. Barbara called John and Louise about her daughter's suggestion, and they agreed to a joint meeting.

The meeting took place a few days later at the couple's home. At Barbara's suggestion, John discussed his feelings of loss and depression related to his physical health. In response to Marsha's questioning, John admitted that Louise got on his "nerves" and that he sometimes yelled at her. He also admitted that the nurse and nursing assistant angered him when they failed to show up on time. Louise stated that she was committed to taking care of her husband but resented his poor treatment of her and the nurses. She said that John was not capable of physical abuse but "his words hurt just as much as a fist." John admitted that his "anger got the best of him at times." During the course of the session, it became clear that John's adaptation would need to be discussed in context with the couple's relationship issues. The clients accepted Barbara's suggestion that they should look at John's adjustment and their relationship concurrently. Louise thought that both problems would be improved if they had a little more help. Initially, this need for assistance had been prioritized as the second target problem to be addressed. John and Louise now agreed that the "help problem" needed immediate attention. Since the visit seemed very emotionally challenging for the clients and several relationship issues had been discussed intensely, the social worker accepted the change of focus and the reprioritizing of target problems. However, she first ensured that the discussion had not stirred up anger or frustration that neither individual could deal with, i.e., feelings that could not wait until the time when relationship issues were the direct focus of intervention.

Barbara suggested that the three of them share with one another their thoughts about how more help might be obtained. Marsha spoke first, saying the priority should be getting the nurse's assistant back. Marsha and her mother discussed how this might be done, e.g., calling her or her supervisor. Noting that John had said nothing, Barbara asked him what ideas he might have. After some hesitation, John said that he might owe the nurse's aide an apology and that he would be willing to call her himself. Marsha, who seemed moved by her father's action, volunteered to work out some regular times to come over in order to give her mother some respite. With prompts from Barbara, a task plan was developed. John would contact the nurse's aide the following day. If she was unwilling to return—a possible obstacle they anticipated—John would contact her supervisor. He would apologize to her as well and ask whether another nurse would be available to provide care. Marsha would start her increased schedule of visits the following week. With John's permission, Barbara agreed to contact his physician about medication for his depression.

At her next visit, Barbara learned that John had apologized to the nurse's aide and that she had agreed to resume service. Marsha was planning to begin her increased schedule of visits later in the week. In a joint session with John and Louise, Barbara and Louise discussed how she might use the respite time that Marsha's visits would provide. She expressed a desire to get out of the house more often but still felt guilty about passing off her responsibilities. This was identified as a possible obstacle to task implementation. However, it was then decided that this should be treated as a separate problem area to work on. Problem exploration and development of task alternatives followed. Barbara asked Louise about her interest in attending a caregivers' support group so that she could share her feelings and problem-solve with others who also provided care. This would also enable her to get out of the house without feeling as guilty, since she would be doing something to improve her care of John. Louise responded positively to this rationale, and John expressed his support for her attending a caregiver support group. Louise said that she would like to try a group because she might "learn some things." The social worker gave her information on the center's weekly support group meeting times as well as one other group that existed in the community. Two tasks were agreed upon: (1) Louise would identify a support group meeting that would work with her schedule; and (2) Louise would attend one support group meeting to see whether she liked it.

By the next session, which took place two weeks later, the nurse's aide had returned. Marsha had also come to help and spend time with her parents. Louise had started her support group. John was a little less depressed and seemed to be responding to the medication. However, it was too early to know whether the medication would bring about long-term improvement in his depression.

This session and the next two were spent largely on John and Louise's relationship problems, which both agreed were more important at this point than issues relating to his adjustment to his illness. A basic problem in their communication was clarified: John would get angry—often because Louise had not done something he thought should have been done—and Louise would respond by withdrawing and ignoring him. This usually made John even angrier. Tasks involving problem-solving communication were used. These were accomplished both in the session and between sessions. The couple would select an issue, usually involving John's care, and try to develop a solution for it. Both were asked to paraphrase what the other had said as a part of developing skills in attentive listening and empathic responding. John was helped to see that at times he expected too much of Louise. Louise agreed to try to continue dialogues with John rather than to withdraw.

In the last session, the couple agreed that considerable progress had been made. Both had benefited from the help provided by the nurse's aide and Marsha. Louise found the support group useful even though she had only gone twice. However, she indicated that she was planning to continue attending. John's feelings about himself and his illness had somewhat improved. The couple was communicating a little better even though their relationship problems had not been completely resolved. They had not done any structured communication exercises during the past week, but they thought they were helpful and planned to continue to do them. John commented that they had been given a "good start" and that "the rest was up to them." (See boxes 9.5 and 9.6 for an overview of the problems and tasks.)

COMMENTS

These cases illustrate task-centered work with caregivers and care recipients in hospital and community settings. In the first two cases service was focused

---

BOX 9.5 PROBLEMS: JOHN, LOUISE, AND MARSHA

PROBLEM STATEMENT	GOAL	PROBLEM IDENTIFIER
John depressed as a result of illness	Relieve feelings of worthlessness and depressed mood	John
The couple's relationship difficulties	Improve communication	John, Louise, Marsha
Louise in need of additional help	Secure additional help for Louise	Louise
Louise's need to get out of the house	Develop out-of-house activities	Louise

---

on the remediation of immediate problems that appeared to be resolvable in the short term. Time limits were not used in all examples, but time estimates were given in one case. In the last case, time limits were employed since the problems with adjustment to illness and the relationship problems were potentially interminable (see chapter 6).

The identification of and focus on specific problems acknowledged by the client—a central feature of task-centered practice—was evident in all cases. Here the social worker tries to help clients define problems that are the most pressing to them and yet are solvable. The case of John, Louise, and Marsha illustrates how problem definitions and priorities may change in the course of an intervention. The problems in their relationship and Louise's need for more outside supports were added as new information emerged during the course of the intervention. Each time a new target problem was identified, the order in which they were to be addressed was reviewed and reprioritized. In all cases described, the identification of and agreement on specific problems provided a clear focus for work that was understood by all parties involved.

In keeping with the model, clients agree to and carry out tasks to resolve their difficulties, thus enabling them to be active rather than passive participants in the intervention process. Practitioners take responsibility for tasks involving special knowledge or skill, such as determining the availability of resources. Even when client tasks are not successfully completed, they may help stimulate other actions. Thus, Catherine was not able to record her feelings about placing Letta, but her attempt to do so stimulated an effort to

---

BOX 9.6 TASKS: JOHN, LOUISE, AND MARSHA

TASK	SUGGESTED	CARRIED OUT	TCR*
1.1.: Have physician prescribe antidepressant medication.	SW	SW	4
2.1 Problem-solving communication to resolve specific issues and to learn problem-solving and communication skills	SW	John and Louise	3
3.1.: Contact nurse's aide to have service resumed	John	John	4
3.2 Marsha to increase time spent with her parents	Marsha	Marsha	4
3.3.: Louise to attend caregiver support group	SW	Louise	2

*Task Completion Ratings 4 = task completely achieved, 3 = substantially achieved, 2 = partially achieved, 1 = not achieved, n = unable to implement task

---

think about the issues and sort them out. We also note how the social worker, Kevin, facilitated her expressions of feeling about the placement and reframed her decision as one that will provide Letta with needed care rather than as an act of rejection. In this way he was able to help her work through a major obstacle to the placement task—her feelings of guilt over her failure to care for her sister.

In all cases, tasks were devised to provide additional help for caregivers and to enable them to develop social contacts and support—a basic strategy in work with caregivers. Finally, we note the use of task planners in two of the cases as a means of identifying possible tasks that might be used for particular problems.

GROUP WORK WITH CAREGIVERS

Practice with caregivers often makes use of a group work approach. Examples include caregiver support groups, educational groups, or planning and advocacy task groups. For reviews of the research and effectiveness of caregiver groups see Bourgeois and associates (1996), Knight and associates (1993), Toseland and Siporin (1986), and Tross and Blum (1988).

Zastrow (1997) categorizes the primary purpose of groups as education, problem solving and decision making, therapy, self-help, socialization, social conversation, recreation-skill building, task, and sensitivity and encounter training. Most commonly, caregiver groups focus on or combine elements of the first five types, i.e., aspects of self-help, education, and problem solving, therapy, and socialization. Members of education groups improve their knowledge and skills regarding specific subject matters. Caregivers learn about topics related to the care recipient's health, mental health, and physical and cognitive conditions. At the same time, learning practical caregiving skills as well as skills for self-preservation is commonly important in educational group work. In problem-solving groups, members develop strategies to resolve specific difficulties. Socializing, although a by-product of most group work, can also be its primary focus.

Groups provide an excellent medium to reduce caregivers' stress and burden. Toseland (1995:228) summarizes the many ways in which support groups can assist caregivers in reducing their levels of stress (see box 9.7).

Caregiver support groups can focus on a wide range of issues. Common topics for support groups that can benefit caregivers of frail older adults are presented in the overview in box 9.8 (Toseland 1995).

TASK-CENTERED GROUP WORK WITH CAREGIVERS

As noted in chapter 6, in task-centered group work the group is used to help individual members to identify problems as well as to plan, implement, and review tasks. Task-centered caregiver groups may also include the educational and skill development components outlined by Toseland above.

ROLE OF GROUP LEADER

The role of the task-centered group worker, albeit similar to that of a practitioner working with individuals, is marked by some noteworthy differences. A practitioner working with groups has to maintain a dual focus on the individual and the group (Toseland and Rivas 2001). On the one hand, the practitioner has to support individual group members in their work toward addressing the problems they are encountering in caregiving, making sure that their personal needs are met and that individual problem solving occurs. On the other hand, she has to be concerned with the process and the goals

---

BOX 9.7 WAYS IN WHICH SUPPORT GROUPS CAN REDUCE CAREGIVER STRESS:

- Provide caregiver with respite
- Reduce loneliness
- Promote ventilation of emotions
- Share feelings in a supportive environment
- Validate, universalize, and normalize thoughts, feelings, and experiences
- Instill hope
- Affirm the significance of the caregiver role
- Educate caregivers about aging process, resources, or health and disability topics
- Teach problem-solving and coping strategies
- Foster the caregiver's capacity for problem solving

---

for the group as a whole. She has to keep the group process moving and ensure that interactions foster a constructive group process.

Since group participants initially tend to direct their interactions toward the practitioner, she has to facilitate communication among the group members. At the same time, she has to prevent a small number of group members from dominating group interactions. Rather, the atmosphere should allow all members to contribute in a meaningful way. Related to this effort is the importance of assisting participants to increase their abilities to listen.

Task-centered practice is collaborative in nature. The same holds true for task-centered group work. While the practitioner facilitates the process and ensures that the group stays on track, group members should see each other as equal partners in their problem-solving efforts. This can be facilitated, for example, by calling on group members to help each other in generating and implementing their tasks.

GROUP CONDITIONS

A leader should take several basic conditions into consideration when planning a caregiving group: the stage of group development, group structure, group process, group culture, group resources, extra-group transactions, group boundaries, and group climate (Garvin 1997). We will provide only a short overview of some of these group conditions. For a more detailed review, see Garvin (1997) and Tolson, Reid, and Garvin (2002).

BOX 9.8 COMMON TOPICS FOR CAREGIVER SUPPORT GROUPS

- Increasing the understanding of the elderly care recipient
- Improving the use of formal and informal supports
- Improving coping abilities
- Assisting caregivers to better take care of themselves
- Improving problematic relationships with the care recipient and other family members
- Learning home care and behavior management skills

Some predictable changes occur within a group as it evolves over time. These transformations are referred to as the stages of group development. During the group formation phase, participants get to know each other and often still feel ambivalent about participating in a group process. Some individuals may interact in a stereotypical manner. Others may be guarded about their communication. Often, this is followed by a period during which group members test the leader and challenge the rules that evolved in the formation process. This phase is often referred to as the integration, disintegration, and conflict phase (Garvin 1997; Hartford 1971). A key activity of the group leader during this phase is to ensure the continued commitment of all members. The third stage of group development is the group functioning and maintenance phase. It is during this phase that most of the treatment activities and task work occur. Finally, the last one to two sessions focus on termination. As in task-centered practice with individuals, these sessions concentrate on reviewing and reinforcing accomplishments. In addition, members are asked to discuss their group experience. For a review of the characteristics and group leader interventions relating to various developmental stages of a task-centered group see Fortune (1985).

Group structure refers to the relationships that develop among group members. These relationships influence group interactions, but they also have an impact on individuals' problem solving. For example, group members may support or hinder the development of an idea based on their like or dislike of the person presenting it. Subgroups may exist or develop over time. For example, some members may have previously attended other caregiver support groups, or they may know each other from the community. The group leader has to be attentive to the group structure and make sure that it fosters an environment conducive to constructive problem-solving work.

Several resources are required for the implementation of a group. They include, among others, staff support and group leadership, physical space, equipment, and assistance for outreach and recruitment. As in practice with individual clients, recording problems, tasks, and task achievements are often an integral part of task-centered group work. These recording instruments should also be available for group members in sufficient numbers.

A decision regarding the group's boundaries, including determination of the group's membership, should be made at the outset. Who will become a group member? Can someone join the group after it starts? Can a group member miss several sessions? At the same time, participants continue interactions outside the group with other persons throughout their group experience. In task-centered group work, a participant may perform a task that involves an outside individual. For example, a caregiver's task may involve the care recipient or other family members as the target of the intervention. At other times, a task may involve the active participation of the care recipient.

Finally, group session activities and a proposal for the group should be developed. Some leaders include a general timeline for each session activity in their outline. While this is generally beneficial, one has to be careful not to hamper the group process by working from a schedule that leaves no room for addressing issues ad hoc. A typical two-hour middle phase group session might be structured as follows: (1) 15 minutes: task review and monitoring of progress, (2) 30 minutes: relevant education and support activities, (3) 60 minutes: generating and agreeing on tasks, (4) 15 minutes: processing and evaluating the group experience (see box 9.9 for an overview).

BOX 9.9 CASE EXAMPLE: OUTLINE OF GROUP SESSIONS ACTIVITIES

SESSION	ACTIVITY
1	Getting to know members, overview of sessions and topics
2–4	Exploring problems, possibly generating initial tasks
3–10	TPIS, S&E, processing group experience
11	TPIS, planning of termination
12	Termination, processing of group experience, celebration

Note: TPIS = work on the task planning and implementation sequence, when it is introduced, will differ from group to group

S&E = Skills training and education

When planning a group, leaders should develop a proposal in which they detail the organizational context of the planned group (Toseland and Rivas 2001). An example of such a treatment group proposal is presented in box 9.10.

PREGROUP PHASE

When setting up a caregiver group, a decision has to be made about potential members. As in the example of a caregiver support group, participants often have problems or needs in common. Similarities among members can enhance the group process. Toseland (1995) even suggests that the concerns and problems of caregivers of persons with mental health problems, such as dementia, differ significantly from those of people taking care of a person with a physical disability. Therefore, if the pool of potential members and the resources allow it, he suggests the creation of separate groups.

A related consideration is the recruitment of group members. Caregivers are not a very visible client population. Some individuals may feel that they are abandoning their caregiving responsibilities if they are leaving the care recipient behind while attending a group session (Toseland 1995). Others may have difficulty receiving care coverage for their time of absence. Outreach efforts should take this into consideration. Providing respite for the caregivers for the time of the group may be as important as a targeted recruitment campaign using multiple channels.

Most group leaders hold a pregroup interview with potential participants. One purpose of this interview is the screening of potential participants. Questions that guide this process include: Do the prospects have problems that fit in with the theme of the group? Will they be able to participate and contribute to the group process? Would they be better suited for group or individual treatment? Other questions may focus on practical aspects of group attendance, such as whether the person has adequate transportation. A second purpose of the interview is the preparation of participants for a task-centered group. One aspect is the preparation for the group experience in general. Another is to introduce the task-centered approach. Some group leaders already begin selecting target problems for group work (Garvin 1985). This initial exploration and selection of problems follows an approach similar to that in task-centered practice with individuals. However, since the group has a specific focus, i.e., caregiver support, the selected problem(s) should fall within this focus. These problems may change during the course of the group, but it is beneficial to start with an area to focus on during the initial phase. The practitioner should let clients know that they will present

BOX 9.10 CASE EXAMPLE: TREATMENT GROUP PROPOSAL

SYNOPSIS:

This proposal is for a task-centered education and support group for caregivers of frail elderly persons residing in the community.

PURPOSE:

Purpose of the group is fourfold: (1) To provide opportunities for individual caregivers' problem solving within a group context, (2) to provide education on topics that relate to caregiving, (3) to provide opportunities to learn caregiving skills, and (4) to establish an environment of exchange and support for caregivers.

SPONSORSHIP:

The group is sponsored by the Grace Street House Senior Service Center. A social worker from this agency will lead the group. A graduate student who is conducting her field placement at the agency will assist her. Guest speakers from within the agency will participate in some group sessions.

MEMBERSHIP:

The group is open to caregivers living in the local community, with a preference given to those who have been providing care for more than six months. Focus of the group is on caregivers of elderly persons, regardless of types of caregiving.

RECRUITMENT:

Various agency programs serve a significant number of caregivers. Group members will be recruited by asking practitioners to identify potential participants. Information about the group will also be shared with staff at other agencies serving elderly persons and caregivers.

GROUP COMPOSITION:

The group will consist of 6–8 caregivers. It will be a closed group since some of the skills training will occur in a gradual and cumulative way. No new members will be added to the group after it commences.

ORIENTATION:

The social worker and her graduate student will conduct an individual pre-group interview with each group member. During this interview they will orient the group member regarding the purpose and process of the group. In addition, potential group members will be introduced to basic information on the task-centered group work approach.

LOCATION:

The group will meet at the small meeting room of Grace Street House.

DURATION:

The group will meet Saturdays from 10–12 A.M. for twelve consecutive weekly sessions.

TRANSPORTATION:

The senior center cannot offer transportation services. If needed, agency staff will assist in organizing senior transportation services for individual group members.

their target problem during the initial phase of the group, usually in the first or second session. At times, it may be helpful to rehearse this presentation with clients. For example, some caregivers may feel uncomfortable sharing personal information in a group setting. This may be especially challenging if it is their first group work experience.

INITIAL PHASE OF TASK-CENTERED GROUPS

As a group develops, group norms evolve. This process commences at the very beginning of the first group session. Group norms are shared beliefs about appropriate and inappropriate behavior in the group setting (Toseland and Rivas 2001). While all group members contribute to the development of the norms in one way or another, the practitioner has a responsibility to promote norms that foster individual and group growth and maintain basic ethical standards. One way of achieving this is by contracting with members on a set of basic group norms (see box 9. 11).

OBTAINING INFORMATION

The group leader obtains basic information from members during the pre-group interview. She takes this information into consideration when planning the group's composition and structure. At the beginning of the first

---

BOX 9.11 CONTRACT ON GROUP NORMS

1. The sanctity and rights of all members should be valued. Thus members are not pressured to say or do anything that they do not wish to say or do.
2. Every member's contribution to the work of the group should be appreciated.
3. Members should seek ways to have caring feelings toward one another.
4. Members should find ways of cooperating rather than competing with one another.
5. The group should seek ways to help rather than exclude members who some find 'difficult.'

Tolson, Reid and Garvin 2002

group session, participants are usually asked to share some information about themselves and their problems. The group facilitator should let group members know beforehand that they will be asked to present this to the group (Tolson, Reid, and Garvin 2002).

She should help the clients decide what to present and how much to reveal. Some group workers are very specific about the amount and type of information to be shared, others ask participants to present what they feel comfortable sharing. A common approach to obtaining information during the first session is to ask group members to interview each other in pairs of two and then present the other person to the group (Tolson, Reid, and Garvin 2002).

SELECTING, PRIORITIZING, AND EXPLORING PROBLEMS

As in task-centered practice with individuals, group participants work on self-acknowledged problems. As noted, some group workers begin selecting target problems during the pregroup interview. In such cases, clients are asked to share their problems during the initial group session. Another option is to identify problems during the first session. Using this approach, clients are asked to think about and list the problems they would like to address. As group members share their problems, others provide feedback. Group members influence each other in this interactive process. Hearing another person's problems may prompt someone to reflect on an issue he or she had not thought about. Through the process of sharing their problems with the group, members increase their commitment to work on them (Garvin 1985).

As a next step, the target problems are prioritized. This process may differ from individual practice in a number of ways. Several group members may have similar problems. They can learn from each other when they address these problems. Yet, the problems may have different meanings and differing levels of importance for different group members. While the same problem may be critical for one group member to address immediately, another participant may have a very different set of circumstances requiring other issues to be addressed first. However, group pressure to conform and the example set by another group member may influence the way individuals prioritize their problems. The leader's role in this context is to point this out and facilitate corrective processes. The more focused a group's theme, the less likely this is to occur. It is more likely to take place in a general caregiver treatment group than, say, in a caregiver support and education group with a specific focus on techniques to prevent burnout.

Another important role of the group leader is to facilitate the process of exploring target problems. In smaller groups, she may ask individuals to present their problems and ask all group members to participate in providing feedback. In larger groups, she may ask a participant to choose one or two group members to assist in the problem exploration. Since the group members do not know each other well at this time, this may feel less intimidating and cause less anxiety.

Once target problems are explored, problem specification begins. Problem specification itself follows the same outline as in task-centered practice with individuals. Taking advantage of the collective, group members can help each other in specifying problems. One approach is to have each participant work with the entire group. Group members provide feedback, taking turns. This approach is most feasible with smaller groups. Another method is to break the group into subgroups. Each of them focuses on the problem specification of the respective subgroup members. A similar approach can be used when using pairs of members.

SETTING GOALS AND CONTRACTING

Setting goals can be achieved through a similar interactive process as problem specification. Participants can set their goals in interaction with the group, with a subgroup, or in pairs. Even when using pairs or subgroups, sharing the final goals with the whole group is beneficial as members can learn from each other. The interest expressed by group peers may also increase the individual's motivation to work toward the stated goal. In sum, contracting on problems and goals is similar to what is done in individual practice. However, the group offers additional opportunities, such as contracts between members and the group or among group members.

MIDDLE PHASE OF TASK-CENTERED GROUPS

GENERATING, SELECTING, AND AGREEING ON TASKS

Once group members are ready to work on the members' respective problems, the focus shifts to the task planning and implementation sequence. The timing may be different for each group as well as for individual group members. Tolson, Reid, and Garvin (2002) suggest several approaches if some group members are ahead of the rest in their readiness to begin task work.

One is to have those participants assist other group members through a buddy system. Another option is to work with some members in a small subgroup. However, since it can interfere with group cohesion, this should option should be exercised with caution.

The features of tasks and their implementation are the same in group work and individual practice. What differs, however, is the process of developing tasks. In groups, members can assist each other in developing tasks. They brainstorm together and help each other by making suggestions. Moreover, problems faced by group members may be very similar in nature. Consequently, group members can draw from a pool of individuals that share some experience in dealing with the problem. Yet, while the problems may be similar, the specific tasks usually differ (Garvin 1985). The social worker has to facilitate the process of task development in such a way that an adequate set of alternatives is developed. For example, group members sometimes home in on one task too early before other options have been presented. Once task alternatives have been developed, group members assist each other in the evaluation of the alternatives. However, the task that is chosen at the end should to be selected by the person who will perform it.

Task agreement usually occurs between the group member and the group rather than with the practitioner. This approach places more value on the task, since all group members have a stake in task completion. Their continued involvement in various aspects of all group members' tasks increases their participation and engagement with each other.

Planning the details of task implementation again includes aspects similar to individual practice. Group members can provide each other with useful information and feedback. Together, they can role-play the performance of a task—one of the major advantages of working with groups. In anticipating obstacles members benefit from the insights and suggestions of others who share similar experiences and have comparable problems.

Finally, summarizing tasks at the end of each session is as essential a step in task-centered group work as it is in individual practice. The numerous tasks of all group members may be hard to remember. Tasks can be summarized using a blackboard or a flip chart. Another approach is to ask each group member to briefly summarize his or her tasks.

REVIEWING TASKS AND TARGET PROBLEMS

Sessions using a task-centered group work format begin with a review of each member's task accomplishments and target problems. Group members assist one another in the appraisal of how well a task was implemented, what worked, and what did not work. If individual tasks were not carried out, the facilitator should ensure that other group members do not reprimand the individual for nonperformance. Target problems are reviewed and evaluated much in the same way. How much time a group can spend each session on reviewing task accomplishments and target problems will vary. While a task review should always be conducted, a group facilitator may decide to perform a review of changes in target problems less frequently. One approach is to review the progress of two or three different group members each week. We would like to conclude this section on the middle phase of group work with caregivers with an example.

CASE EXAMPLE: MIDDLE PHASE SESSION OF CAREGIVER GROUP

The Caregiver Education and Support Group is a twelve-week group that meets at the local senior center. It is led by the senior center's social worker and her graduate student. Occasionally, guest speakers are invited to speak on specific topics. The group consists of nine caregivers, six women and three men. Their ages vary from 57 to 78 years. All have been providing care for longer than eight months. The participants were identified and recommended to the group by staff of the senior center as well as by practitioners in other agencies providing services to older adults. The group is meeting on a weekly basis. An individual pregroup session was held with each participant. The group's first sessions focused on getting to know each other and presentation of some of the issues and problems the caregivers were facing. The following five sessions focused on individual problem-solving tasks, aimed at helping caregivers address their problems and needs. A second set of five sessions had a more educational focus, intending to teach caregivers skills that would make their lives easier and prevent burnout.

The seventh session, which will be examined in detail, began with a review of the task accomplishments of each group member. Since tasks had focused on individual problems and a more extensive review of problem changes was conducted, a little more than the usually allotted fifteen minutes were used for this part of the session. Most group members had accomplished their tasks at least to a considerable extent. However, two group members had made only little progress on their tasks. Group members discussed additional ways that these tasks could be performed with more success. The process ended with two slightly revised tasks that these individuals agreed to undertake by the following group session.

After a short talk by the social worker about the transition into the more educational part of the group process—group members had received a detailed outline after the screening interview—the second part of the session focused on ways that caregivers could unwind and relax after a long day of providing care. The social worker talked for about twenty-five minutes and introduced several relaxation techniques and breathing exercises. She then opened up the group for a discussion of the strategies that members typically use to relax. This was followed by the development of individual relaxation tasks. During this process, one group member suggested that relaxation tasks could also be a joint activity by caregiver and care recipient. A discussion followed in which group members expressed diverging opinions whether separate caregiver tasks would be better in providing respite. After the discussion went on for some time, the group leader refocused and reminded the group that next week's entire session would focus on caregiver respite and that they could include more discussion on this topic.

Tasks that were developed by group members fell into three categories. Two group members wanted to carry out tasks with their respective care recipients. One of them planned to set aside an hour each afternoon, prepare some tea, and jointly reminisce with her husband. The second developed shared tasks for him and his wife to pick a short story or poem each day that they would read to each other. Most group members generated tasks that related to trying out some of the relaxation techniques they had learned during the middle part of the session. Finally, the two group members who had difficulty with their previous tasks decided that they would focus primarily on them. Thus, rather than having a daily relaxation task, they were to perform it a least once during the following week.

The session ended with a review of the group process. One group member indicated her uneasiness with the group's time management. She indicated that the group usually started a few minutes late and then ran over the time. Since she had to rely on a friend for transportation, it caused her some additional stress. The group agreed to make an effort to start on time.

FINAL PHASE OF TASK-CENTERED GROUPS

Termination in task-centered groups occurs during the last one or two sessions. In these sessions the group members conduct a final problem and task review, reinforce one another's accomplishments, and discuss future plans. They also discuss the group experience and say their good-byes.

The final problem review and reinforcing of accomplishment is a joint group activity. Again, group members provide feedback and learn from one another during this process. They share with each other what they valued about the way tasks were achieved and what changes they saw occurring as a result. At the same time, the accomplishments of the group itself should be reinforced. The practitioner should point out how the group members helped each other solve problems. She should also highlight the ways they participated in the group process and how the group as a whole benefited from each member's contributions.

Finally, future plans are discussed. Relationships will have developed during the course of the group. These new relationships can be incorporated into future planning. For example, group members can develop a "buddy support system" in which they help each other in the future. Occasionally, some or all group members decide to continue as a group, for example as a caregiver self-help group. The practitioner can assist group members in getting started. Many groups celebrate their ending, for example, by bringing food or going out after completion of the last session.

CHAPTER 10

PRACTICE IN LONG-TERM CARE SETTINGS

Debra Lacey

T HE PURPOSE of this chapter is to examine how a task-centered model can be implemented in long-term care settings. In previous chapters the practice model was discussed in its use as an intervention with older adults or their caregivers in the community. In this chapter, long-term care facilities are the environment under discussion. The first part of this chapter will address relevant differences between long-term care settings and independent living. The second part of this chapter will illustrate the model by discussing two case situations.

RELEVANT CHARACTERISTICS OF FACILITIES AND RESIDENTS

In this country, the term *nursing home* is often used generically to apply to all facilities that provide residence and some services to older adults. People new to long-term care are often unaware that in long-term care terminology is important, and there are often vast differences between nursing or skilled nursing facilities, commonly known as nursing homes, and lesser levels of care, often referred to as assisted living, residential care, board and care, and foster care.

Skilled nursing facilities are on the one end of the long-term care continuum, providing the greatest amount of medical and personal care to older adults. Currently, about 1.4 million older adults live in about 16,500 nursing homes throughout the country (Federal Interagency Forum on Aging-Related Statistics 2000). Almost all nursing homes operate under strict federal and state regulations that broadly dictate the facilities' policies. Directives extend from documentation requirements and residents' rights to designated size of meal portions and acceptable water temperatures. Nursing homes are also required to provide individualized care, yet the preponderance of regulations often results in limited flexibility in the provision of services.

Nursing homes historically have cared for older adults who are among the most frail and impaired in this country, and in recent years the overall degree of frailty and impairment has risen among nursing home residents (Federal Interagency Forum on Aging-Related Statistics 2000). This has occurred partly as a result of efforts by many states to limit nursing home care to the most frail (Hawes, Rose, and Phillips 1999), the geometric growth of the "old-old"—those 85 and older—and an increase in community services that enable many frail older adults to delay nursing home placement until they are extremely impaired.

Medicare and Medicaid—two primary insurance programs used by older adults—provide the policy framework for nursing homes and help pay for the care of many nursing home residents. Medicare typically covers posthospital rehabilitative and/or nursing services for a limited period of time. Medicaid is the primary payer of custodial care for individuals who have become indigent. In 1999 about 68 percent of all nursing home residents were Medicaid recipients (Harrington et al. 2000).

Partly due to these reimbursement structures, many nursing homes serve two distinctively different types of older adults—those who are admitted for short (up to three months) rehabilitative stays, and those who will stay there permanently. Recent trends indicate that there has been an increase in older adults using nursing homes for short rehabilitative stays and a slight decrease in the overall percentage of older adults living permanently in nursing homes (Federal Interagency Forum on Aging-Related Statistics 2000; Kane et al. 1999). Such trends are expected to continue. However, with the aging of the baby boom generation, the number of older adults requiring nursing home care will more than triple in the next thirty years (Maloney et al. 1996). Therefore, clinicians increasingly will need to understand long-term care environments if they are to work effectively with an aging population.

Despite significant improvements in care over the past decade, nursing homes in this country often still have a dismal public image (Fries et al. 1997). A popular newsmagazine recently referred to nursing homes as "mortuaries" (Goldstein 2001:49). Not surprisingly, families often feel guilty and burdened when they move older relatives, friends, or spouses into nursing homes (Forbes, Bern-Klug, and Gessert 2000).

Many nursing homes, particularly older facilities, lack the homelike atmosphere that residents and families prefer. Older nursing homes, in particular, often appear hospital-like with large, impersonal common spaces, long wards of double bedrooms with hospital beds, and staffing consisting largely of nursing personnel in uniforms. Newer facilities are often designed with more personal and homelike spaces and with greater sensitivity to the environmental needs of people with dementia.

Still, despite improvements in care and ambiance, nursing homes are often considered an undesirable long-term care alternative, and this has, in part, fueled the rise of assisted living facilities throughout the country. Currently, there are about 11,500 assisted living facilities in the United States. Together they serve more than 500,000 older adults (Hawes et al. 1999). Considered one of the fastest growing industries in the 1990s (United States GAO 1997; Hawes et al. 1999), these facilities vary widely in size, ambiance, and services although all provide fewer services than nursing homes. Assisted living facilities typically provide housing, some protective oversight, medication administration, and many provide limited personal assistance. Currently, assisted living facilities are regulated only by state agencies. The degree of oversight varies significantly from state to state (United States GAO 1997). Marketers of assisted living facilities promote their differences from nursing homes, e.g., they often are marketed as more upscale, more homelike, more private and freer from the burdensome regulations of nursing homes (United States GAO 1997; Goldstein 2001; Pruchno and Rose 2000). A comprehensive study of assisted living facilities across the country found that only about 11 percent of the facilities actually fit this description. Another 60 percent of facilities described as assisted living were characterized by minimal privacy and varying amounts of personal service and may have been formerly labeled as board and care homes for the aged (Hawes et al. 1999).

More freedom from regulation allows assisted living facilities greater flexibility than nursing homes in their provision of services. This freedom from regulation often translates into less accountability for resident care (United States GAO 1997; Goldstein 2001). In recent years charges of poor resident care in some assisted living facilities have begun to mirror similar longtime complaints in nursing homes. Still, assisted living remains popular with older adults and family members as a desired long-term care option that delays or prevents nursing home placement (United States GAO 1997; Goldstein 2001).

Most assisted living facilities in this country are private pay only, meaning that older adults with low incomes usually do not have access to these facilities (Hawes et al. 1999). Anecdotal reports and limited research indicates that in some parts of the country older adults who have the functional ability to live in assisted living facilities move into nursing homes because of payment issues (Pruchno and Rose 2000). However, on average, nursing home residents are more cognitively and functionally impaired than residents of assisted living facilities (Hawes et al. 1999; Reinardy and Kane 1999).

For practitioners, the implications of the long-term care environment are significant. In nursing homes practitioners and clients may have limited ability to change aspects of the resident's daily routine because of the regulations, policies, and practices that often dictate nursing home life. At the same time, more professional staff is often available (e.g., nurse aides, nurses, social workers, activities staff), and they are more accountable to plans of care for residents. Practitioners may be working with residents with short-term rehabilitative needs, with those who will be permanently placed, or with both groups. They often need a degree of expertise in dementia to work successfully with residents, families, and staff of nursing homes.

In assisted living facilities practitioners and clients may have greater flexibility in addressing problems related to the resident's daily routine. At the same time, fewer on-site professional staff may be available to address problems in the residence. The staff that is present may be less accountable in regard to resident care issues. Practitioners may be working with residents suffering from similar but less severe functional and cognitive problems as nursing home residents. However, as residents' functional abilities worsen over time, they may need to move to a nursing home. At least 25 percent of assisted living residents eventually move to a nursing home (Hawes et al. 1999).

THE PLACEMENT PROCESS

The decision to place a family member in a nursing home or an institutional setting is not easily made. In fact, most families postpone this decision until they become too overwhelmed with the daily caregiving tasks and are no longer able to provide adequate care (see Naleppa 1996 for a review). A significant amount of research has tried to establish predictors for the risk of institutional placement. The most important contributing factors are the caregiver's subjective distress at being overwhelmed by twenty-four-hour caregiving demands (Brown, Potter, and Foster 1990; Chenoweth and Spencer 1986; Cohen et al. 1993; Lieberman and Kramer 1991; McFall and Miller 1992; Montgomery and Kosloski 1994). Other factors include the caregiver's health and mental health (Colerick and George 1986; Pratt, Wright, and Schmall 1987), lack of spousal support (Cohen et al. 1993; Colerick and George 1986; Dolinsky and Rosenwaike 1988; Shapiro and Tate 1988; Liu and Manton 1989). Caregivers who do not accept their caregiving role are more likely to favor institutional placement (Cohen et al. 1993; Pruchno, Michael, and Potshnik 1990). The living arrangement of the person has been identified as a good predictor. Persons living alone are more likely to enter a long-term care facility than those living with spouses, family members, or friends (Branch and Jette 1982; Hanley et al. 1990; Montgomery and Kosloski 1994; Morycz 1985; Smallegan 1985).

Earlier research on predictors of institutionalization by Colerick and George (1986) indicates that caregivers' characteristics and the caregiving environment are better predictors than the characteristics of the care recipient. Nonemployed elderly spouses are the group with the highest tendency of continued in-home caregiving (Colerick and George 1986; Montgomery and Kosloski 1994). This group also reports comparatively high life satisfaction (Colerick and George 1986).

For the male elderly, marital status is a strong predictor. Unmarried and never married men are at the highest risk of entering a nursing home (Dolinsky and Rosenwaike 1988; Hanley et al. 1990). Some studies found that the presence of children in the elderly person's life reduced the placement risk (Dolinsky and Rosenwaike 1988; Wan and Weissert 1981), but another study identified the combination of a spousal and child caregiver unit to increases the likelihood of institutionalization (Lieberman and Kramer 1991). A child as primary caregiver increases the probability for entering long-term care (Colerick and George 1986; Lieberman and Kramer 1991), especially if the child is a son (Montgomery and Kosloski 1994).

The move into an institutional setting is emotionally taxing for all involved and should be considered as equivalent to a family crisis (Schneewind 1990; Zarit and Whitlatch 1992). Despite this, however, it should be considered part of the normal family life cycle (Naleppa 1996; Schneewind 1990). Many placements are arranged in a very short time period from the hospital or a rehabilitation facility, rather than from the client's home. Numerous service providers and professionals (e.g., social workers, nurses, physicians, and case managers) may be involved in the placement decision, adding to the stress and feelings of being overwhelmed.

ADJUSTMENT ISSUES

One of the most common issue for practitioners in long-term care is helping residents of nursing homes and assisted living facilities adjust to their new environment. Even if the move is temporary, older adults are faced with new physical environments that are sometimes difficult to negotiate, with a host of unfamiliar staff, and with the loss of familiar surroundings that may have provided an important anchor of the older adult's sense of self. Practitioners need to understand the painful emotions of loss and grief that many older adults experience when they move into a long-term care setting. However, it can be anticipated that older adults who move into nursing homes with the expectation of returning home will have a less stressful period of adjustment than those residents who have no expectation of returning home.

When a person moves into a nursing home or assisted living facility, he or she often has to leave behind a comforting environment and many cherished possessions that may have been an important source of stability, comfort, and identity. Some new residents may feel an impending sense of mortality as the "content" of their lives is scaled down after they move from a house or an apartment into one room or a shared room in a facility. Residents typically have far less privacy in the facility and may have difficulty navigating in a new environment.

Early in the admission process, particularly if a placement is undesired by the elderly person, practitioners may need to spend time with the resident and family members, validating their grief and finding positive ways to help residents adjust successfully to their relocation. Practitioners can incorporate therapeutic interventions in a task-centered approach to adjustment problems (as will be discussed in the case scenarios).

As mentioned, new residents may suffer from identity-related problems. In nursing homes this may be most acute early in the admissions process. Residents may be identified by their medical diagnoses, rather than by the self-images that they constructed over a lifetime. For instance, a resident who always thought of himself as a painter, basketball coach, and father, is now described by the staff as the new resident with congestive heart failure in room 4. Over time, this resident's identity reasserts itself, as he becomes familiar to the staff. Yet this is usually not evident to the resident at the time of admission. Practitioners can help ease this transition by making sure that staff persons know about relevant aspects of residents' histories. Learning about residents' histories often provides opportunities for staff to become sensitive to and bonded with new residents.

New residents often experienced a recent acute episode (e.g., stroke, hip fracture). Thus they may feel an increased sense of helplessness, dependence, and physical pain, and related to this, a sense of loss regarding who they were before—independent and mobile—and who they are now—physically dependent on others. These residents may require additional psychosocial support from staff and family as they adjust to a changed self.

For older adults in general, strengths-based interventions such as the task-centered model may be particularly effective. Older adults are likely to have a reservoir of coping and adaptation skills that "contains strengths that can be drawn upon in coping with adversity in later life" (Gatz and Zarit 2002:18).

Helping newly placed older adults maintain or regain a sense of personal control may be central to the adjustment process. Research suggests that residents who have a stronger sense of personal competence (i.e., self-efficacy) adjust better and cope more effectively with nursing home placement than those with a lowered sense of personal competence (Johnson et al. 1998).

ADJUSTMENT: RELATIONSHIPS WITH FAMILY

Families are an important source of emotional and instrumental support for older adults moving to a long-term care setting, continuing the caregiving role they play in the community (Naleppa 1996). Family ties continue after entering long-term care facilities but include a shift of obligation (Zarit and Whitlatch 1992). Yet a move to a nursing home or assisted living facility also often changes dynamics in family relationships. Spouses may be living apart for the first time in half a century, parents may be living much further away or much closer to their adult children. Some older adults move into a facility after sharing a family home with a sibling for many years. Thus, the change in physical environment often has significant ramifications for family relationships, which may be positive or negative or have elements of both. For instance, new residents and family members may grieve the loss of intimate relationships, family members may feel guilty for not keeping their relative at home. Some residents may feel abandoned by their families, and others may be relieved to be in a setting with twenty-four-hour care. New residents with cognitive impairments may have a particularly difficult time adjusting to an unfamiliar environment. Yet, family members may find renewed energy for the emotional aspects of the relationship after they have less responsibility for hands-on care.

Despite myths to the contrary, family caregivers do not abandon their relatives after placement in a long-term care setting. In fact, family caregivers report a continued sense of responsibility and involvement after an older relative is moved into a nursing home (Forbes, Bern-Klug, and Gessert 2000; Kane et al. 1999; Naleppa 1996). However, for those who are permanently placed, there may be an emotional toll. In one study, family caregivers of nursing home residents reported feeling greater emotional distance from their relative over time (Kane et al. 1999).

In assisted living facilities, family members of frail older adults may provide frequent hands-on assistance to their relatives, who otherwise might only receive minimal personal care from the staff. Providing hands-on care has been found to be initially emotionally rewarding for family members, but over time the responsibility may cause increased stress for the caregiver

(Kane et al. 1999). Thus, practitioners need to be sensitive to the changes that occur in relationships after admission to the nursing home or assisted living facility and to the emotional changes that may occur in family relationships over time.

Adjustment—short-term or long-term—is dependent on many factors, including the circumstances that precipitated the placement, the goal of the resident and family at placement, the cognitive capacity of the resident, and the resident's and family members' relationship history and coping styles. Because of the heterogeneity of experiences of older adults and their family members around institutional placement, practitioners need to understand the dynamics specific to each individual and his or her family system.

ADJUSTMENT: RELATIONSHIPS WITH STAFF

An often ignored but critical component of the adjustment process involves another aspect of relationships—the relationship of the new resident to the staff. In long-term care settings, older adults depend on paid staff to provide meals, medication administration, and laundry services. In nursing homes and in some assisted living facilities staff persons assist residents with bathing and personal hygiene. Staff persons are typically expected to familiarize themselves with residents' preferences in these areas and to treat residents with respect and dignity, regardless of the resident's attitude or behavior toward staff. Thus, staff and residents are typically engaged in relationships marked by both intimacy as well as power and control issues. These issues may peak during the initial adjustment period, when staff and residents are adjusting to each other's routines and personalities. For example, in a nursing home, a new resident may expect staff to help her get up at 7 A.M.—her life-long morning routine. However, staff may be locked into a different schedule. They are getting other longtime residents up at 7 A.M. and cannot get to her until 7:30 or 8 A.M. This resident may feel powerless in the situation and may react by becoming verbally abusive to staff for coming "late" to her room. Such situations are not infrequent, but over time staff and residents usually find a workable compromise to such problems. However, adjustment occurs more quickly if practitioners address such problems early in the resident's stay. As staff and residents learn to work together, they often develop strong emotional bonds, and many staff members perceive themselves as the residents' second families.

Not surprisingly, issues of power and control also extend to relationships between family members and nursing home staff. Caregivers often continue to perceive themselves as such when the older adult is placed. Some caregivers continue providing significant amounts of personal care. Others see their "new" role more as a caregiver-manager rather than a hands-on caregiver (Hoffman and Platt 1991; Kane et al. 1999). Thus, there is a potential for staff and family members to have conflicts in decision making in regard to who is actually "in charge" of the resident's care (Hoffman and Platt 1991). This may be particularly problematic when a resident lacks decisional capacity and staff and family disagree about what constitutes good care or what constitutes the "best interest" of the resident. Sometimes these problems are exacerbated by poor communication between staff and family members. In these instances, practitioners can be helpful in ensuring that both families and staff feel heard and supported, regardless of the problem's outcome. For instance, an adult daughter might become upset with staff when her mother, who is functionally declining, begins having falls. The daughter may blame the staff for the falls. She may insist that her mother have rigorous physical therapy to improve her functioning. Staff members, feeling defensive, may curtly tell the daughter this is not possible without providing a full explanation of the evaluation that led to the medical determination. A skilled practitioner can help facilitate a nonthreatening, nonblaming meeting in which the daughter can begin to understand and grieve for her mother's irreversible decline and staff persons can articulate the measures they are taking to maximize the mother's safety and functional ability.

In general, staff and families maintain relatively positive relationships. Most staff members recognize that family members are the primary emotional supports and the residents' remaining links to their former communities. When they have good relationships, family members can provide insight to staff persons by sharing stories about a resident's history, habits, and previous lifestyle. This is particularly helpful for residents with cognitive impairments. Staff, in turn, may provide the family with information about an older adult's medical and functional assessments and the medical, rehabilitative, and psychosocial plans of care.

ADJUSTMENT: RESIDENT-RESIDENT RELATIONSHIPS

For many people moving into nursing homes and assisted living facilities the most challenging aspect of initial adjustment involves changing from living in a private home environment to a setting where privacy may be minimal. In many nursing homes and assisted living facilities, residents share bedrooms and bathrooms. Even when residents have private rooms, staff usually have total access to these areas for tasks including cleaning, bringing in laundry, and assisting with personal care. Many facilities serve congregate meals, requiring residents to eat in public groupings at least twice daily. As a result, people who may have lived alone for fifty years may now have to adjust to eating breakfast, lunch, and dinner with up to a hundred or more people.

When residents share rooms, they have to adjust to living with someone else's daily habits. As one might expect, conflicts with roommates are not uncommon. For instance, one resident may prefer to go to sleep at 8 P.M. in a quiet room while her roommate prefers to watch television until midnight. These residents may find ways to adjust to each other's preferences (e.g., the "night owl" resident may agree to wear television headphones), or they may decide that they are incompatible. Thus, resident-to-resident adjustment issues always involve accommodation and compromise, and sometimes several room changes before compatibility is achieved.

Complicating relationships among residents is the presence of dementia in most facilities. In nursing homes, usually 60 percent or more of residents have moderate to severe cognitive impairments (Alzheimer's Disease Statistics Fact Sheet 1996). In assisted living facilities, about 37 percent of residents are cognitively impaired (Hawes et al. 1999). People with dementia often have behaviors that are difficult to deal with for staff and for residents who are cognitively intact. It is not uncommon for residents with dementia to wander into others' rooms, fall asleep in others' beds, and rummage through others' belongings. While this is rarely a problem for other residents with dementia, these behaviors understandably can cause great consternation for residents who are cognitively intact or only mildly cognitively impaired. Residents who are cognitively intact may be frustrated with, angered by, or frightened of cognitively impaired residents. They may also worry about these residents' safety and feel protective of them. In some facilities, the cognitively impaired residents with the most intrusive behaviors live in separate units. In many long-term care settings, however, populations are mixed. The practitioner's role in these situations may be to ensure that all residents are safe, and that the psychosocial needs of both the cognitively impaired and cognitively intact residents are being met.

POTENTIAL ISSUES AFTER THE ADJUSTMENT PERIOD

Often, problems that occur during the initial adjustment process (e.g., grief, power and control issues, changing relationships) continue to replay themselves, albeit in different forms, during a resident's stay in a long-term care facility. Grief and loss may be a particularly recurring theme in the lives of residents, staff, and families. Long-term care residents typically have multiple chronic health conditions that worsen over time. They, their family members, and staff may periodically grieve these losses and need to readjust various aspects of their relationships. Residents often develop friendships with each other, and they often grieve when their friends die or leave the facility. Staff turnover is a rampant problem in the long-term care industry, and residents and families may feel abandoned by departing staff with whom they developed a caring and trusting relationship. Residents and families may also reexperience power and control adjustment issues with new staff.

Because older adults in long-term care settings often live with multiple medical problems and chronic illnesses, practitioners must keep in mind the clinical issues that are likely to affect a person's quality of life and abilities. These include the often coexisting conditions of depression and chronic pain (Hoyer, Rybash, and Roodin 1999). Several recent studies indicate that many nursing home residents are undertreated for pain (Miller, Gozalo, and Mor 2000; Won et al. 1999). Moreover, the presence of untreated chronic pain may be associated with greater functional disability and mood disorders (Won et al. 1999). Although these studies were conducted in nursing homes, it is likely that similar conditions may exist for older adults in assisted living facilities. Because pain and depression are often treatable, practitioners in long-term care should always assess for the presence of these debilitating problems.

Ultimately, the quality of older adults' experiences in long-term care settings is largely dependent on the professionalism of the staff and the quality of the relationships between residents, family members, and the facility staff. Recognizing the centrality of these relationships, practitioners who work with older adults in long-term care settings strive to enhance the relationships between residents, families, and staff by encouraging meaningful communication as well as mutual respect and understanding.

TASK-CENTERED PRACTICE IN LONG-TERM CARE SETTINGS

As described elsewhere in this book, the task-centered model emphasizes the client's autonomy and strengths. Box 10.1 presents some of the most relevant aspects of task-centered practice in long-term care (Reid 1996).

A cornerstone of task-centered practice is the focus on the autonomy of the client and on the client's ability to develop and carry out tasks leading to a resolution of his or her problem under the facilitation and/or guidance of the practitioner (Reid and Fortune 2002). As Naleppa and Reid (2000) point out, frail elderly clients may have limited abilities or resources with which they can effect change in their lives. Older adults in long-term care facilities are more impaired than the general population. Many are in failing health and have cognitive impairments. Poor health in very old adults has been

---

BOX 10.1 IMPORTANT ASPECTS OF TASK-CENTERED PRACTICE IN LONG-TERM CARE

- Collaborative relationship between the practitioner and the client
- Focus on problems identified by the client
- Time-limited intervention period
- Clearly defined sequence of tasks carried out by the client and practitioner
- Preference for empirically tested methods and theories
- Focus on the current obstacles blocking the resolution of the client's problems rather than on dealing with the historical origins of the problem

---

found to be associated with a preference for deferring important medical decisions to providers and family members (Puchalski et al. 2000). Older adults with moderate and severe cognitive impairment have deficits in memory and judgment abilities, impairing their ability to plan and follow through with decisions.

At the same time, practitioners cannot assume that frail older adults do not want to participate in decisions that affect aspects of their lives that are still important to them. Research has shown that elderly persons who have positive feelings of well-being also feel that they have control over specific problems central in their lives (Hoyer, Rybash, and Roodin 1999; Johnson et al. 1998). Thus, the notion of autonomy with institutionalized older adults is not an all-or-nothing proposition. Rather, it is a matter of determining together with the older adult which problems the person has the ability and interest to focus energy on. A useful framework for this endeavor is the autonomy framework described in chapter 5 (Collopy 1988). In this framework, it will be recalled, autonomy can be decisional or executional. In decisional autonomy, a person has the ability to participate in a decision but not its implementation, and in executional autonomy the person may lack the ability to formulate the decision, but he or she may be able to participate in its implementation. The following case scenarios will exemplify how the task-centered model is applied with older adults using the framework.

CASE EXAMPLE: NURSING HOME

The following case scenario describes a nursing home situation in which complications arise regarding a potential discharge of a resident who was admitted for a rehabilitative stay. June Smith is a 78-year-old woman who came to the nursing home after she fractured her hip at home. She had surgery in the hospital and needed rehabilitation before she could return home. June had advanced osteoarthritis but was otherwise relatively healthy. Prior to the hospitalization and nursing home placement, June lived in a two-story home with her longtime husband, Hal. He was 80 and had heart problems and some mild memory impairment. June and Hal had two children, Doris, 56, who lived locally with her family, and Alex, 53, who lived with his family about two hours away from his parents' home. At the time of the admission, June identified Doris as the family member to contact for financial and discharge issues.

June had been admitted to the nursing home with the expectation that she would participate in a rehabilitation program to build up her strength and mobility. After that, she was to return home. About one week into her stay, the nursing home social worker was asked by staff to intervene with June and her family.

According to the staff report, June had refused physical therapy for the past two days. June kept saying she wanted to go home. Staff indicated that June was not independent enough yet to return home. If June did not resume therapy within a day or two, she would lose her Medicare funding for the rehabilitative stay. Therapy staff said that Hal—who took the Senior Van almost daily for visits to the nursing home—was too frail and too forgetful to follow through on the therapists' instructions for helping June ambulate safely at home. Staff indicated that June's daughter was not returning their phone calls regarding the discharge of her mother. Moreover, staff described June as "lazy" and a "complainer."

A key tenet of the task-centered model is collaboration between the practitioner and the client and a focus on problems identified by the client. To that end, the social worker agreed to meet with June, not to persuade her to resume therapy, but to see if she could collaborate with her in addressing her immediate issues. The social worker's goal of the first meeting was assessment, i.e., collecting information that might aid her and June in developing a plan to address June's current problems.

The staff social worker met with June and explained that she had been asked by therapy and nursing staff to see her and that she was interested in helping June address the issues that were important to her. June acknowledged that she had refused physical therapy for several days. She said she wanted to go home, and she asked the social worker to call her daughter who would "take care of everything." Upon further probing, June told the social worker that she refused physical therapy for the past several days because she was in pain. The exercises were "too hard," and "the physical therapist doesn't like me." Further questions revealed that she felt depressed about her situation, i.e., her loss of independence and her reliance on staff and her daughter.

Having gathered this information, the social worker made a quick assessment of the situation. She discussed her assessment openly but tactfully. The social worker said she believed that June could go home successfully and safely but not within the next few days. She also said that she thought June's feelings of depression might be contributing to her discouragement and difficulty with planning. After some discussion, the social worker and June agreed on two goals. The first goal was to get June discharged home as soon as could safely be arranged. The second goal was to help June regain her sense of control about her life. Because June was feeling so overwhelmed, the social worker suggested that they should start with small tasks.

The social worker explained to June that to meet the first goal, they had to deal with the physical therapy issue. Regarding the second goal—increasing June's sense of control—the social worker asked June if she would be willing to participate in a joint meeting later that day to include the physical therapist and the head nurse. June reluctantly agreed but also said that she was a little intimidated. The social worker helped June prepare for her first task through a rehearsal of the meeting. Taking the role of the physical therapist, she asked June about her refusal to participate in therapy. In her role play response, June blurted out angrily "Because I don't want to!" The social worker acknowledged her resentment at being asked to do physical therapy but wondered if she might not want to use this opportunity to tell the therapist about the pain she felt while doing the exercises. In a repetition of the role play June gave a calm explanation of the discomfort she experienced.

Prior to the afternoon meeting, the social worker met briefly with the head nurse and the therapist and explained that they were working toward increasing June's decisional autonomy. The social worker also mentioned that June had several behavioral indicators of depression—tearfulness, hopelessness, lack of motivation, and June's self-identified depression—and that a depression could explain some of the behaviors that were labeled as "lazy" and "complaining." Therapist and head nurse agreed to be mindful of facilitating June's role in the decision-making process. The head nurse agreed to ask June if she would be willing to meet with a doctor regarding her depressive feelings.

That afternoon, the social worker, June, the head nurse, and the physical therapist met in June's room. With prompting from the social worker, June calmly explained her resistance to therapy. After some discussion, plans were made to try therapy again the next day. According to the task plan, June would receive pain medication about an hour before therapy, the therapist would modify the exercises, and June would let the therapist know if she was still in pain or uncomfortable with an exercise. The therapist, who had been frustrated with June in therapy, said she would try to cultivate a more positive working relationship with her. In response to the nurse's question, June agreed to meet with a doctor regarding her depression.

During this meeting June also disclosed that she was unhappy with her table assignment at lunch. Hal was often there for lunch, but they had no privacy to talk. The head nurse—mindful of the importance of June's decision-making—asked June if she preferred to eat in her room with Hal. June thought about this suggestion for a minute and then said that she would prefer this option. The nurse said that the new lunch arrangement could start the next day.

The next afternoon the social worker met briefly with June, who reported that the pain medication helped her tolerate of the physical therapy. She was getting along better with the therapist since the meeting the day before. June had met with the physician, who diagnosed her with moderate depression. June agreed to try out antidepressant medication. The social worker and June also arranged to further plan for June's discharge early the next week. June gave permission to contact Doris, her daughter, regarding discharge planning. June said that Doris had been visiting her regularly in the evenings.

As the social worker became more involved in helping June make the transition to her home, she realized that her family relationship necessitated a more family-oriented task-centered approach. The social worker recognized that Doris' behavior—visiting her mother in the evening, but avoiding talking to day staff about discharge—signaled the importance of reaching out to Doris in a nonthreatening manner. In keeping with the task-centered model, the social worker also recognized that it was important for this family to focus on present, immediate concerns and to avoid becoming mired in a rehashing of old resentments.

The social worker left a message for Doris asking her to call and discuss her concerns about her mother returning home. This time, Doris returned the social worker's call. Doris said she was overwhelmed with the responsibilities for her parents, especially her father, whose dementia was worsening. Doris complained that her brother was not helpful at all and that her mother was too dependent. At the same time, she acknowledged that she had difficulty relinquishing control of her responsibilities. After some discussion, Doris said she wanted the social worker's assistance in addressing her issues around June's discharge. They agreed on a goal to improve communication between Doris, her mother, and her brother regarding Doris' concerns. Doris and the social worker agreed on initiating a family meeting "just to talk" about discharge concerns. Doris also agreed to two tasks: (1) To call her brother and make sure he would attend, and (2) to prepare for the meeting by developing a list of immediate concerns.

The social worker met early the next week with June who said that she was having continued success with therapy. This was helping her feel more hopeful. The social worker and June discussed the upcoming family meeting. After some discussion, June agreed to complete a task for the meeting, i.e., developing her own list of concerns about her return home. June also volunteered to introduce the social worker to her husband Hal later that day. The social worker agreed, and she met Hal that afternoon. June asserted that the staff's perception of Hal as "pleasantly confused" seemed accurate. It was questionable to what extent he might be able to participate in decision making regarding June's return home.

Later that week, June, her family, and the nursing home staff (the social worker, head nurse, physical therapist, and nursing assistant) held a meeting. The social worker began the meeting by explaining its purpose as addressing immediate issues related to June's return home. The therapist discussed June's progress in physical therapy, but she also mentioned her concerns about her report of the lack of assistive devices in her home (e.g., no raised toilet seat, grab bars in the shower, etc.). Doris discussed the concerns she had about her continued ability to help her parents without extra support. She also said she was hoping that her brother could be more helpful. Doris' brother Alex and his wife said they could offer some limited assistance, but they were not sure what they could do. June brought her list of concerns. She said that her primary concern was managing Hal as well as the housework that was increasingly difficult to perform because of her osteoarthritis. After much discussion—during which the social worker emphasized present concerns and not old interpersonal resentments—the family group agreed on the following tasks. Alex and his wife would take over all aspects of financial management from Doris. They also agreed to be responsible for getting assistive devices in the home. Finally, they would take Hal to their home for a long weekend visit every two months to provide some respite for June. Hal was agreeable to this plan. Doris and her mother agreed to perform the following tasks after June's discharge. Doris said she would contact an acquaintance from the church that was a paid housecleaner. June's task would then be to interview the housecleaner to make sure she felt comfortable having her assist with housecleaning every two weeks. Doris and June assumed joint task responsibility for visiting a local adult day care center to see if it would be an appropriate place for Hal to spend one day a week. This could potentially provide needed respite for June and be an opportunity for positive socializing for Hal, who was often isolated at home. At this point, the group set a discharge date for the beginning of the following week.

The social worker met one more time with June prior to her discharge. As June's mood and outlook improved, she continued to maximize her decisional autonomy in making decisions about tasks related to her return home. As her functional ability improved, she also began to have increased executional autonomy. For example, June called her pastor as a reference for the housecleaner that she was considering hiring. June was discharged successfully later that week.

TASK-CENTERED GROUPS IN LONG-TERM CARE SETTINGS

Task-centered practice is as applicable to groups as it is to clinician-client dyads. As discussed in the previous chapter, task-centered groups are defined by use of the group process to help individuals solve specific personal issues or problems. The group exists largely for mutual support in resolving personal issues. In other words, "the ultimate change target against which success is measured is not interaction of group members outside the session but rather resolution of the separate problems of each" (Reid 1996:631).

While task-centered group work may be particularly applicable to older adults and caregivers (chapter 9), certain caveats apply to its use in long-term care settings (see box 10.2).

BOX 10.2 CONSIDERATIONS FOR GROUP WORK IN LONG-TERM CARE SETTINGS

- Older adults are more likely to have hearing and visual difficulties than younger people. Thus clinicians must find meeting spaces with good acoustics, bright light without glare, and minimal distractions. They should check with residents during group sessions to make sure they are seeing and hearing adequately.
- Many older adults in long-term care have health problems that fluctuate in intensity and could affect their ability to participate consistently in meetings.
- Many older adults in long-term care settings have dementia. Task-centered groups for older adults in these settings need to be modified. Groups should adjust their focus to include more activities like reminiscing, sensory-oriented endeavors, and social activities that foster the residents' remaining cognitive strengths.
- Old age is developmentally distinct from middle age and young adulthood. A number of theories suggest that a task in later life is to find meaning and put one's life in context (Hoyer, Rybash, and Roodin 1999). To that end, a task-centered group may be part of a larger focus on establishing acceptance for one's past and present life.

CASE SCENARIO: TASK-CENTERED GROUP
IN AN ASSISTED LIVING FACILITY

A social worker contracted with Oak Lawn, an assisted living facility with about one hundred residents, to provide eight weekly group sessions. The target audience included any residents who were having problems in their adjustment to the facility or their relationships with family members. However, the group was to be open to all residents who wished to join. This particular case scenario focuses on the issues of Joe, one of the six participants who signed up for the group. The example illustrates use of key methods of task-centered groups even though not all components of the model (such as individual screening interviews) were used. In practice, the task-centered group work model may be modified to incorporate other components, such as education, as illustrated in the previous chapter, or to meet purposes specific to the setting, as in the present case.

Prior to the first session, the social worker made sure that the meeting room was appropriate for the sensory needs of the participants. She also verified that refreshments would be served at each session.

In the introductory session, the social worker focused on explaining the purpose of the group, which included problem identification, assistance in addressing whatever problems were identified, and group support. Much of the balance of the session involved introductions of the residents. A good deal of time was devoted to this activity to enable residents, if they wished, to express themselves in terms of their lifelong identity. This exercise also helped the social worker assess the problems, strengths, and coping styles of the participants. At the end of the introductions, the social worker discussed group rules with the participants. Using a flip chart, she wrote in large type all suggestions for group rules. Participants then identified the most important rules, including attending sessions regularly and taking turns in discussions.

In previous groups, the social worker had experienced that sessions sometimes ended with sadness and some participants left feeling disconnected. Since then, she included an ending ritual for each session. Each member would offer one example of "what I am grateful for in my life today." In the social worker's experience this exercise helped many participants leave the group more content and satisfied.

In the second session, Joe, the only male member of the group, began a diatribe against his adult children, particularly his daughter. The other group members were silent and seemed to vacillate between sympathy and discomfort as Joe vented his anger toward his children for about ten minutes. Finally, as one woman tried to interrupt, Joe cut her off and continued talking. At this point, the social worker intervened.

The social worker gently reminded Joe that a primary purpose of the group was to focus on present problems. She asked, if a recent event had precipitated Joe's display of anger. Joe said he was angry because evening staff was refusing to give him his cigarettes. Joe called his daughter, who said he shouldn't be smoking at all with his emphysema. She had told the staff not to allow him to smoke. Upon further questioning, Joe disclosed that staff held his cigarettes because he had been caught smoking in his room on several occasions. (Smoking was not allowed in the building.)

The social worker asked other members for their responses. The room was silent. Joe tried to resume talking, but the social worker asked him to wait. Finally, one woman said that she was upset by his smoking indoors and that she was afraid that he could cause a fire if he was careless. Another woman supported her. Joe started becoming angry again and told the women they did not know what they were talking about. The social worker, attempting to defuse Joe's defensiveness, validated his frustration with losing control over something important to him. After a short silence, one group member said, "I think Joe's angry that his wife is in a nursing home, and he's taking it out on all of us." Joe looked at her and began crying. "You don't understand," he cried, "we've been married fifty-four years, and she doesn't even know me anymore."

Immediately, one woman said, "I do understand. My husband had Alzheimer's and for the last two years of his life, he didn't know me." Another woman said, "My husband was very sick before he died. I wanted to believe he knew I was there, but I knew that he didn't." Joe continued weeping and said little else as the other participants discussed their stories of their losses of spouses.

As the discussion continued, the social worker asked participants to identify what helped them get through these difficult times and how they thought they made a difference as caregivers. The social worker's goal at this time was to encourage the participants' recognition of their strengths, their contributions, and their coping skills. Also, when a participant minimized her role as a caregiver, others were quick to identify her contributions. Group members praised Joe for the strength of his commitment to his wife and the importance of his continued visits with her. The group then concluded the second meeting with the gratitude ritual.

At the third session, the social worker reviewed the content and process of the second session. Then she asked the participants about problems they were finding difficult to resolve by themselves. Group members identified problems including perceived insensitivity on the part of the staff to a participant's visual impairment, coping with residents with worsening dementia, and complaints about meals and food service. Joe identified three problems—the smoking conflict, his difficult relationship with his children complicated by the third problem, his reliance on his children to take him to the nursing home twice weekly to visit his wife. Joe said he wanted to visit more often but did not have transportation.

Over the next several sessions, the social worker helped participants identify and clarify particular tasks they were undertaking to address their problems. Members in turn suggested tasks they could carry out with other members, offering suggestions about how these tasks could be done or alternative tasks that might be tried. Through this process each member worked out an action plan, which the social worker recorded. With support from the social worker, group members held each other accountable for their plans. After discussion with the group, Joe decided to address the smoking issue first. With input from the group, Joe decided that a reasonable approach involved a meeting with the social worker, administrator, and evening staff regarding a smoking contract. Joe said he still did not understand why he could not smoke in his room, but after listening to group members, he said he would adhere to a contract to only smoke outside if evening staff would cooperate. With the help of group members, he rehearsed the position he would be taking in the meeting. Joe had previously rejected suggestions that he try to quit smoking.

At the next meeting, Joe reported to the group that he was successful at the meeting, and he was now smoking outside in the evenings—much to the consternation of his daughter. As the group became more cohesive and as all members, including Joe, became more adept in using group process skills, Joe became more respectful of the women in the group. He began to interrupt less and to listen more.

In the sixth session, Joe and the group discussed his desire to visit his wife in the nursing home more frequently. Joe had insisted that his children should be responsible for increasing his visits, but the group strongly encouraged him to consider other options, e.g., using a paid driver.

Joe said his first task would involve talking with his son about what he could afford. He would do this by the next session. He also indicated that he would talk to the facility administrator about helping him recruit a paid driver.

During the next sessions, the social worker again facilitated group discussions regarding task obstacles, plans, progress, and achievements. She also continued to work with the group in enhancing mutual respect. By the end of this seventh session, she began termination of the group by reminding the members that the next session would be the last meeting.

The social worker prepared for the last group session by reviewing individual successes since the first session, as well as the progress they had made as group members. She began the last session by asking group members to discuss their perceptions regarding the progress made toward resolving their individual problems. Members also discussed other rewards from the group, including validation of both their grief and their strengths. Joe said that he was thankful to the group for listening to him and helping him see his continued value to his wife. He said that the administrator was helping him find a driver, and he was looking forward to spending more time with his wife in the time she had left. The social worker asked him about his relationship with his children. He said he was still angry with them but less so than at the start of the group.

The last group ended with an adapted weekly group ritual during which group members, including the social worker, expressed gratitude for what they learned in the group.

CONCLUSION

One purpose of this chapter has been to describe common issues practitioners encounter in the different types of long-term care facilities. For instance, practitioners need to be aware of the differences in policy and care practices between skilled nursing facilities or nursing homes and lesser levels of care, such as assisted living. Understanding how these facilities function helps practitioners understand the kinds of interventions that may be acceptable or appropriate in these settings.

Adjustment to changes in residence was discussed as well as the roles practitioners play in helping new residents and their family members adapt to new and often undesired circumstances. Practitioners often need to validate the losses that precede or accompany moves to long-term care environments and help older adults and their family members work through feelings including grief and guilt during the adjustment process. Grief and loss issues resurface periodically during a stay in a long-term care environment. Thus, practitioners need to continue working with residents and families around such issues.

Task-centered practice in long-term settings can be challenging, as a cornerstone of this model is the value placed on the client's autonomy in the practitioner-client relationship. In many long-term care settings older adults are limited by the dictates of their environment as well as by their functional limitations. The case scenarios presented in this chapter offered examples of how practitioners can use task-centered practice with clients by understanding how "autonomy" and "tasks" can be modified to best serve the interests and the goals of frail older adults in long-term care residences.

PART III

TASK PLANNERS

As has been discussed earlier in the book, task planners are intervention modules that can be drawn upon in work with the elderly and caregivers in regard to specific issues. A task planner consists of brief descriptions of the problem, references to relevant literature, and a "menu" of possible actions the client can take to resolve the problem as well as suggestions of what the practitioner can do to facilitate these problem-solving actions or to initiate others (Reid 2000).

Task planners essentially provide a range of tasks that may be applicable to the problem at hand. Some may be more useful than others. In most cases they will need to be modified to the client's specific needs and situation.

Tasks are stated as suggestions directed to the client, but they may contain technical terms that might need to be interpreted or recast in discussing the tasks with clients. Unless otherwise specified, it is assumed that the client is the elderly person. By this means we try to reinforce the notion that the elderly person should be in charge of activities aimed at alleviating his or her problems. However, it is recognized that caregivers or others may frequently need to play a role in the actual implementation of the tasks. Some tasks, such as tasks to "identify" or to "learn about" may be begun in the session, but it is assumed that such tasks can be continued after the session.

Under *Elaboration* we provide additional information about the task, which might include its rationale or details about how the task might be implemented. Under *Practitioner's Role* we list suggestions about how the practitioner can facilitate the client's implementation of the task. The section *Practitioner's Role* is used selectively to indicate the practitioner's activities specific to the task; basic intervention methods are normally not included. Some task planners include Web sites that may be accessed for further information. A categorized listing of over two hundred Web sites useful in work with the elderly is included in the appendix.

The task planners are listed under five main headings: Resources and Planning, Home and Personal Safety, Caregiving and Respite, Living and Care Arrangements, and Health and Mental Health. The exact location of each is given in the table of contents at the front of the book. Drafts of most task planners were prepared by master's and doctoral students and by geriatric social workers, as indicated by the names at the end of the task planners.

ADVANCE DIRECTIVES:
HEALTH CARE PROXY AND DNR ORDERS

In 1991 the United States Congress passed the Patient Self-Determination Act. This legislation mandated that hospitals, nursing homes, and other health care providers receiving Medicare and Medicaid as payment for service must develop written policies regarding advance directives. They are required to ask patients whether they have prepared an advance directive and have to provide written material regarding their right to execute these documents (Freeman 1994; Sansone and Phillips 1995). The two most common forms of advance directives are the living will and the durable power of attorney for health care. The living will outlines the patient's desires regarding medical treatment if he or she should become medically unable to make such decisions. The durable power of attorney for health care (health care proxy in some states) appoints a person of the patient's choosing to make decisions regarding health care if the patient becomes medically unable to do this (Soskis 1997). Studies have shown that the utilization rate of advance directives is very low among the elderly, ranging from 0 percent to 18 percent (Gamble, McDonald, and Lichstein 1991; High 1993). Among the reasons cited for this low usage are a lack of information and a lack of encouragement from families and health care professionals (Emanuel and Emanuel 1989; Murphy 1990; Zweibel and Cassel 1988), a lack of trust that health care professionals will respect such documents (Freeman 1994), the misinterpretation of the meaning of advance directives (Freeman 1994), and a lack of follow-through in the completion of the documents (Soskis 1997; High 1993).

Most people have a definite idea about the kind of medical care they want as they reach their later years. Some people want to fight for every minute of life under any circumstances. Other people are fearful of high-tech medical interventions that would artificially prolong the dying process. Individuals vary along a continuum between these extremes and at different times in their health status or disease process. In the absence of clear instructions to the contrary, aggressive medical treatments will usually be applied. It is therefore important that people complete advance directives and educate their loved ones, caregivers, and health care providers about their wishes before a medical emergency occurs. Advance directives are instructions in the event that there is a terminal condition with no reasonable expectation of recovery or in the event of a persistent vegetative state. This may authorize the provision, withdrawal, or withholding of care, or it may stipulate the opposite decision to artificially prolong life by any means; advance directives can also authorize any option in between these extremes.

Assigning a health care proxy is designed to make sure that medical choices will be honored. The mandate of the Durable Medical Power of Attorney (DMPOA) is to ensure that the decisions of the patient are honored if the patient cannot speak for him– or herself (see "Advance Planning: Power of Attorney"). The DMPOA is not really making the decisions; he is describing the decisions already made by the patient. This is at least a three-part process: thinking through one's general medical framework (see "End-of-Life Decision Making"), deciding how to formally address these decisions within the legal framework of state statutes, and informing critical persons of this thought process. Because decisions become more or less clear over time and circumstances, it is very important to share one's general thinking on these issues as decisions evolve. This way loved ones know the general framework from which decisions are being made.

Three common components of an advance directive are the living will, health care proxy, and the decision to make an anatomical donation. A "Do Not Resuscitate Order" (DNR) is a physician's order based on the patient's and/or health care proxy's instructions to not initiate cardiopulmonary resuscitation (CPR) in the event of a cardiac arrest. This decision is made when the patient's quality of life is such that he or she does not want it to be artificially extended. A patient may also request a DNR when he or she is relatively independent but anticipates a period of decline, debility, and death. Under these circumstances, if the patient's heart stops for any reason, the physician's order prohibits CPR and the resultant intubation or venting on life support machines. Under all circumstances, patients can expect and demand aggressive pain and symptom management until the moment of death.

Literature: Freeman (1994); Gamble, McDonald, and Lichstein (1991); High (1993); Sansone and Phillips (1995); Soskis (1997); Zweibel and Cassel (1988).

Web Sites: www.choices.org (Choices in Dying), www.ghc.org/health_info/adv_dir/advpage.html

See also: "Advanced Planning: Power of Attorney," "End-of-Life Decision-Making," "Financial and Personal Records"

TASK MENU

1. Learn about the different types of advance directives.

Elaboration: You can complete any or all of an Advance Directive as you decide which is appropriate. You may make a decision regarding the living will portion, assigning a medical power of attorney, or anatomical donation.

Practitioner's role: Educate the client on the different options and what they entail and provide written information on living wills and health care proxies. Every hospital and most physicians' offices can provide the forms. One does not need to hire an attorney or even have the forms notarized in most states. Determine which sections of advance directives are appropriate. Know the standard state legal documentation for advance directives. Provide several copies of completed forms for clients to file with their physician, hospital, and to share with primary caregivers.

2. Review your current medical status with your physician.

Elaboration: Discuss your preferences for end-of-life care and DNR orders. Explore your physician's comfort level with respecting your wishes.

Practitioner's role: Support the patient in securing information and acceptable medical advocates.

3. Determine whether your DNR status is temporary, for this admission or surgery, or to be honored under all circumstances and subsequent hospital admissions.

4. Contact an elder law attorney if needed.

Elaboration: Although it is not necessary for the execution of advance directives, an elder law attorney is familiar with the legal issues regarding these documents and can assist with correct wording. This will help to ensure that the client's wishes will be properly respected.

Practitioner's role: Provide client with a list of local attorneys that specialize in elder law.

5. Contact Choices in Dying to obtain advance directive documents specific to the state of residence if needed.

Elaboration: Choices In Dying is a national organization that provides state-specific advance directive forms and instructions for their completion. Information can be obtained from their Web site (www.choices.org).

6. Learn about relevant medical treatments and their effects from the physician.

Elaboration: Understanding relevant medical treatments, such as ventilators, cardiopulmonary resuscitation, feeding tubes, and other similar treatments and their effects can help the client decide whether or not he or she wishes to receive them. The more specific the health care wishes are spelled out in the advance directives, the easier it is to follow the client's intent.

7. Choose a person to be designated as a health care proxy.

Elaboration: This decision should be discussed with the designated person first to make sure that he or she would be comfortable in this role.

Practitioner's role: Encourage the client to reflect on the choice of a health care proxy who is well acquainted with the client's wishes stated in the advance directives.

8. Inform family members of the existence of the advance directives and the provisions therein.

Elaboration: Discuss contents of advance directives with family members and significant others. This can initiate a very meaningful and profound sharing of your wishes about care in the event of a terminal illness and other quality of life issues.

9. File a copy with your primary care physician and hospital of choice.

10. Provide additional copies of advance directives to other physicians, the person designated to be the health care proxy, and family members.

Elaboration: If all parties have the information, it will lessen the likelihood of misunderstanding regarding the client's wishes in a medical emergency.

11. Consider completing a power of attorney (see task planner "Advance Planning: Power of Attorney").

—Anne Margolis and Janet Coleman

ADVANCE PLANNING: POWER OF ATTORNEY

An older adult may need assistance with financial and organizational tasks, such as keeping track of bills, filing income tax returns, submitting medical claims, obtaining public benefits, and making doctor's appointments. Engaging in advance planning can help the elderly person reduce uncertainty and put into place the personal care and asset management strategies he or she desires in the event that incapacity or disability occurs. The most compelling reason for advance planning is to avoid that a person succumbs to illness or cognitive impairment without having provided another person with the authority to make decisions regarding his or her financial and personal affairs. Caregivers and family members are then faced with having to make those decisions, but they may lack the authority to do so. They may obtain guardianship when the person becomes incapacitated, but this can be time consuming, expensive, and emotionally challenging. It is possible that the appointed guardian might not be someone the older person would have chosen. Moreover, in such an arrangement the guardian may not make decisions according to the older person's wishes. Thus, a court-appointed legal guardian should be viewed as a last resort.

There are two components to advance planning, i.e., financial planning and health care planning. See "Advance Directives" for health care planning. Several components are necessary for financial planning: organizing financial records (see "Financial and Personal Records"), making a living will, and creating a power of attorney (POA). A power of attorney is a contract between two parties in which one person gives the other person the legal authority to handle certain financial or legal affairs. The power of attorney acts as an "agent" in carrying out the person's wishes. This can range from a very narrow focus, such as just handling the checking account for day-to-day money management, to a very broad focus that covers a wide range of financial and legal responsibilities. The POA needs to be notarized, a service provided by attorneys and some banks, among others. It needs to be filed at the county clerk office in the county of residence. A POA can be limited (only for a limited time period) or general (no restrictions on what the POA can do). Furthermore, one can distinguish between three basic types of power of attorney: regular, durable, and springing durable power of attorney.

A regular power of attorney carries out decisions made by the client. This function is performed as long as a client is cognitively able to make decisions. The durable power of attorney carries out the same functions as the regular power of attorney, but additionally has the mandate and authority to do so even after a person becomes too incapacitated to make decisions. A springing durable power of attorney only assumes the power of attorney functions after a person becomes unable to make and implement decisions.

Literature: Arnason, Rosenzweig, and Koski (1995); Cohen and Cohen (1990); Harrison (1994); High (1993); Hoffman (1994); Overman and Stoudemire (1993); Patterson, Baker, and Maeck (1993); Wacker (1995).

Web Sites: www.aarp.org (AARP)

See also: "Advance Directives," "Financial and Personal Records"

TASK MENU

1. Learn about power of attorney and the conditions under which one can be created.

Elaboration: A power of attorney is a contract between two persons in which one person gives the other the legal authority to handle his or her financial affairs. This second person acts as an "agent" in carrying out the first person's wishes. One can decide what range of authority is given with the power of attorney. A power of attorney can only be created if the person is of sound mind and is acting according to his or her own free will.

Practitioner's role: Explain the benefits of advance planning and creating a power of attorney. Educate the client about the differences between power of attorney, durable power of attorney, springing durable power of attorney, living will, health care proxy, and advance directives. Provide information about helpful resources (e.g., Area Agency on Aging, AARP, local Alzheimer's Association, Choice in Dying, National Academy of Elderlaw attorneys). Establish that the client is capable of appointing a power of attorney.

2. Decide who should be appointed as power of attorney.

Elaboration: It is important to trust the person that is appointed as power of attorney. It can be a family member or a friend who is capable of managing your affairs and has the time and inclination to do so. It is beneficial to appoint someone who lives nearby. Appointing two or more persons as POA is possible. If you appoint two or more people to act as your agent, you can decide whether you want them to act jointly (e.g., both signatures are required at all times), or whether they can act separately.

Practitioner's role: Facilitate discussion about the POA with client and family members. Help the client to think about persons who would be best suited for the role and would be willing and able to take it on.

3. Decide whether to appoint a regular, durable, or springing durable power of attorney.

Elaboration: The regular power of attorney is only valid while a person has the mental capacity to tell the agent what to do and to supervise his or her actions. A durable power of attorney stays in place even after the person becomes incapable of directing the agent. The POA continues to take care of the affairs when the person who appointed him or her is least able to do so. A springing durable power of attorney has the same powers as a durable power of attorney, except he or she will only "spring" into action in the case of some future time or event that you determine beforehand. This means that you can appoint someone as POA now but not expect him or her to gain access to any financial affairs until some later date. The POA would only become active when the appointed time or situation arrives.

4. Create the power of attorney.

Elaboration: A standard form to create a POA can be used. The form needs to be filled out, notarized, and filed with the county clerks' office in the client's county of residence.

Practitioner's role: Supply the client with a standard POA form. Explain terms that may be unclear. Assist the client with filing the POA. This can require contacting the client's lawyer, a legal aid service, or a local bank.

5. Decide who should be given authority to make health care decisions if you do not have the ability to make them yourself.

Elaboration: This can be a different person than your POA. Since decisions about financial affairs require different skills and emotional involvement than decisions about your health care issues, you may want to appoint different people for these two tasks. (See "Advance Directives").

—*Jenny Overeynder*

END-OF-LIFE MEDICAL DECISION MAKING

Modern medical care includes near miracles of technological possibilities. Some of the advances in cardiac care and major organ transplants would have sounded like science fiction only ten years ago. While these advances can extend a meaningful quality of life, the death rate is still 100 percent. There comes a time when the options available in this high-tech environment are no longer "done for us" but increasingly "to us."

Consumers of this advanced medical care are encouraged to become increasingly educated in how to advocate for the best medical care. Publicity on incidences of medical error and concern over the influence of managed care exacerbate our anxiety. Elderly health care consumers of today were conditioned to trust their physicians implicitly, but future generations of elderly consumers are more likely to insist on active participation in medical decision making. The baby boom children of today's elderly are increasingly demanding that a benefits-versus-burden conversation accompany all medical decision making for their loved ones.

Initiating a discussion about one's end-of-life care preferences is appropriate at any age and medical status, and it is of great benefit to have considered the topic before a medical crisis occurs. Discussions should include fears about dying, understanding prognosis, achieving important end-of-life goals, and attending to physical needs in accordance with the patient's wishes and values (Balaban 2000).

The benefits-versus-burden framework, quality of life framework, and life-prolonging versus death-prolonging framework are three possible constructs that may help in medical decision making. While almost everyone wants his or her life prolonged, few want their deaths prolonged. The "trick" is to decide when the living part is over and the dying part of one's life has begun. This is different for everyone, and the only people who can determine which phase patients are in are the patient and those who love and know them. Everyone defines his or her quality of life uniquely. For some, quality of life is dependent upon the ability to read or enjoy music. For another person, it may be an issue of independence and relative dependence on other people. Another patient may define his quality of life as the ability to give and receive love.

Literature: Balaban (2000); Dunn (2000); Emanuel (2000); Reichel (1999).

TASK MENU

1. Involve family members as much as possible in the discussions.

Elaboration: Educate significant others about your wishes. When family members are included, they can become advocates for the patient. They are then released from the burden of making medical decisions later but can instead honor the stated wishes of the patient. Disagreement can be minimized and family bonds strengthened by a commitment to open communication.

2. Gather helpful health care professionals and loved ones.

Elaboration: Be aware of those professional and lay caregivers who may have pertinent information and expertise and invite their participation as you feel it is appropriate. Locate knowledgeable facilitators of medical decision making. This may be a physician, social worker, or nurse.

Practitioner's role: Create a safe environment with the goal of eliciting the patient's preferences and then respecting them. Facilitate open communication with the patient and other professional advisors.

3. Obtain information about diagnosis, expected disease process, and prognosis.

Elaboration: Keep seeking those professionals who can meet your needs and communication style.

Practitioner's role: Insist that honest assessments are shared with the patient and family to the extent they desire, realizing that experts can be wrong at times. Understand that even designated professionals (one's attending MD) may have difficulty engaging in such direct conversation.

4. Address the psychological, social, and spiritual aspects of end-of-life decision making.

Practitioner's role: Information that enhances the understanding of the family system, spiritual beliefs, and coping and communication styles can greatly enhance the ability to facilitate constructive decision making. Seek input from other professionals and team members regarding family functioning. Provide a supportive environment for a patient and family who will likely be in a state of stress. Recognize that life goals may change in the context of a serious illness, but there may still be an opportunity for a life that includes hope. There is always something we can do. It may not be a cure but may not be any less profound for the patient's quality of life. Being a model for compassionate truth-telling is a vital role for the professional. As Emanuel (2000:797) describes this gift of bearing witness: "Healers can hear pain, healers give people permission to show pain, healers are not afraid to see pain."

5. Decide on a framework for decisions.

Elaboration: See frameworks described above.

6. Develop a process that respects and includes the patient (unless he or she is absolutely unwilling or unable to participate, e.g., in a persistent vegetative state.

Elaboration: Some patients are capable of open communication but choose not to know the medical realities of their case. This choice must be respected just like the choice to know and decide on everything directly. In all cases, the object is to clarify the wishes and goals of the patient. The patients should be in charge of orchestrating their own last years, weeks, or hours. The others are engaged in playing our appointed parts.

7. Obtain information on the financial, ethical, and legal issues involved.

Elaboration: There are many resources for learning about the financial, ethical, or legal issues related to a specific decision topic. For example, hospital ethics committees and patient advocates, Medicaid workers and attorneys, and physicians and social workers can provide valuable advice and information. Do not be reluctant to ask about the financial impact of medical decision making. For instance, planning for the care of a patient with a very short prognosis may be very different from making a plan to use finite financial and family resources for a protracted illness.

Practitioner's role: The practitioner must be able to provide education on the financial, legal, and ethical repercussions of the patient's choices. Until this substantial information is obtained, the practitioner must "know who knows" and make the information available to patient and family. It is incumbent upon the professional helper to become aware of his or her own biases, fears, and discomfort in dealing with death and dying in order to provide competent assistance. This responsibility is just as important as knowing the state Medicaid regulations or the local nursing homes that provide hospice care.

—*Janet Coleman*

FINANCIAL AND PERSONAL RECORDS

While the majority of elderly persons who are heads of households still own their homes, they may become too incapacitated and incompetent to continue handling some or all of their daily affairs. There may be problems with paying bills and attending to other financial matters. Having financial and personal records in order may make the difference between living independently and living in an institutional setting (Bassuk 2001). Arrangements regarding the handling of personal and financial matters should be made early on. A responsible and trusted person should be selected to assist the older adult in managing his or her financial affairs. Completing a living will and establishing a health care proxy are two ways in which elderly persons can take responsibility for their health before they can no longer make decisions regarding their medical wishes. Becoming old often involves unsettling role transitions. These may become especially evident when turning over part of one's financial and personal records, since such records are usually kept confidential and personal throughout one's life. Even adult children often have little access to their parents' records. As practitioner you may need to spend additional time looking at the effects that these role transitions may have on the elderly client.

If family members are not available or the person does not like to involve them in handling financial and personal records, daily money managers or financial planners can assist a client in these tasks. They can help the person in creating filing systems and organizing bills, straightening out payments, preparing bank deposits and money transfers, and helping with applications and paperwork for entitlement and other programs (Bassuk and Lessum 2001).

Literature: Bassuk and Lessum (2001); Moroney and Krysik (1998); Gilbert and Terrell (1998).

Web Sites: www.aadmm.com (American Association of Daily Money Managers)

See also: "Advance Directives: Health Care Proxy," "Advance Planning: Power of Attorney"

TASK MENU

1. Create a "financial records" file.

Elaboration: File information regarding insurance policies (life, homeowners, automobile, health, etc.), all policy numbers, as well as each agent's name and phone numbers.

2. Make a list of your financial resources.

Elaboration: List all income, pension, interest, rental property, stocks and bonds, and any other sources of financial support.

3. Have bank account statements and their balances in the file.

4. Create separate files for information on Social Security, Medicare, and Medicaid.

Practitioner's role: Educate client on the rights and policies of Social Security, Medicare, and Medicaid. Elderly clients often do not have sufficient information regarding these programs. Have information available from each of these programs.

5. Know where your safe deposit boxes are and keep the information in the file.

6. Keep your most recent tax return on file.

7. Make a list of recurring expenses.

Elaboration: List when each bill is due and the typical amount. Keep a copy of the last bill or statement on file.

8. Have phone numbers for each creditor on file.

9. Make a list of property taxes and their amounts.

10. Share the information with a trusted person.

Practitioner's role: Encourage clients to confide in someone regarding their financial affairs. Seek help for ambiguous areas of their financial situation. If necessary, encourage the client to begin allowing a trusted family member to take over some of the responsibility of attending to financial matters. Explain how knowing about financial and personal records ahead of time can save the caretaker or power of attorney time if the client becomes incapacitated. Let the client know that turning over one's affairs is a natural part of the aging process and that it does not mean giving up total control of the situation.

11. Create a "personal records" file.

Elaboration: This file should contain the following (if applicable): living will, birth certificate, marriage certificate, divorce papers, names of children, grandchildren, friends, and their addresses and phone numbers. The file should also contain a list of your employers and the dates you were employed, as well as educational and military records, the name of your church and religious leader. Include names of lawyers, doctors, dentists, and financial advisors as well as your funeral and burial request.

12. Keep all files stored in one safe place.

13. Share the location with a trusted person.

14. Consider establishing a power of attorney and advance directives.

Elaboration: See task planners on Advance Directives and Power of Attorney.

—*Sharon Bagg-Kerrigan*

HOSPICE

Hospice acknowledges that dying is a normal part of life and focuses on maintaining the quality of the remaining life. It does not hasten nor prolong death. Hospice is a kind of home care that focuses on caring for a client during the final phase of their illness (Butler et al. 1996; National Hospice and Palliative Care Organization 2000; Simpson, Fox, and Lynn 2000). Hospice home care has additional features beyond regular home care services, such as psychosocial support, chaplain services, volunteer assistance, and bereavement support for families or caregivers after the death of a client. Hospice concentrates on palliative care (pain and symptom management) and providing comfort to the patient in a home setting or distinct hospice facility. Hospice care affirms life and regards dying as a normal process. It offers a support system to help the patient live as actively as possible until death while helping family members cope during the patient's illness and later in their bereavement.

Admission criteria for hospice programs funded by Medicare and Medicaid require that the patient no longer be pursuing curative treatment and that a physician attests to a prognosis of six months or less (Friedrich 1999; Reichel 1999). If a patient lives longer than six months, hospice care may continue if the patient still has a need and a prognosis of less than six months.

Hospices now care for over half of all Americans who die from cancer and for a growing number of patients with other chronic, life-threatening illnesses, such as end-stage heart or lung disease (Simpson, Fox, and Lynn 2000). America's hospices were leaders in caring for terminally ill patients with HIV/AIDS (Mesler 2000; Simpson, Fox, and Lynn 2000). More than 90 percent of hospice days of care are provided in patients' homes, substituting for more expensive hospitalizations. For hospice patients served in 1995, 77 percent died in their own personal residence, 19 percent died in an institutional facility, such as a hospital or nursing home, and 4 percent died in other settings (NHPCO 2000).

The major barriers to hospice and palliative care programs are cultural, ethical, educational, technological, financial, bureaucratic, and regulatory. Referrals are often made too late for the patient and family to benefit fully from optimal hospice and palliative care services. When patients are admitted before the actively terminal phase of their illness, they have the advantage of developing a trusting relationship with their hospice nurse and staff before a crisis arises. This greatly enhances the effectiveness of available support from caring professionals.

More than one-fifth of hospice patients nationwide are diagnosed with a disease or condition other than cancer. In urban areas hospices serve a large number of HIV/AIDS patients. Hospices also serve families coping with the end-stages of chronic diseases like emphysema, Alzheimer's, cardiovascular, and neuromuscular diseases. Hospices serve a majority of older clients, but they also serve all ages. Many hospices have clinical staff with expertise in pediatric care. Hospice offers a family-centered concept of care that pays as much attention to the grieving family as it does to the dying patient. Many of the grief services that hospices provide are offered to the community at large, serving schools, churches and the workplace. Many hospices coordinate community resources to make home care possible because they realize that terminally ill people may live alone. Hospices also can help to find an alternative location where the client can safely receive care, such as nursing facilities and adult care residences. Most hospices in the United States are certified by Medicare, which requires that they employ experienced medical and nursing personnel with skills in symptom control. Hospices provide state-of-the-art palliative care, using advanced technologies to prevent or alleviate distressing symptoms.

Persons affected by a terminal illness may struggle to come to terms with death. The hospice staff is always available to discuss all options and facilitate the needs and preferences of all families. Care providers must also address their own comfort level when talking with clients about hospice and issues of death and dying (Brinson and Brunk 2000; Byock 1997; Reese 2000). Often clients may not have verbalized it, but on some level they have probably thought about their own death. In most cases a client will experience relief when the care provider or family members begin to openly talk about hospice, death, or dying issues (Byock 1997; Lattazani-Licht, Mahoney, and Miller 1998; Reese 2000; Reichel 1999).

Literature: Brinson and Brunk (2000); Butler et al. (1996); Byock (1997); Emanuel and Emanuel (1998); Friedrich (1999); Kovacs and Bronstein (1999); Lattazani-Licht, Mahoney, and Miller (1998); Mesler (2000); National Hospice and Palliative Care Organization (2000); Nolen-Hoeksema, Larson, and Bishop (2000); Reese (2000); Reichel (1999); Simpson, Fox, and Lynn (2000).

Web Sites: www.dying.well.org (hospice and palliative care resources); www.partnershipforcaring.org (Partnership for Caring); www.aahpm.org (American Academy of Hospice and Palliative Medicine); www.rwjf.org (Robert Wood Johnson Foundation); www.abcd-caring.com (Americans for Better Care of the Dying)

TASK MENU*

1. Become well informed of the hospice concept, its comprehensive services, and its financial aspects.

Elaboration: Hospice care takes place wherever the need exists. About 80 percent of hospice care takes place in the client's home. Hospice care can also be provided in a nursing home or adult care residence (see description above).

2. Aid families and caregivers in negotiating the financial aspects of hospice care.

Elaboration: Most people who use hospice are over 65 and are entitled to the Medicare Hospice Benefit (NHPCO 2000; Brinson and Brunk 2000). Hospice is also covered by most managed care policies, state Medicaid programs, and most hospices provide care regardless of the ability to pay. Covered services are: skilled nursing, social work, home health aide, pharmacy, durable medical equipment (hospital beds, oxygen, etc.), pastoral counseling, volunteer support, and bereavement services. Under Medicare and Medicaid, there are provisions for respite, acute care admissions, and continuous care in crisis circumstances. A 5 percent copayment is allowed, but many hospices do not charge any amount.

3. Address legal concerns. (See task planner on advance directives)

4. Evaluate communication patterns among all parties involved.

Elaboration: It is important that the client's needs are clearly stated and communicated to caregivers and the agency that will provide the hospice services; otherwise the services will not be provided in a consistent manner (Reese 2000).

5. Specify the services that are available to the client.

Elaboration: Regulations require that patient and family will be informed at the time of admission about the nature and frequency of services to be provided. Visits are usually intermittent (1–2 hours in length, 1–5 times a week, depending on the plan of care). Many clients and family members erroneously believe that in-home hospice care entails twenty-four hours, seven days a week coverage if they have ample insurance coverage. It is unlikely that such extensive coverage is possible. A concise explanation of the designated services will help the client to understand the services more completely (Byock 1997; NHPCO 2000; Friedrich 1999; Nolen-Hoeksema, Larson, and Bishop 2000).

6. Become involved in the health care reform movement.

Elaboration: Managed care companies play a major role in the way that home care and hospice care is provided in this country. Because cost effectiveness is an increasingly important aspect for these companies, we must ensure that quality and provision of client care is not undermined or eliminated. Service providers must assure that the necessary supports and systems operate in ways that provide respect, integrity, and optimum services for clients and their families (Butler et al. 1996; Kovacs and Bronstein 1999; Lattazani-Licht, Mahoney, and Miller 1998; NHPCO 2000).

—*Janet Coleman and Monica Zdimal*

*Tasks of this menu are for practitioners.

NUTRITION PROGRAMS: MEALS-ON-WHEELS

Deficits in nutrition can negatively affect an elderly person's health and aging process. Yet many elderly persons lack a regular and balanced diet. This in turn leads to the prevalence of a number of different nutritional deficiencies. In order to address the problem meals and nutritional services are provided to senior citizens through several programs. Many of the nutrition programs are funded through the Older Americans Act (OAA) Title III. Programs covered by the OAA have to comply with specific nutrition standards.

Nutritional screening and assessment are an important part of many programs. Those that are funded through the OAA use a brief ten-question nutrition checklist. Recently, a National Nutrition Screening Initiative has developed and made available additional nutrition screening tools. Some clients have nutritional needs that may require a detailed assessment by a professional nutritionist.

Factors that affect one's nutritional status include physical health (e.g., problems with digestion or chewing), psychological health (e.g., loneliness, depression), and financial problems (e.g., lack of sufficient income to buy food). When developing a meal plan or selecting a nutrition program, these factors should be taken into consideration. Depending on the agency providing the service, meals may be prepared by a registered dietician who can prepare meals according to the client's special dietary needs. The following are the most common nutrition and meals programs.

FOOD STAMP PROGRAM The food stamps program is an income-based program aimed at diminishing malnutrition among low-income populations of all ages. Older adults who receive SSI benefits automatically qualify for food stamps. Food stamps are used to purchase food items in regular stores and supermarkets. While there are a few limitations, the person using food stamps can decide which food items to buy. Unfortunately, many users of food stamps continue to feel stigmatized when having to pay with them.

CONGREGATE MEALS Congregate meal sites are located in a variety of community-based settings, including senior centers, churches, schools, and some restaurants. Congregate meals are open to persons 60 years and older and their spouses (Wacker, Roberto, and Piper 1997). In addition to serving a nutritionally balanced diet for a small donation, these programs also offer nutritional screening, education, and information on other programs. While all congregate meal sites offer lunch, only a small percentage offers breakfast or dinner.

HOME-DELIVERED MEALS AND MEALS-ON-WHEELS One of the best known programs of home-delivered meals is meals-on-wheels, a service that is offered by county, community, and private providers. Once individuals become participants in a home-delivered meals program, they can receive meals on a short-term or long-term basis, depending on their personal situation. Usually, two meals a day are available, one cold and one hot meal. Some agencies charge or ask for donations for the meals or the delivery; however, they usually offer a sliding scale fee schedule. The eligibility requirements for home-delivered meals vary. Programs receiving funding through the OAA Title III must focus on serving the elderly aged 60 years and older. Home-delivered meals are often distributed by volunteers. These volunteers may also serve as a social contact and support function for the elderly client (Wacker, Roberto, and Piper 1997).

FOOD BANKS Like food stamps, food banks serve low-income persons of all ages. The food comes from a variety of sources, including donations by individuals, restaurants, grocery stores, manufacturers, and government commodities.

SHOPPING ASSISTANCE PROGRAMS Lack of transportation and mobility problems may make it difficult for an elderly person to go shopping independently. A growing number of shopping assistance programs are available to assist older adults in getting to the store and back, assisting with the shopping, or having groceries delivered to the home. Some local grocery stores may also provide delivery services to older adults. Senior transportation programs can help elderly clients in getting to and from the store for shopping (see task planner on transportation).

Literature: Wacker, Roberto, and Piper (1997)

Web Sites: www.meals.org; www.theumbrella.org; www.meals-on-wheels.org; www.
members.aol.com/mealwheels/services.htm
See also: "Senior Transportation"

TASK MENU

1. Complete a nutritional screening.
Elaboration: Such screenings are best conducted by nutritionists. Several screening and assessment tools are available through the Nutrition Screening Initiative.
2. Learn about the nutrition and meals programs.
Practitioner's role: Provide information about the local nutrition programs. Explain the service they provide. Review the eligibility requirements.
3. Contact program and apply for services.
Practitioner's role: Make referral, if needed, and provide necessary information.
4. If home-delivered meals are requested, arrange for delivery time.
Elaboration: Meals are delivered five to seven days per week. Some programs offer frozen meals that are delivered less frequently. Consider that you should be home at the time of delivery. Schedule the delivery time accordingly.
Practitioner's role: Initially monitor service delivery. Assess whether the client improves eating habits after meal delivery begins. Reassess the client's nutritional needs if warranted. Since meals may differ significantly from the type of cooking the client is used to, weight gain or weight loss may occur. If this happens, review alternatives together with the client (e.g., requesting a lower calorie meal plan from meals-on-wheels service provider).
5. If a congregate meal program is selected, arrange for transportation.
Practitioner's role: Assist client in making transportation arrangements.
6. Monitor service delivery and regularly reassess nutrition needs.

SENIOR TRANSPORTATION

While many urban areas offer public transportation, this service may be very limited in suburban and rural areas. Furthermore, an elderly person may not be able to utilize public transportation because of functional or cognitive limitations. Elderly individuals who no longer drive depend on a range of transportation service providers (e.g., public transit authorities, for-profit and non-profit organizations, religious groups, informal support systems). The following are the basic types of transportation services currently available.

FIXED-ROUTE SYSTEM Most public transportation services use fixed-route systems. In this approach, a specially equipped bus or van follows the same route and schedules.

DEVIATED-FIXED-ROUTE SYSTEM Using this model, the bus or van operates on a fixed route, but the driver deviates from this route if an eligible rider makes a request.

PARATRANSIT OR DEMAND-RESPONSIVE SYSTEMS This option has strict eligibility criteria. It is usually offered only to persons who fulfill certain age or disability criteria. Using this approach, a rider is transported from one specific location to another. Demand-responsive systems can operate on short notice (a few hours in advance), or they may require twenty-four-hour advance notice. Depending on the provider, the driver will stop at the curb or come to the door to pick up a passenger.

INCIDENTAL TRANSIT Incidental transit is the transportation that many human service organization offer to their clients. A typical example is a van that brings older adults to an adult day care center.

Literature: Naleppa (2001b); U.S. Department of Transportation (1997); Wacker, Roberto, and Piper (1997).

Web Sites: www.nhtsa.dot.gov/people (U.S. Department of Transportation); www.aoadhhs.gov/Factsheets/transportation.html (Administration on Aging)

See also: "Travel Disability" (Reid 2000)

TASK MENU

1. Select the senior transportation service you want to use.

Practitioner's role: Educate the client about senior transportation options available in the community. If alternatives exist, review the advantages and disadvantages of each transportation service with the client. Review how the client will pay for senior transportation.

Elaboration: User costs for transportation vary significantly. Door-to-door transportation costs up to twice the regular fare. Off-peak public transportation costs half the usual fare. Medicaid may cover transportation to a medical provider if the client lacks individual transportation. Many human service providers charge only a nominal fee for incidental transit.

2. Gather required documentation.

Elaboration: The documentation requirements vary, depending on the type of transportation needed and the local eligibility requirements. In some cases, an eligibility letter from a physician is needed.

Practitioner's role: "The procedure for assisting clients in accessing transportation services is as varied as the systems in place. Typically, the process begins with assessment of the client's individual needs. Does the client have specific physical or cognitive limitations that need to be addressed? What are the client's reasons for seeking senior transportation services? The practitioner should then educate the client about the available local transportation and senior transportation systems. Which service matches the client's individual transportation needs? Does the client fit the eligibility requirements? Typical eligibility requirements are age-related (e.g., 60 years and older) or depend on certain levels of disability or chronic illness" (Naleppa 2001b).

3. Complete and submit application.

4. If required, call and confirm transportation the day before using it.

Practitioner's role: Rehearse with the client how to use senior transportation. If needed, provide the client with a list of the procedures (calling transportation service, setting up pick-up time and location, using transportation passes, etc.).

5. Utilize senior transportation service.

Elaboration: Bring along eligibility letter and required documentation.

Practitioner's role: If necessary, arrange for someone to accompany the client the first time he/she uses the transportation service.

RETIREMENT: SUCCESSFULLY MAKING THE TRANSITION

The impact of retirement on the health and mental health of older adults is often neglected in the counseling arena (Zuehlsdorff and Baldwin 1995). In most industrial countries retirement is a normative part of the life cycle (Bosse, Spiro, and Levenson 1997). Many retired persons report experiencing discomfort and dissatisfaction with the transition into retirement (Weiss 1997). Even the preretirement process can be a time of considerable challenge to mentally prepare for the transition (Zuehlsdorff and Baldwin 1995). One in every three retirees finds retirement to be stressful (Bosse 1998). Recent research has identified factors that place a retiree at risk for experiencing the transition as stressful (Bosse 1998). These include early or unexpected retirement, socioeconomic status, retirement from a white-collar occupation, daily hassles, and stressful life events around the time of retirement (Bosse 1998). The need for improved planning, education, and counseling services for those considering retirement persists (Zuehlsdorff and Baldwin 1995).

Social and psychological aspects of life can be negatively affected during retirement (Zuehlsdorff and Baldwin 1995). Some retirees experience the benefits of retirement as deprivations (Weiss 1997). No longer being required to come to work can invoke in some persons a sense of no longer being needed. During the preretirement years, people may tend to maintain relationships based on their occupation. Following retirement, these relationships can vanish quickly, sometimes resulting in social isolation. Retirement can also lead to a diminished sense of self-worth. The lack of a set schedule and routine can be problematic for some. Furthermore, the activities now available may feel less engaging than those at work (Weiss 1997).

Retirement may give rise to loneliness, depression, and anxiety, which could all be due to the multiple losses experienced—e.g., loss of identity, income, and social status and support (Bosse 1998). Retirement has been implicated as a potential contributing factor in the higher rates of suicide among older people, particularly older men (Bosse 1998).

The American Association of Retired Persons (AARP) is a good resource concerning retirement life. AARP is a nonprofit organization dedicated to providing information and resources for people over 50 years of age. Besides maintaining an informative Web site (*AARP Webplace*), AARP publishes magazines (*Modern Maturity, My Generation*) and a monthly newspaper. It produces prime-time radio and *Mature Focus Radio* programs that offer information on current topics. AARP coordinates local self-help chapters and orchestrates legislative, judicial, and consumer advocacy.

Literature: Bosse (1998); Bosse, Spiro, and Levenson (1997); Jensen-Scott (1993); Richardson (1993); Riker and Myers (1990); Weiss (1997); Zuehlsdorff and Baldwin (1995).

Web Sites: www.aarp.org

TASK MENU

1. Write down your thoughts and feelings about retirement.

Elaboration: Making such a list helps you become more aware of your thoughts and feelings and may provide a good starting point for discussing how your perception of retirement relates to your concerns.

Practitioner's role: Beliefs about retirement may affect the client's use of coping strategies to deal with retirement. This can affect the amount of distress experienced during the transition into retirement. Become aware of how the client perceives retirement by exploring feelings about the change as well as the value the client places on work as a way of achieving personal goals (Jensen-Scott 1993). Sample questions include: What are your typical thoughts and feelings when you think about retirement? How do you feel about retirement? It may help to discuss these questions in the context of the client's feelings about growing older since this too impacts on a successful transition (Richardson 1993). Additional questions include: What would you do if you didn't have to work? What kind of things do you do on your days off? What do you like and dislike about your job? What will you miss and or not miss about your job? How can positive experiences from your job be incorporated into your retirement life? Are there things you always wanted to do but never could? Would you like to try doing those things during your retirement? This probing can provide an opportunity to validate concerns while challenging irrational beliefs concerning retirement.

2. Recognize and accept a new self-definition based on something other than competence within your occupation.

Elaboration: When adapting to retirement, it is important to try to redefine your sense of self, so that the ending of your professional or work career becomes easier to accept (Weiss 1997). Our self-concept, as well as how we perceive others, tends to be greatly influenced by what we do for a living (Bosse, Spiro, and Levenson 1997). Our occupations serve as a marker by which we define ourselves, maintain our self-identity, and relate to each other. For example, when we meet new people, a question that typically arises early in the conversation relates to what one does for a living (Bosse, Spiro, and Levenson 1997). Part of a successful adaptation to retirement requires accepting ourselves as no longer being active in the world of work (Weiss 1997).

Practitioner's role: Explain to the client that the first goal of intervention is to reorganize how he or she defines him or herself. Although what we do during our career is important to our sense of self, there are other things in our lives that help define our sense of self. Try to help the client present examples of things in his or her life—other than work—that have contributed to his or her sense of self (e.g., family, lifelong friends, recreational activities, community involvement). Point out that relationships with members of the client's former work community can be maintained in different ways and outside the work environment. Help the client identify activities that foster his or her self-worth. Projects that lack challenge and social support may be less beneficial than those that have these characteristics.

3. Learn more about what life after retirement has to offer.

Elaboration: By learning about retirement, one can move toward coping with the change. A positive step toward coping with retirement may be to join AARP. Further information concerning membership and additional benefits can be obtained from AARP's Web site or by contacting them at: AARP, 601 E Street, NW, Washington, DC 20049, phone: (800) 424–3410, email: member@aarp.org, Web address: http://www.aarp.org.

Practitioner's role: The client may lack knowledge or have misperceptions regarding retirement. Be prepared to offer information and empower the client to learn more about issues related to retirement (e.g., lifestyle options, changes in relationships, perspectives on aging, adult development).

4. Prepare yourself for the change in lifestyle.

Elaboration: Once a date is set for retirement, prepare yourself for the transition period by planning things such as hobbies, longer vacations, spending more time with families and friends, joining new groups, and trying new leisure activities (Richardson 1993).

5. Make a list of leisure activities that interest you.

Elaboration: Retirement is often a sudden shift from full-time work to full-time leisure (Weiss 1997). This is not necessarily a negative trade-off (Riker and Myers 1990). Satisfying leisure activities can help to (1) provide alternate means for achieving status, (2) meet needs previously satisfied by work, (3) maintain time management skills, (4) contribute to an increased sense of well-being, (5) enhance self-esteem, (6) contribute to a sense of purposefulness and meaning, and (7) present opportunities for socializing with people of various ages (Riker and Myers 1990).

Practitioner's role: A problem encountered by some retirees has less to do with available opportunities and more with a lack of experience in doing leisurely activities (Riker and Myers 1990). Assist the client in finding activities that are adequately engaging. Help the client successfully replace activities related to work with volunteer activities, self-improvement activities, travel, hobbies that involve other people, classes, etc.

6. Attend a retirement planning group or seminar.

Elaboration: Retirement planning groups are offered by various community-based organizations. Some groups focus primarily on financial planning; others also include information on various aspects of transitioning from work to retirement.

7. If applicable, invite your partner to retirement planning sessions.

Elaboration: Including your partner in retirement planning can enable him or her to realize the degree of your concerns and can facilitate a collaborative effort and discussion to address your concerns. Issues of domain responsibility and of closeness and separateness may have to be reconsidered

(Weiss 1997). For example, as a couple you could ask yourselves how the retirement of one partner will affect household roles (e.g., the household division of labor) and lifestyle roles.

8. Join a self-help support group for retirees.

Elaboration: Retirees often develop new needs for companionship and support (Weiss 1997). Self-help groups provide support from others in a similar situation. Group members benefit from opportunities to: (1) Interact with other people who share similar interests and life experiences, (2) discuss common concerns, (3) share information, (4) become involved in their communities, (5) offer companionship, and (6) influence policy decisions relevant to their age group.

Practitioner's role: Encourage the client to join a local support group for retirees. Emphasize the benefits of such a group, e.g., making him or her feel validated, understood, and supported. The group can serve as an opportunity to learn new methods of coping.

9. Review options for phasing in retirement or transitioning to part-time work.

Elaboration: While retirement used to be a final decision to leave the work force, more and more individuals move from full-time to part-time status or return to work after some time of retirement.

—*Brian Freidenberg*

ELDER ABUSE AND MISTREATMENT

Elder abuse encompasses a wide range of problems. Although descriptions of elder abuse contain common elements, no single, consistent definition exists (Sanchez 1996). Paveza (2001) identifies five types of elder mistreatment: elder abuse, sexual abuse, neglect, emotional abuse, and financial exploitation. Elder abuse consists of behavior that is aimed at harming the other person through actions like hitting, punching, or using a weapon. Sexual abuse entails unwanted sexual actions. Elder neglect involves the lack of providing needed care. One can differentiate between self-neglect, active neglect, i.e., intentional neglect by a caregiver, and passive or unintentional neglect (Paveza 2001). Emotional abuse involves the intentional use of verbal communication to cause a person emotional or psychological anguish. Finally, financial exploitation may be referred to as material, financial, economic, or fiduciary abuse (e.g., theft, extortion, or blocking access to resources). There are wide cultural variances as to what are normal family financial interactions. Screening instruments for financial exploitation that may be valid from a white, middle-class perspective may not work well in minority communities (Sanchez 1996).

Cases of elder abuse, as understood from a family systems approach, cast the abused elder as the identified client and the abuse as a result of family dynamics and environmental pressures on caregiver and client. This conception suggests that the dynamics can be identified and addressed. For caregivers, task planners on anger and stress management may be useful (See Reid 2000). Some tasks for elder abuse assume that the elderly individual is competent while other tasks assume that he or she is cognitively impaired. Elders are not likely to report abuse themselves. At least 70 percent of reported cases come to official attention because of third-party observers (Berliner 1999).

Literature: Filinson and Ingman (1989); Kosberg (1983); Krummel (1996); Miller and Veltkamp (1998), Paveza (2001). A particularly useful article that provides a framework for identifying older people subject to financial abuse is: Wilber and Reynolds (1996).

Web Sites: www.lifelinecairns.org.au/elderabuse.htm; www.gbla.org/abuse.html; www.oaktrees.org/elder/help.shtml; www.seniorlaw.com/elderabuse.htm; www.aoa.dhhs.gov/Factsheets/abuse.html

See also: The following task plannners in Reid (2000): "Caregiving: Burden on one family member," "Anger and stress management," "Anger management and aggression control: Adult," "Couple or family conflict."

TASK MENU: FOR ELDERS AND CAREGIVERS

1. Identify elements of abuse.

Practitioner's role: Be aware of the mandated reporting requirements if abuse is found to exist. Make clients aware of your professional responsibilities in this area. Explain what constitutes verbal, emotional, psychological, physical, sexual, and financial abuse and then assist clients in identifying abuse.

2. List separately assets owned or controlled by caregivers and abused elderly person.

Elaboration: Assets can be utilized for various exchanges (e.g., living arrangements, legal assistance, hiring individuals outside the family to assist with activities of daily living, grocery shopping, etc.). A separate listing may be necessary to determine whether financial abuse is actually taking place.

3. Identify agencies that may offer help.

Practitioner's role: Be aware of the formal and informal resources that are available and refer clients if appropriate. Agencies to interact with in cases of elder abuse are the Office of the Aging, Area Agencies on Aging, Social Security office, public or mental health clinics, local hospitals, and legal services offices. If needed, accompany the client or caregiver to the appropriate agency.

4. Contact and visit support groups in your area.

Practitioner's role: Communicate that the client's problems are not unique. Suggest that the elderly person and caregiver visit support groups that have members with problems similar to their own (e.g., senior support groups and caregiver support groups).

5. Identify the nature and sources of conflict.

6. Learn about role reversal and reframe it as role reformation.

Elaboration: Adults caring for elderly parents may interpret the situation as a role reversal in which they are now parenting the parent. This can lead to resentment on both sides as well as to feelings of shame, guilt, and frustration. Reframing the situation as a role reformation helps to reflect the changing roles of both while also respecting the parent-child relationship that existed prior to assuming a caregiver-care recipient relationship (Krummel 1996).

Practitioner's role: Normalize the situation as a natural process.

7. Learn about how the aging process may affect the elder's capacities.

Elaboration: Caregivers need to adjust their expectations in relation to the elder's physical and mental capacities.

8. Try to resolve conflict through face-to-face negotiation.

Practitioner's role: Make use of the task planner on couple or family conflict (Reid 2000).

9. Learn about nonviolent coping behaviors.

Elaboration: People can become so angry that they see no coping mechanisms available other than verbal or physical violence. Rage and frustration can incapacitate individuals and lead them to react in violent and hurtful ways.

Practitioner's role: Teach the caregiver alternative coping methods such as *progressive relaxation* techniques, calmly discussing the situation with the elder, and taking a respite period from caregiving.

10. Begin giving each other emotional support or encouragement on a daily basis.

11. Identify conflicts or crises you think may occur and come up with plans how they could be handled.

12. Identify the possible activities and resources that might alleviate stress.

Elaboration: Both elder and caregiver should enlist help available from formal and informal support systems. Possible activities include visits to senior centers, churches, or other community settings, and out-of-house activities for the caregiver. Resources to alleviate stress include home care or overnight care with friends or family, respite (see task planner on respite), use of volunteer and homemaker services (meals and housekeeping), and neighbors. Caregivers may be able to trade duties with other caregivers.

13. Discuss with caregiver or care recipient the activities they may want to do outside the home and encourage them to pursue these.

14. If necessary, discuss long-term care options.

TASK MENU: CONCERNED RELATIVES, FRIENDS, NEIGHBORS WHO SUSPECT ELDER ABUSE

1. Discuss with elders current conditions in their lives to get an understanding of what may be occurring and to assess their degree of cognitive functioning.

Elaboration: Is the elder's memory, judgment, or reasoning impaired? How is his or her mobility, energy level, and ability to read or write? Does he or she have vision or hearing problems? Is the elder emotionally vulnerable and seeking others to help cope with loneliness, bereavement, or loss of self-esteem from illness? All these are factors that may leave elders vulnerable to abuse, particularly financial abuse (Wilber and Reynolds 1996).

2. Discuss the elder with the caregiver to determine if there are any suspicious attitudes or if some other individual may be suspected of taking advantage of the elder.

Elaboration: Is the suspect a family member who is no longer following previous norms of exchange or reciprocity (indications may be a suddenly improved or a deteriorating relationship)? Is the suspect a friend or neighbor, and if so, who initiated the relationship? Is the individual in a position of professional trust and subject to ethical standards that prohibit conflict of interest? Is it a fiduciary relationship (e.g., one that requires the caregiver to ensure that the elder's best interest is pursued) based on a trust or written instructions, such as power of attorney, of the elder? (Wilber and Reynolds 1996).

3. If there is reason to suspect some form of abuse, contact proper authorities (Office of Aging or an abuse hotline).

—*Bruce Parker, Pamela Zettergren, and James Golden*

Adapted from Reid (2000)

———————————

EMERGENCY INFORMATION: VIAL-OF-LIFE

Many persons, including elderly individuals, lack easily accessible emergency information. This can become especially problematic when elderly persons are living alone. Timely provision of certain health information may be crucial in an emergency situation. The vial-of-life is a free and simple option to make such emergency information easily accessible. It consists of a plastic vial containing a one-page emergency information sheet. This sheet covers information that may be important in an emergency, e.g., personal information, medical conditions, medications taken, allergies, special nutrition requirements, primary care physician, and phone number of a contact person. The vial-of-life is placed into a person's refrigerator door, and a small sticker indicating that a vial-of-life exists is placed on the outside apartment door and the refrigerator door. When emergency workers see a vial-of-life sticker on the door, they know to look for the vial-of-life in the person's refrigerator door.

Literature: Weaver (1994)

Web Sites: Vial Of Life on the Web Project's Web site: www.stormnet.com/~kerry/kpage/vial.html; American Senior Safety Agency: www.seniorsafety.com/vial.html; www.seniorcitizens.com/k/eprs.html

See also: "Telephone Reassurance"

TASK MENU

1. Review current provisions for emergency situations.

Practitioner's role: Integrate this review with a general assessment of the client's personal safety and emergency information. For example, it may be useful to assess whether an emergency response system, such as LifeLine, is needed. You may also consider conducting an environmental assessment of the client's home safety. Without provoking unnecessary anxiety, present the client with possible emergency scenarios and find out how the client would handle these situations. Assist the client with developing strategies to master possible emergency situations.

2. Assess whether the vial-of-life would be a useful addition to your personal safety.

Practitioner's role: Educate the client about the benefits of accessible emergency information. Explain and explore vial-of-life as an option to increase personal safety.

3. Obtain a vial-of-life.

4. Fill out vial-of-life.

Practitioner's role: Assist client in completing information if necessary. The completion of information on the person's health status and personal information can be used as an opportunity to review the client's needs and whether they have been appropriately addressed.

5. Place vial-of-life in refrigerator and place stickers on refrigerator and outside door.

6. Update the vial-of-life information if changes to your health status occur.

Practitioner's role: Facilitate the information update if learning of any changes in the client's life that should be entered in the vial-of-life. Reviewing the vial-of-life information can become part of the regular reassessment process.

HOME SAFETY: ENVIRONMENTAL ASSESSMENT

If environmental demands exceed the capabilities of an older person, some degree of function will be lost. This can result in an unnecessary loss of independence. It can also increase the risk of falls and accidents. It is important to make sure that an older person's physical environment is both *accessible,* as well as *usable.* An accessible environment is one that can be easily reached, is "friendly" (available to a person in a physical as well as a psychological sense), and can be appropriately used by the older individual. In addition to being accessible, an environment needs to be usable. Usability is a characteristic of an environment that allows a person to perform functions that are normally associated with that environment. Once the person has been able to get into a particular place, e.g., a bathroom, the person has to be able to use that place. In a usable environment, the functional abilities of an individual are fully compatible with that environment. There are many ways in which an environment can be made accessible and usable. These range from simple adaptive devices to major renovations and sophisticated adaptations.

Literature: Bishop and Machemer (1997); Cohen and Cohen (1990); Lawton (1999).
Web Sites: www.aarp.org (AARP); www.mdch.state.mi.us/mass/HSC/hsccover.html
See also: "Falls and Accidents," "Home Safety: Repairs"

TASK MENU

1. Learn about age-related changes that may impact on the ability to function in a physical environment.

Elaboration: Examples of age-related changes include vision (needing more light to see, increased sensitivity to glare), hearing (e.g., difficulty in screening out background noises, hearing high-pitched sounds, and hearing very low tones), physical strength (e.g., grip strength decreases), and a decrease in the sense of taste and smell.

Practitioner's role: Educate the client about age-related changes. Provide written educational materials.

2. Become familiar with the concept of "environmental press."

Elaboration: Some physical environments are harder to negotiate than others. As one grows older, the physical surroundings have a greater influence on one's ability to function. The challenge is to create a living space that is taxing to a certain degree but continues to remain as comfortable and familiar as possible.

Practitioner's role: Educate the client about the concept of "environmental press." Give some examples and ask the client to describe his/ her home environment.

3. Check the accessibility of your physical environment.

Elaboration: Check the home and grounds as well as those places often visited by the person. Some areas that should be assessed include:

(a) Outside of home: Is the driveway level? Are there steep slopes or sharp edges that may be difficult to negotiate? Do all steps and stairways have railings? Is the outside well lit? Is there an easy way to enter the home in bad weather conditions? Are the doors easy to open?

(b) Inside home: Are rooms well lit? Do problems with glare exist? Are the colors of sufficient contrast, so one can clearly see where one is going? Are there any scatter rugs or other obstacles on the floor (e.g., wires, electrical cords)?

(c) Bathrooms: Are there grab bars in the shower and bathtub? Is there a safety mat on the floor of the tub? Is there a stool in the shower to sit on? Are the sinks and faucets easy to reach and easy to open and close? Is the toilet high enough, so one can easily get up?

(d) Everyday objects: (telephones, kitchen utensils, remote controls, etc.). Are they easy to use? Are they light enough to handle? Are they safe to use?

Practitioner's role: Ask to make a home visit to assess the client's physical environment. Review with the client what changes could be made to improve safety and prevent accidents. Supply the client with literature on safety improvements that can easily be made. Two useful sources of information include: The Home Safety Checklist of the U.S. Consumer Products Safety Commission, Washington, D.C. 20207, (800) 638–2772, and the gadget book from AARP, available through their Web site at www.aarp.org.

4. Make the home handicap accessible, if needed.

Elaborations: Often, there is no reimbursement for the expenses of home modifications. In certain instances, however, Medicaid or Medicare can reimburse some of the costs. Contact the local Area on Aging or the local Center for Independent Living for information on eligibility and resources.

Practitioner's role: The practitioner's role usually is to conduct an initial assessment and act as mediator and advocate. Major modifications should be supervised and undertaken by specialized contractors.

5. Become familiar with resources that may be needed.

Practitioner's role: Connect the client with resources available in the area. Get feedback from the client as to the usefulness of these resources.

—*Jenny Overeynder*

FALLS AND ACCIDENTS

Accidents are the sixth leading cause of death in persons over 65 years of age, and falls account for two thirds of these deaths (Steinweg 1997). Falls also account for the majority (40 percent) of traumatic injuries occurring in the elderly population. As people age, the incidence of falls increases. The annual incidence of falls is approximately 30 percent in persons over the age of 65 who are living independently. This rate increases to 50 percent in persons over 80 years of age (Steinweg 1997). Approximately 5 percent of falls result in fractures and 5–10 percent result in serious injuries that require medical attention. Over two-thirds of those who fall will fall again in the following six months (Baraff 1998). Even when no injury or fracture occur, the fear of falling again increases. In some cases this leads to social isolation and a reduction of physical activities (Corrigan and Brennan 2001).

Age-related changes that contribute to the risk of falling include: Changes in vision and hearing, decreased reaction time, reduced muscle strength, difficulties in gait and balance, decreased bladder control, and orthostatic hypotension (Corrigan and Brennan 2001). Other intrinsic risk factors include dementia, neurological disease, musculoskeletal disabilities, arthritis, medications, and alcohol use. Environmental factors also play an important role. Common environmental hazards include loose rugs, unstable or improperly placed furniture, poor lighting, slippery surfaces, clutter, cords, improper footwear, and shelves that are difficult to reach.

Factors a practitioner should take into consideration during an assessment include: previous falls, prescriptions and over-the-counter medications, vision, mobility, osteoporosis, flexibility and muscle strength, and chronic diseases. Persons who witnessed the fall should be interviewed on how it happened since events and symptoms preceding a fall provide important clues for the prevention of future falls. The Hendrich Fall Risk Assessment Tool (Hendrich, Kippenbrock, and Soja 1995) provides a useful instrument for assessing risk factors.

Literature: Baraff (1998); Corrigan and Brennan (2001); Hendrich, Kippenbrock, and Soja (1995); Steinweg (1997).

Web Sites: www.srhip.on.ca/bgoshu/Injury/InjuryFallsReportFS.html; www.celos.psu.edu/Research/falls.htm; www.cdc.gov/ncipc/duip/falls.htm; www.nihs.go.jp/acc/cochrane/revabstr/ab000340.htm

See also: "Home Safety: Environmental Assessment," "Exercise, Fitness and Health," "Senior Living Alternatives," "Assisted Living," "Nutrition: Meals-on-Wheels"

TASK MENU

1. Meet with primary care physician to determine any injuries.

Practitioner's role: Review medical history with patient and determine the cause of the fall. Assess whether repeated falls have occurred. Conduct an environmental assessment to evaluate whether improvements can be made to increase the client's personal safety.

2. Discuss concerns or fears.

Elaboration: Communicate with health care practitioners, family members, and social supports. Discuss the impact of the fall and how it affects your day-to-day activities.

3. Seek out available services.

Elaboration: Clients may benefit from additional services, such as physical therapy, nutritional assessment and meals programs, home health, or a personal care aide.

Practitioner's role: Assess the client's needs and assist in accessing required services. Coordinate in-home support services.

4. Learn to compensate for functional limitations and attend physical therapy.

Elaboration: Physical therapists can provide individualized training that helps increase mobility, gait, balance, and muscle strength as well as techniques to compensate for functional limitations. They can also teach safer ways to get up from a chair, walk around a room, go up and down stairs, and use adaptive devices. Based on their professional experience, physical therapists may provide useful advice on how to improve the home environment to better meet the client's needs.

5. Reduce environmental risk factors.

Elaboration: Review the entire home for potential environmental hazards (see task planner "Home Safety: Environmental Assessment"). Modify the home to forestall future falls. Install appropriate safety devices, including handrails in hallways and stairways, good lighting, grab bars for the shower, raised toilet seats with handrails, chairs, and sofas that the person can easily stand up from. Provide client with a home safety checklist.

6. Obtain adaptive or protective devices.

Practitioner's role: Assess which devices could benefit the client. If necessary, make sure the client receives training by a physical therapist in how to properly use adaptive devices. For some dementia patients, protective devices such as wheelchair seatbelts can be used to reduce the risks of further falls and wandering.

7. Review and adjust medications if needed.

Elaboration: Medications may have side effects that can cause balance and gait problems, drowsiness, decreased cognitive abilities, and delayed reaction. Identify any recent changes in medications, i.e., increased dosage as well as new prescriptions. Review medication pamphlets with client. If necessary, consult physician or pharmacist.

8. Learn strategies to control pain if necessary.

Elaboration: Many older adults endure pain from arthritis and other diseases. Pain may cause a person to move less securely or with improper balance and gait. It may reduce the person's mobility and over time decrease the ability to walk. See task planner on chronic pain (Reid 2000).

9. Assess potential sensory deficits and correct them as needed.

Elaboration: An age-related reduction in visual acuity contributes to the increased likelihood of falls among the elderly. Some of these visual problems can be reduced.

Practitioner's role: Encourage patient to get eyes examined.

10. Exercise to increase balance, strength, and overall mobility.

Elaboration: See task planner "Exercise, Fitness, and Health."

11. Prepare an individual fall prevention plan.

Elaboration: Corrigan and Brennan (2001) suggest the creation of a fall prevention plan that takes into consideration the client's risk factors:

(a) Brighter rooms, more light, and family visits in the late afternoon may help those elderly who experience increased confusion in the evening.

(b) Early visits may benefit clients with Parkinson's disease because their medication effects wear off in the morning.

(c) Toilet training and utilizing a regular schedule may reduce the risk factors for elderly persons with incontinence.

(d) Electronic warning devices can assist caregivers in monitoring elderly persons with mobility problems.

12. Develop an emergency plan in case of another fall.

Practitioner's role: Educate the client about ways to call for help in case a fall occurs. Provide information on telephone emergency response systems (see task planner "Telephone Reassurance").

13. If needed, consider alternative living arrangements.

Elaboration: Moving to a skilled nursing home, an assisted living facility, or moving in with family may be safer for the client (see task planners on senior living alternatives and assisted living).

—*Yolanda King*

EMERGENCY RESPONSE SYSTEMS: TELEPHONE REASSURANCE

In an emergency situation, an elderly person may need to call for help but could be unable to reach a phone. A typical case would be a person who had a fall and is unable to get up. Emergency telephone services are available to assist in such situations. An example of one such service is LifeLine, a two-way emergency response system (www.lifelinesys.com). Other examples are the Mobile Locator and the Safe Return programs. Usually, the client wears a transponder the size of a small button on a cord around the neck or on a bracelet. This transponder is linked to a twenty-four-hour telephone service that can be accessed for help in case of an emergency by pushing a button. Most services require the client to push a call button once a day as an indicator that he or she is doing well. If the person does not push that button, the service provider calls the elderly person and, if there is no response, sends out an emergency medical response team. In addition to their direct benefits in emergency situations, telephone response systems also enhance clients' feelings of security and enable them to live independently for a longer period of time. Emergency telephone services are easily installed and cost comparatively little.

Literature: Portland Multnomah Commission on Aging (1994); Kropf and Grigsby (1999); Hamill (1998); Roush and Teasdale (1997).

Web Sites: www.lifelinesys.com (LifeLine Emergency Response System); www.seniorcitizens.com/k/eprs.html; www.seniorsafety.com/vial.html

TASK MENU

1. Assess your personal safety needs.

Elaboration: If you have problems in getting around in your home or if you are afraid you might fall and not be able to get up to call for help, an emergency telephone system such as Life Line can be very helpful. It will give you peace of mind and the security to know that if something happens, help will be on the way in a very short time. It may also enable you to maintain your independence longer.

Practitioner's role: Discuss the desirability of an emergency response system and assess whether the client is ready and willing to use it.

2. Research local providers of emergency response systems and apply for the one that best fits your needs.

Elaboration: Services differ from community to community. It is important to get a service from a reputable agency at a reasonable cost. Some services are offered directly by telephone companies. Your local Alzheimer's Association is a good source of information. They may also provide these services. Other program examples include: LifeLine, Mobile Locator, and Safe Return.

Practitioner's role: Find out where the client can apply for an emergency telephone system. Contact the hospital department of social work, the Alzheimer's resource center, or the Area Agency on Aging for information about local providers. Assist the client in applying for the service and make sure the installation goes smoothly.

3. Install an emergency telephone system in your home.

Elaboration: There usually is a one-time installation fee as well as a monthly subscription fee.

4. Practice the use of your emergency telephone system.

Elaboration: You will be required to wear a push button. Whenever you need help, one press of the help button activates a small in-home unit called a communicator. It puts you in touch with a person called a LifeLine monitor. He or she will talk to you to find out what kind of help you need. You will be asked to provide the names and phone numbers of several "responders," people that know you very well and live nearby. They will have a key to your home. The person at LifeLine will call one of your "responders" who will come over and check on you. In the event that you press your button and cannot speak, the police or ambulance service will be notified, and they will come over immediately. In all instances, the LifeLine monitor will be able to ask for additional help if needed.

Practitioner's role: Offer to practice the use of the LifeLine with the elderly person. From time to time, ask whether the client always wears the button and remembers its purpose. If needed, troubleshoot reasons for not wearing the button. Common reasons include: being cumbersome in bed at night, irritating the skin, and being ashamed of having to use it.

SENIOR LIVING ALTERNATIVES: HOUSING OPTIONS AND LONG-TERM CARE FACILITIES

A client's physical, health, or financial situation may require a change in his or her living arrangements. Typical reasons include high rent, sale of the apartment/house by owner, problems accessing the house, need for extensive repairs, mobility problems, problems living independently, and changes in the availability of caregivers. In addition to personal difficulty with the current situation, many clients have problems finding a suitable new living arrangement. A common task in case management with elderly clients is to find an appropriate alternative living arrangement. Various reasons for a change in the living situation include a wish for increased socializing and the fear of being alone, need of assistance in activities of daily living, and need for personal or nursing care. Several levels of alternative living arrangements are available. The most common options are listed below.

SENIOR APARTMENTS Target groups are seniors who can live independently. Apartments are usually private. Often, there is no assistance for meals or medication, home health aides, or other direct support. Some senior apartment buildings have meal sites, i.e., a warm meal can be purchased on the premises. They may provide transportation to shopping or doctors, community rooms, and access to senior programs. Senior apartments are sometimes subsidized and may offer rent on a sliding scale.

RETIREMENT COMMUNITIES Target groups are seniors who can live independently. Apartments or homes are typically private. Retirement communities often offer meals and light housekeeping services. Usually there is no assistance on site for meals or medication, home health aides, or other direct support. They often provide transportation to shopping or doctors, community rooms, and access to senior programs.

ADULT HOMES Target groups are seniors in need of some assistance. Adult homes usually have individual bedrooms (sometimes semiprivate). Help with medications and meals is provided as well as around-the-clock supervision. Seniors are free to leave the facility independently. Nursing and medical staff is usually available on an on-call basis.

ASSISTED LIVING Target groups are older adults who can live independently, semi-independently, or are in need of regular assistance. There are several names for assisted living, including board and care, residential care, enriched housing, and domiciliary care (Mitty 2001a). Services include scheduled and unscheduled assistance, availability of twenty-four-hour support and supervision, coordination of personal services and personal care, recreational activities, and health-related services (Mitty 2001a).

HEALTH-RELATED NURSING FACILITIES Target groups are seniors in need of nursing care and assistance with activities of daily living. Rooms are private or semiprivate. Residents share living room and dining room. Medications, meals, and personal care are provided. Therapeutic services are provided as needed.

SKILLED NURSING FACILITIES This is the type of facility offering the highest level of care. It is geared to elderly who need a high level of assistance through around-the-clock nursing care and assistance with activities of daily living. Rooms are private or semiprivate. Residents share living room and dining room. Medications, meals, and personal care are provided. Therapeutic services are provided as needed. Nursing homes can be certified by Medicaid or Medicare and in some instances by both (Mitty 2001b). Medicaid and sometimes Medicare may pay for skilled nursing care (see also chapter 10).

Literature: Mitty (2001a); Mitty (2001b).
Web Sites: www.aarp.org (AARP); www.familycareamerica.com (Family Care America)
See also: "Resident Adjustment to Nursing Home Placement," "Assisted Living Facility/Placement"

TASK MENU

1. Learn about senior housing and alternative living options.
   Elaboration: Services and housing options for the elderly can be found through local resources (e.g., library, senior service agencies, local resource manuals) and Web-based materials. The AARP Web site provides useful

information (www.AARP.com). A comprehensive listing of facilities and their addresses can be found at the Web site of Family Care America (www.familycareamerica.com).

2. Consider your needs and goals regarding housing and alternative living options.

Elaboration: Try to narrow your choices by assessing what you desire and what your present housing and living needs include. Develop a checklist of the pros and cons of various housing options.

3. Visit sites and obtain application materials.

Practitioner's role: Assist the client and caregivers in the preparation of the visit. Develop a list of questions to ask. Develop a list of things that are most important for the client and caregivers in making their decision.

4. Gather documentation required for the application process.

Elaboration: A range of documents are required if the elder is accessing subsidized housing or looking to enter a nursing facility. The elderly person needs to gather documents such as tax returns, Social Security pay stubs, and bank statements.

5. If required for the application, schedule a medical appointment to have a doctor complete requested medical information.

Elaboration: Many subsidized housing residences and nursing facilities require documentation of medical needs to assess eligibility, possible financial subsidization, and acceptance into a treatment facility.

6. Complete and submit application.

Practitioner's role: It may be useful to follow-up on status of application. Find out whether the application was received, was complete, and how long it will take to find out the prospects of being accepted.

7. Consider the impact of the changes that might occur due to the move.

Elaboration: The process of relocation can bring about many issues, such as loss of self, loss of autonomy, intense feeling of mortality, sense of burden, etc. (See task planner "Relocation").

8. If necessary, plan the "downsizing" of your household.

Elaboration: Since the move may include a reduction of living space, the household may need to be "downsized." Letting go of personal belongings can cause strong emotional reactions. Involving family members or friends may provide beneficial emotional support for the client.

9. Make arrangements to move belongings.

Practitioner's role: Assist the client and caregiver in planning for the transition (see task planner "Resident Adjustment to Nursing Home Placement"). Conduct a follow-up visit with the client after the move.

—*James Golden*

ADULT FOSTER CARE: BOARD AND CARE FACILITIES

Adult foster care is a noninstitutional alternative for the elderly person. It represents one of the intermediate options between independent living and nursing homes. In some areas adult foster care homes are also called board and care facilities and adult group homes. An adult foster home is a private residentially zoned house with a live-in caregiver who is not related to the individuals receiving room and board (Mion and Ondus 2001). Foster homes are usually located in residential neighborhoods.

Adult foster care provides residents with a private, homelike environment with some level of supervision and oversight. Adult foster care is generally designed for those individuals who are less functionally and cognitively impaired than those in nursing homes. In adult foster homes, residents usually have their own room, participate in general household tasks, maintain outside contact with friends and relatives, and continue to be connected with the extended community (Mehrota and Kosloski 1991). In selecting an adult foster home, it is important that clients choose a home that allows them independence, individual well-being, and quality of life. For those individuals requiring high levels of around-the-clock care, a nursing home may be the more appropriate senior living alternative. The costs for adult foster care include basic fees for room and board as well as additional fees for specific services such as telephone or laundry. Some adult foster homes can accept Medicaid payment.

Literature: Bourland and Lundervold (1990); Mehrota and Kosloski (1991); Mion and Ondus (2001); Michigan Adult Foster Care (1999).

Web Sites: www.miafc.com (foster care resource directory); www.alfnet.com (Assisted living network)

See also: "Alternative Living: Senior Housing," "Assisted Living," "Adjustment to Placement"

TASK MENU

1. Determine if your physical functioning and mental health is appropriate for adult foster care.

Elaboration: Adult foster care is an alternative housing option for individuals who desire a structured living environment but are not so disabled that they require nursing home care. It is important to assess the level of care that is required at the initial stage of considering adult foster care.

Practitioner's role: Facilitate assessment process. Obtain a client release to speak with medical and other relevant professionals.

2. Research available adult foster care options.

Elaboration: The Michigan Adult Foster Care Web site includes information about adult foster care and directions for inquiring about facilities across the country (www.miafc.com—go to "Public Help—Adult Foster Care")

Practitioner's role: Share knowledge about resources and educate the client and family about available adult foster care placements.

3. Plan a visit to potential foster homes.

4. Write a list of questions to ask foster caregivers.

Elaboration: It is important that you and your family conduct thorough interviews with caregivers to learn about how they run the adult foster home. Questions should focus on the match between the foster family's and the client's expectations, the responsibilities of the elderly individual, financial arrangements, etc.

Practitioner's role: Assist the client in developing a list of questions to ask.

5. Visit foster homes to meet potential caregivers and look at the living environments.

Elaboration: Make sure to speak with the caregivers, assess the home and its surrounding community, and think about the environmental fit. Some areas to evaluate during the visit include the physical shape of the facility, safe entrances and emergency exits, well-lighted hallways, rooms, parking areas, wheelchair access, safety features like handrails, smoke detectors, and the overall impression of the building (Mion and Ondus 2001). If a private room is a consideration, the client should specifically ask if one is available.

Practitioner's role: Accompany the client on the visit and act as a liaison with caregivers if needed. Help facilitate the interviewing process. Make sure that the elderly person has all required information to make an informed decision.

6. Appraise the positive and negative aspects of the adult foster care homes visited.

Practitioner's role: After visiting foster homes, the client should have a clearer idea about what an adult foster placement would be like. Elicit the client's feelings about living in an adult foster home and facilitate an open discussion. Assist the client in developing a list of pros and cons for each home that was visited.

7. Review financial costs.

Elaboration: The costs of adult foster care vary greatly. In some circumstances, Medicaid reimbursement may be available.

8. Review the last survey report, if available.

Elaboration: A licensed adult foster care home should be able to furnish a survey report. Any deficiencies of the facility would be noted in this document (Mion and Ondus 2001).

9. Select an adult foster care home.

10. Complete application and contract with foster home.

Elaboration: In addition to completing the contract, also consider how the contract can be terminated if needed. For example, the resident's medical condition may require nursing home placement at a later point in time.

11. Move to foster home.

See "Adjustment to Placement" and "Relocation."

—Mary Kate Schneider

ASSISTED LIVING FACILITIES: PLACEMENT

Assisted living facilities are currently overtaking nursing homes as the primary source of elder care (Meyer 1998). This model offers care that is managed by a professionally licensed staff for individuals who do not require twenty-four-hour nursing assistance but need help with some activities of daily living. Admission requirements for assisted living vary widely. Many states have licensure requirements; however, these are not uniform. Assisted living is a relatively new residential care option. It is costly and is still primarily a part of the private pay market (Tinsley 1996), but some states are developing financing schemes to assist elders with lower income (Mitty 2001a). Room and board costs are usually paid through personal income, VA compensation or pension, and SSI while service costs can be financed through other sources such as Medicaid, state subsidies, and private or public long-term-care insurance (Lasfargues 1996). Personal care for low-income elders may be covered through Medicaid.

Placing an elderly person into this type of alternative living situation can be a difficult decision for a spouse and family members. As the person's condition is deteriorating, the caregiver may know that the individual requires an environment where professional assistance is available. However, it may still be difficult to let go since caregivers are not certain of the treatment the elderly person will receive (Siebert 1998). One advantage of assisted living is that the care recipient and the caregiving spouse can move in together. Thus, it can provide respite for the person who primarily provides care, needed services for the person requiring assistance, and a supportive environment with opportunities for recreational activities and socializing for both. Assisted living facilities offer a promising new model of care for the elderly, but it is important for their loved ones to be reassured about the quality of services that they will receive in any facility they choose.

Literature: Greene et al. (1997); Lasfargues (1996); Meyer (1998); Mitty (2001a); Siebert (1998); Tinsley (1996).

Web Sites: www.familycareamerica.com (Family Care America)

See also: "Nursing Home Placement," "Senior Living Alternatives"

TASK MENU

1. Obtain information about assisted living.

Elaboration: Utilize available resources to find out more about assisted living. Addresses of local facilities can be found through local resource guides or at the Family Care America Web site (www.familycareamerica.org).

Practitioner's role: Utilize knowledge of outside resources to educate the client and the client's family about assisted living and available placements.

2. Evaluate the available alternatives.

3. Call promising facilities for more information.

4. Make appointments at facilities that sound promising and meet the budget requirements.

Elaboration: For clients with low incomes, assisted living may not be an affordable alternative.

Practitioner's role: Assist the client system in developing a plan in which family members can accompany the elderly individual and their family to the facilities.

5. Make personal visits to assisted living facilities and take a full tour.

Elaboration: To gain a good picture of the facility, a full tour should include looking at rooms available for potential residents as well as at all supportive facilities (recreational, health, personal care, congregate meals site, etc.).

Practitioner's role: Assist the clients in determining what key issues to highlight during the visit.

6. Evaluate the staff's level of interaction with the residents.

Elaboration: From the family's perspective, issues such as staff knowledge and training, communication patterns with residents, attitude, turnover, and continuity are important decision-making factors. Staff-to-resident ratios are another area of significance in assessing quality of care.

Practitioner's role: Work with the clients to formulate a list of questions that they can ask staff members and residents during their visit.

7. Schedule the visit so you can go to the dining room during mealtime and sample the food that is served.

Elaboration: The food served influences an individual's health and physical well-being. It is also good to speak with a dietician if a special diet is required.

8. Check access to services within the facility.

9. Check availability of transportation to outside appointments and services.

Elaboration: While many services are provided on-site, it is still important to have easy access to the outside community. For example, many residents of assisted living facilities continue to see their own physician rather than the onsite doctors.

10. Ask assisted living staff to set up an appointment to speak with a family member of a current resident.

Elaboration: It may be beneficial to talk with a person who has already placed a family member in the residence. This would allow the client's family to learn about financial aspects as well as obtain a second opinion about the operations within the facility.

Practitioner's role: Act as a liaison between the families to facilitate a productive conversation in which helpful information is exchanged.

11. Apply for assisted living placement and complete service agreement.

Elaboration: At admission to an assisted living facility, a service agreement should be completed. The agreement should include an assessment of the current service needs, a description of the respective services, the costs, and the payment structure (Mitty 2001a).

12. Prepare move to assisted living facility.

Elaboration: See "Senior Living Alternatives" and "Nursing Home Placement."

—Mary Kate Schneider

RESIDENT ADJUSTMENT TO NURSING HOME PLACEMENT

Placement in a nursing home can be a traumatic experience. Many view moving to a nursing home as the "end of the line." Emotionally, it is a difficult time for clients as they are separated from home, familiar surroundings, family, and friends. Each individual has to deal with a change of residence, daily routine, and support network in addition to health issues. Entering a nursing home is a major life transition for both the elderly person and family members. The placement decision is usually made only after all other alternatives have been exhausted, caregivers are unable to continue their caregiver involvement, or the condition of the person has deteriorated and now presents greater needs than the family can address (Naleppa 1996). This decision for placement involves feelings of guilt, grief, and loss for all the parties involved. It is one of the most difficult decisions for families and is often associated with significant family conflict and distress.

Goodness of fit between the motivational style of the resident and the nursing home is important. For example, a self-determined motivational style fits well with nursing homes that allow freedom and choice while less self-determined individuals may do better in more constrained environments (O'Connor and Vallerand 1994). Several negative consequences have been associated with placements, most importantly increased mortality and decreased psychological wellness (Tobin 1991).

Adjustment to nursing home life can take many months or even longer. The degree of change in environment is correlated with psychological stress. The resident is usually concerned about how much control will be lost over his or her life. There is particular concern with the control over events surrounding one's death. The meaning of life is often questioned (Starck 1992). Much of the literature surrounding adjustment to nursing home placement focuses primarily on the transition for family members. However, group work with newly admitted residents provides the opportunity for them to become familiar with and receive support from others who are experiencing similar difficulties. Hence, involvement in such groups can help new residents have a more positive adjustment to the nursing home.

Literature: Crose (1990); Dye and Erber (1981); Grossmann and Weiner (1988); Harris (1997); McCallion, Toseland, and Freeman (1999); Naleppa (1996); Porter and Clinton (1992); Taft and Nehrke (1990); Timko and Moos (1989); Tobin (1991); Yoder, Nelson, and Smith (1989); Rehfeldt, Steele, and Dixon (2000); Manion and Rantz (1995); DePaola and Ebersole (1995); Fisher (1991); Erwin (1996); Ronch and Crispi (1997); Brown-Watson (1999).

Web Sites: www.retirement-living.com/main.html; www.seniorlink.com; senioroptions.com; www.hcoa.org/nagec; www.nih.gov/nia; www.aahsa.org; www.alfa.org; ccal.org)

See also: "Alternative Living: Relocation"

TASK MENU (FOR RESIDENT):

1. Attend a group for new residents.

Elaboration: Begin to form new support networks with other residents and staff.

Practitioner's role (if part of residential staff): Organize a group for new residents to assist them in their adjustment to the home. Schedule regular group sessions. Limit group size, as larger groups tend to increase hearing difficulties and lessen attention span. Establish meeting time and place. Track new residents and invite them to participate. Introduce the new resident to other residents and staff. Facilitate group involvement by offering support, empathy, and assistance in problem solving. Provide follow-up visit(s) to residents after the final group session.

2. At the first group session introduce yourself and explain how you came to reside in the nursing home.

Practitioner's role: Make sure that group members participate. If necessary, set time limits for each resident to speak so that all group members can share their personal information.

3. Bring to the group discussion your own experiences and problems with placement.

Elaboration: Discuss what the change means for you. Express your feelings around change of residence, change of routine, loss of cognitive or physical abilities, etc. Use a self-monitoring diary to keep track of situations, people, or events that you wish to discuss or remember.

Practitioner's role: Facilitate discussion of the meaning of the placement for the resident. Focus on these issues during the second, third, and fourth sessions.

4. Listen with empathy and offer support to others.

Practitioner's role: Discourage any one resident from monopolizing discussion. Redirect discussion when necessary.

5. Identify some of your own strengths and coping abilities with respect to the placement process and bring them to the group for discussion.

Practitioner's role: Allow sufficient time for all group members to recognize their own strengths and assist those residents that are unable to express their thoughts. Provide support to each resident. Encourage residents to voice their own opinions.

6. Bring to group your own ideas for solving problems discussed at previous sessions and share with other group members.

Practitioner's role: Organize ideas on large chalkboard or overhead to facilitate understanding. Condense ideas generated throughout previous sessions and encourage residents to voice concerns to nursing home staff when difficulties arise. Offer ideas on how to utilize these strategies in the future when faced with problems within the nursing home. Model or role-play problem-solving skills.

7. Identify previous forms of enjoyment, hobbies, and activities.

Practitioner's role: Explore past interests with the resident to make a good fit between the person and the environment.

8. Join activities in the nursing home that fit with your interests.

9. Become a member of the Residents' Council to provide input about programming, care, services, etc.

Practitioner's role: Encourage the resident to exercise as much choice as is possible. The resident should be in control of as much as he or she can in order to maintain dignity and self-esteem (Tobin 1991).

10. Discuss feelings and thoughts about your situation with your family.

11. Use progressive relaxation or meditation when there are situations or people who are upsetting.

Elaboration: Sometimes other residents are impaired in ways that you may find distressing. If possible, go to another section of the nursing home when such residents are in close proximity.

Practitioner's role: Teach client techniques of progressive relaxation.

TASK MENU: (FOR FAMILY)

1. Establish a visiting schedule.

Elaboration: This is particularly important when a family member is first placed in the nursing home and is adjusting to the new living situation.

2. Establish an open and honest relationship with staff.

Practitioner's role: Maintain contact with family to discuss placement issues and concerns and to provide support.

3. Listen attentively and empathically when the family member (resident) expresses thoughts and feelings about placement.

4. Encourage the family member (resident) to become involved in nursing home life and activities.

5. If possible, take the nursing home resident out on day trips.

6. Address questions and concerns to appropriate staff (e.g., social worker, head nurse, nurses' aide, physician, etc.).

7. Treat all staff members courteously.

Elaboration: Speaking kindly to nursing home staff may ensure that the family member is treated better.(See also chapter 10.)

—*Maura Barrett*

Adapted from Reid (2000)

RELOCATION

Older adults are often faced with having to relocate from one living environment to another where they can receive more care, such as an adult home, assisted living apartment, or nursing home. Because of reimbursement patterns, it is also becoming more common for seniors who already reside in residential homes to be transferred to other facilities that provide higher, lower, or more affordable levels of care. Moving from one residential home to another can be difficult and challenging in several ways. For the person moving, the situation and process represents a loss of control and a need to adjust to a new environment. Relocation can cause significant levels of stress. The level of stress associated with the move depends on factors such as how the change alters the caregiving relationship (Zarit and Whitlatch 1992) and the involvement of the person in the placement or moving decision. It is also associated with increased mortality and decreased physical and mental capabilities (Danermark and Ekstroem 1990). The term "transfer trauma" is frequently used with respect to the difficulties associated with moving elderly individuals. Families that were involved in the person's life and caregiving, usually continue to do so after a decision to move into an institutional setting (Naleppa 1996). Using a preparation program and providing seniors with a sense of control can assist in alleviating these concerns. Some have suggested that rituals to mark the transition and relocation can ease the burden of the move (see Schneewind 1990).

Literature: Blasinsky (1998); Danermark and Ekstroem (1990); McCallion and Toseland (1995); Naleppa (1996); Schneewind (1990); Soares and Rose (1994).

See also: "Adjustment to Placement."

TASK MENU

1. Ask questions about the new facility and discuss options with practitioner.
   Practitioner's role: Provide information to the elderly person and act as liaison between him or her and the staff at the facilities.
2. If a choice between facilities is available, list pros and cons of each, discuss them with family or others, and make a decision.
   Practitioner's role: Assist in decision making by educating the resident and family members about services available at the facilities.
3. Speak with the practitioner at the new facility and request a tour.
   Practitioner's role: Provide telephone numbers, arrange for transportation, and accompany the client on a tour of the facility if desired.
4. Visit new facility to familiarize yourself with new surroundings and staff.
   Practitioner's role: Familiarize the resident with the new setting by facilitating site visits. Accompany the resident on a site visit and introduce him or her to staff. Review activities offered. Educate the resident about location of facility (distance from present location and family members).
5. Identify concerns or fears.
   Practitioner's role: Identify and correct potential misconceptions about the move. Prepare resident emotionally for move using counseling techniques. Also offer such services to family members.
6. Seek out special services for the elderly and for caregivers.
   Practitioner's role: Link clients and families to special services and address psychosocial barriers to the acceptance of such services. For example, discuss losses, vulnerabilities, defenses, and dependency issues.
7. Identify impact of relocation.
   Practitioner's role: Discuss impact of relocation with client, family, or caregivers.
8. Attend support groups, workshops, social, and recreational groups.
   Practitioner's role: Offer information on mutual support groups, psychoeducational workshops, social and recreational groups, and service and advocacy groups (McCallion and Toseland 1995).
9. Make requests for specific room or roommate, if desired and possible.
   Practitioner's role: Work with social worker from new facility to create a smooth transition.
10. Decide on preferred mode of transportation to new facility.
    Practitioner's role: Assist in making arrangements for transportation.
11. Set time aside to say farewell to other residents and staff members.

Practitioner's role: Assist resident with packing belongings and saying good-byes to other residents and staff members. Provide follow-up visit if desired.

12. Plan a ritual to mark the transition and relocation.

Elaboration: Rituals that mark the transition from one environment and life phase to the next can reduce the burden and stress felt by the person relocating (Schneewind 1990). Examples of such rituals include a farewell dinner, writing thank-you notes, taking a group picture with friends at the time of the departure, and having family members or friends accompany the person to the new location.

—*Maura Barrett and Jennifer Hescheles*

Adapted from Reid (2000)

ADULT CHILDREN: COMMUNICATION AND CAREGIVING

Adult children provide a considerable amount of assistance and care to their aging parents. Moreover, they provide more difficult care to parents over much longer periods of time than they did when life expectancy was forty-seven years and elders comprised only 4 percent of the population (Stone, Cafferata, and Sangl 1987). This is the first time in the history of the United States that couples on average have "more parents than children." In 1900 a caregiver spent an average of eight years caring for an elder. Today a woman can expect to spend eighteen years caring for an older family member, a sim-ilar amount of time as spent on raising children before they leave home (Stone, Cafferata, and Sangl 1987).

When adult children or family members take on a caregiving role, they are often challenged when trying to establish and maintain constructive com-munication. The relationship that one has with a parent may be strained from years of unresolved anger or resentment. When an adult child is unex-pectedly forced into the role of caregiver, many aspects of that relationship will be changed (Beckerman and Tappen 2000; Biegel, Sales, and Schulz 1991; Schroots 1993). This time period is one of potential healing and growth, but effective dialogue is necessary in order to initiate resolution.

Care recipients may be angry and struggling with the realities of aging and illness that confront them (Beckerman and Tappen 2000; Cowles 2000). Caregiving adult children, on the other hand, may be overwhelmed and unprepared to deal with the multiplicity of current and future issues that will impact the status of their aged parents (Beckerman and Tappen 2000; Gallo et al. 1999; Novak 1997). During this time period communication is essential, but discussions around sensitive issues are even more difficult to initiate. Yet, if the caregiver can obtain a level of comfort and ease in talking about issues such as housing, finances, or medical care, the experience of helping and providing care will be more gratifying (Biegel, Sales, and Schulz 1991; Novak 1997).

See also: www.careguide.net; www.nfcacares.org (National Family Caregivers Association).

Literature: Beckerman and Tappen (2000); Cowles (2000); Gallo et al. (1999); Novak (1997); Schroots (1993); Stone, Cafferata, and Sangl (1987).

TASK MENU (FOR CAREGIVER, FAMILY MEMBER)

1. Evaluate and accept your personal limitations.

Elaboration: Recognize that while you are extending an important service to your parent, this should not define all aspects of your life. Avoid treating parents like children just because they require assistance or may not be able to cognitively function at the highest level.

2. Respect your parent's wishes as far as possible.

Elaboration: Decisional autonomy is the ability to make a self-determined decision, and executional autonomy involves the self-determined implementation of the decision. When one or the other is lost or diminished, the person is too often treated as if both have been lost. For example, not being able to carry out a decision should not limit the person's freedom to make that decision.

Practitioner's role: Assist in differentiation between decisional and executional autonomy and ensure that both are sufficiently considered.

3. Initiate reciprocal and respectful communication exchanges.

Elaboration: Facilitate discussions about what your parent or care recipient wants and what frightens or concerns the person. Talk, listen, and share your feelings. The following suggestions can help encourage the communication exchange:

(a) Set time aside to talk with your parent or care recipient when you will not be interrupted, and you are both rested and prepared.

(b) Be considerate and open regarding medical prognosis, financial issues, and your ability to help.

(c) Encourage the elderly individual to express any concerns or fears.

(d) Encourage the elder to make his or her own decisions for as long as possible. Let the person know that you are there to assist in any way possible.

(e) Listening is an integral aspect of developing a communicative relationship.

(f) Terminate any discussion that agitates the elder.

4. If you are not able to develop this type of rapport with your parent or care recipient, try to find someone who can.

Elaboration: It is essential to have open lines of communication. You may want to consult a family friend, clergyperson, or mental health professional to help you negotiate the steps listed above.

5. Make recommendations, *not* decisions, when communicating with your elderly parent or care recipient.

Elaboration: Sometimes one has to avoid "doing too much," i.e., assisting with activities care recipients can do for themselves. Excessive caregiving can create dependency, but more independence is usually the goal. The following issues should be addressed when communicating with the elder or care recipient:

(a) Identify the elder's primary concerns.

(b) Ask your elderly parent how important it is to remain in his or her home and if other options would be acceptable.

(c) Based on the current situation, ask your elderly parent about his or her financial situation and whether he or she can afford expensive medical bills. Inquire about long-term care coverage (see task planner on long-term care insurance).

(d) Make sure that your elderly parent has an updated and valid living will.

(e) Make sure that your elderly parent has established a durable power of attorney that will designate a person to make legally binding decisions in case he or she becomes incapacitated (see task planner on power of attorney).

(f) Discuss establishing advance directives, which outline a patient's wishes and medical care instructions as they relate to life-sustaining procedures (see task planner on advance directives).

6. Improve your caregiving experience through better communication.

Elaboration: Consider the following when communicating with your elderly parent or care recipient:

(a) Be prepared and find the right environment.

(b) Relax and maintain eye contact.

(c) Encourage your parent to talk.

(d) Avoid interrupting or criticizing.

(e) Focus on feelings.

(f) Speak clearly.

(g) Ask one question at a time.

(h) Have patience and allow sufficient time for a response.

7. Get organized, educated, and take care of yourself in a way that prevents burnout.

Elaboration: (see task planners on short-term respite and long-term respite).

8. Take time to identify resources.

Elaboration: Create a master phone list of friends, doctors, agencies, and supports in the community.

9. Educate yourself regarding your elderly parent's or care recipient's ailments.

10. Identify other people who can look in on your elderly parent or care recipient.

—Kimberly Karanda

CAREGIVING: BURDEN ON ONE FAMILY MEMBER

Even under the best circumstances, caregiving is a physically and emotionally demanding task. When it becomes the primary responsibility of one family member, it can be overwhelming. The responsibilities impact family life, leisure time, work life, personal finances, and in some cases physical and mental health. Emotional burdens of caregivers include grief, anger, anxiety, guilt, depression, embarrassment, and altered family dynamics (Mellins et al. 1993; National Alliance for Caregiving 1997). As the care recipient's condition declines and providing care becomes more involved, the situation tends to become increasingly tense for the care provider. One study of caregiving daughters showed that having multiple roles in addition to caregiving, specifically those of worker and mother, was associated with feelings of overload. However, resentment about the caregiving role was highest for those who had fewer roles apart from eldercare, especially when they had to quit work to provide care and did not have a partner to talk with. Life satisfaction was higher for partnered and working caregivers (Murphy et al. 1997).

Primary caregivers frequently cite that they need more time for themselves, but many do not utilize respite services. Service utilization rates were lowest among Asian caregivers. African-Americans and Hispanics were more likely than whites or Asians to cite caregiving as a financial hardship (National Alliance for Caregiving 1997). Compared with white caregivers, nonwhite caregivers are more likely to be an adult child, friend, or other family member rather than a spouse. Nonwhite individuals also report lower levels of caregiver stress, burden, and depression and endorse more strongly held beliefs about filial support. Nonwhite caregivers use prayer, faith, or religion as coping mechanisms more frequently than white caregivers (Connell and Gibson 1997).

One study found that spouses preferred in-home respite over adult day care (Cotrell 1996). The majority of spouses saw overnight family care as appropriate only for emergencies while adult children saw overnight care as appropriate for social and recreational activities. Adult children who resided with the care recipient reported employment and caregiver stress and their resulting exasperation as an impetus for utilizing services. Studies of interventions to reduce caregiver burden suggest that individual interventions may be more effective than group interventions (Knight, Lutzky, and Macofsky 1993; Toseland and Smith 1991).

Literature: Clark and Rakowski (1983); Connell and Gibson (1997); Cotrell (1996); Gendron et al. (1996); Mellins et al. (1993); Murphy et al. (1997); National Alliance for Caregiving (1997); Toseland and Smith (1991); Zarit and Edwards (1996); Berg-Weger, Rubio, and Tebb (2000); O'Rourke and Tuokko (2000); White, Townsend, and Stephens (2000); Zarit, Gaugler, and Jarrott (1999); Rogers (1999); Cox (1998); Weaver (1994).

Web Sites: www.nfcacares.org/; www.caregiving.com/articles/index.htm; www.caregiving.com/newslet/index.htm; www.careplanner.org; www.aarp.org/indexes/health.html#caregiving; /www.familycareamerica.com; www.caregiver.org.

See also: "Adult Day Care," "Socializing Opportunities," "Respite Services/General," "Respite/Short-Term," "Respite/Long-Term."

TASK MENU

1. Communicate the problem of being overburdened to other family members.

2. Express feelings about providing care to other family members.

Practitioner's role: Discussing this can entail strong emotional reactions as it may include feelings of guilt or anger by caregivers, care recipient, or other family members less involved in providing assistance. Thus, the practitioner may have to play a very active role in facilitating this task. Less involved family members may or may not know about the caregiver's feeling of being overwhelmed.

3. Identify ways to better balance the caregiving role with other family members.

4. Designate other responsible caregivers.

Elaboration: Asserting oneself is particularly important in unbalanced caregiving relationships (Gendron et al. 1996).

5. Split caregiving tasks among family members.

Practitioner's role: Prepare the client for increased tension and conflict that will likely result from this task. Have the client remind family members that this situation, if handled with a positive attitude, can result in increased closeness, social support, and time spent together among family members (Mellins et al. 1993).

6. Set up a family care plan, including who will be responsible for what type of assistance, and establish a process of monitoring to make sure that the needs of the care recipient are being met.

7. Discuss as a family (including the care recipient) the possibility of requesting outside services, including respite care.

Elaboration: Two types of respite currently exist, short-term and longterm services. Short-term respite may last from an hour to an entire day and may be provided at home or in a community setting. Long-term respite usually lasts from a few days to a week and usually involves a stay at a residential facility, such as a nursing home or an adult foster home (see task planners "Respite: Short-Term" and "Respite: Long-Term").

8. If relevant, designate family member(s) to investigate services available and arrange for an initial contact.

9. Discuss as a family (including the care recipient) the possibility of placement in long-term care if relevant.

10. Designate family member(s) to investigate long-term care facilities and arrange initial contact if relevant.

11. Explore ways to recover personal time.

Elaboration: Set aside blocks of personal time during which caregiving responsibility is covered by someone else (family member, adult day care, respite care).

—*Holly Hokanson*

Adapted from Reid (2000)

RESPITE: LONG-TERM

A common problem for caregivers is the need for some respite from the demands placed on them by the daily intensive care for a dependent elderly person. Respite is usually discussed in the context of adult day care services that provide respite to the caregiver. However, respite can also be needed for a longer period of time, e.g., when a caregiver wants or needs to travel or has an illness that temporarily prevents him or her from providing the required care.

Long-term respite is usually provided in a structured setting that the elderly individual can stay in for a number of days at a time, in most cases from two days to a week (Mace and Rabins 1991). Short-term and long-term respite have been proven to improve caregivers' attitudes and feelings of well-being. Moreover, they enhance caregivers' ability to provide care (Cox 1997). For further details about the benefits of respite, see the task planner on short-term respite. Caregivers often utilize long-term respite services in order to take some time for themselves, travel, have time to deal with other important family matters, or to have extra time around the holidays (Mace and Rabins 1991; Cotterill et al. 1997). Long-term respite offers the elderly person an opportunity to enjoy the company and social activities with other older adults (Cotterill 1997). Places that offer long-term respite include: hospitals, nursing homes, foster homes, adult respite homes, and arrangements with family or friends who will provide care for an extended period of time (Cotterill et al. 1997; Mace and Rabins 1991).

Literature: Cotterill et al. (1997); Cox (1997); Mace and Rabins (1991).

Web Sites: www.familycareamerica.com

See also: "Respite: Short-Term," "Relocation."

TASK MENU

1. If you are considering respite, discuss it with all involved.

Elaboration: Although less emotionally laden than a nursing home placement, this decision still can lead to feelings of ambiguity, guilt, and abandonment in caregivers and clients. It is important to bear in mind that caregivers often begin to look for respite after having reached emotional and physical exhaustion. It is helpful for all involved in the person's care to be present when discussing opinions and concerns about respite. It is also important to consider and address the care recipient's personal feelings regarding respite. When introducing respite as a potential option to the elderly family member, it may be useful to emphasize those benefits for the person that go beyond "being taken care of" (e.g., it may help to highlight the adult activities that the person will enjoy).

Practitioner's role: If necessary, help facilitate a family meeting to ensure that the concerns and opinions of all involved are heard. Educate caregiver(s) and care recipient about adjustment issues that the elderly person may have to temporary relocation. (See task planner on relocation.)

2. Learn more about community respite options.

Elaboration: As there may be a number of places that offer long-term respite in your area, it is important to know the local respite service alternatives. Options may include hospitals, nursing homes, and informal settings. Call your local Office for the Aging or check the phone listings under "aging" or "respite." The ARCH (Access to Respite Care and Help) phoneline is a nationwide service that will connect you with resources within your community (800–773–5433). The ElderCare Locator is another phone service providing similar assistance (800–677–1116).

Practitioner's role: Educate family and elderly person about community resources that provide respite options. Note that some communities may still have few formal respite resources.

3. Gather information about available resources.

Elaboration: Determine how often respite is needed and for how long, what services are offered, how arrangements are made, application requirements, fees for service, and who provides medical care if it is needed. Write down specific questions before calling facilities.

Practitioner's role: Facilitate this process and advocate for the family.

4. Consider financial issues associated with respite care.

Elaboration: Fees associated with respite care vary depending upon the type of respite and care needed. Often, respite services need to be paid for privately. Medicare may pay for nursing home visits if a skilled nursing care need exists and an individual requires treatment for a specific condition (Mace and Rabins 1991). However, Medicare usually does not pay for nursing home visits for the sole purpose of respite for a caregiver. A limited number of federal and state agencies have grants that assist with the costs associated with respite care.

Practitioner's role: Understand the current policy of Medicare and Medicaid as it relates to payment for respite care. Educate the family about available grants or funding. This information may be obtained through the local Office for the Aging. Discuss alternative payment options with the respite facility. Advocate for the family as needed.

5. Determine which facility is best for the care recipient and caregiver.

Practitioner's role: Facilitate a discussion about available options with all relevant parties. Be available to answer questions and facilitate the decision-making process by making sure that all parties have input. Set up visits if necessary.

6. Contact the facility about application process.

7. Complete necessary application.

8. Visit facilities to learn more about them.

Practitioner's role: Facilitate this visit. It may be helpful to develop a list of questions that the caregiver and client should ask when visiting the facility. If several options are available, keeping a list of pros and cons can assist in making the decision.

9. At the time of respite placement, communicate clearly with the intake worker about the nature of the elderly person's condition and any other potential problems.

Elaboration: It may be necessary to provide written information on the elderly person's needs (e.g., on special diets, ambulatory needs, toileting needs, behavioral issues, medications, and activities enjoyed).

10. Provide the facility with emergency contact numbers.

Elaboration: Include phone numbers for the caregiver, other family members, and medical care providers.

11. Pack personal clothing, personal items, medications, reading material, and pictures.

Elaboration: The facility usually provides information on what is appropriate for their facility.

12. Visit client at respite placement.

Elaboration: As with long-term placements (e.g., nursing home), initial visits help to ease the transition. Review the task planner on relocation regarding how to assist the elderly person in the transitional process.

—*Holly Hokanson*

RESPITE: SHORT-TERM

A common problem for caregivers is the need for respite from the demands placed on them by the daily intensive care for a dependent elderly person. Respite is usually discussed in the context of adult day care services that provide respite to the caregiver. However, respite can also be needed for a longer period of time, e.g., when the caregiver wants to go on a vacation trip or has an illness that temporarily prevents her or him from providing the required care.

Many families have strong feelings about placing their elderly relatives in an institutional setting and provide care in the home as long as it is possible. However, social, economic, physical, and psychosocial factors impact on the caregivers' ability to provide care. Respite is a concept that allows caregivers to take some time for themselves while a care recipient is being cared for safely, thus reducing the caregiver's stress and burden. Two types of respite currently exist, short-term and long-term services. In short-term respite, a professional may come into the home and care for the elderly person. In many cases, however, respite occurs outside of the home in a structured setting, such as an adult day care facility. Short-term respite may last from one hour to a whole day. Respite has been found to improve caregivers' attitudes, decrease caregivers' stress, and minimize depression as well as health and relationship problems (Cox 1997). Respite has also been found to decrease the probability of long-term care placement (Cox 1997). In addition, respite offers the older adult time to spend with others, make new social contacts and friends, increase social behaviors, enhance feelings of self-esteem and self-worth, and increase independence from caregivers (Cotterill et al. 1997).

Literature: Cotterill et al. (1997); Cox (1997); Geriatric Patient Education Resource
    Manual (1992); Mace and Rabins (1991); Naleppa (2001a); Nankervis et al. (1997).
Web Sites: www.familycareamerica.com
See also: "Adult Day Care," "Relocation," "Respite: Long-Term," "Relocation."

TASK MENU

1. Decide what type of short-term respite is desired.

Elaboration: There are various types of short-term respite, including in-home respite by home health aides, other caregivers, or community volunteers, or respite in more structured settings, such as adult day care or other community programs. Involve the patient and caregivers in the discussion and decision-making process.

Practitioner's role: Assess the needs of care recipient and caregiver. Provide education on short-term respite options.

2. Determine how much respite time is desired.

Elaboration: It is important to consider the care recipient's functional and health conditions, the caregiver's needs, and the availability of resources.

3. Seek out information about local resources.

Elaboration: Locally, the Office on Aging, senior service centers, other caregivers, churches, support groups, community mental health centers, nursing homes, hospitals, and newspapers may be able to offer information about resources. The ARCH (Access to Respite Care and Help) phoneline is a nationwide service that will connect you with resources within your community (800–773–5433). The ElderCare Locator is another phone service that provides similar assistance (800–677–1116). It is important to consider financial aspects at this time.

Practitioner's role: Educate and connect the elderly person and family with area resources.

4. Choose a respite option.

Practitioner's role: Facilitate the decision-making process, ensuring that all parties involved have the opportunity to present their desires and concerns.

5. Become familiar with the respite choice.

Elaboration: If the choice is in-home respite, it may be helpful to be available for the first visit. If a more structured environment in the community is selected, visit the facility, talk with staff, inquire about the qualifications and training of staff members, observe how problems are dealt with, and review the normal daily schedule of the facility (see task planner on relocation).

Practitioner's role: Act as a liaison between family and facility. Educate family about the types of respite options.

6. Visit respite facility.

Practitioner's role: Facilitate this visit. It may be helpful to develop a list of questions that the caregiver and client should ask when visiting the facility. If several options are available, keeping a list of pros and cons can assist in making the decision.

7. Pick a starting date and a proposed weekly schedule for respite.

8. Communicate with the elderly person about anticipated concerns.

Practitioner's role: Address the elderly client's concerns.

9. Ask the visitor or facility about information needed to care for the patient.

Elaboration: Be sure to include any behavioral problems, favorite foods, enjoyed activities, rest times, emergency contacts, special dietary concerns, the elderly person's likes and dislikes, medical condition, and any special assistance that is needed.

10. Develop a written document with all necessary information.

Practitioner's role: Provide education and information on facility.

11. Prior to the starting date, gather all necessary information and medications, and organize them for the visitor or the facility.

Practitioner's role: Required paperwork, medical records, etc. vary from facility to facility. Assist the client in gathering the required documentation. Arrange for transportation and help if needed.

12. Discuss arrangements with family and facility or visitor to make sure that all issues have been addressed.

13. Begin respite schedule and monitor service delivery.

—*Holly Hokanson*

ADULT DAY CARE

Taking on the responsibility of caring for an elderly relative in the home can be a difficult and taxing task. It requires a significant time commitment and effort on the part of the caregiver and can be a major physical and emotional burden. Caregiving can take away from normal activities of daily living including, in some cases, full-time employment. Adult day care is a concept that was introduced to provide elderly individuals with a variety of support services during any part of the day. These community-based programs give people an opportunity for socializing through peer-support and supervised activities. They may also offer specialized care such as nursing, speech therapy, physical therapy, and counseling (Cohen-Mansfield et al. 1994). Another important function of adult day care is to provide a much needed respite option to the caregiver. Family functioning can be enhanced when the elderly individual is able to maintain his or her usual place of residence but can spend some time in a community care system. This allows the caregivers time to work, run errands, or perform other tasks that might not get completed otherwise. For the elderly person, adult day care represents an arena for enhancing his or her physical and mental well being longer and at a higher level of functioning than is likely in an institutional setting (Kaye and Kirwin 1990). Services are provided for up to twelve hours per day. Currently, no uniform national standards exist for adult day care. Programs that use Medicaid funding for part of their services are required to be certified by Medicaid.

A distinction is made between two basic forms of adult day care: the social model and the medical model of adult day care. However, this distinction is becoming less clear as most programs today mix social and medical adult day care concepts (Naleppa 2001b).

SOCIAL ADULT DAY CARE The social model of adult day care is for elderly persons who benefit from opportunities to socialize as well as from creative programming, meals and nutritional services, and in some cases medication management under the supervision of nursing or social work staff. The participants are usually able to manage all or most of their personal care needs.

MEDICAL ADULT DAY CARE The medical day care model is for those elderly persons who need medical, nursing, physical, or occupational therapy and require more intensive personal care. Physician's orders are required to receive medical services.

MIXED MODEL ADULT DAY CARE The mixed model combines elements of both approaches. In practice, the distinction between the three models is often difficult since many variations exist.

Literature: Child and Elder Care Directory (1999); Cohen and Eisdorfer (1993); Cohen-Mansfield et al. (1994); Kaye and Kirwin (1990); Naleppa (2001b).

Web Sites: www.careguide.net

See also: "Respite: Short-Term," "Respite: Long-Term," "Relocation."

TASK MENU

1. Obtain information about adult day care.

Elaboration: Contact the Child and Elder Care Directory (www.careguide. net). This directory allows an individual to complete a free personal profile. The person provides personal information as well as the type of adult day care facility of interest. The person is then provided with a list of facilities in the respective geographic area. This Web site also contains other resources and information regarding frequently asked questions. Another useful contact is the National Institute of Adult Day Care c/o National Council on the Aging, 1409 Third St. S.W., Suite 200, Washington D.C., 20024, phone (800) 424–9046.

Practitioner's role: Educate the client and provide information on how programs operate, what services are provided, who is eligible, and what costs are entailed. Assist the client in gathering the necessary data about the different adult day care options available in the local community.

2. Contact local facilities that provide requested services and make appointments to visit.

Practitioner's role: Help clients review the available alternatives and discuss which programs would fit their needs.

3. Visit the adult day care facility.

Elaboration: Make an appointment to speak with administrative staff to learn about financial requirements, meals, medical related services, and support services.

Practitioner's role: Accompany the family on their visit if needed.

4. Spend time with staff and day care residents.

Elaboration: This will enable clients to witness staff and resident interactions, social dynamics, and self-sufficiency levels of the people the facility serves. A visit of the facility is often a key factor in determining the appropriateness of a potential day care placement.

5. Attend a group if possible.

6. Speak with members of the medical staff to inquire about the care offered to visitors.

Elaboration: Many adult day care programs have a medical emphasis, offering specialties in physical therapy, occupational therapy, psychiatry, and physician assessments (Kaye and Kirwin 1990). Find out whether the therapies the client requires are provided. Other questions to address include: What is the staff-to-client ratio? What are the qualifications of the service personnel? Is the facility easily accessible?

7. Determine the availability of transportation for program participants.

Practitioner's role: Many facilities provide transportation for participants in adult day care. If transportation services are not provided by the facility, inquire about local senior service transportation (see task planner on senior transportation).

8. Apply to adult day care program.

Elaboration: If medical services are required, a physician's order is required.

Practitioner's role: Educate the client about the terms of the contract. Assist the client and caregiver in completing the application.

9. Monitor service provision over time.

—*Mary Kate Schneider*

DEMENTIA, ALZHEIMER'S DISEASE, AND DELIRIUM: SPOUSE AND FAMILY ADJUSTMENT

DEMENTIA Dementia describes a category of usually slowly progressing cognitive disorders that involve memory loss and loss in intellectual and mental functioning. The DSM-IV characterizes dementia as "the development of multiple cognitive deficits" that includes impairment in memory (American Psychiatric Association 1994:133). Dementia mostly afflicts older adults. Five percent of persons over 65 years and 20 percent of those over 80 years experience dementia (Kaplan and Sadock 1998).

ALZHEIMER'S DISEASE Senile dementia of the Alzheimer's type (SDAT) is the most common type of irreversible dementia. It accounts for about 50–60 percent of all dementia cases and is a diagnosis for 50 percent of all nursing home residents (Kaplan and Sadock 1998). SDAT is characterized by a slowly progressing loss of cognitive functioning and an increasing disorientation to time and place. In the early phases of SDAT, many individuals continue to live independently. Memory loss is evident, and the ability to learn new material is impaired. A decline from one's previous level of functioning occurs. For example, individuals may lose items, become easily lost in unfamiliar places, or leave food cooking on the stove. Some individuals show increased irritability and other personality changes. Even as the disease progresses, many individuals suffering from SDAT remain at home and can be cared for by a spouse or a family member. However, it becomes more and more evident that individuals are forgetting previously learned material. They can become lost in familiar neighborhoods and have difficulty with shopping or paying bills. In the later stages an individual may forget his or her schooling, occupation, birthday, family members (e.g., spouses, children), and eventually even his or her own name. Gait or other motor disturbances can develop. End stage Alzheimer's disease may result in the inability to maintain basic hygiene and personal care, self-feeding, and even language skills. The person may eventually be "reduced" to a vegetative state, becoming mute and bedridden.

Throughout the course of the disease, some individuals experience delirium, delusions, or depressed mood in combination with the SDAT. As the disease progresses, caring for the person and management of behavior may become overwhelming for the caregivers. Alzheimer's disease is one of the most trying mental health conditions for family members. They witness their loved one slowly lose his or her memory and increasingly become confused and disoriented. Fears, stressors, and losses for the family and spouses are enormous. The average duration of the disease from onset until death is from one to ten years. Realities of the day-to-day caregiving and planning needs for the individual with SDAT become increasingly burdensome as the condition progresses.

DELIRIUM Delirium is an impairment of consciousness with a sudden onset. It follows a brief, fluctuating course but has the potential for rapid improvement when treated. The person experiencing delirium is temporarily disoriented and may have delusions or hallucinations. Causes of delirium include diseases of the central nervous system, systemic diseases such as heart failure, and intoxication or withdrawal from toxic or pharmaceutical agents (Kaplan and Sadock 1998). It has been estimated that between 30–40 percent of all hospitalized patients over the age of 65 experience an episode of delirium (Kaplan and Sadock 1998).

Literature: American Psychiatric Association (1994); Brechling and Schneider (1993); Carstensen, Edelstein, and Dornbrand (1996); Foltz-Gray (1997); Hamill (1998); Katzman (1987); McCallion, Toseland, and Diehl (1994); McCallion, Toseland, and Freeman (1999); Tobin (1999); Toseland and McCallion (1998).

Web Sites: www.aoa.dhhs.gov/factsheets/alz.html; www.biostat.wustl.edu/alzheimer/; www.alz.org/; www.alzheimers.org/

See also: "Relocation," "Respite: Short-term," "Hospice."

TASK MENU

1. Secure information from physicians regarding provisional diagnosis to rule out other causes of dementia and to assess the patient's competency and the stage of the disease.

Practitioner's role: Assist health care professionals in gathering information needed to make provisional diagnosis.

2. Provide support, nurturing, and reassurance regarding provision of care to patient.

Practitioner's role: Provide counseling for spouse and family in order to facilitate their adjustment to the changes taking place in the individual with Alzheimer's disease.

3. If the individual is in the early stages of Alzheimer's disease, develop a plan for the execution of advance directives for personal, financial, social, and medical needs.

Elaboration: Obtain legal advice as needed. In the early stages of dementia, individuals are usually capable of understanding the implications of their illness and may be willing to review personal health and financial commitments in anticipation of future incapacity. Someone in the early stage of dementia who is confused or disoriented in time and place is still be capable of making most decisions and expressing preferences about most aspects of his or her health care (Brechling and Schneider 1993). (See task planners about advance directives and power of attorney.)

Practitioner's role: Be able to respond to questions concerning advance directives and legal resources.

4. File for guardianship (conservatorship in some states) if the patient is in an advanced stage of dementia and has not utilized advance directives.

5. Read *The 36-Hour Day* by Nancy Mace and Peter Robins.

Elaboration: This book gives a realistic outlook of what managing an individual with Alzheimer's disease entails.

6. Join a support or stress management group.

Elaboration: Support groups can reduce your levels of stress and provide an opportunity to share with other caregivers and learn more about caring for a family member with dementia.

7. If the patient's condition is advanced, discuss options for behavioral and medical management with physician.

Elaboration: Small doses of neuroleptics are sometimes sufficient to ameliorate severe depression, agitation, aggressiveness, and paranoia. The medications may, however, produce extrapyramidal side effects and marked psychomotor retardation (Katzman 1987). Medications may need to be complemented with behavior modification techniques.

Practitioner's role: Practice or demonstrate through role play the techniques of progressive relaxation and coping imagery. Such techniques may be used to assist the family in behavior modification of an individual with Alzheimer's disease, or they can be used to aid the family in stress reduction.

Help spouse and family to identify triggers that prompt agitation in the individual with Alzheimer's disease so they can be avoided.

8. Discuss living arrangements and plan for long-term care needs as the disease progresses.

Elaboration: If considering institutionalization, research costs, availability, and quality of care provided by potential settings. Some nursing homes do not accept patients with behavior problems. Make site visits as necessary. (See task planner on relocation.)

9. Improve the quality of the patient's physical environment.

Elaboration: It is important to create an environment that is nonthreatening and predictable by using nightlights, clocks, calendars, etc. (Tobin 1999). Additionally, in the early stages of Alzheimer's disease it is helpful to provide an ordered environment, as it assists the individual in externally organizing what he or she once organized internally.

10. Read sections on preservation of self in Tobin (1991).

Elaboration: This publication provides helpful information on how to allow an individual with Alzheimer's disease to maintain as much of his or her dignity as is possible.

11. Continue to treat the person as you always have.

Elaboration: This reinforces the preservation of self for the individual with Alzheimer's disease. Taking part in simple pleasures seems to facilitate adaptation (Tobin 1999).

12. Identify meanings of the patient's behavior, particularly in the middle to late stages, to assist the patient in retaining a sense of self.

Elaboration: Bizarre behavior of patients often has meaning that relates to the striving for the preservation of self. Once this principle is understood, it becomes possible for families to interpret bizarre behavior as the patients' effort to maintain their identity and retain their sense of self. This makes it easier for family members to tolerate unusual behaviors (see Tobin 1999 for examples).

13. Consider respite or adult day care programming.

Elaboration: See task planners on short-term respite and adult day care.

14. Consider hospice for the person in final stage Alzheimer's disease.

Elaboration: See task planner on hospice.

Practitioner's role: Initiate referral to hospice program. Provide counseling to spouse and family for anticipatory grief and loss issues. Discuss possibility of continued counseling with family and spouse in regard to grief and loss following the death of the elderly person.

—Tammy Rucigay

Adapted from Reid (2000)

EXERCISE, FITNESS, AND WELL-BEING

Elderly people today show a strong interest in various kinds of fitness and health promotion programs. Researchers link heart conditions, osteoporosis, obesity, depression, and early aging to "disuse" of the body (Busby-Whitehead 1999; Harriss et al. 1989). Research shows strong support for the positive effects of exercise in later life (Busby-Whitehead 1999; Lee, Hsieh, and Paffenbarger 1995). Although researchers had initially thought that cardiovascular ability declined steadily among older adults, more recent studies demonstrate that regular exercise can reduce the rate of decline (Huffman 2000; Kemper and Binkhorst 1993). Some studies found no decline over a decade or more in cardiovascular performance among elders who are highly trained in physical activity (Kemper and Binkhorst 1993). Elders with hypertension show a decrease in blood pressure even from engaging in a limited walking program (Harriss et al. 1989; Lee, Hsieh, and Paffenbarger 1995). Exercise increases an individual's aerobic capacity, increases cardiac output, and leads to better use of muscles (Huffman 2000; Kemper and Binkhorst 1993; Lee, Hsieh, and Paffenbarger 1995). Exercise can strengthen the heart and circulatory system while improving the health of heart attack patients and preventing another attack (Lee, Hsieh, and Paffenbarger 1995). Despite these benefits from exercise, many people reduce the amount of physical activity they engage in as they age. Physically challenging activities are still seen by many as not appropriate for older people. However, this attitude is beginning to change. Two indicators of these changes are the growing number of older adult members of fitness clubs and the increased availability of exercise equipment in assisted living and other long-term care facilities.

Literature: Busby-Whitehead (1999); Harriss et al. (1989); Huffman (2000); Kemper and Binkhorst (1993); Lee, Hsieh, and Paffenbarger (1995).

Web Sites: www.asktransitions.com/articles/aerobics1.html; www.swmed.edu/home_pages/library/consumer/eldxr3.htm; www.iamfitforlife.com/

TASK MENU:

1. List current or recent physical activities and identify additional activities you could engage in.

Elaboration: It is important to obtain pertinent information regarding previous lifestyle and exercise functioning in order to gauge at what level of intensity the current programming should be set (Busby-Whitehead 1999; Huffman 2000). If an elderly person has no previous exercise or activity history, a more gradual initiation into a regime will be necessary. Assessing attitudes or perceived barriers will facilitate appropriate interventions (Huffman 2000). If an elderly person is too afraid to walk in the neighborhood, making a referral to a local health club or a mall walking group for this activity would be more appropriate. If the elderly person has health conditions that may limit the type and amount of physical activity he or she can carry out, a physician should be involved in the decision.

2. Obtain information about the benefits and importance of exercise.

Elaboration: Older people of all ages and physical conditions have a lot to gain from exercise and from staying physically active. They can also lose substantially if they are physically inactive due to a decrease in health and abilities. Researchers have found that exercise and physical activity can improve the health of people who are 90 years of age or older, who are considered frail, or who are suffering from some diseases (Kemper and Binkhorst 1993).

3. Design a leisure or exercise program that will reduce physical and psychological risks.

Elaboration: Physical risks include injury (especially falls and fractures), severe fatigue, and in some situations death. Psychological risks include the fear of failure, ridicule, or embarrassment. Programs that enhance a sense of self-efficacy prove to be the most successful. As elderly people experience self-efficacy, they will take on more challenging tasks and expend more effort on the scheduled activity.

4. Integrate endurance, strength, balance, and stretching exercises.

Elaboration: Endurance activities will increase heart rate and breathing for prolonged periods of time. Strength exercises will increase the physical power and thus enable elderly persons to complete and to do things they like to do. Balance exercises are instrumental in fall prevention (falling is a major cause of serious injury or death in elders). Finally, stretching will keep the elder's body flexible, thus preventing muscle strain or injury.

5. Think about nontraditional activities to include in an exercise and leisure repertoire.

6. Seek out programs that have a social interaction component.

Elaboration: Research shows that elders will join and stay with programs if they include a social interaction piece (Huffman 2000). Many elders will participate in physical activities in order to be with other elders.

7. Ensure that leisure or exercise program leaders design individualized programming that is in tune with your requests and needs.

Elaboration: It is common that the elderly person's goals will differ from those of younger people in exercise, fitness, or sports programs. Some senior centers provide exercise programs that support independence and social contact (Busby-Whitehead 1999).

—Kimberly Karanda

URINARY INCONTINENCE

Between 15 percent and 35 percent of the elderly living at home experience urinary incontinence (Steeman and Defever 1998). The amounts of urine leaked can range from drips to a high volume of urine loss (Burgio 1998). There are four types of incontinence: stress, overflow, urge, and functional incontinence. Stress incontinence refers to the leakage of urine during exercise, sneezing, coughing, laughing, or any other type of body movement. Overflow incontinence refers to minimal amounts of urine leaked from a constantly filled bladder. This tends to occur in older men who have a blockage due to an oversized prostate gland. Urge incontinence refers to situations where an individual is unable to reach the toilet in time. Many elderly people suffer from this type of incontinence. It is associated with individuals who may not remember to urinate or have difficulty reaching the toilet in time due to physically or cognitively disabling conditions. Functional incontinence refers to situations when an individual is in an acute medical situation and is unable to reach the bathroom.

Several treatments can assist an individual in dealing with urinary incontinence. They include medical treatment, behavioral therapy, pharmacological treatment, and surgery. Several types of incontinence aids can be used for urinary incontinence that cannot be cured. They include pads, adult diapers, and other absorbent devices as well as catheters and other drainage devices. Since treatments for the different types of incontinence vary significantly, it is necessary to obtain an accurate medical assessment of the cause and type of urinary incontinence.

Literature: Burgio (1998); Steeman and Defever (1998).

Web Sites: www.nafc.org (National Association for Continence)

TASK MENU

1. Meet with your primary care provider to diagnose the symptoms of incontinence.

Elaboration: During the time of assessment, your health care provider will discuss your medical history and urinary behaviors. To obtain a clear picture of your incontinence, the health care provider may conduct a physical exam and urine tests. Your health care provider may prescribe medication.

Practitioner's role: Encourage medical assessment and support the client throughout this process. Explain existing incontinence tests and procedures. More information about incontinence can be found at the National Kidney Foundation Web site at www.niddk.nih.gov/health/kidney/nkudic.htm.

2.Learn about your type of incontinence.

Elaboration: Since several types of incontinence exist, it is helpful to learn more about your type and associated factors. You may want to look into the existing types of treatment, including medication, behavior therapy, and surgery.

Practitioner's role: Educate the client about his or her type of incontinence and existing treatments.

3. Learn behavioral techniques that help you control your bladder and sphincter.

Elaboration: The two main types of behavioral therapy for incontinence are bladder training and pelvic muscle exercises. Bladder training refers to scheduling visits to void and being aware of when and where you most often have accidents (see tasks 4 and 5). Pelvic muscle exercises and Kegel exercises assist an individual in strengthening weak muscles in the bladder area. One can identify the weak muscles by stopping urine flow midstream. The muscles used in this process can be strengthened by tightening them to a count of four. Repeat the tightening ten to fifteen times several times a day. It is important to discuss these treatments with a medical provider.

Practitioner's role: Connect the client with appropriate resources or provide education about behavioral techniques.

4. Urinate throughout the day at specific times rather than waiting for the urge to urinate.

Elaboration: Develop a schedule that allows for you to urinate every two or four hours as needed. Even if you do not have the urge to urinate, it is important to keep on schedule. It may be helpful to set a timer to remind you of scheduled times. Adjust the schedule as you learn what best fits your own needs.

Practitioner's role: Assist and support the client in developing and following this schedule. Be sensitive to the client's feelings around the new daily schedule.

5. Keep a written record of urinary habits, including each urination and incontinent occurrences.

Elaboration: This record will provide you and your health care provider with information about the frequency and indicators of your incontinent occurrences.

Practitioner's role: Support and remind the client of keeping records of urinary habits.

6. Follow exercise and medication treatments recommended by health care provider.

Practitioner's role: Discuss treatment regime with clients and make sure that they understand it.

7. Be aware of where the closest bathroom is when you are not at home.

8. Make it easier to get to your bathroom at home.

Elaboration: Remove any objects that may be in your path so you can reach the bathroom quickly. Install a night-light and grab bars in the bathroom to assist you when you may be in a hurry.

Practitioner's role: Help the client identify obstacles in the home that may prolong his or her ability to get to the toilet.

9. Drink a sufficient amount of fluids.

Elaboration: It is essential to drink enough fluids throughout the day. Cutting back on fluid intake will not cure incontinence and may be harmful to one's health.

10. Utilize incontinence pads if necessary

Elaboration: It is important to change these pads regularly. Discuss pad options with health care provider.

—Holly Hokanson

MEDICATION MANAGEMENT AND TREATMENT ADHERENCE

Nonadherence (noncompliance) is defined as client behavior that does not "coincide with medical or health advice" as a result of the interaction among the "regimen, the clinician, the patient, and the home environment" (Vandereycken and Meerman 1988:186). Nonadherence comprises a broad range of behaviors from dropping out of care precipitately to minor alterations in the treatment regimen. According to Vandereycken and Meerman (1988), nonadherence tends to occur when therapeutic requirements conflict with the client's usual behaviors or personal belief system or when the client receives care over a long period of time, such as in the case of a chronic substance abuse problem or a mental illness. In long-term care, nonadherence is generally characterized by a progressive "slippage" from cooperative to uncooperative behavior. An example is the client having surgery as recommended by a physician and failing to keep scheduled follow-up appointments. For many disorders, long-term outcomes are largely a function of treatment compliance (Sperry 1995).

The health conditions of many elderly clients require them to regularly rely on prescribed medications. In addition, elderly persons often have to take a number of medications concurrently. Not taking the medication can lead to severe health complications. Elderly individuals with memory loss or forgetfulness may have problems remembering what medications to take and the prescribed intervals between dosages. Reasons that call for efforts to manage a client's medication include a client's confusion about what to take and when, forgetfulness and memory problems, need to take a large number of different medications, resistance to take medication, and lacking the prescribed medication. Helping the client to establish procedures for regular intake of medications is especially important if the medication is live saving and the client has problems remembering to take it.

One study showed that as much as one third of all hospitalizations related to adverse drug effects and half of all reports of fatalities due to inappropriate use of prescription medication involved elderly individuals (Lamy 1990). Nursing home admissions have also been linked to elderly persons' inability to manage medications at home (Hammond and Lambert 1994). Some elderly clients may not take medication due to their costs. Several prescription benefit programs are available that are specifically targeted at low-income older adults.

Clients with psychiatric problems have particular difficulty in complying with treatment regimens (Sperry 1995). Medications that control psychiatric symptoms may be abandoned by the client for a variety of reasons, such as denial of mental illness with its associated stigma, discomfort with the medication's side effects, and a lack of understanding regarding the need to continue medications even after psychiatric symptoms have abated (Campbell and Daley 1993). For many clients, facilitating adherence to a drug schedule is a key element of treatment.

Literature: Barusch (1991); Campbell and Daley (1993); Casper and Regan (1993); Connelly and Dilonardo (1993); Massaro, Pepper, and Ryglewicz (1994); Meichenbaum and Turk (1987); Olfson, Hansell, and Boyer (1997); Salzman (1993); Kail (1992); Noyes, Lucas, and Stratton (1996); Mitchell et al. (2001).

Web Sites: www.aoa.gov/naic/Notes/caregivingforelderly.html; www.healthycaregivers. com/; www.medicare.gov

TASK MENU

1. Learn about medical condition and medication (most effective time to take, dosage, side effects).

Elaboration: A general resource is the Merck Manual of Medical Information, Home Edition. The Internet can also be used to gather information on medications (e.g., Yahoo—Medical—Search). If medication is prescribed for mental health problems, learn about the interaction effects between the disorder, addictive substances (if taken), and medications taken concurrently.

Practitioner's role: Make sure that the client has an accurate understanding of his or her condition as well as the interaction and potential side effects of prescription and over-the-counter medications or other substances (e.g., alcohol).

2. Review medication pamphlet or contact physician or pharmacist for directions, dosage, and side effects.

Elaboration: Important information covered in the medication pamphlet includes: possible side effects, typical dosage, regimen for missed dosages, drug interactions, and possible behavioral side effects.

Practitioner's role: Review this information with the client. Explain any unknown or unclear terminology to the client. Educate the client about the need to take medications as prescribed. Help the client establish reasons that could lead to irregular intake of medication.

3. Write a list of all medications to be taken.

Elaboration: Include medication name, dosage, and the times to take it.

4. Identify reasons for nonadherence.

Elaboration: Reasons may include unpleasant side effects, fear of dependence or long-term harm, forgetfulness, and doubts about the efficacy of the medication.

Practitioner's role: Help the client correct misconceptions about medication. Consult with physician when reasons appear to have a realistic basis.

5. Learn how to monitor status of your health condition.

Elaboration: For conditions such as hypertension and diabetes learn to take blood pressure or test blood sugar. Chart blood pressure, injections, or medications taken.

6. Combine taking medication dosages and prescribed therapeutic activities with daily habits and rituals.

Elaboration: If you must take medication in the morning on an empty stomach, have pills beside the bed with an empty glass. Make it part of the morning ritual to fill the glass with water and take your pill immediately. For medication that must be taken with food, have it timed to be part of your meal activity. If relaxation exercises or other recommended treatments are part of your ongoing therapy, pair them with daily habits and rituals in the same manner.

7. Describe signs and outcomes of mental illness relapse and compare them to your experience when not taking medications (if medication is taken for mental health problem).

Elaboration: Use self-monitoring of behavior to write descriptions. Discuss them with others to gain insight into the correlation between psychiatric relapse and noncompliance in taking medications.

8. Identify meaningful rewards for adhering to treatment recommendations.

Practitioner's role: Some clients have difficulty thinking of what they enjoy, so have a list of alternatives available.

9. Enlist a friend or significant other to assist with monitoring progress.

10. If there is a period of time when adherence is not working, use self-monitoring to become aware of the reasons.

11. Develop a list of advantages and disadvantages of taking medications as prescribed.

12. Discuss with physician or others involved if it is possible to simplify or better tailor the treatment regimen to the individual (Sperry 1995).

Elaboration: Make sure that oral and written directions for medication(s) and treatment(s) are given. Ask if there is any form of the medication being used that may be taken once daily or in long-lasting injectable form. If your literacy level is low, you have poor vision, or your dexterity is limited, identify and use problem-solving skills to find ways to compensate or correct these limiting factors (Hussey 1991).

Practitioner's role: Discuss with physician or psychiatrist prescribing medications how best to tailor or customize information and schedule to the client's personality style and circumstances.

13. Explore options for managing medication intake.

Elaboration: Some ways to organize medication management include developing a schedule to manage medication intake, storing the medication in a visible place (e.g., kitchen table, top of night drawer), drawing a chart or weekly calendar with check-off columns for the medications taken, and drawing a big enough reminder sign. If deemed beneficial, color-code medication bottles (e.g., for clients with vision problems).

14. Obtain a compartmentalized pill box to reduce errors in pill taking.

15. If caregivers are involved, designate a caregiver who is responsible for medications.

Elaboration: If the condition of the elderly person requires it, closely monitor compliance. Regulate amount and time for medications to be taken.

16. Monitor medication usage.

Elaboration: This includes monitoring potential side effects, periodically checking the expiration date of medications, discarding medications when they reach the expiration date, and restocking on time.

—Diane Austen and Pamela Zettergren

Adapted from Reid (2000)

TINNITUS: COPING WITH THE SOUNDS

Tinnitus is the perception of sounds (e.g., ringing or buzzing) in one's own ears or head in the absence of relevant external acoustic stimuli (Henry and Wilson 1998). It is more commonly referred to as "ringing in the ears" (Jastreboff and Jastreboff 2000). Tinnitus is one of the most common medical complaints among the elderly population (Billue 1998). One in three people over 65 years of age report tinnitus (Salomon 1989). Although it can be experienced at any age, most cases of tinnitus occur in those between the ages of 40 and 80 (Peifer, Rosen, and Rubin 1999).

It is not unusual for people to experience tinnitus only periodically, though the duration of the sounds is usually brief, i.e., only a few seconds (Pinchoff et al. 1998). However, for about 2 percent of the population, the sounds can be unrelenting and persistent (Pinchoff et al. 1998). Its persistence can be as debilitating as hearing loss (Griest and Bishop 1996). This type of tinnitus is sometimes referred to as "chronic severe" or simply "chronic" tinnitus (Erlandsson and Hallberg 2000). The cause of tinnitus is often uncertain (Peifer, Rosen, and Rubin 1999) and currently no cure exists (Jastreboff and Jastreboff 2000). Thus, medical professionals often advise chronic sufferers that they will have to "live with it" (American Tinnitus Association 1993).

The presence of tinnitus can lead to severe psychological or emotional distress (Andersson and McKenna 1998) and seems to increase the likelihood of having a coexisting mental disorder (Hiller and Goebel 1992). Problems such as anxiety, depression, and irritability have been found to be more common among tinnitus sufferers than the general population (Andersson 1997; Scott and Lindberg 2000). Chronic tinnitus sufferers also experience excessive stress as well as sleeping problems (Folmer and Griest 2000), difficulty concentrating (Scott and Lindberg 2000), decreases in social and occupational functioning (Saunders 1996), a decrease in quality of life (Erlandsson and Hallberg 2000), and even suicide (Moller 2000). Sufferers report that stress can exacerbate their tinnitus so that sounds seem more noticeable than usual (Gabriels 1996; Hazelby 1996; Saunders 1996; Sourgen and Ross 1998). If sufferers are unable to cope with stressful situations, they are more likely to be annoyed by the tinnitus (Dineen, Doyle, and Bench 1997). The primary goal of tinnitus management is to provide relief from tinnitus and to help the client overcome the psychosocial problems associated with tinnitus (Newman, Jacobson, and Spitzer 1996). Thus, learning how to manage stress seems essential (Hazelby 1996).

Literature: American Tinnitus Association (1993); Andersson (1997); Andersson and McKenna (1998); Billue (1998); Davies, McKenna, and Hallam (1995); Dineen,

Doyle, and Bench (1997); Erlandsson and Hallberg (2000); Erlandsson, Hallberg, and Axelsson (1992); Folmer and Griest (2000); Gabriels (1996); Goebel and Hiller (1996); Griest and Bishop (1996); Hazelby (1996); Henry and Wilson (1998); Hiller and Goebel (1992); Jastreboff and Jastreboff (2000); Kroner-Herwig et al. (1995); Laurikainen et al. (2000); Lindberg et al. (1987); Moller (2000); Neher (1991); Newman, Jacobson, and Spitzer (1996); O'Connor and Zappia (1993); Ong (1994); Peifer, Rosen, and Rubin (1999); Pinchoff et al. (1998); Salomon (1989); Saunders (1996); Scott and Lindberg (2000); Slater and Terry (1987); Sourgen and Ross (1998); Stouffer and Tyler (1990); Stouffer et al. (1991); Tyler (1997); Wilson, Bowen, and Farag (1992).

Web Sites: www.ata.org (American Tinnitus Association); www.ohsu.edu/ohrc/ (Oregon Hearing Research Center)

TASK MENU

1. Recognize that presently no cure for tinnitus exists, but you can learn how to cope with the condition.

Practitioner's role: Explain to the client that the aim of intervention will not be to cure the tinnitus but to reduce some of its unpleasant effects. Explain to the client that he or she will learn how to cope with the sounds.

2. Learn about tinnitus.

Elaboration: By learning about tinnitus, one moves toward coping with it. The American Tinnitus Association (ATA) has a wealth of information (e.g., books, brochures, videos, local self-help groups, newsletter and a quarterly journal, *Tinnitus Today*). Information and brochures can be acquired via ATA's Web site (www.ata.org) or through ATA, P.O. Box 5, Portland, OR 97207, phone: (800) 634- 8978. Another source for tinnitus information is the Oregon Hearing Research Center (OHRC). OHRC can be contacted at Oregon Health Sciences University, 3181 S.W. Sam Jackson Park Road, Portland, OR 97201–3098, phone: (503) 494–8032, Tinnitus Clinic phone: (503) 494–7954, -0910, Web: www.ohsu.edu/ohrc/.

3. Write down your beliefs about tinnitus.

Elaboration: Beliefs about tinnitus may affect the client's motivation for using coping strategies to deal with his or her tinnitus (Erlandsson, Hallberg, and Axelsson 1992). This in turn could affect the amount of distress produced by tinnitus (Lindberg et al. 1987).

Practitioner's role: Become aware of how the client perceives the tinnitus. This can help to further understand the problems, can be an opportunity to provide relevant information, and can be the basis for challenging inaccurate beliefs concerning tinnitus (Sourgen and Ross 1998)

4. Learn and practice progressive muscle relaxation.

Elaboration: Stress exacerbates the symptoms of tinnitus. Progressive relaxation has been found to be helpful in improving sufferers' ability to cope with their tinnitus (Davies, McKenna, and Hallam 1995; Gabriels 1996; Goebel and Hiller 1996; Kroner-Herwig et al. 1995; Wilson, Bowen, and Farag 1992). In these studies, progressive relaxation has helped in decreasing self-reported annoyance, distress, discomfort, anxiety, and it has contributed to improve the subjects' mood.

Practitioner's role: Implement progressive relaxation as a major component of treatment. Be sure to inquire about any movements or postures that may cause pain. Adjust relaxation techniques accordingly to suit the client's physical capacities.

5. Keep a tinnitus diary and record conditions that contribute to changes in the severity of tinnitus.

Elaboration: Since factors that aggravate or reduce tinnitus vary—quiet places can reduce the severity for some while aggravating it for others—this strategy helps identify situations or places that should be avoided or sought out. Once connections between certain conditions or situations and tinnitus severity have been established, one can plan actions that alleviate the tinnitus and avoid those activities that exacerbate it.

Practitioner's role: Ask the client to keep a record of activities and occasions when tinnitus severity is increased or reduced. Before beginning the diary, inform the client that he or she will likely encounter more circumstances that increase tinnitus severity than those decreasing it (Stouffer et al. 1991). Conditions where severity is increased or reduced should be discussed after having been recorded for several weeks. Encourage the client to minimize the amount of time spent in activities or conditions where severity is increased and to maximize time spent in activities or conditions where severity is reduced.

6. Invite family members into sessions.

Elaboration: Including family members in your treatment can enable them to realize the validity and severity of this condition. It can also facilitate the development of strategies to reduce situations that aggravate the tinnitus.

7. Join a tinnitus support group.

Elaboration: In tinnitus self-help groups, members share a common condition, realize that their problems are not unique, learn that people react to their tinnitus in different ways, and provide emotional support for each other. To learn more about ATA tinnitus self-help groups that may be in your area, visit the ATA Web site www.ata.org.

Practitioner's role: Encourage the client to join a support group. Emphasize that such a group could help in making him or her feel validated, understood, and supported. The group could also serve as a resource for learning new methods of coping.

—*Brian Freidenberg*

STROKE: COPING DURING THE AFTERMATH

Each year 400,000 Americans suffer a stroke (Hinds 2000). Stroke occurs when there is an interruption in the blood supply to the brain. The most common cause is a blockage of an artery, but bleeding that occurs in the brain can also cause a stroke. In either case, a stroke often results in some brain damage (Glass et al. 2000). Stroke is the leading cause of serious disability in the U.S. (National Center for Health Statistics 1996). Disruption of psychosocial functional capacities is common following stroke (e.g., communication, emotional regulation, cognition, memory, attention, and coping ability; Glass et al. 2000). Such psychosocial factors seem to greatly influence long-term adjustment (Astrom, Adolfsson, and Asplund 1993; Colantino et al. 1993). Psychosocial functioning has been determined to be a critical component in physical recovery and the coping process (Andersen et al. 1995; Astrom 1996).

Although physical disabilities can occur following stroke, the mental effects are often considered to be more significant. Most of the disabilities caused by stroke are of a mental or cognitive nature, rather than physical (Birkett 1998). Depression is a common side effect of stroke. It affects half of all stroke survivors (Hinds 2000), and depression has been found to be a major risk factor for death among survivors (Goldberg 1998).

As stroke fatalities have declined over the past few decades, more attention is being given to the development of nonpharmacological interventions that aim at reducing disability and enhancing functioning following a stroke (Glass et al. 2000). Physicians assert that medical intervention alone is not sufficient for stroke management and that other services (e.g., psychological interventions, physical rehabilitation) are required to maximize rehabilitative outcomes (Kaufman and Becker 1991). Stroke survivors can benefit from interventions designed to assist in coping with the disruption of their psychosocial functioning. It has been suggested that intervening in this area may improve their emotional well-being and morale as well as enhance the success of their overall recovery (Birkett 1998; Frasure-Smith and Prince 1989; King 1996).

Literature: Andersen et al. (1995); Anderson, Deshaies, and Jobin (1996); Astrom (1996); Astrom, Adolfsson, and Asplund (1993); Colantino et al. (1993); Evans, Bishop, and Haselkorn (1991); Evans et al. (1994); Frasure-Smith and Prince (1985); Glass (1990); Glass et al. (2000); Glass and Maddox (1992); Glass et al. (1993); Hanger and Mulley (1993); Hinds (2000); Kaufman and Becker (1991); Kawachi et al. (1996); King (1996); National Center for Health Statistics (1996); Rao, Ozer, and Toerge (2000); Santus et al. (1990); Sife (1998); Sipski and Alexander (1997).

Web Sites: www.stroke.org; www.strokeassociation.org

TASK MENU:

1. Include your family in the treatment process.

Elaboration: Family dynamics have been shown to have a significant effect on the extent and pace of the survivor's functional and psychological recovery (Anderson et al. 1996; Glass et al. 1993). Stroke can have a substantial impact on family dynamics (Evans et al. 1994). Family members, particularly those who become caregivers following the stroke, can experience sleep problems, social isolation, anxiety, and depression (Birkett 1998).

Practitioner's role: Family-focused psychosocial intervention is strongly recommended. Recognize that the family caregiver may not know how to respond to a loved one following his or her stroke (Hinds 2000). Encourage the client to include a close family member in the treatment. Caregivers' inclusion in therapy may not only benefit their own mental health, but it will likely help them learn how to better communicate and respond to the survivor's needs. While the tasks below are to be used with the stroke survivor, there are some instances where the family caregiver should participate in the tasks.

2. Calmly describe any emotional reactions that you have concerning the stroke and its aftereffects.

Elaboration: Recovery frequently requires close attention to the emotional and psychological reactions to the stroke. Poor emotional functioning after a stroke has been found to have a significant negative impact on functional recovery (Glass et al. 2000). Common reactions include anger, frustration, despair, anxiety, fatigue, loneliness, hopelessness, depression, and feelings of loss and grief (Glass et al. 2000). These reactions result in part from the profound and sudden challenge that a stroke presents to the survivor and in part from the direct physiological impact on the brain (Glass et al. 2000; Glass and Maddox 1992). These negative reactions are often directed toward those family members who are trying to be helpful while struggling with their own reactions to the stroke (Glass et al. 2000). This can be a concern, since compassion and empathy by family members is associated with a faster rate of recovery (Glass et al. 2000). The opportunity to express these emotional reactions and at times experiencing them during sessions facilitates empathy and compassion for the other (Glass et al. 2000). It should also be noted that you and your family might experience the same stages of mourning (Heller 1998).

Practitioner's role: Solicit emotional reactions of the stroke survivor and the caregiver, including any possible fears (e.g., concerning another stroke, death, etc.) and concerns they may have developed since the stroke (Glass et al. 2000). Encourage survivor and caregiver to openly discuss their emotional experiences. Validate and normalize their reactions. Reframe them as important but temporary coping mechanisms. Facilitating such discussion can enhance feelings of closeness and solidarity, which in turn has been found to be associated with increased psychological and physical recovery (Glass 1990).

3. Learn more about stroke and resources for stroke survivors and their families.

Elaboration: You may lack a clear understanding of what has happened following your time in the hospital. It is common to have questions about stroke and critical to have those questions answered. Inadequate knowledge about stroke has been associated with life dissatisfaction (Evans, Bishop, and Haselkorn 1991; Hanger and Mulley 1993). Several resources can help you learn more about stroke. One organization is the American Stroke Association (ASA). ASA provides information and services to stroke survivors and their caregivers. ASA distributes newsletters and other educational materials. Contact ASA at American Stroke Association, 7272 Greenville Avenue, Dallas, TX 75231, phone: (800) 553–6321 (to contact the Stroke Connection which offers educational books, videos, and audiotapes) or (888) 4-STROKE (to contact the Stroke Family Support Network), email: strokeassociation@heart.org, Web: www.strokeassociation.org. Another resource is the National Stroke Association (NSA). NSA offers complimentary as well as low-cost publications concerning stroke. They also provide information on stroke prevention, treatment, and rehabilitation. NSA can be contacted at National Stroke Association, 9707 E. Easter Lane, Englewood, Co. 80112, phone: (800)-STROKES, fax: (303) 649–1328, Web: www.stroke.org.

Practitioner's role: Educate client and caregiver about the causes, natural history, and epidemiological facts about stroke. Discuss warning signs, risk factors, and emergency plans for responding to a new stroke. Recovery timetables emphasizing the timing and process of recovery should be addressed as well (Glass et al. 2000).

4. Accept role changes.

Elaboration: Stroke often alters one's ability to perform social and family roles (Glass et al. 2000). What may be especially difficult to accept are "role reversals" in the family. While you may have been responsible for certain tasks before the stroke (e.g., handling finances, household chores), a family member may now be responsible for them. This may be difficult to accept. Additionally, you may perceive that your family members are making important decisions without your input or consent. Be candid about your feelings and ask family members to keep you informed of any decisions they make concerning your life (Bullard-Bates, Bozzo, and Davies Hendricks 2000).

Practitioner's role: Help client and caregiver assess the limits of the survivor's independence. Ask the survivor what he or she can still do for himself or herself. Help client and caregiver assess prestroke family and social roles and facilitate a discussion on redefining these roles (Glass et al. 2000).

5. Learn and practice muscle relaxation techniques.

Elaboration: Muscle relaxation has been recommended to reduce stress in stroke survivors (Bullard-Bates, Bozzo, and Davies Hendricks 2000). This helps you better cope with the impact of the stroke.

Practitioner's role: Teach the client progressive relaxation techniques. Be sure to inquire about any movements that are not feasible or produce pain. Adjust relaxation techniques to suit the client's physical capacities.

6. Optimize social supports in your life by expanding your social network.

Elaboration: There are numerous beneficial effects of social networks and social support (Glass et al. 2000). The presence of a strong social support network has been associated with improved recovery from serious illness, reduced risk of poststroke depression, less risk for nursing home placement, improved quality of life, better overall psychological adjustment, and lower mortality rates (Anderson, Deshaies, and Jobin 1996; Glass et al. 2000; Goldberg 1998; Kawachi et al. 1996; King 1996). Set up a support system. One approach would be to connect with other stroke survivors and their families through ASA. Accept offers of help when they are extended.

Practitioner's role: Assess client's previous support patterns in times of stress or illness (Glass et al. 2000). Conduct a social network assessment. Brainstorm on how client and caregiver can recruit extended network members. Assess social needs and potential barriers to recruiting additional support. Help the client reintegrate into social activities that are commensurate with the client's physical status. Emphasize the intrinsic value of returning to valued social activities. Help the client accept remaining deficits. Assist client in seeking meaning in the crisis of the stroke (Glass et al. 2000).

7. Join a self-help support group.

Elaboration: Stroke survivor support groups can be beneficial to the recovery process. They can provide an additional resource for expanding your social network (Birkett 1998; Glass et al. 2000). ASA offers stroke club support groups, and NSA can refer survivors to local support groups. Support groups, like those offered by CAPS and the Well Spouse Foundation, may benefit your family members (Heller 1998).

Practitioner's role: Encourage client and caregivers to join a local stroke survivor support group. Provide education on the social and educational value of such groups. Highlight the benefits of such groups, e.g., offering empathy, validation, and support, and learning of new coping methods to combat poststroke stress.

—*Brian Freidenberg*

APPENDIX: SELECTED WEB SITES
FOR WORK WITH THE ELDERLY
Compiled by Miranda Koss

Web sites regularly change and may disappear after some time. Nevertheless, it is useful to present the reader with a list of Internet resources that have useful information for practice with older adults. The Web sites are presented alphabetically by topic areas.

ADJUSTMENT TO GROWING OLD

www.onlineathens.com/1998/110298/1102.a2carter.html
www.ettaclarkphotography.com/
seniors-site.com/library/growold.html
webdata2.soc.hawaii.edu/growold/
members.tripod.com/nutrition_4/index.html
www.ncpa.org/pi/health/hcoct98i.html
www.cyber-north.com/health/growing.htm

ADVANCE DIRECTIVES

www.choices.org
www.ghc.org/health_info/adv_dir/advpage.html
www.rights.org/deathnet/LWC.html
www.ama-assn.org/public/booklets/livgwill.htm
www.euthanasia.org/lwvh.html
www.mindspring.com/~Escottr/will.html
www.ahca.org/info/advdir.htm
www.wnet.org/archive/bid/sb-advance.html
www.abanet.org/elderly/myths.html

ADULT DAY CARE

www.health-center.com/english/senior/livingoptions/aaday.htm
www.charlotte.com/observer/family/bestread/adultcare.htm
www.healthinformatics.com/docs/english/SHA/adaycare.sha.asp
www.amcity.com/stlouis/stories/1998/11/23/focus1.html
www.newlifestyles.com
www.hospicomm.com/adultdaycare.htm
www.ohioline.ag.ohio-state.edu/~Eohioline/lifetime/lt4–1f.html
www.aoa.dhhs.gov/AOA/webres/adultday.htm
www.libertynet.org/adcg
www.amcity.com/stlouis/stories/1998/11/23/focus1.html
www.aoa.dhhs.gov/factsheets/default.htm

AFRICAN-AMERICAN

www.census.gov/pubinfo/www/afamhot1.html
www.josseybass.com/catalog/isbn/0–7879–0351–5/praise.html
www.blackfamilies.com/living/family_relationships/census_role.html
aafp.org/afp/970300ap/abs_9.html
www.cudenver.edu/public/library/reference/afam.html
www.prostatecancer.com/otherinfo/abstracts/2/1701.html
www.aoa.dhhs.gov/AOA/dir/68.html
www.thirdmil.org/program/aars_pr.html
www.toptags.com/aama/docs/jcrow.htm
www.isr.umich.edu/rcgd/prba/persp/sp97/structure.html
medicine.ucsf.edu/divisions/cadc/mission/index.shtml
iml.umkc.edu/casww/blackeld.htm
www.psa-rising.com/medicalpike/menus/africanam.htm

AGE DISCRIMINATION

www.aoa.dhhs.gov/factsheets/ageism.html

AGING WITH DEVELOPMENTAL DISABILITIES

thearc.org/faqs/vision.html

ALCOHOL AND DRUGS

www.health.org/pubs/elderly/elderly.htm
www.health.org/samsha.htm

www.ias.org.uk/factsheets/elderly.htm
www.nattc.org/internet.html
www.health.org/links.htm
www.dhs.state.ut.us/edo/othrlnks.htm
www.samhsa.gov/csat/csat.htm
www.niaaa.nih.gov
www.health.org/index.htm
www.jointogether.org
www.health.org/index.htm
www.aoa.gov/aoa/pages/agepages/alcohol.html
www.casacolumbia.org
www.health.org/pubs/resguide/olderams.htm#sec1
www.health.org/pubs/resguide/olderams.htm#sec2
www.health.org/pubs/resguide/olderams.htm#sec3
www.health.org/pubs/mbcu/mbcu.htm
www.health.org/pubs/elderly/trends2.htm
www.jointogether.org/sa/
alcoholism.about.com/msubonline.htm?pid=2750&cob=home
alcoholism.about.com/gi/dynamic/offsite.htm?site=http://aaforum.org
alcoholism.about.com/mbody.htm?cob=home&terms=elderly+alcohol+
    abuse&pm=112_200_t
www.alcoholismhelp.com/index/html/sgp92.html
www.baptisteast.com/CHD002.htm

ALZHEIMER'S DISEASE

my.webmd.com/content/asset/chat_transcript.522383
www.isl.net/~Ehoffcomp/Welcome.html
www.alzwell.com/Thisweek.html
www.zarcrom.com/users/alzheimers/index1.html
www.alzwell.com/welcome.html
www.aoa.dhhs.gov/factsheets/alz.html
www.coa.uky.edu/ADReview/
www.ices.on.ca/docs/fb3390.htm
home.online.no/~Edusan/diseases/alzheimers/index.html
www.biostat.wustl.edu/alzheimer/
www.geocities.com/HotSprings/3004/
www.virtuallawoffice.com/journal.html
www.alz.org/
www.alzheimers.org/

ARTHRITIS

my.webmd.com/content/dmk/dmk_article_55408

ASSISTED LIVING

www.aspe.os.dhhs.gov/daltcp/reports/indepth.htm
www.aspe.os.dhhs.gov/daltcp/reports/litrev.pdf
www.aspe.os.dhhs.gov/daltcp/reports/98state.htm
www.calregistry.com/tips.htm
www.alfnet.com/tips/whatalf.htm
www.alfnet.com/elr_home.htm
www.alfnet.com/menu_page.htm
www.assistedlivinginfo.com/members.html
www.ahca.org/info/con-astl.htm
www.retiree-living.com/introasst.html
www.whca.org/alfbrochure.htm
www.elderlycarekonnection.com/

CANCER AND ELDERLY

www.wanonline.com/life/life1534.html

CAREGIVERS

my.webmd.com/content/dmk/dmk_article_43004
ericps.crc.uiuc.edu/npin/respar/texts/parfami/famcare.html
www.caregiving.com/index.html
www.nfcacares.org/
www.caregiving.com/articles/index.htm
www.caregiving.com/newslet/index.htm
www.alz-nova.org/tips.htm
www.tcaging.org/caregive.htm
heartsongbooks.com/carebk3.html
www.nfivc.org/old/other.htm
www.aoa.dhhs.gov/elderpage/locator.html
www.caregivers.com/
www.aoa.dhhs.gov/May99/caregiver.html

CAREGIVER ISSUES

www.elderlycarekonnection.com/articles.htm
www.elderlycarekonnection.com/
www.aoa.dhhs.gov/elderpage/locator.html
caregivers.com/
www.aoa.dhhs.gov/May99/caregiver.html
www.bmj.com/cgi/content/full/313/7053/364
www.bmj.com/cgi/content/full/312/7024/153
iml.umkc.edu/casww/specpops.htm

CHEMICAL ABUSE AND THE ELDERLY

www.health.org/pubs/elderly/trends2.htm
www.casacolumbia.org
www.casacolumbia.org
www.casacolumbia.org/publications1456/publications_show.htm?
   doc_id=5882
www.statcan.ca/english/ads/11–008-XIE/drugs.html
www.baptisteast.com/chd000.htm
www.baptisteast.com/CHD003.htm
www.baptisiteast.com/CHD010.htm
www.ctclearinghouse.org/felder.htm
www.health.org/pubs/elderly/index.htm
www.health.org/pubs/elderly/medreports.htm
www.aoa.dhhs.gov/aoa/pages/agepages/medicine.html
www.mayo.edu/geriatrics-rst/Drug.html
www.sirius.com/~Enakelley/welcome/powwow.html
www.egna.com
http://dir.yahoo.com/Health/Diseases_and_Conditions/Narcotics_
   Addiction/Narcotics_Anonymous
www.healthsquare.com/pdrfg/pd/chapters/fg4ch23.htm

CHRONIC PAIN

www.medinfo.ufl.edu/cme/hmoa2/pain/slide32.html
www.nurseweek.com/ce/ce711a.html
www2.rpa.net/~Elrandall/index.html

www.chronicpainsolutions.com/articles/cowanspr98.htm
www.tznet.com/busn/advocate/pain.html
www.pulsus.com/Pain/02_03/gagl_ed.htm
www.goedhart.com/painresource/index.html
www.mednwh.unimelb.edu.au/a-report/95_96/pubs.htm
www.macmcm.com/ascp/ascp98-agsgmp.htm
www.hr.state.or.us/pain/
wwwhost.gu.se/geriatrik/disputationer/Hall-Lord.html

DEATH

www.globalideasbank.org/death.html
online96.com/seniors/dying.html
www.elder-law.com/1996/issue341.html
www.cacf.org/wwwboard/messages/205.html
www.msn.fullfeed.com/~Ejstllmnk/bishop/deathdyg.html
freethought.org/org/ar/articles/mignacca.html
euthanasia.com/mchugh.html
www.kirstimd.com/bookdead.htm
www.psy.fsu.edu/~Echarness/courses/aging/6919s99/death/index.htm

DEPRESSION

www.psycom.net/depression.central.elderly.html
www.shpm.com/articles/aging/agdep1.html
www.findarticles.com/cf_0/m3225/n5_v57/20460464/p1/article.jhtml
www.nami.org/helpline/elddepres.htm
www.agenet.com/depression_elderly.html
www.mentalhealth.com/book/p45-dp01.html
www.bmj.com/cgi/content/full/312/7041/1298/c
www.bmj.com/cgi/content/full/313/7064/1058

DIABETES

www.agenet.com/fit_facts_elder_action.html
ohioline.ag.ohio-state.edu/ss-fact/0166.html
www.macmcm.com/ags/ags98-ecmepdfbb.htm
www.niddk.nih.gov/health/diabetes/pubs/cookbook/cookbook.htm
www.diabetes.org/ada/diabetesinfo.asp
www.diabetes.org/ClinicalDiabetes/v17n11999/Pg19.htm

DENTAL CARE

www.mdmanagement.ca/cmaj/vol-157/issue-2/0127b.htm

DEPRESSION

www.uncg.edu/edu/ericcass/depress/docs/older.htm
www.uncg.edu/edu/ericcass/depress/docs/latelife.htm

DEVELOPMENTALLY DISABLED: ELDERLY PARENTS

seattletimes.nwsource.com/news/local/html98/altsher_19990527.html
userpages.umbc.edu/~Eechen1/

DRUGS: LOW COST

www.ec-online.net/Knowledge/Articles/drugcosts2.html

ELDER ABUSE

www.oaktrees.org/elder/
www.lifelinecairns.org.au/elderabuse.htm
www.gbla.org/abuse.html
www.hagenbaugh.com/nb0296.html
www.oaktrees.org/elder/help.shtml
www.seniorlaw.com/elderabuse.htm
www.aoa.dhhs.gov/Factsheets/abuse.html
www.aoa.dhhs.gov/abuse/default.htm
www.aphsa.org/hotnews/neais.htm
www.mincava.umn.edu/elderv.asp
www.add.nsw.gov.au/releases/9808_abuse.htm
www.aoa.gov/abuse/default.htm
da.co.la.ca.us/seniors/crimes.htm
www.aoa.dhhs.gov/factsheets/abuse.html
www.hc-sc.gc.ca/hppb/healthcare/pubs/clinical_preventive/pdf/s11c77e.pdf

ELDER LAW

www.seniorlaw.com/index.htm
www.nsclc.org/
www.mhaging.org/involved/index.html

EMPLOYMENT

www.aoa.dhhs.gov/factsheets/employment.html

EXERCISE

nursinghome.org/closeup/cupdocuments/cu104.htm
www.asktransitions.com/articles/aerobics1.html
www.swmed.edu/home_pages/library/consumer/eldxr3.htm
www.iamfitforlife.com/

EYE CARE

www.cma.ca/cmaj/vol-152/1211e.htm
www.pnc.com.au/~Egetwell/eyes.htm
www.agenet.com/Visual_Changes.html
www.laeyeworks.com/visioncare/popeye.html
www2u.biglobe.ne.jp/~Edrnaomi/default.htm
pharminfo.com/pubs/msb/amd.html
www.aoa.gov/aoa/pages/agepages/eyes.html
www.penpages.psu.edu/reference/28507/285072114.HTML
www.more.abcnews.go.comsections/newsuese/wnt_eyetreat_intro

FALLS AND ELDERLY

www.srhip.on.ca/bgoshu/Injury/InjurySP.html#Prevention
www.srhip.on.ca/bgoshu/Injury/InjuryFallsReportFS.html
www.jr2.ox.ac.uk/bandolier/band20/b20–5.html
www.hcn.net.au/healthbrochures/prevsteps.htm
www.hcn.net.au/healthbrochures/whattodo.htm
www.celos.psu.edu/Research/falls.htm
taiwan.vh.org/Patients/IHB/IntMed/ABA30/1994/falling.html
www.cdc.gov/ncipc/duip/falls.htm
www.aafp.org/afp/971101ap/steinweg.html
www.colostate.edu/Depts/CoopExt/PUBS/CONSUMER/10242.
    htmlhttp://www.ices.on.ca/docs/fb4490.htm
www.acep.org/public/fc009818.htm
www.nihs.go.jp/acc/cochrane/revabstr/ab000340.htm

FINANCIAL AND PERSONAL RECORDS

www.dollar4dollar.com/98–0518/tx0518.htm
www.ptclub.com/Trusts.html

GENERAL INFORMATION AND KNOWLEDGE

www.ageofreason.com
www.aoa.dhhs.gov/AOA/webres/craig.htm
seniors-site.com
www.aoa.dhhs.gov
www.bmj.com
www.aoa.dhhs.gov/AOA/webres/craig.htm

HEALTH ISSUES

www.healthfinder.org/justforyou/seniors.htm
www.niddk.nih.gov/health/diabetes/pubs/cookbook/cookbook.htm
www.diabetes.org/ada/diabetesinfo.asp
my.webmd.com/content/dmkdmk_article_51884
www.aoa.dhhs.gov/aoa/eldractn/foodfact.html
www.agcom.purdue.edu/AgCom/Pubs/HE/HE-605.html
www.thirdage.com/health/
www.elderweb.com/default.php3?PageID=152
disabilities.nashp.org/papers/0002.htm

HOBBIES AND RECREATIONAL ACTIVITIES

www.his.com/~Epshapiro/computers.and.elderly.html
www.aifs.org.au/institute/pubs/WP15.html

HOME MAINTENANCE

www.sunsentinel.com/daily/1022.htm
www.penpages.psu.edu/reference/28507/285072114.html
ww.-home.calumet.york.ca/pbrugnat/www/problems.htm
www.christmasinapril.org/

HOME SAFETY

www.mdch.state.mi.us/mass/HSC/hsccover.html

HOSPICE, DEATH, AND DYING

www.hopsicenet.org

HOUSING OPTIONS

www.aoa.dhhs.gov/factsheets/housing.html
www.acsu.buffalo.edu/drstall
www.seniorsites.com/
www.hud.gov/senior.html

JOBS

www.aoa.dhhs.govfactsheets/volunteer.html

LITERACY

www.cal.org/NCLE/DIGESTS?GROW_OLD.HTML

LONG-TERM CARE

www.aspe.hhs.gov/daltcp/reports/diseldes.htm
my.webmd.comcontentdmkdmk_article_43006
my.webmd.com/content/dmk/dmk_article 43024
my.webmd.com/content/dmk/dmk_article_51884
www.aspe.hhs.gov/daltep/reports/diseldes.htm

MEDICATIONS

www.healthsquare.com/pdrfg/pd/chapters/fg4ch23.htm

MENTAL HEALTH

www.bmj.com/cgi/content/full/315/7105/413
www.frii.com/~Eshetler/dx.htm

NUTRITION

www.thai-otsuka.co.th/pxnews/0498nl01.
www.maff.gov.uk/inf/newsrel/1998/981021b.htm
www.psghs.edu/pubtips/N/NUTRITIONANDELDERLY.html
www.caregiver.on.ca/cghdnt.html
www.i5ive.com/article.cfm/elderly_caregiving/4136
www.healthline.com/articles/hl9405dt.htm
www.aoa.gov//pr/enpevpr.html
www.penpages.psu.edu/reference/12101/12101667.HTML

www.joe.org/joe/1992fall/iw3.html
www.colloidal.com.au/library/section1/nutrition.htm
www.postgradmed.com/issues/1997/11_97/pn_nutr.htm
www.health.org/insight/elderlym.htm
www.looksmart.com/edu1/eus534
www.wews.com/yourhealth/yourhealth-90831–160926.html
www.familyhave.com/health/elderlym.html
www.ificinfo.health.org/insight/elderlym.htm
www.aoa.dhhs.gov/factsheets/enp.html
www.jsonline.com/alive/nutrition/1111savvy.stm
persephone.agecom.purdue.edu/agcom/pubs/he/he-605.html

NURSING HOMES

www.angelfire.com/tn/NursingHome/

PERSONAL AND HEALTH RECORDS

www.capmed.com/

RELATIONSHIPS

www.aifs.org.au/institute/pubs/WP15.html
www.agenet.com
www.aifs.org.au/institute/pubs/WP15.html
www.aoa.dhhs.gov/factsheets/grandparents.html
www.aoa.dhhs.gov/may97/Grandparents.html

RELOCATION

www.placestoretire.com/
cgi.chicago.tribune.com/business/smallbusiness/article/0%2C2669%2C2–
    36335%2CFF.html
www.relojournal.com/may2000/atlassurvey.htm
www.cgcgroup.com/emoves/
www.2c.com/wb_hrpages/hr_gen_moving.html

SCAMS AND FRAUDULENT ACTIVITIES AGAINST THE ELDERLY

www.sunsentinel.com/daily/1022.htm
www.aoa.gov/aoa/eldractn/homemodf.html

www.theindependent.com/Archive/073098/stories/073098/New_scams30.
 html
tahoe.com/appeal/archive/stories.1.17.97/news/1a10snow17Jan1294.html
www.state.me.us/ag/clg21.htm
www.fraud.org/welcome.htm
www.fraud.org/elderfraud/eldset.htm
www.adultcare.com/Library/GrassleyOnCharityfraud.asp?TopicID=
 FL&Topic=Financial?legal

SEXUALITY

www.mcauley.acu.edu.au/-yuri/aged/Eder1.htm
www.alznsw.asn.au/library/rlsex.htm
www.aoa.dhhs.gove/aoa/pages/agepages/sexuality.html

STROKE AND CEREBROVASCULAR ACCIDENT (CVA)

my.webmd.com/content/dmkdmk_article_51884

TRANSPORTATION NEEDS

www-home.calumet.yorku.ca/pbrugnat/www/problems.htm
www.aoa.dhhs.gov/factsheets/Transportation.html

VOLUNTEERING

www.aoa.dhhs.govfactsheets/volunteer.html

WOMEN AND AGING

www.asaging.org/at/at-203/spirit.html

REFERENCES

Abramson, J. 1988. Participation of elderly patients in discharge planning: Is self-determination a reality? *Social Work* 33:443–448.

Adler, K. A., T. L. Patterson, and I. Grant. 2002. Physiological challenges associated with caregiving among men. In B. J. Kramer and E. H. Thompson, eds., *Men as caregivers: Theory, research, and service implications*. New York: Springer.

Aldwin, C. M. 1991. Does age affect the stress and coping process? Implications of age differences in perceived control. *Journal of Gerontology* 46:P174–P180.

Alzheimer's Disease Statistics Fact Sheet. 1996. [Online] Available: http://www.alz.org/dinfo/factsheet/ADS.html.

American Nurses Credentialing Center. 2002. Levels of Credentialing. Retrieved July 31, 2002, from http://www.nursingworld.org/ancc/certify/cert/cofcred.htm.

American Occupational Therapist Association. 2002. *About Occupational Therapy* Retrieved July 31, 2002, from http://www.aota.org/featured/area6/.

American Psychiatric Association. 1994. *Diagnostic and statistical manual of mental disorders.* 4th ed. Washington, D.C.: American Psychiatric Association.

American Tinnitus Association. 1993. *Results of the 1992 tinnitus patient survey: Booklet for tinnitus patients.* Portland: American Tinnitus Association.

Andersen, G., K. Vestergaard, M. Ingeman-Nielsen, and L. Lauritzen. 1995. Risk factors for post-stroke depression. *Acta Psychiatrica Scandinavica* 92:193–198.

Anderson, D., G. Deshaies, and J. Jobin. 1996. Social support, social networks, and coronary artery disease rehabilitation: A review. *Canadian Journal of Cardiology* 12:739–744.

Andersson, G. 1997. Cognitive-behavioral treatment for tinnitus: A difficult case. *Scandinavian Journal of Behavior Therapy* 26:86–92.

Andersson, G., and L. McKenna. 1998. Tinnitus masking and depression. *Audiology* 37:174–182.

Andresen, E., B. Rothenberg, and J. G. Zimmer, eds. 1997. *Assessing the health status of older adults.* New York: Springer.

Anker-Unnever, L. 1999. An effective managed care strategy: Case managers in partnership with primary care physicians. In: F. E. Netting and F. G. Williams, eds., *Enhancing primary care of elderly people.* New York: Garland.

Applebaum, R., and C. D. Austin. 1990. *Long-term care case management: Design and evaluation.* New York: Springer.

Arnason, S., E. Rosenzweig, and A. Koski. 1995. *The legal rights of the elderly.* New York: Practicing Law Institute.

Astrom, M. 1996. Generalized anxiety disorder in stroke patients: A three-year longitudinal study. *Stroke* 27:270–275.

Astrom, M., R. Adolfsson, and K. Asplund. 1993. Major depression in stroke patients: A three-year longitudinal study. *Stroke* 24:976–982.

Austin, C. D. 1983. Case management in long-term care: Options and opportunities. *Health and Social Work* 8:16–32.

Austin, C. D. 1988. History and politics of case management. *Generations* 12:7–10.

Austin, C. D. 1990. Case management: Myths and reality. *Families in Society* 71:398–407.

Austin, C. D. 1993. Case management: A systems perspective. *Families in Society: The Journal of Contemporary Human Services* 74:451–459.

Austin, C. D. 2001. Case management. In M. E. Mezey, ed., *The encyclopedia of elder care: The comprehensive resource on geriatric and social care,* pp. 121–124. New York: Springer.

Balaban, R. B. 2000. A physician's guide to talking about end-of-life care. *Journal of Geriatric Internal Medicine* 15:195–200.

Bandura, A. 1982. Self-efficacy mechanism in human agency. *American Psychologist* 37:122–147.

Baraff, L. 1998. Emergency department management of falls in the elderly. *The Western Journal of Medicine* 168:183–184.

Barusch, A. S. 1991. *Elder Care: Family training and support.* Newbury Park: Sage.

Bassuk, K., and J. Lessum. 2001. Collaboration of social workers and attorneys in geriatric community-based organizations. *Journal of Gerontological Social Work* 34 (3): 93–108.

Baum, M., and M. Page. 1991. Caregiving and multigenerational families. *Gerontologist* 31:762–769.

Bayles, K. A., and C. K. Tomoeda. 1991. Caregiver report of prevalence and appearance order of linguistic symptoms in Alzheimer's patients. *Gerontologist* 31: 210–216.

Beaton, S. R., and S. A. Voge. 1998. *Measurements for long-term care: A guidebook for nurses.* Thousand Oaks: Sage.

Beck, A. T., C. H. Ward, M. Mendelson, J. Mock, and J. Erbaugh. 1961. An inventory for measuring depression. *Archives of General Psychiatry* 44:53–62.

Beck, A. T., and R. W. Beck. 1972. Screening depressed patients in family practice: A rapid technique. *Postgraduate Medicine* 52:81–85.

Beckerman, A. G., and R. M. Tappen. 2000. *It takes more than love: A practical guide to taking care of an aging adult.* Baltimore: Health Professions Press.

Belsky, J. K. 1990. *Psychology of aging: Theory, research, and interventions.* 2d ed. Pacific Grove, CA: Brooks/Cole.

Benbenishty, R., and A. Ben-Zaken. 1988. Computer-aided process of monitoring task-centered family interventions. *Social Work Research and Abstracts* 24:7–9.

Bender, M., P. Bauckham, and A. Norris. 1999. *The therapeutic purposes of reminiscence.* Thousand Oaks, CA: Sage.

Bergner, M., R. A. Bobbitt, W. B. Carter, and B. S. Gibson. 1981. The Sickness Impact Profile: Development and final revision of a health status measure. *Medical Care* 19:787–805.

Berg-Weger M., D. M. Rubio, and S. S. Tebb. 2000. Living with and caring for older family members: Issues related to caregiver well-being. *Journal of Gerontological Social Work* 33:47–62.

Berkman, B., S. Chauncey, W. Holmes, A. Daniels, E. Bonander, S. Sampson, and M. Robinson. 1999. Standardized screening of elderly patients' needs for social work assessment in primary care: Use of the SF-36. *Health and Social Work* 24:9–16.

Berliner, H. 1999. Clinical Reference System: Senior health advisor. [Online] Available: http://www.patienteducation.com/level3/senorsa1.html

Biegel, D. E., E. Sales, and R. Schulz. 1991. *Family caregiving in chronic illness: Alzheimer's disease, cancer, heart disease, mental illness, and stroke.* Newbury Park, CA: Sage.

Billue, J. S. 1998. Subjective idiopathic tinnitus. *The International Journal of Clinical Excellence for Nurse Practitioners* 2:73–82.

Birkett, D. P. 1998. The psychiatry of stroke. In W. Sife, ed., *After stroke: Enhancing quality of life.* New York: Haworth.

Bishop, K., and R. Machemer. 1997. Environment and aging. In R. Machemer, ed., *Understanding aging and developmental disabilities: An inservice curriculum*, pp. 75–105. Rochester, N.Y.: University of Rochester.

Bitzan, J. E., and J. M. Kruzich. 1990. Interpersonal relationships of nursing home residents. *Gerontologist* 30:385–390.

Blasinsky, M. 1998. Family dynamics: Influencing care of the older adult. *Activities: Adaptation and Aging* 22:65–72.

Bloom, B. 2000. Planned short-term psychotherapies. In C. R. Snyder and R. E. Ingram, eds., *Handbook of psychological change*, pp. 429–454. New York: Wiley.

Bosse, R. 1998. Retirement and retirement planning in old age. In I. H. Nordhus, G. R. VandenBos, S. Berg, and P. Fromholt, eds., *Clinical geropsychology*, pp. 155–159. Washington, D.C.: American Psychological Association.

Bosse, R., A. Spiro, and M. R. Levenson. 1997. Retirement as a stressful life event. In T. W. Miller, ed., *Clinical disorders and stressful life events*, pp. 325–250. Madison: International Universities Press.

Bourgeois, M. S., R. Schulz, and L. Burgio. 1996. Interventions for caregivers of patients with Alzheimer's disease: A review and analysis of content, process, and outcomes. *International Journal of Aging and Human Development* 43:35–92.

Bourland, G., and D. Lundervold. 1990. The caring family home: A behavioral model of adult foster care. *Adult Residential Care Journal* 4:95–108.

Brammer, L. M., E. L. Shostrom, and P. J. Abrego. 1989. *Therapeutic psychology: Fundamentals of counseling and psychotherapy.* 5th ed. Englewood Cliffs, N.J.: Prentice Hall.

Branch, L. G., and A. M. Jette. 1982. A prospective study of long-term care institutionalization among the aged. *American Journal of Public Health* 72:1373–1378.

Brechling, B. G., and C. A. Schneider. 1993. Preserving autonomy in early state dementia. *Journal of Gerontological Social Work* 20:17–33.

Brennan, J. P., and C. Kaplan. 1993. Setting new standards for social work case management. *Hospital and Community Psychiatry* 44:219–222.

Brinson, S. V., and Q. Brunk. 2000. Hospice family caregivers: An experience in coping. *The Hospice Journal* 15:1–13.

Brody, E. M. 1981. Women in the middle and family help to older people. *Gerontologist* 21:471–480.

Brody, E. M. 1985. Parent care as a normative family stress. *Gerontologist* 25:19–29.

Brody, E. M., N. P. Dempsey, and R. A. Pruchno. 1990. Mental health of sons and daughters of the institutionalized aged. *Gerontologist* 30:212–219.

Brody, J. A., and E. L. Schneider. 1986. Diseases and disorders in aging: A hypothesis. *Journal of Chronic Disability* 39:871–876.

Brown, L. J., J. F. Potter, and B. G. Foster. 1990. Caregiver burden should be evaluated during geriatric assessment. *Journal of the American Geriatrics Society* 38:455–460.

Brown-Watson, A. V. 1999. *Still kicking: Restorative groups for frail older adults.* Baltimore: Health Professions Press.

Bullard-Bates, P. C., H. Bozzo, and J. Davies Hendricks. 2000. Quality of life after stroke. In P. R. Rao, M. N. Ozer, and J. E. Toerge, eds., *Managing stroke: A guide to living well after stroke*, pp. 171–204. Arlington, VA: ABI Professional Publications.

Burgio, K. L. 1998. Behavioral vs. drug treatment for urge urinary incontinence in older women: A randomized controlled trial. *Journal of the American Medical Association* 280 (23): 1995–2000.

Burnside, I., and M. Schmidt. 1994. *Working with older adults: Group process and techniques.* 3d ed. Boston: Jones and Bartlett.

Busby-Whitehead, J. 1999. Exercise for older patients. In J. J. Gallo, J. Busby-Whitehead, P. V. Rabins, R. A. Silliman, J. B. Murphy, and W. Reichel, eds., *Reichel's care of the elderly: Clinical aspects of aging*, pp. 141–146. 5th ed. Philadelphia: Lippincott Williams and Wilkins.

Butler, R. N., R. Burt, K. M. Foley, and R. S. Morrison. 1996. Palliative medicine: Providing care when cure is not possible. *Geriatrics* 51:33–39.

Byock, I. 1997. *Dying well: Peace and possibilities at the end of life.* New York: Riverhead Books.

Campbell, F., and D. C. Daley. 1993. *Coping with dual disorders: Addiction and emotional or psychiatric illness.* Center City, MN: Hazeldon Educational Materials.

Cantor, M. H. 1983. Strain among caregivers: A study of the experience in the United States. *Gerontologist* 23:597–604.

Cantor, M. H. 1991. Family and community: Changing roles in an aging society. *Gerontologist* 23:597–604.

Carman, M. B. 1997. The psychology of normal aging. *Psychiatric Clinics of North America* 20:15–24.

Carstensen, L. L., B. A. Edelstein, and L. Dornbrand. 1996. *The practical handbook of clinical gerontology.* Thousand Oaks, CA: Sage.

Carter, R., and K. Golant. 1994. *Helping yourself help others: A book for caregivers.* New York: Random House.

Casper, E. S., and J. R. Regan. 1993. Reasons for admission among six profile subgroups of recidivists on inpatient services. *Canadian Journal of Psychiatry* 38:657–661.

Chenoweth, B., and B. Spencer. 1986. Dementia: The experience of family caregivers. *Gerontologist* 26:267–272.

Child and Elder Directory. 1999. *Adult day care.* [Online] Available: http://www.careguide.net.

Christenson, M. 1990. *Aging in the designed environment.* Binghamton N.Y.: Haworth.

Clark, N. M., and W. Rakowski. 1983. Family caregivers of older adults: Improving helping skills. *Gerontologist* 23:637–642.

Cohen, C. A., D. P. Gold, K. I. Shulman, J. T. Wortly, G. McDonald, and M. Wargon. 1993. Factors determining the decision to institutionalize dementing individuals: A prospective study. *Gerontologist* 33:714–720.

Cohen, D., and C. Eisdorfer. 1993. *Caring for your aging parents: A planning and action guide.* New York: Penguin.

Cohen, L. K. 1977. *Communication aids for the brain-damaged adult.* Minneapolis: Sister Kenny Institute.

Cohen, U., and G. D. Weisman. 1990. Experimental design to maximize autonomy for older adults with cognitive impairments. *Generations* 14 (suppl.): 75–78.

Cohen-Mansfield, J., J. Besansky, V. Watson, and L. Bernhard. 1994. Underutilization of adult day care: An exploratory study. *Journal of Gerontological Social Work* 22:21–39.

Colantino, A., S. A. Kael, A. M. Ostfield, and L. F. Berkman. 1993. Psychosocial predictors of stroke outcomes in an elderly population. *Journal of Gerontology* 48:5261–5268.

Colerick, E. J., and L. K. George. 1986. Predictors of institutionalization among caregivers of patients with Alzheimer's Disease. *Journal of the American Geriatrics Society* 34:493–498.

Collopy, B. J. 1988. Autonomy in long-term care: Some crucial distinctions. *Gerontologist* 28:655–672.

Congressional Budget Office. 1999. Projections of expenditures for long-term care services for the elderly. [Online] Available: http://www.cbo.gov.

Connell, C. M., and G. Gibson. 1997. Racial, ethnic, and cultural differences in dementia caregiving: Review and analysis. *Gerontologist* 37:355–364.

Connelly, C. E., and J. D. Dilonardo. 1993. Self-care issues with chronically ill psychotic clients. *Perspectives in psychiatric care* 29:31–35.

Corcoran, K., and J. Fisher. 2000. *Measures for clinical practice: A sourcebook*. 3d ed. New York: Free Press.

Cormican, E. J. 1977. Task-centered model for work with the elderly. *Social Casework* 58:490–494.

Cormier, W. H., and L. S. Cormier. 1998. *Interviewing strategies for helpers: Fundamental skills and cognitive behavioral interventions*. 4th ed. Pacific Grove, CA: Brooks/Cole.

Corrigan, B., and M. Brennan. 2001. Falls prevention. In M. E. Mezey, ed., *The encyclopedia of elder care: The comprehensive resource on geriatric and social care*, pp. 253–254. New York: Springer.

Cotrell, V. 1996. Respite use by dementia caregivers: Preferences and reasons for initial use. *Journal of Gerontological Social Work* 26:35–55.

Cotterill, L., L. Hayes, M. Flynn, and P. Sloper. 1997. Reviewing respite services: Some lessons from the literature. *Disability and Society* 5:20–37.

Cowles, L. A. F. 2000. *Social work in the health field: A care perspective*. New York: Haworth.

Cox, C. 1998. Experience of respite: meeting the needs of African-American and white caregivers in a statewide program. *Journal of Gerontological Social Work* 30:59–72.

Cox, C., and A. Monk. 1990. Minority caregivers of dementia victims: A comparison of Black and Hispanic families. *Journal of Applied Gerontology* 41:778–784.

Cox, C. 1993. Service needs and interests: A comparison of African-American and white caregivers seeking Alzheimer assistance. *American Journal of Alzheimer's Disease* (May/June): 33–40.

Cox, C. 1997. Findings from a statewide program of respite care: A comparison of service users, stoppers, and nonusers. *Gerontologist* 37:511–518.

Crose, R. 1990. Establishing and maintaining intimate relationships among nursing home residents. *Journal of Mental Health Counseling* 12:102–106.

Crum, R. M., J. C. Anthony, S. S. Bassett, and M. F. Folstein. 1993. Population-based norms for the mini mental state examination by age and educational level. *JAMA* 269:2386–2391.

Dalaker, J. 1999. *Poverty in the United States: 1998. Table 2*. U.S. Census Bureau, Current Population Reports P60–207. Washington, D.C.: U.S. Government Printing Office.

Danermark, B. and M. Ekstroem. 1990. Relocation and health effects on the elderly: A commented research review. *Journal of Sociology and Social Welfare* 17:25–49.

Davies, S., L. McKenna, and R. S. Hallam. 1995. Relaxation and cognitive therapy: A controlled trial in chronic tinnitus. *Psychology and Health* 10:129–143.

Davis, I. P. 1975. Advice-giving in parent counseling. *Social Casework* 56:343–347.

DePaola, S. J., and P. Ebersole. 1995. Meaning in life categories of elderly nursing home residents. *International Journal of Aging and Human Development* 40: 227–236.

Dierking, B., M. Brown, and A. E. Fortune. 1980. Task-centered treatment in a residential facility for the elderly: A clinical trial. *Journal of Gerontological Social Work* 20:43–55.

Dineen, R., J. Doyle, and J. Bench. 1997. Audiological and psychological characteristics of a group of tinnitus sufferers, prior to tinnitus management training. *British Journal of Audiology* 31:27–38.

Dinerman, M. 1992. Managing the maze: Case management and service delivery. *Administration in Social Work* 16:1–9.

Dolinsky, A. L., and I. Rosenwaike. 1988. The role of demographic factors in the institutionalization of the elderly. *Research on Aging* 10:235–257.

Dreher, B. B. 2001. *Communication skills for working with elders.* New York: Springer.

Duke University Center for the Study of Aging and Human Development. 1978. *Multidimensional functional assessment: The OARS methodology.* Durham, NC: Duke University.

Dunn, H. 2000. *Hard choices for loving people.* Herndon, VA: A and A Publishers.

Dupree, L. W. 1994. Geropsychological modular treatment: Back to the future. *Journal of Gerontological Social Work* 22:211–220.

Dye, C. J., and J. T. Erber. 1981. Two group procedures for the treatment of nursing home patients. *Gerontologist* 21:539–544.

Elliott, R. 1984. A discovery-oriented approach to significant change in psychotherapy: Interpersonal process recall and comprehensive process analysis. In L. N. Rice and L. S. Greenberg, eds., *Patterns of change: Intensive analysis of psychotherapy process.* New York: Guilford.

Elliott, R. 1986. Interpersonal process recall (IPR) as a psychotherapy process research method. In L. Greenberg and W. Pinsof, eds., *The psychotherapeutic handbook: A research handbook.* New York: Guilford.

Emanuel, L. 2000. The privilege and the pain. *Annals of Internal Medicine* 122:797–798.

Emanuel, E. J., and L. L. Emanuel. 1992. Proxy decision making for incompetent patients: An ethical and empirical analysis. *JAMA* 267:2067–2071.

Emanuel, E. J., and L. L. Emanuel. 1998. The promise of a good death. *The Lancet* 351:21–30.

Emlet, C. A., J. L. Crabtree, V. A. Condon, and L. A. Treml. 1996. *In-home assessment of older adults: An interdisciplinary approach.* Gaithersburg, MD: Aspen.

Erlandsson, S. I., and L. R. M. Hallberg. 2000. Prediction of quality of life in patients with tinnitus. *British Journal of Audiology* 34:11–20.

Erlandsson, S. I., L. R. M. Hallberg, and A. Axelsson. 1992. Psychological and audiological correlates of perceived tinnitus severity. *Audiology* 31:168–179.

Erwin, K. 1996. *Group techniques for aging adults: Putting geriatric skills enhancement into practice.* Washington D.C.: Taylor and Francis.

Evans, R. L., D. S. Bishop, and J. K. Haselkorn. 1991. Factors predicting satisfactory home care after stroke. *Archives of Physical Medicine and Rehabilitation* 72:144–147.

Evans, R. L., R. T. Connis, D. S. Bishop, R. D. Hendricks, and J. K. Haselkorn. 1994. Stroke: A family dilemma. *Disability and Rehabilitation* 16:110–118.

Farran, C. J., E. Keane-Hagerty, S. Sallowat, S. Kupferer, and C. S. Wilken. 1991. Finding meaning: An alternative paradigm for Alzheimer's disease family caregivers. *Gerontologist* 31:483–489.

Farran, C. J., B. H. Miller, J. E. Kaufman, and L. Davis. 1997. Race, finding meaning, and caregiver distress. *Journal of Aging and Health* 9:316–333.

Federal Interagency Forum on Aging-Related Statistics. 2000. *Older Americans 2000: Key indicators of well-being.* Washington, D.C.: U.S. Government Printing Office.

Federal Interagency Forum on Aging-Related Statistics. 2002. Older Americans 2000: Key indicators for well-being, Indicator 6. [Online] Available: www.agingstats.gov/chartbook2000/economics.

Feinstein, A. R., B. R. Josephy, and C. K. Wells. 1986. Scientific and clinical problems in indexes of functional disability. *Annals of Internal Medicine* 105:413–420.

Filinson, R., and S. R. Ingman. 1989. *Elder abuse: Practice and policy.* New York: Human Sciences Press.

Fillenbaum, G. G. 1988. *Multidimensional functional assessment of older adults: The Duke Older Americans Resources and Services procedures.* Hillsdale, N.J.: Lawrence Erlbaum.

Finch, C. E., and R. E. Tanzi. 1997. Genetics of aging. *Science* 278:407–411.

Fisher, B. J. 1991. *It's not quite like home: Illness career descent and the stigma of living at a multilevel care retirement facility.* New York: Garland.

Fisher, J., and K. Corcoran. 2000. *Measures for clinical practice: A sourcebook.* 3d ed. New York: Free Press.

Fokemer, D., A. Jensen, L. Lipson, M. Stauffer, and W. Fox-Grage. 1996. *Adult foster care for the elderly: A review of state regulatory and funding strategies.* Washington D.C.: American Association of Retired Persons.

Folmer, R. L., and S. E. Griest. 2000. Tinnitus and insomnia. *American Journal of Otolaryngology* 21:287–293.

Folstein, M. F., S. E. Folstein, and P. R. McHugh. 1975. Mini mental state: A practical method for grading the cognitive state of patients for the clinician. *Journal of Psychiatric Research* 12:189–198.

Foltz-Gray, D. 1997. One step at a time. *Contemporary Long Term Care* 20:54–55.

Forbes, S., M. Bern-Klug, and C. Gessert. 2000. End-of-life decision making for nursing home residents with dementia. *Journal of Nursing Scholarship* 32 [On-Line], Available: InfoTrac Web: Expanded Academic ASAP.

Fortune, A. E. 1981. Communication processes in social work practice. *Social Service Review* 55:93–128.

Fortune, A. E. 1985. *Task-centered practice with families and groups.* New York: Springer.

Fortune, A. E., and E. Rathbone-McCuan. 1981. Education in gerontological social work: Application of the task-centered model. *Journal of Education for Social Work* 17:98–105.

Fortune, A. E., and W. J. Reid. 1999a. *Research in social work.* 3d ed. New York: Columbia University Press.

Fortune, A. E., and W. J. Reid. 1999b. *Teaching research: An instructor's manual for research in social work.* 3d ed. New York: Columbia University Press

Fortune, A. E., B. Pearlingi, and C. D. Rochelle. 1992. Reactions to termination of individual treatment. *Social Work* 37:171–178.

Frank-Stromberg, M., ed. 1992. *Instruments for clinical nursing research.* Boston: Jones and Bartlett.

Fraser, M. C. 1992. Measuring mental status and level of consciousness. In M. Frank-Stromberg, ed., *Instruments for clinical nursing research*, pp. 86–113. Boston: Jones and Bartlett.

Frasure-Smith, N., and R. Prince. 1989. The ischemic heart disease life stress monitoring program: Impact on mortality. *Psychosomatic Medicine* 47:431–445.

Freeman, M. 1994. Helping homebound elderly clients understand and use advance directives. *Social Work in Health Care* 20:61–72.

Friedrich, M. J. 1999. Experts describe optimal symptom management for hospice patients. *JAMA* 282:1213–1219.

Fries, B. A., C. Hawes, J. N. Morrins, C. D. Phillips, V. Mor, and P. S. Park. 1997. Effect of the National Resident Assessment Instrument on selected health conditions and problems. *Journal of the American Geriatrics Society* 45:994–1001.

Functional Living. 1995. *Geriatric patient education eesource manual.* Gaithersburg, MD: Aspen.

Gabriels, P. 1996. Tinnitus, hyperacusis, and the family. In G. E. Reich and J. A. Vernon, eds., *Proceedings of the fifth international tinnitus seminar*, pp. 563–567. Portland, OR: American Tinnitus Association.

Gallo, J. J., J. Busby-Whitehead, R. V. Rabins, R. A. Silliman, and J. B. Murphy, eds. 1999. *Reichel's care of the elderly: Clinical aspects of aging.* Philadelphia: Lippincott Williams and Wilkins.

Gallo, J. J., T. Fulmer, G. J. Paveza, and W. Reichel. 2000. *Handbook of geriatric assessment.* 3d ed. Gaithersburg, MD: Aspen

Gamble, E. R., P. J. McDonmald, and P. R. Lichstein. 1991. Knowledge, attitudes, and behavior of elderly persons regarding living wills. *Archives of Internal Medicine* 151:277–280.

Garvin, C. D. 1974. Task-centered group work. *Social Service Review* 48:494–507.

Garvin, C. D. 1985. Practice with task-centered groups. In A. E. Fortune, *Task-centered practice with families and groups*, pp. 45–77. New York: Springer.

Garvin, C. D. 1997. *Contemporary group work.* 3d ed. Needham Heights, MA: Allyn and Beacon.

Gatz, M., V. L. Bengston, and M. J. Blum. 1990. Caregiving families. In J. E. Birren and K. W. Schaie, eds., *Handbook of the psychology of aging.* 3d ed. San Diego: Academic Press.

Gatz, M., and S. H. Zarit. 2002. A good old age: Paradox or possibility? Unpublished manuscript.

Gelfand, D. E. 1998. *The aging network: Programs and services.* 5th ed. New York: Springer.

Gendron, C., L. Poitras, D. P. Dastoor, and G. Perodeau. 1996. Cognitive-behavioral group intervention for spousal caregivers: Findings and clinical considerations. *Clinical Gerontologist* 17:3–19.

George, L. K., and L. P. Gwyther. 1986. Caregiver well-being: A multidimensional examination of caregivers of demented adults. *Gerontologist* 26:253–259.

Gerety, M., J. E. Cornell, C. D. Mulrow, M. Tuley, H. P. Hazuda, M. Lichtenstein, C. Aguilar, A. Kadri, and J. Rosenberg. 1994. The Sickness Impact Profile for Nursing Homes (SIP-NH). *Journal of Gerontology, Medical Sciences* 49:M2–M8.

Geriatric Patient Education Resource Manual. 1992. *Care of the Caregiver, Supplement #2.* Gaithersburg, MD: Aspen.

Gilbert, N., and P. Terrell. 1998. *Dimensions of social welfare policy.* 4th ed. Boston: Allyn and Bacon.

Glass, T. A., and G. L. Maddox. 1992. The quality and quantity of social support: Stroke recovery as psychosocial transition. *Social Science and Medicine* 34: 1249–1261.

Glass, T. A. 1990. *Stroke, social support, and rehabilitation: Settings and sequences.* Durham, NC: Duke University.

Glass, T. A., B. Dym, S. Greenberg, D. Rintell, C. Roesch, and L. F. Berkman. 2000. Psychosocial intervention in stroke: Families in recovery from stroke trial (FIRST). *American Journal of Orthopsychiatry* 70:169–181.

Glass, T. A., D. B. Matchar, M. J. Belyea, and J. R. Feussner. 1993. Impact of social support on outcome in first stroke. *Stroke* 24:64–70.

Goebel, G., and W. Hiller. 1996. Effects and predictors of a psychotherapeutic inpatient treatment for chronic tinnitus. In G. E. Reich and J. A. Vernon, eds., *Proceedings of the fifth international tinnitus seminar,* pp. 568–574. Portland, OR: American Tinnitus Association.

Goldberg, D. P., and V. F. Hiller. 1979. A scaled version of the General Health Questionnaire. *Psychological Medicine* 9:139–145.

Goldberg, D. P. 1972. *The detection of psychiatric illness by questionnaire.* London: Oxford University Press.

Goldberg, I. K. 1998. How common is depression following stroke? In W. Sife, ed., *After stroke: Enhancing quality of life.* New York: Haworth.

Goldstein, A. 2001, August 13. Time in depth: How not to grow old. *Time* 158 (6): 48–53.

Gonyea, J. G., and N. M. Silverstein. 1991. Role of Alzheimer's disease support groups in families' utilization of community services. *Journal of Gerontological Social Work* 16:43–55.

Gottlieb, G. L. 1995. Geriatric psychiatry. In H. H. Goldman, ed., *Review of general psychiatry,* pp. 483–491. 4th ed. Norwalk, CT: Appleton and Lange.

Greenberg, L. S., and W. M. Pinsof, eds. 1986. *The psychotherapeutic process: A research handbook.* New York: Guilford.

Greene, A., C. Hawes, M. Wood, and C. Woodsong. 1997. How do family members define quality in assisted living facilities? *Generations* 21:1–15.

Greenwald, A. B. 1984. *Lipreading made easy.* Washington, D.C.: Alexander Graham Bell Association.

Griest, S. E., and P. M. Bishop. 1996. Evaluation of tinnitus and occupational hearing loss based on twenty-year longitudinal data. In G. E. Reich and J. A. Vernon, eds., *Proceedings of the fifth international tinnitus seminar,* pp. 381–394. Portland, OR: American Tinnitus Association.

Grossman, H. D., and A. Weiner. 1988. Quality of life: The institutional culture defined by administrative and resident values. *Journal of Applied Gerontology* 2:389–405.

Guccione, A. 1999. What is a physical therapist? *Physical Therapist Magazine.* Retrieved July 30, 2002. Available online: http://internet.apta.org/pt_magazine/oct99/closer.html.

Gwyther, L. P. 1988. Assessment: Content, purpose, outcomes. *Generations* 12:11–15.

Haley, W. E., E. G. Levine, L. Brown, J. W. Berry, and G. H. Hughes. 1987. Psychological, social, and health consequences of caring for a relative with senile dementia. *Journal of the American Geriatrics Society* 35:405–411.

Haley, W. E., D. L. Roth, M. I. Coleton, G. R. Ford, and C. A. C. West. 1996. Appraisal, coping, and social support as mediators of well-being in Black and White family caregivers of patients with Alzheimer's Disease. *Journal of Consulting and Clinical Psychology* 64:121–129.

Hall, E. T. 1966. *The hidden dimension.* Garden City, N.Y.: Doubleday.

Hamill, C. T. 1998. Quality assurance: Utilizing technology to ensure safety. *Continuing Care* 17:14–15.

Hammond, S. L., and B. L. Lambert. 1994. Communicating about medications: Directions for research. *Health Communication* 6 (4): 247–251.

Hanger, H. C., and G. P. Mulley. 1993. Questions people ask about stroke. *Stroke* 24:536–538.

Hanley, R. J., L. M. Alecxih, J. M. Wiener, and D. L. Kennell. 1990. Predicting elderly nursing home admissions: Results from the 1982–1984 National Long-Term Care Survey. *Research on Aging* 12:199–227.

Harper, B. 1995. Report from the national task force on access to hospice care by minority groups. *Hospice Journal* 10:1–9.

Harrington, C. H., H. M. Carrillo, S. C. Thollaug, P. R. Summers, and V. Wellin. 2000. Nursing Facilities, Staffing, Residents, and Facility Deficiencies, 1993–1999 [On-Line].

Harrington, C., S. Woolhandler, J. Mullan, H. Carrillo, and D. U. Himmelstein. 2001. *American Journal of Public Health* 91:1452–1455.

Harris, P. B. 1997. A support group in a home for the elderly. In T. S. Kerson et al., *Social work in health care settings: Practice in context,* pp. 635–648. 2d ed. Binghamton, NY: Haworth.

Harris, P. B. 1998. Listening to caregiving sons: Misunderstood realities. *Gerontologist* 38:342–352.

Harrison, E. 1994. Is article 81 in your client's future? *Elder Law Attorney* 42:4–6.

Harriss, S. S., C. J. Caspersen, G. H. DeFriese, and H. Estes. 1989. Physical activity counseling for healthy adults as a primary preventive intervention in the clinical setting. *JAMA* 261:3590–3598.

Hartford, M. 1971. *Groups in social work.* New York: Columbia University Press.

Hash, K. M. 2001. Caregiving and post-caregiving experiences of midlife and older gay men and lesbians. Ph.D. diss., Virginia Commonwealth University, Richmond, VA.

Haug, M. R., A. B. Ford, K. C. Stange, L. S. Noelker, and A. D. Gaines. 1999. Effect of giving care on caregivers' health. *Research on Aging* 21:515–538.

Haupt, B. 1997. *Characteristics of patients receiving hospice care services: United States, 1994.* Hyattsville, MD: National Center for Health Statistics.

Hawes, C., J. N. Morris, C. D. Phillips, V. Mor, B. E. Fries, and S. Nonemaker. 1995. Reliability estimates for the Minimum Data Set for nursing home facility resident assessment and care screening (MDS). *Gerontologist* 35:172–178.

Hawes, C., M. Rose, and C. D. Phillips. 1999. *A National Study of Assisted Living for the Frail Elderly.* Beachwood, Ohio: Myers Research Institute. [Online] (World-Cat: Accession No. OCLC:465672480).

Hayslip, B., and J. Leon. 1992. *Hospice care.* Newbury Park, CA: Sage.

Hazelby, J. 1996. Education and tinnitus management counseling: A case study. In G. E. Reich and J. A. Vernon, eds., *Proceedings of the fifth international tinnitus seminar,* pp. 629–636. Portland, OR: American Tinnitus Association.

Heller, J. M. 1998. The role of the social worker on a stroke rehabilitation unit. In W. Sife, ed., *After stroke: Enhancing quality of life.* New York: Haworth.

Hendrich, N. A., T. Kippenbrock, and M. E. Soja. 1995. Hospital falls: Development of a predictive model for clinical practice. *Applied Nursing Research* 8:129–139.

Hendricks, J., ed. 1995. *The meaning of reminiscence and life review.* Amityville, N.Y.: Baywood.

Henry, J. L., and P. H. Wilson. 1998. An evaluation of two types of cognitive intervention in the management of chronic tinnitus. *Scandinavian Journal of Behaviour Therapy* 27:156–166.

Hepworth, D. H., R. H. Rooney, and J. A. Larsen. 2001. *Direct social work practice: Theory and skills.* 6th ed. Pacific Grove: Brooks/Cole.

Hess, J. P. 1991. Health promotion and risk reduction for later life. In R. F. Young and E. A. Olson, eds., *Health, illness, and disability in later life: Practice issues and interventions,* pp. 25–44. Newbury Park, CA: Sage Publications.

High, D. M. 1993. Advance directives and the elderly: A study of intervention strategies to increase use. *Gerontologist* 33:342–349.

Hiller, W., and G. Goebel. 1992. Psychiatric disorders and their degree of severity in patients with severe tinnitus and pain syndromes. In J.-M. Aran and R. Dauman, eds., *Tinnitus 91: Proceedings of the fourth international tinnitus seminar,* pp. 441–444. Amsterdam: Kugler.

Hinds, D. M. 2000. *After stroke: The complete, step-by-step blueprint for getting better.* London: Thorsons.

Hinrichsen, G. A., and M. Ramirez. 1992. Black and white dementia caregivers: A comparison of their adaptation, adjustment, and services utilization. *Gerontologist* 32:375–381.

Hoffman, S. B., and C. A. Platt. 1991. *Comforting the confused: Strategies for managing dementia*. New York: Springer.

Hoffman, M. K. 1994. Use of advance directives: A social work perspective on the myth versus the reality. *Death Studies* 18:229–241.

Hooyman, N. R., and N. A. Kiyak. 1999. *Social gerontology: A multidisciplinary perspective*. Boston: Allyn and Beacon.

Horowitz, A. 1985. Family caregiving to the frail elderly. In C. Eisdorfer, M. P. Lawton, and G. Maddox, eds., *Annual review of gerontology and geriatrics*, 5:194–246. New York: Springer.

Hospice Foundation of America. 2001. *What is Hospice?* [Online] Retrieved July 30, 2002. Available: http://www.hospicefoundation.org/what_is/.

Hoyer, W. J., J. M. Rybash, and P. A. Roodin. 1999. *Adult development and aging*. 4th ed. Boston: McGraw Hill.

Huffman, G. B. 2000. Guidelines: Prescribing exercise for the older patient. *American Family Physician* 62:1166–1169.

Hummert, M. L. 1990. Multiple stereotypes of elderly and young adults: A comparison of structure and evaluations. *Psychology and Aging* 5:183–193.

Hummert, M. L. 1993. Age and typicality judgments of stereotypes of the elderly: Perceptions of young versus elderly adults. *International Journal of Aging and Human Development* 37:217–226.

Hummert, M. L. 1994. Stereotypes of the elderly and patronizing speech. In M. L. Hummert, J. M. Wiemann, and J. L. Nussbaum, eds., *Interpersonal communication in older adulthood: Interdisciplinary theory and research*, pp. 162–184. Thousand Oaks, CA: Sage.

Hummert, M. L., J. M. Wiemann, and J. L. Nussbaum, eds. 1994. *Interpersonal communication in older adulthood: Interdisciplinary theory and research*. Thousand Oaks, CA: Sage.

Hussey, L. C. 1991. Overcoming the clinical barriers of low literacy and medication noncompliance among the elderly. *Journal of Gerontological Nursing* 17 (3): 27–29.

Huttman, E. 1985. *Social services for the elderly*. New York: The Free Press.

Intagliata, J. 1982. Improving the community care for the chronically mentally disabled: The role of case management. *Schizophrenia Bulletin* 8:655–674.

Jastreboff, P. J., and M. M. Jastreboff. 2000. Tinnitus retraining therapy (TRT) as a method for treatment of tinnitus and hyperacusis patients. *Journal of the American Academy of Audiology* 11:162–177.

Jensen-Scott, R. 1993. Counseling to promote retirement adjustment. *The Career Development Quarterly* 41:257–267.

John, R., and B. McMillian. 1998. Exploring caregiver burden among Mexican Americans: Cultural prescriptions, family dilemmas. *Journal of Aging and Ethnicity* 1:93–111.

John, R., C. H. Hennessy, T. B. Dyeson, and M. D. Garrett. 2001. Toward the conceptualization and measurement of caregiver burden among Pueblo Indian family caregivers. *Gerontologist* 41:210–219.

Johnson, B. D., G. L. Stone, E. M. Altnaier, and L. D. Berdahl. 1998. The relationship of demographic factors, locus of control, and self-efficacy to successful nursing home adjustment. *Gerontologist* 38:209–216.

Jordan, C., and C. Franklin. 1995. *Clinical assessment for social workers: Quantitative and qualitative methods.* Chicago: Lyceum.

Kagan, N., and H. Kagan. 1990. IPR: A validated model for the 1990s and beyond. *The Counseling Psychologist* 18:436–440.

Kahn, R. L., A. I. Goldfarb, M. Pollack, and A. Peck. 1960. Brief objective measures for the determination of mental status in the aged. *American Journal of Psychiatry* 117:326–328.

Kail, B. L., ed. 1992. *Special problems of non-compliance among elderly women of color.* New York: Edwin Mellen.

Kane, R., and R. Kane. 2000. *Assessing older persons: Measures, meaning, and practical applications.* Oxford: Oxford University Press.

Kane, R. A., J. Reinardy, J. D. Penrod, and S. Huck. 1999. After the hospitalization is over: A different perspective on family care of older people. *Journal of Gerontological Social Work* 31:119–141.

Kantner, J. 1987. Mental health case management: A professional domain? *Social Work* 32:461–462.

Kaplan, H. I., and B. J. Sadock. 1998. *Synopsis of psychiatry: Behavioral sciences/clinical psychiatry.* 8th ed. Philadelphia: Lippincott Williams and Wilkins.

Karp, D. A., and V. Tanarugsachock. 2000. Mental illness, caregiving, and emotion management. *Qualitative Health Research* 10:6–25.

Katz, S., A. B. Ford, D. M. Quick, R. W. Moskowitz, B. Jackson, and M. W. Jaffe. 1963. Studies of illness in the aged - The index of ADL: A standardized measure of biological and psychosocial function. *JAMA* 185:914–919.

Katzman, R. 1987. Alzheimer's disease: Advances and opportunities. *American Geriatrics Society* 35:69–73.

Kaufman, S. R., and G. Becker. 1991. Content and boundaries of medicine in long-term care: Physicians talk about stroke. *Gerontologist* 31:238–245.

Kawachi, I., G. A. Colditz, A. Ascherio, E. B. Rimm, E. Giovannucci, M. J. Stampfer, and W. C. Willett. 1996. A prospective study of social networks in relation to total mortality and cardiovascular disease in men in the USA. *Journal of Epidemiology and Community Health* 50:245–251.

Kaye, L. W., and J. S. Applegate. 1990. *Men as caregivers for the elderly: Understanding and aiding unrecognized family support.* Lexington, MA: Lexington Books.

Kaye, L. W., and P. M. Kirwin. 1990. Adult day care services for the elderly and their families: Lessons from the Pennsylvania experience. *Journal of Gerontological Social Work* 15:167–183.

Kemper, H. C. G., and R. A. Binkhorst. 1993. Exercise and the physiological consequences of the aging process. In J. J. F. Schroots, ed., *Aging, health, and competence: The next generation of longitudinal research.* New York: Elsevier.

Kemper, S., and K. Lyons. 1994. The effects of Alzheimer's dementia on language and communication. In M. L. Hummert, J. M. Wiemann, and J. L. Nussbaum, eds., *Interpersonal communication in older adulthood: Interdisciplinary theory and research*. Thousand Oaks, CA: Sage.

Kemper, S. 1992. Language and aging. In F. I. Craik, and T. A. Salthouse, eds., *Handbook of aging and cognition*, pp. 213–270. Hillsdale, N.J.: Lawrence Erlbaum.

Kemper, S., D. Kynette, S. Rash, and K. O'Bryan. 1989. Life-span changes to adults' language: Effects of memory and genre. *Applied Psycholinguistics* 10:49–66.

Kiecolt-Glaser, J., R. Glaser, E. C. Shuttleworth, C. S. Dyer, P. Ogrocki, and C. E. Speicher. 1987. Chronic stress and immunity in family caregivers of Alzheimer's Disease victims. *Psychosomatic Medicine* 49:523–535.

King, R. B. 1996. Quality of life after stroke. *Stroke* 27:1467–1472.

Kinney, J. M., and M. A. P. Stephens. 1989. Caregiving hassles scale: Assessing the daily hassles of caring for a family member with dementia. *Gerontologist* 29: 328–332.

Kiresuk, T. J., and R. E. Sherman. 1968. Goal attainment scaling: A general method for evaluating comprehensive mental health programs. *Community Mental Health Journal* 4:443–453.

Knight, B. G., S. M. Lutzky, and U. F. Macofsky. 1993. Meta-analytic review of interventions for caregiver distress: Recommendations for the future. *Gerontologist* 33:240–248.

Knight, B. G., M. Silverstein, T. J. McCallum, and L. S. Fox. 2000. A sociocultural stress and coping model for mental health outcomes among African-American caregivers in Southern California. *Journal of Gerontology* 55B:P142–P150.

Kosberg, J. I. 1983. *Abuse and maltreatment of the elderly: Causes and interventions.* Boston: John Wright.

Koss, M. P., and J. Shiang. 1994. Research on brief psychotherapy. In A. Bergin and S. Garfield, Eds., *Handbook of psychotherapy and behavior change*, pp. 664–700. 4th ed. New York: Wiley.

Kovacs, P. J., and L. R. Bronstein. 1999. Preparation for oncology settings: What hospice social workers say they need. *Health and Social Work* 24:57–65.

Kramer, B. J. 1997. Differential predictors of strain and gain among husbands caring for wives with dementia. *Gerontologist* 37:239–249.

Kroner-Herwig, B., G. Hebing, U. Van Rijn-Kalkmann, A. Frenzel, G. Schilkowsky, and G. Esser. 1995. The management of chronic tinnitus: Comparison of a cognitive-behavioural group training with yoga. *Journal of Psychosomatic Research* 29:153–165.

Kropf, N. P., and R. K. Grigsby. 1999. Medicine for older adults. *Home Health Care Services Quarterly* 17:1–11.

Krummel, S. 1996. Abuse of the elderly by adult children. In D. M. Busby, ed., *The impact of violence on the family: Treatment approaches for therapists and other professionals*, pp. 123–148. Boston: Allyn and Bacon.

Lamy, P. P. 1990. Adverse drug effects. *Clinical Pharmacology* 6 (2): 293–307.

Lasfargues, J. 1996. Assisted living choices: More residential care options for people with disabilities mean nursing homes aren't the only Game in town. *Paraplegia News* 50:12–18.

Lattazani-Licht, M., J. J. Mahoney, and G. W. Miller. 1998. *The hospice choice: In pursuit of a peaceful death.* New York: Fireside.

Laurikainen, E., R. Johansson, E. Akaan-Penttila, and J. Haapaniemi. 2000. Treatment of severe tinnitus. *Acta Otolaryngology*, Supplement, 543:77–78.

Lawton, M. P. 1999. Environmental design features and the well-being of older persons. In M. Duffy, ed., *Handbook of counseling and psychotherapy with older adults.* New York: Wiley.

Lawton, M. P., and E. M. Brody. 1969. Assessment of older people: Self-maintaining and instrumental activities of daily living. *Gerontologist* 9:179–186.

Lawton, M. P., D. Rajagopal, E. Brody, and M. H. Kleban. 1992. The dynamics of caring for a demented elder among black and white families. *Journal of Gerontology* 27:S156–S164.

Lazarus, L. W., B. Stafford, K. Cooper, B. Cohler, and M. Dysken. 1981. Pilot study of an Alzheimer patients' relatives discussion group. *Gerontologist* 21:353–358.

Lee, I. M., C. Hsieh, and R. S. Paffenbarger. 1995. Exercise intensity and longevity in men. *JAMA* 273:1179–1184.

Lee, Y. R., and K. T. Sung. 1998. Cultural influences on caregiving burden: Cases of Koreans and Americans. *International Journal of Aging and Human Development* 46:125–141.

Liberman, R. P., K. Mueser, and S. Glynn. 1988. Modular behavioral strategies. In I. R. Falloon, ed., *Handbook of behavioral family therapy.* New York: Guilford Press.

Lichtenberg, P. A. Ed. 2000. *Handbook of assessment in clinical gerontology.* New York: Wiley.

Lieberman, M. A., and L. Fisher. 1999. The impact of a parent's dementia on adult offspring and their spouses: The contribution of family characteristics. *Journal of Mental Health and Aging* 5:207–222.

Lieberman, M. A., and J. H. Kramer. 1991. Factors affecting decisions to institutionalize demented elderly. *Gerontologist* 31:371–374.

Lindberg, P., B. Scott, L. Melin, and L. Lyttkens. 1987. Long-term effects of psychological treatment of tinnitus. *Scandinavian Audiology* 16:167–172.

Linsk, N. L., B. Miller, R. Pflaum, and A. Ortigara-Vicik. 1988. Families, Alzheimer's disease, and nursing homes. *Journal of Applied Gerontology* 7:331–349.

Litwak, E. 1985. *Helping the elderly: The complimentary roles of informal networks and formal systems.* New York: Guilford.

Liu, K., and K. G. Manton. 1989. The effect of nursing home use on Medicaid eligibility. *Gerontologist* 29:59–66.

Loewenstein, D. A., and B. J. Mogosky. 2000. The functional assessment of the older adult patient. In P. A. Lichtenberg, ed., *Handbook of assessment in clinical gerontology*, pp. 529–554. New York: Wiley.

Loewenstein, D. A., E. Amigo, R. Duara, A. Guterman, D. Hurwitz, N. Berkowitz, F. Wilkie, G. Weinberg, B. Black, B. Gittelman, and C. Eisdorfer. 1989. A new scale for assessment of functional status in Alzheimer's disease and related disorders. *Journal of Gerontology: Psychological Sciences* 44:114–121.

Lowy, L., and J. Doolin. 1990. Multipurpose and senior centers. In A. Monk, ed., *Handbook of gerontological services*. 2d ed. New York: Columbia University Press.

Lubben, J. E. 1988. Assessing social networks among elderly populations. *Family Community Health* 11:45–52.

Mace, N., and P. Rabins. 1981, repr. 1991. *The 36-hour day: A guide to caring for persons with Alzheimer's disease, related dementing illnesses, and memory loss in later life*. Baltimore: John Hopkins University Press.

MacLennan, B., S. Saul, and M. Weiner. Eds. 1988. *Group therapies for the elderly*. Madison, CT: International Universities Press.

Magee, J. J. 1988. *A professional's guide to older adults' life review: Releasing the peace within*. Lexington: Lexington Books.

Mahoney, F. I., and D. W. Barthel. 1965. Functional evaluation: The Barthel Index. *Maryland State Medical Journal* 14:61–65.

Maloney, S. K., J. Finn, D. L. Bloom, and J. Andresen. 1996. Personal decision-making styles and long-term care choices. *Health Care Financing Review* 18:141–155.

Manion, P. S., and M. J. Rantz. 1995. Relocation stress syndrome: A comprehensive plan for long-term care admissions *Geriatric Nursing* 16:108–112.

Manton, K. G., and B. J. Soldo. 1985. Dynamics of health changes in the oldest old: New perspectives and evidence. *The Millbank Quarterly* 63:206–285.

Manton, K. G., J. C. Vertrees, and R. F. Clark. 1993. A multivariate analysis of disability and health, and its change over time in the National Channeling Demonstration data. *Gerontologist* 33:610–618.

Martin, K. S. 2000. Home health care, outcomes management, and the land of Oz. *Outcomes Management for Nursing Practice* 3:7–12.

Massaro, J. B., B. Pepper, and H. Ryglewicz. 1994. *Alcohol, street drugs, and emotional problems*. Center City, MN: Hazeldon Educational Materials.

Maurer, R. E., and J. H. Tindall. 1983. Effect of postural congruence on client's perception of counselor empathy. *Journal of Counseling Psychology* 30:158–163.

Mayo Foundation for Medical Education and Research. 2002. Retrieved July 31, 2002, from www.mayo.edu/geriatrics-rst/NH.RTF.html.

McCallion, P., and R. W. Toseland. 1995. Supportive group intervention with caregivers of frail older adults. *Social Work with Groups* 18:11–25.

McCallion, P., R. W. Toseland, and M. Diehl. 1994. Social work practice with caregivers of frail older adults. *Research on Social Work Practice* 4:64–88.

McCallion, P., R. W. Toseland, and K. Freeman. 1999. Evaluation of a family visit education program. *Journal of the American Geriatrics Society* 47:203–214.

McDonald, P. A., and M. Haney. 1997. *Counseling the older adult*. San Francisco: Jossey-Bass.

McFall, S., and B. H. Miller. 1992. Caregiver burden and nursing home admission of frail elderly persons. *Journal of Gerontology: Social Sciences* 47:S73–S79.

McKinlay, J. B., S. L. Crawford, and S. L. Tennstedt. 1995. The everyday impacts of providing informal care to dependent elders and their consequences for the care recipients. *Journal of Aging and Health* 7:497–528.

McNally, S., S. Ben and S. Newman. 1999. Effects of respite care on informal carers' well-being: A systematic review. *Disability and Rehabilitation* 21:1–14.

Mehrota, C., and K. Kosloski. 1991. Foster care for adults: Issues and evaluations. *Home Health Care Services Quarterly* 12:115–136.

Meichenbaum, D., and D. C. Turk. 1987. *Facilitating treatment adherence: A practitioner's guidebook.* New York: Plenum Press.

Mellins, C. A., M. J. Blum, S. L. Boyd-Davis, and M. Gatz. 1993. Family network perspectives on caregiving. *Generations* 17:21–24.

Meltzer, L. J., and J. R. Rodrigue. 2001. Psychological distress in caregivers of liver and lung transplant candidates. *Journal of Clinical Psychology in Medical Settings* 8:173–180.

Mesler, M. A. 2000. Hospice and assisted suicide: The structure and process of an inherent dilemma. *Death Studies* 24:135–155.

Meyer, H. 1998. The bottom line on assisted living. *Hospitals* and *Health Networks* 72:22–27.

Michigan Adult Foster Care. 1999. Adult Foster Care. [Online] Retrieved June 10, 2000. Available: http://www.miafc.com.

Miller T. W. and L. J. Veltkamp. 1998. *Clinical handbook of adult exploitation and abuse.* Madison, CT: International Universities Press.

Miller, B., and S. Guo. 2000. Social support for spouse caregivers of persons with dementia. *Journals of Gerontology: Series B: Psychological Sciences and Social Sciences* 55B:S163–S172.

Miller, B. 1990. Gender differences in spouse caregiver strain: Socialization and role expectations. *Journal of Marriage and the Family* 52:311–321.

Miller, S. C., P. Gozalo, and V. Mor. 2000. Outcomes and utilization for hospice and non-hospice nursing facility decedents. [Online]. Available: http://aspe.hhs.gov/daltcp/reports/oututil.htm. (Prepared by the Center for Gerontology and Health Care Research, Brown University, under DHHS contract # 100–97–0010).

Mion, L. C., and K. A. Ondus. 2001. Adult foster care homes. In M. E. Mezey, ed., *The encyclopedia of elder care: The comprehensive resource on geriatric and social care,* pp. 16–18. New York: Springer.

Mitchell, J., H. F. Mathews, L. M. Hunt, K. H. Cobb, and R. W. Watson. 2001. Mismanaging prescription medications among rural elders: The effects of socioeconomic status, health status, and medication profile indicators. *Gerontologist* 41:348–356.

Mittelman, M. S., S. H. Ferris, E. Shulman, G. Steinberg, and A. Ambinder. 1995. Comprehensive support program: Effect on depression in spouse-caregivers of AD patients. *Gerontologist* 35:792–802.

Mitty, E. L. 2001a. Assisted living. In M. E. Mezey, ed., *The encyclopedia of elder care: The comprehensive resource on geriatric and social care*, pp. 73–75. New York: Springer.

Mitty, E. L. 2001b. Nursing homes. In M. E. Mezey, ed., *The encyclopedia of elder care: The comprehensive resource on geriatric and social care*, pp. 452–456. New York: Springer.

Moller, A. R. 2000. Similarities between severe tinnitus and chronic pain. *Journal of the American Academy of Audiology* 11:115–124.

Monahan, D. J. 1995. Informal caregivers of institutionalized dementia residents: Predictors of burden. *Journal of Gerontological Social Work* 23:65–82.

Montgomery, R. J. V., and K. Kosloski. 1994. A longitudinal analysis of nursing home placement for dependent elders cared for by spouses vs adult children. *Journal of Gerontology: Social Science* 49:S62–S74.

Montgomery, R. J., J. G. Gonyea, and N. R. Hooyman. 1985. Caregiving and the experience of objective and subjective burden. *Family Relations* 34:19–26.

Moody, H. R. 1994. *Aging: Concepts and controversies*. Thousand Oaks, CA: Pine Forge Press.

Moroney, R. M., and J. Krysik. 1998. *Social policy and social work: Critical essays on the welfare state*. Hawthorne, N.Y.: de Gruyter.

Morris, J. N., C. Hawes, B. E. Fries, C. D. Phillips, V. Mor, S. Katz, K. Murphy, M. L. Drugovich, and A. S. Friedlot. 1990. Designing the national resident assessment instrument for nursing home facilities. *Gerontologist* 30:293–307.

Morrow-Howell, N. 1992. Clinical case management: The hallmark of gerontological social work. *Journal of Gerontological Social Work* 18:119–131.

Morycz, R. K. 1985. Caregiving strain and the desire to institutionalize family members with Alzheimer's disease: Possible predictors and model development. *Research on Aging* 7:329–361.

Moxley, D. P. 1989. *The practice of case management*. Newbury Park, CA: Sage.

Murphy, B., H. Schofield, J. Nankervis, S. Bloch, H. Herrman, and B. Singh. 1997. Women with multiple roles: The emotional impact of caring for aging parents. *Ageing and Society* 17:277–291.

Murphy, D. J. 1990. Improving advance directives for healthy older people. *Journal of the American Geriatrics Society* 38:1251–1256.

Myers, A. M., P. J. Holliday, K. A. Harvey, and K. S. Hutchinson. 1993. Functional performance measures: Are they superior to self-assessment? *Journal of Gerontology* 48:M190–M206.

Naleppa, M. J. 1995. Task-centered case management for the elderly in the community: Developing a practice model. Ph. D. diss., State University of New York at Albany.

Naleppa, M. J. 1996. Families and the institutionalized elderly: A review. *Journal of Gerontological Social Work* 27:87–111.

Naleppa, M. J. 1999. *Client autonomy in task-centered case management*. Unpublished Manuscript.

Naleppa, M. J. 2001a. Adult day care. In M. E. Mezey et al., ed., *The encyclopedia of elder care: The comprehensive resource on geriatric and social care*, pp. 12–14. New York: Springer.

Naleppa, M. J. 2001b. Transportation. In M. E. Mezey et al., ed., *The encyclopedia of elder care: The comprehensive resource on geriatric and social care*, pp. 646–648. New York: Springer.

Naleppa, M. J., and K. Hash. 2002. Home-based practice with older adults: Challenges and opportunities in the home environment. *Journal of Gerontological Social Work* 35:71–88.

Naleppa, M. J., and W. J. Reid. 1998. Task-centered case management for the elderly: Developing a practice model. *Research on Social Work Practice* 8:63–85.

Naleppa, M. J., and W. J. Reid. 2000. Integrating case management and brief-treatment strategies: A hospital-based geriatric program. *Social Work in Health Care* 31:1–23.

Nankervis, J., H. Schofield, H. Herrman, and S. Bloch. 1997. Home-based assessment for family carers: A preventive strategy to identify and meet service needs. *International Journal of Geriatric Psychiatry* 12:17–28.

Nathanson, I., and T. Tirrito. 1998. *Gerontological social work: Theory into practice.* New York: Springer.

National Academy on an Aging Society. 2000. *Hypertension: A common condition for older Americans.* Washington, D.C.: National Academy on an Aging Society.

National Alliance for Caregiving and American Association of Retired Persons. 1997. *Family caregiving in the U. S.: Findings from a national study.* Washington D.C.: National Alliance for Caregiving and American Association of Retired Persons.

National Association of Social Workers. 1992. *Standards for social work case management.* Washington, D.C.: National Association of Social Workers.

National Association of Social Workers. 2002. Choices: Careers in social work. Retrieved December 7, 2002, from: http://www.socialworkers.org/pubs/choices/choices2.htm. Washington D.C.

National Center for Health Statistics. 1993. *Health, United States, 1993.* Hyattsville, MD: Public Health Service.

National Center for Health Statistics. 1996. *Health, United States 1995.* Hyattsville, MD: Public Health Service.

National Council Licensure Examination for Practical/Vocational Nurses. 2001. NCLEX-PN. Examination Test Plan National Council of State Boards of Nursing. Retrieved July 31, 2002, from http://www.ncsbn.org/public/resources/res/Nclexpn2.pdf.

National Council of State Boards of Nursing. 1998. Approval of Nursing Education Programs by Boards of Nursing. National Council Position Paper. Retrieved July 31, 2002, from http://www.ncsbn.org/public/regulation/nursing_education_accreditation.htm.

National Eldercare Institute on Transportation. 1994. *Meeting the challenge: Mobility for elders.* Washington, D.C.: Author.

National Hospice and Palliative Care Organization (NHPCO). Homepage of the National Hospice and Palliative Care Organization. [Online]. Available: www. nhpco/general12.htm [2000, November 10].

Neher, A. 1991. Tinnitus: The hidden epidemic, a patient's perspective. *The Annals of Otology, rhinology, and laryngology*, 1004:327–330.

Netting, F. E. 1992. Case management: Service or symptom? *Social Work* 37:160–164.

Netting, F. E., and F. G. Williams. 1999. Implementing a case management program designed to enhance primary care physician practice with older persons. *Journal of Applied Gerontology* 18:25–45.

Neundorfer, M. M., M. J. McClendon, K. A. Smyth, J. C. Stuckey, M. E. Strauss, and M. B. Patterson. 2001. A longitudinal study of the relationship between levels of depression among persons with Alzheimer's disease and levels of depression among their family caregivers. *Journals of Gerontology: Series B: Psychological Sciences and Social Sciences* 56B:301–313.

Newman, C. W., G. P. Jacobson, and J. B. Spitzer. 1996. Development of the tinnitus handicap inventory. In G. E. Reich and J. A. Vernon, eds., *Proceedings of the fifth international tinnitus seminar*, pp. 186–192. Portland, OR: American Tinnitus Association.

Nolen-Hoeksema, S., J. Larson, and M. Bishop. 2000. Predictors of family members' satisfaction with hospice. *The Hospice Journal* 15:29–48.

Norbeck, J. S., A. M. Lindsi, and V. L. Carrieri. 1981. The development of an instrument to measure social support. *Nursing Research* 30:264–269.

Novak, M. 1997. *Issues in aging: An introduction to gerontology*. New York: Longman.

Noyes, M. A., D. S. Lucas, and M. A. Stratton. 1996. Principles of geriatric pharmacotherapy. *Journal of Geriatric Drug Therapy* 10:5–35.

O'Connor, G. C. 1988. Case management: System and practice. *Social Casework* 69:97–106.

O'Connor, B. P., and Vallerand. R. J. 1994. Relative effects of actual and experienced autonomy on motivation in nursing home residents. *Canadian Journal on Aging* 13:528–538.

Olfson, M., S. Hansell, and C. A. Boyer. 1997. Medication noncompliance. In D. Mechanic, ed., *Improving inpatient psychiatric treatment in an era of managed care*, pp. 39–49. San Francisco: Jossey-Bass.

Oncology Nursing Society and Association of Oncology Social Work. 2002. Joint Position on End-Of-Life Care. Retrieved March 4, 2002. http://www.aosw.org/ publications/ons-aosw.html.

Ong, T. J. 1994. Approaches to tinnitus management. *Scottish Medical Journal* 39:131–134.

O'Rourke, N., and H. Tuokko. 2000. Psychological and physical costs of caregiving: the Canadian study of health and aging. *Journal of Applied Gerontology* 19: 389–404.

Ossip-Klein, D., B. M. Rothenberg, and E. M. Andresen. 1997. Screening for depression. In E. Andresen, B. Rothenberg, and J. G. Zimmer, eds., *Assessing the health status of older adults*. New York: Springer.

Overman, W., and A. Stoudemire. 1993. Legal, financial, and ethical issues in Alzheimer's disease and other dementias. In R. Park and R. Zec, eds., *Neuropsychology of Alzheimer's disease and other dementias*, pp. 615–625. New York: Oxford University Press.

Parkerson, G. R., Jr., W. E. Broad, and C. K. J. Tse. 1991. Development of the 17-item DUKE Health Profile. *Family Practice* 8:396–401.

Patterson, S. L.; M. Baker, and J. P. Maeck. 1993. Durable powers of attorney: Issues of gender and health care decision making. *Journal of Gerontological Social Work* 21:161–177.

Paveza, G. J. 2001. Elder mistreatment: Overview. In M. E. Mezey, ed., *The encyclopedia of elder care: The comprehensive resource on geriatric and social care*, pp. 231–233. New York: Springer.

Paveza, G. J., D. Cohen, M. Hagopian, T. Prohaska, C. J. Blaser, and D. Brauner. 1989. A brief assessment tool for determining eligibility and need for community-based long-term care services. *Behavior, Health, and Aging* 1:133–139.

Paveza, G. J., T. Prohaska, M. Hagopian, and D. Cohen. 1989. *Determination of need revision: Final report.* Chicago: Gerontology Center, University of Illinois at Chicago.

Pearlin, L. I., J. T. Mullan, S. J. Semple, and M. M. Skaff. 1990. Caregiving and the stress process: An overview of concepts and their measures. *Gerontologist* 30:583–594.

Peifer, K. J., G. P. Rosen, and A. M. Rubin. 1999. Tinnitus etiology and management. *Clinics in Geriatric Medicine* 15:193–204.

Peters-Davis, N. D., M. S. Moss, and R. A. Pruchno. 1999. Children-in-law in caregiving families. *Gerontologist* 39:66–75.

Pfeiffer, E. 1975. A short portable mental status questionnaire for the assessment of organic brain deficit in elderly patients. *Journal of the American Geriatrics Society* 23:433–441.

Phillips, C. D., and C. Hawes. 1996. Nursing homes. In L. A. Vitt, J. K. Siegenthaler, N. E. Cutler, and S. Golant, eds., *Encyclopedia of financial gerontology*, pp. 385–390. Westwood, CT: Greenwood.

Pinchoff, R. J., R. F. Burkard, R. J. Salvi, M. L. Coad, and A. H. Lockwood. 1998. Modulation of tinnitus by voluntary jaw movements. *The American Journal of Otology* 19:785–789.

Pomeroy, E. C., A. Rubin, and R. J. Walker. 1995. Effectiveness of a psychoeducational and task-centered group intervention for family members of people with AIDS. *Social Work Research* 19:129–152.

Porter, E. J., and J. F. Clinton. 1992. Adjusting to the nursing home. *Western Journal of Nursing Research* 14:464–481.

Portland Multnomah Commission on Aging. 1994. *Senior Helpline: 24 hour access to critical services.* Portland: Portland Multnomah Commission on Aging.

Poulshock, S. W., and G. T. Deimling. 1984. Families caring for elders in residence: Issues in the measurement of burden. *Journal of Gerontology* 39:230–239.

Pratt, C., S. Wright, and V. Schmall. 1987. Burden, coping, and health status: A comparison of family caregivers to community-dwelling and institutionalized Alzheimer's patients. *Journal of Gerontological Social Work* 10:99–112.

Pruchno, R. A., and N. L. Resch. 1989. Husbands and wives as caregivers: Antecedents of depression and burden. *Gerontologist* 29:159–165.

Pruchno, R. A., and M. S. Rose. 2000. The effect of long-term care environments on health outcomes. *Gerontologist* 40:422–428.

Pruchno, R. A., J. E. Michael, and S. L. Potshnik. 1990. Predictors of institutionalization among Alzheimer disease victims with caregiving spouses. *Journal of Gerontology: Social Sciences* 45:S259–S266.

Puchalski, C. M, Z. Zhong, M. M. Jacobs, E. Fox, J. Lynn, J. Harrold, A. Galanos, R. S. Phillips, R. Califf, and J. M. Teno. 2000. Patients who want their family and physician to make resuscitation decisions for them: Observations from SUPPORT and HELP. *Journal of the American Geriatrics Society* 48:S84–S90.

Rao, P. R., M. N. Ozer, and J. E. Toerge. 2000. *Managing stroke: A guide to living well after stroke*. Arlington, VA: ABI Professional Publications.

Rathbone-McCuan, E. 1985. Intergenerational family practice with older families. In A. E. Fortune, ed., *Task-centered practice with families and groups*. New York: Springer.

Rau, M. T. 1993. *Coping with communication challenges in Alzheimer's disease*. San Diego: Singular.

Raveis, V. H., D. Karus, and S. Pretter. 1999. Correlates of anxiety among adult daughter caregivers to a parent with cancer. *Journal of Pyschosocial Oncology* 17:1–26.

Redinbaugh, E. M., R. C. MacCallum, and J. K. Kiecolt-Glaser. 1995. Recurrent syndromal depression in caregivers. *Psychology and Aging* 10:358–368.

Reese, D. J. 2000. The role of primary caregiver denial in inpatient placement during home hospice care. *The Hospice Journal* 15:15–33.

Rehfeldt R. A., A. Steele, and M. R Dixon. 2000. Transitioning the elderly into long-term care facilities: A search for solutions. *Activities, Adaptation, and Aging* 24:27–40.

Reichel, W. 1999. End-of-life care and family practice. *American Family Physician* 59:1388–1392.

Reid, W. J. 1975. A test of a task-centered approach. *Social Work* 20:3–9.

Reid, W. J. 1978. *The task-centered system*. New York: Columbia University Press.

Reid, W. J. 1985. *Family problem solving*. New York: Columbia University Press.

Reid, W. J. 1992. *Task strategies: An empirical approach to clinical social work*. New York: Columbia University Press.

Reid, W. J. 1994. Field testing and data gathering on innovative practice interventions in early development. In J. Rothman and E. J. Thomas, eds., *Intervention Research*, pp. 245–264. New York: Haworth.

Reid, W. J. 1996. Task-centered social work. In F. J. Turner, ed., *Social work treatment: Interlocking theoretical approaches*, pp. 617–640. New York: Free Press.

Reid, W. J. 1997. Research on task-centered practice. *Social Work Research* 21:132–137.

Reid, W. J. 2000. *The taskplanner*. New York: Columbia University Press.

Reid, W. J., and C. Bailey-Dempsey. 1994. Content analysis in design and development. *Research on Social Work Practice* 4:101–114.

Reid, W. J., and L. Epstein, eds. 1972. *Task-centered casework*. New York: Columbia University Press.

Reid, W. J., and L. Epstein, eds. 1977. *Task-centered practice*. New York: Columbia University Press.

Reid, W. J., and A. E. Fortune. 2002. The task-centered model. In A. Roberts and G. Greene, eds., *Social worker's desk reference*. New York: Oxford University Press.

Reid, W. J., and A. Shyne. 1969. *Brief and extended casework*. New York: Columbia University Press.

Reinardy, J., and R. A. Jane. 1999. Choosing an adult foster home or a nursing home: Residents' perceptions about decision making and control. *Social Work* 44:571–585.

Reisberg, B., S. H. Ferris, and M. J. De Leon. 1982. The Global Deterioration Scale (GDS): An instrument for the assessment of primary degenerative dementia (PDD). *American Journal of Psychiatry* 139:1136–1139.

Reuben, D. B., and A. L. Siu. 1990. An objective measure of physical functioning of elderly outpatients: The physical performance test. *Journal of the American Geriatrics Society* 38:1105–1112.

Richardson, V. E. 1993. *Retirement counseling: A handbook for gerontology practitioners*. New York: Springer.

Richmond, M. 1917. *Social diagnosis*. New York: Russell Sage Foundation.

Riddick, C. C., J. Cohen-Mansfield, E. Fleshner, and G. Kraft. 1992. Caregiver adaptations to having a relative with dementia admitted to a nursing home. *Journal of Gerontological Social Work* 19:51–76.

Riker, H. C., and J. E. Myers. 1990. *Retirement counseling: A practical guide for action*. New York: Hemisphere.

Riley, M. W. 1987. On the significance of age in sociology: American Sociological Society, 1986 Presidential Address. *American Sociological Review* 52:1–14.

Robinson, B. C. 1983. Validation of a caregiver strain index. *Journal of Gerontology* 38:344–348.

Rockwood, K. 1994. Setting goals in geriatric rehabilitation and measuring their attainment. *Reviews in Clinical Gerontology* 4:141–149.

Rogers, N. B. 1999. Family obligation, caregiving, and loss of leisure: The experiences of three caregivers. *Activities, Adaptation, and Aging* 24:35–49.

Rogers, N. B. 1999. Caring for those who care: Achieving family caregiver wellness through social support programs *Activities, Adaptation, and Aging* 24:1–12.

Ronch, J. L., and E. L. Crispi. 1997. Opportunities for development via group psychotherapy in the nursing home. *Group* 21:135–158.

Rooney, R. H. 1992. *Strategies for working with involuntary clients*. New York: Columbia University Press.

Rothman, J. 1991. A model of case management: Toward empirically based practice. *Social Work* 36:520–528.

Rothman, J. 1992. *Guidelines for case management: Putting research to professional use.* Itasca: Peacock.

Rothman, J. 1994. *Practice with highly vulnerable clients: Case management and community-based service.* Englewood Cliffs: Prentice Hall.

Rothman, J., and E. J. Thomas, eds. 1994. *Intervention research: Design and development for human service.* Binghamton, N.Y.: The Haworth.

Roush, R. E., and T. A. Teasdale. 1997. Reduced hospitalization rates of two sets of community-residing older adults after use of a personal response system. *Journal of Applied Gerontology* 16:355–366.

Rowe, J. W., and R. L. Kahn. 1998. *Successful aging.* New York: Random House.

Rubin, A. 1987. Case management. *Social Work* 28:49–54.

Ryan, E. B., H. Giles, G. Bartolucci, and K. Henwood. 1986. Psycholinguistics and social psychological components of communication by and with the elderly. *Language and Communication* 6:1–24.

Ryan, E. B., S. Kwong See, W. B. Meneer, and D. Trovato. 1992. Age-based perceptions of language performance among younger and older adults. *Communication Research* 19:423–443.

Ryan, E. B., S. Kwong See, W. B. Meneer, and D. Trovato. 1994. Age-based perceptions of conversational skills among younger and older adults. In M. L. Hummert, J. M. Wiemann, and J. L. Nussbaum, eds., *Interpersonal communication in older adulthood: Interdisciplinary theory and research.* Thousand Oaks, CA: Sage.

Salamon, M. J. 2000. Evaluating functional and behavioral health. In P. A. Lichtenberg, ed., *Handbook of assessment in clinical gerontology.* New York: Wiley.

Salomon, G. 1989. Hearing problems and the elderly. *Dan Medical Bulletin* 33 (suppl. 3): 1–22.

Saltz, C. C., T. Schaefer, and D. M. Weinreich. 1998. Streamlining outpatient geriatric assessment: Essential social, environmental, and economic variables. *Social Work in Health Care* 27:1–14.

Salzman, B. 2001. *Psychiatric medications for older adults: The concise guide.* New York: Guilford.

Sanchez, Y. M. 1996. Distinguishing cultural expectations in assessment of financial exploitation. *Journal of Elder Abuse and Neglect* 8 (2): 49–59.

Sansone, P., and M. Phillips. 1995. Advance directives for elderly people: Worthwhile cause or wasted effort? *Social Work* 40:397–401.

Santo Pietro, M. J. S. and E. Ostuni. 1997. *Successful communication with Alzheimer's disease patients: An in-service training manual.* Newton, MA: Buttersworth-Heinemann.

Santus, G. A., A. Ranzenigo, R. Caregnato, and M. R. Inzoli. 1990. Social and family integration of hemiplegic elderly stroke patients one year after stroke. *Stroke* 21:1019–1022.

Saunders, J. F. 1996. Biofeedback therapy and psychological counseling in the treatment of tinnitus. In G. E. Reich and J. A. Vernon, eds., *Proceedings of the fifth international tinnitus seminar*, pp. 637–638. Portland, OR: American Tinnitus Association.

Scharlach, A. E. 1985. Social group work with institutionalized elders: A task-centered approach. *Social Work with Groups* 8:33–47.

Scharlach, A., B. Lowe, and E. Schneider. 1991. *Elder care and the workforce: Blueprint for action*. Lexington, MA: Lexington Books.

Scharlach, A. E., E. L. Sobel, and R. E. L. Roberts. 1991. Employment and caregiver strain: An integrated model. *Gerontologist* 31:778–787.

Schmid, H., and Y. Hasenfeld. 1993. Organizational dilemmas in the provision of home-care services. *Social Service Review* 67:40–54.

Schneewind, E. H. 1990. The reaction of the family to the institutionalization of an elderly family member: Factors influencing adjustment and suggestions for easing the transition into a new life phase. *Journal of Gerontological Social Work* 15:121–136.

Schneider, R. L., N. P. Kropf, and A. J. Kisor. 2000. *Gerontological social work: Knowledge, service settings, and special populations*. 2d ed. Belmont, CA: Wadsworth.

Schroots, J. F., and J. E. Birren. 1990. Concepts of time and aging in science. In J. E. Birren and K. W. Schaie, eds., *Handbook of the psychology of aging*, pp. 45–64. 3d ed. San Diego: Academic Press.

Schroots, J. J. F., ed. 1993. *Aging, health, and competence: The next generation of longitudinal research*. London: Elsevier.

Scott, J. P. 1990. Sibling interactions in later life. In T. H. Brubaker, ed., *Family relationships in later life*, pp. 86–99. Newbury Park, CA: Sage.

Scott, B., and P. Lindberg. 2000. Psychological profile and somatic complaints between help-seeking and non-help-seeking tinnitus subjects. *Psychosomatics* 41:347–352.

Seltzer, M. M., L. C. Litchfield, L. R. Kapust, and J. B. Mayer. 1992. Professional and family collaboration in case management: A hospital-based replication of a community-based study. *Social Work in Health Care* 17:1–22.

Seniorresource.com. 2002. http://www.seniorresource.com/index.html. Retrieved March 20, 2002.

Shapiro, E., and R. Tate. 1988. Who is really at risk of institutionalization? *Gerontologist* 29:237–245.

Shaw, W. S., T. L. Patterson, M. G. Ziegler, J. E. Dimsdale, S. J. Semple, and I. Grant. 1999. Accelerated risk of hypertensive blood pressure recordings among Alzheimer caregivers. *Journal of Psychosomatic Research* 46:215–227.

Sheikh, J. I., and J. A. Yesavage. 1986. Geriatric Depression Scale (GDS): Recent findings and development of a shorter version. *Clinical Gerontologist* 5:165–173.

Sherman, E. 1991. *Reminiscence and the self in old age*. New York: Springer.

Sherman, S. R., and E. S. Newman. 1988. *Foster families for adults: A community alternative in long-term care*. New York: Columbia University Press.

Shewan, C. M. 1990. The prevalence of hearing impairment. *American Speech Language and Hearing Association* 32:62–75.

Shultz, R., P. Visintainer, and G. M. Williamson. 1990. Psychiatric and physical morbidity effects of caregiving. *Journal of Gerontology* 45:181–191.

Siebert, L. 1998. Making the right decision: Placing your spouse in assisted living. *Real Living With Multiple Sclerosis* 6:12–15.

Siegler, I. C., L. W. Poon, D. J. Madden, and K. A. Welsh. 1996. Psychological aspects of normal aging. In E. W. Busse and D. G. Blazer, eds., *The American Psychiatric Press textbook of geriatric psychiatry*, pp. 105–122. 2d ed. Washington, D.C.: American Psychiatric Press.

Sife, W. 1998. *After stroke: Enhancing quality of life*. Binghamton, N.Y.: Haworth.

Simpson, D. A., E. Fox, and J. Lynn. 2000. Prognostic criteria for hospice eligibility. *JAMA* 283:2527–2531.

Sinoff, G., and L. Ore. 1997. The Barthel Activities of Daily Living Index: Self-reporting versus actual performance in the old-old. *Journal of the American Geriatric Society* 45:832–836.

Sipski, M. L., and C. J. Alexander. 1997. *Sexual functioning In people with disability and chronic illness: A health professional's guide*. Gaithersburg, MD: Aspen.

Slater, R., and M. Terry. 1987. *Tinnitus: A guide for sufferers and professionals*. London: Croom Helm.

Smallegan, M. 1985. There was nothing else to do: Needs for care before nursing home admission. *Gerontologist* 25:364–369.

Smyer, M. A., B. F. Hofland, and E. A. Jonas. 1979. Validity study of the Short Portable Mental Status Questionnaire for the elderly. *Journal of the American Geriatric Society* 27:263–269.

Soares, H. H., and M. K. Rose. 1994. Clinical aspects of case management with the elderly. *Journal of Gerontological Social Work* 22:143–156.

Social Security Administration. 2000. *Income of the population 55 or older, 1998*. Tables VIII.4 and VIII.11. Washington, D.C.: U.S. Government Printing Office.

Soldo, B. J., and E. M. Agree. 1988. America's elderly. *Population Bulletin* 43:1–51.

Sommers-Flanagan, R., and J. Sommers-Flanagan. 1999. *Clinical interviewing*. 2d ed. New York: Wiley.

Soskis, C. W. 1997. End-of-Life decisions in the home care setting. *Social Work in Health Care* 25:107–116.

Sourgen, P. M., and E. Ross. 1998. Perceptions of tinnitus in a group of senior citizens. *The South African Journal of Communication Disorders* 45:61–75.

Sperry, L. 1995. *Psychopharmacology and psychotherapy: Strategies for maximizing treatment outcomes*. New York: Brunner/Mazel.

Starck, P. L. 1992. Suffering in a nursing home: Losses of the human spirit. *International Forum for Logotherapy* 15 (2): 76–79.

Steeman, E., and M. Defever. 1998. Urinary continence among elderly persons who live at home. *Nursing Clinics of North America* 33:441–455.

Steinfeld, E., and S. Danforth, eds. 1999. *Enabling environments: Measuring the impact of environment on disability and rehabilitation.* New York: Kluwer Academic, Plenum.

Steinweg, K. 1997. The changing approach to falls in the elderly. *American Family Physician* 56:1815–1817.

Stephens, M., A. L. Townsend, L. M. Martire, and J. A. Druley. 2001. Balancing parent care with other roles: Interrole conflict of adult daughter caregivers. *Journals of Gerontology: Series-B: Psychological Sciences and Social Sciences* 56B:P24–P34.

Stone, R., G. L. Cafferata, and J. Sangl. 1987. Caregivers of the frail elderly: A national profile. *Gerontologist* 27:616–626.

Stouffer, J. L., and R. S Tyler. 1990. Characterization of tinnitus by tinnitus patients. *Journal of Speech and Hearing Disorders* 55:439–453.

Stouffer, J. L., R. S. Tyler, P. R. Kileny, L. E. Dalzell. 1991. Tinnitus as a function of duration and etiology: Counseling implications. *The American Journal of Otology* 12:188–194.

Stouffer, J. L., and R. S. Tyler. 1990. Characterization of tinnitus by tinnitus patients. *Journal of Speech and Hearing Disorders* 55:439–453.

Strom-Gottfried, K. 2001. The final phase: Termination. In D. H. Hepworth, R. H. Rooney, and J. A. Larson, eds., *Direct social work practice: Theory and skills.* 6th ed. Pacific Grove: Brooks/Cole.

Taft, L. B., and M. F. Nehrke. 1990. Reminiscence, life review, and ego integrity in nursing home residents. *International Journal of Aging and Human Development* 10:189–196.

Teresi, J. A., M. P. Lawton, D. Holmes, and M. Ory, eds. 1997. *Measurement in elderly chronic care populations.* New York: Springer.

Thompson, E. H., A. M. Futterman, D. Gallagher-Thompson, J. M. Rose, and S. B. Lovett. 1993. Social support and caregiving burden in family caregivers of frail elders. *Journal of Gerontology* 48:245–254.

Timko, C., and R. H. Moos. 1989. Choice, control, and adaptation among elderly residents of sheltered care settings. *Journal of Applied Social* Psychology 12:636–655.

Tinsley, R. 1996. Sizing up assisted living. *Nursing Homes* 45:9–12.

Tobin, S. S. 1991. *Personhood in advanced old age.* New York: Springer.

Tobin, S. S. 1999. *Preservation of the self when very old.* New York: Springer.

Tolson, E. R., W. J. Reid, and C. D. Garvin. 2002. *Generalist practice: A task-centered approach.* 2d ed. New York: Columbia University Press.

Toseland, R. W., and P. McCallion. 1998. *Maintaining communication with persons with dementia.* New York: Springer.

Toseland, R. W., and R. F. Rivas. 2001. *An introduction to group work practice.* 4th ed. New York: Macmillan.

Toseland, R. W., and M. Siporin. 1986. When to recommend group treatment: A review of the clinical and the research literature. *The International Journal of Group Psychotherapy* 36:171–201.

Toseland, R. W. 1995. *Group work with the elderly and family caregivers.* New York: Springer.

Toseland, R. W., and M. Coppola. 1985. A task-centered approach to group work with older persons. In A. E. Fortune, ed., *Task-centered practice with families and groups,* pp. 101–114. New York: Springer.

Toseland, R. W., and G. Smith. 1991. Family caregivers of the frail elderly. In A. Gitterman, ed., *Handbook of social work practice with vulnerable populations,* pp. 549–583. New York: Columbia University Press.

Tross, S., and J. Blum. 1988. A review of group therapy with the older adult: Practice and research. In B. MacLennan, S. Saul, and M. Weiner, eds., *Group therapies for the elderly,* pp. 3–32. Madison, CT: International Universities Press.

Tyler, R. S. 1997. Perspectives on tinnitus. *British Journal of Audiology* 31:381–386.

U. S. Census Bureau. 1996. *65+ in the United States: Current population reports (P23-190).* Washington, D.C.: Government Printing Office.

U.S. Census Bureau. 1997. *Population projections of the U.S. by age, sex, race, and Hispanic origin: 1995 to 2050. P25-1130.* Washington, D.C.: Government Printing Office.

U. S. Census Bureau. 2000. *The census 2000 brief series: Population change and distribution, 1990–2000* [PDF] (C2KBR/01–2). 2000. [Online] Available: http://www.census.gov/prod/2001pubs/c2kbr01–2.pdf. U.S. Government Printing Office.

U.S. Census Bureau. 2000. The 65 Years and Over Population: 2000. Census 2000 Brief [PDF] (C2KBR/01–10). Retrieved July 31, 2002 http://www.census.gov/population/www/cen2000/briefs.html.

U.S. Department of Transportation. 1997. *Report No. DOT-P10–97–01.* Washington, D.C.: Author.

United States General Accounting Office. 1997. *Long-term care: Consumer protection and quality-of-care issues in assisted living* (GAO/HEHS-97–93). Available online at http://www.gao.gov.

Vandereycken, W., and R. Meermann. 1988. Chronic illness behavior and noncompliance with treatment: Pathways to an interactional approach. *Psychotherapy and Psychosomatics* 50 (4): 182–191.

Verderber, K. S., and R. F. Verderber. 2001. *Inter-Act: Interpersonal communication concepts, skills, and contexts.* 9th ed. Belmont CA: Wadsworth.

Villaume, W. A., M. H. Brown, and R. Darling. 1994. Presbycusis, communication, and older adults. In M. L. Hummert, J. M. Wiemann, and J. L. Nussbaum, eds., *Interpersonal communication in older adulthood: Interdisciplinary theory and research,* pp. 83–106. Thousand Oaks, CA: Sage.

Voeks, S. K., C. M. Gallagher, E. H. Langer, et al. 1990. Hearing loss in the nursing home: An institutional issue. *Journal of the American Geriatrics Society,* 38.

Vourlekis, B. S., and R. R. Greene, eds. 1992. *Social work case management.* New York: De Gruyter.

Wacker, R. 1995. Legal issues and family involvement in later-life families. In R. Blieszner, ed., *Handbook of aging and the family*, pp. 284–306. Westport, Ct.: Greenwood Press.

Wacker, R. R., K. A. Roberto, and L. E. Piper. 1997. *Community resources for older adults: Programs and services in an era of change.* Thousand Oaks: Pine Forge.

Walker, K. 1998. Preventing falls. *RN* 61:40–41.

Wallhagen, M. I., W. J. Strawbridge, R. D. Cohen, and G. A. Kaplan. 1997. An increasing prevalence of hearing impairment and associated risk factors over three decades of the Alameda County Study. *American Journal of Public Health* 87:440–442.

Wan, T. T., and W. G. Weissert. 1981. Social support networks, patient status, and institutionalization. *Research on Aging* 3:240–256.

Ware, J. E., and C. C. Sherbourne. 1992. The MOS 36-item short form health survey (SF-36): Conceptual framework and item selection, part 1. *Medical Care* 30:473–481.

Watzlawick, P, J. H. Beavin, and D. D. Jackson. 1967. *Pragmatics of human communication: A study of interactional patterns, pathologies, and paradoxes.* New York: Norton.

Weaver, J. W. 1994. Temporary housing: Adult daycare and respite services. In W. E. Folts and D. E. Yeatts, eds., *Housing and the aging population: Options for the new century*, pp. 203–220. New York: Garland.

Weil, M. 1985. Key components in providing efficient and effective services. In M. Weil and J. M. Karls, eds., *Case management in human service practice: A systematic approach to mobilizing resources for clients*, 29–71. San Francisco: Jossey Bass.

Weil, M., and J. M. Karls. 1985. *Case management in human service practice: A systematic approach to mobilizing resources for clients.* San Francisco: Jossey Bass.

Weimer, J. 1997. Many elderly at nutritional risk. *Health Statistics, National Center for Health Statistics*, series 10 http://www.ers.usda.gov/publications/foodreview/jan1997/jan97g.pdf. Retrieved March 20, 20002.

Weinberger, M., G. P. Samsa, K. Schmader, S. M. Greenberg, D. B. Carr, and D. S. Wildmand. 1992. Comparing proxy and patient's perceptions of patients' functional status: Results from an outpatient geriatric clinic. *Journal of the American Geriatric Society* 40:585–588.

Weiss, R. S. 1997. Adaptation to retirement. In I. H. Gotlib and B. Wheaton, eds., *Stress and adversity over the life course: Trajectories and turning points.* Cambridge, UK: Cambridge University Press.

White, T. M., A. L. Townsend, and M. A. P. Stephens. 2000. Comparisons of African-American and white women in the parent care role. *Journal* 40:718–728.

Whitlatch, C. J., S. H. Zarit, and A. von Eye. 1991. Efficacy of interventions with caregivers: A reanalysis. *Gerontologist* 31:9–14.

Wiener, J. M., R. J. Hanley, R. Clark, and J. F. Van Nostrand. 1990. Measuring the activities of daily living: Comparisons across national surveys. *Journal of Gerontology* 45:229–237.

Wight, R. G. 2002. AIDS caregiving stress among HIV-infected men. In B. J. Kramer, ed., *Men as caregivers: Theory, research, and service implications*. New York: Springer.

Wilber, K. H., and S. L. Reynolds. 1996. Introducing a framework for defining financial abuse of the elderly. *Journal of Elder Abuse and Neglect* 8:61–80.

Williams, M. E. 1995. *The American Geriatrics Society's complete guide to aging and health*. New York: Harmony Books.

Williamson, G. J., D. R. Shaffer, and R. Schulz. 1998. Activity restriction and prior relationship history as contributors to mental health outcomes among middle-aged and older spousal caregivers. *Health Psychology* 17:152–162.

Wilson, P. H., M. Bowen, and P. Farag. 1992. Cognitive and relaxation techniques in the management of tinnitus. In J. M. Aran, and R. Dauman, eds., *Tinnitus 91: Proceedings of the fourth international tinnitus seminar*, pp. 489–491. Amsterdam: Kugler.

Wolfe, J. R. 1993. *The coming health care crisis: Who will pay for the care of the aged in the twenty-first century*. Chicago: Chicago University Press.

Won, A., K. Lapane, G. Gambassi, R. Bernabei, V. Mor, and L. Lipsitz. 1999. Correlates and management of nonmalignant pain in the nursing home. *Journal of the American Geriatrics Society* 47:936–942.

Wood, J. B., and I. A. Parham. 1990. Coping with perceived burden: Ethnic and cultural issues in Alzheimer's family caregiving. *Journal of Applied Gerontology* 9:325–339.

Wykle, M., and M. Segall. 1991. A comparison of black and white family caregivers' experience with dementia. *Journal of the National Black Nurses Association* 5:29–41.

Yesavage, J. A., T. L. Brink, T. L. Rose, O. Lum, V. Huang, M. Adey, and V. O. Leirer. 1983. Development and validation of a geriatric depression screening scale: A preliminary report. *Journal of Psychiatric Research* 17:37–49.

Yoder, R. M., D. L. Nelson, and D. A. Smith. 1989. Added-purpose versus rote exercise in female nursing home residents. *American Journal of Occupational Therapy* 9:581–586.

Zarit, S. H., and A. B. Edwards. 1996. Family caregiving: Research and clinical intervention. In R. T. Woods, ed., *Handbook of the clinical psychology of aging*, pp. 333–368. New York: Wiley.

Zarit, S. H., and C. J. Whitlatch. 1992. Institutional placement: Phases of the transition. *Gerontologist* 32:665–672.

Zarit, S. H., and J. M. Zarit. 1990. The memory and behavior checklist and the burden interview. Cited in S. R. Beaton, and S. A. Voge. 1998. *Measurements for long-term care: A guidebook for nurses*. Thousand Oaks: Sage.

Zarit, S. H., R. C. Birkel, and E. MaloneBeach. 1989. Spouses as caregivers: stresses and interventions. In M. Goldstein, ed., *Family involvement in treatment of the frail elderly*, pp. 23–62. Washington, D.C.: American Psychiatric Press.

Zarit, S. H., J. E. Gaugler, and S. E. Jarrott. 1999. Useful services for families: research findings and directions. *International Journal of Geriatric Psychiatry* 14:165–181.

Zarit, S. H., K. E. Reever, and J. Bach-Peterson. 1980. Relatives of the impaired elderly: Correlates of feelings of burden. *Gerontologist* 20:649–655.

Zarit, S. H., P. A. Todd, and J. M. Zarit. 1986. Subjective burden of husbands and wives as caregivers: A longitudinal study. *Gerontologist* 26:260–266.

Zastrow, C. 1997. *Working with groups.* 4th ed. Chicago: Nelson-Hall.

Zuehlsdorff, H. W., and C. Baldwin. 1995. *Retirement counseling: Preparing for the "Golden Years."* Washington, D.C.: U.S. Department of Education. Retrieved from ERIC database.

Zweibel, N. R., and C. K. Cassel, eds. 1988. *Care of the nursing home patient: Clinical and policy concerns.* Philadelphia: W. B. Saunders.

AUTHOR INDEX

SUBJECT INDEX